John Howard Schütz

Paul and the Anatomy of Apostolic Authority

New Introduction by Wayne A. Meeks

W9-DAK-265

Westminster John Knox Press
LOUISVILLE • LONDON

Scripture quotations from the Revised Standard Version of the Bible are copyright © 1946, 1952, 1971, and 1973 by the Division of Christian Education of the National Council of the Churches of Christ in the U.S.A. and are used by permission.

Book design by Jennifer K. Cox

Westminster John Knox Press edition
Published by Westminster John Knox Press
Louisville, Kentucky

This book is printed on acid-free paper that meets the American National Standards Institute Z39.48 standard. ⊗

PRINTED IN THE UNITED STATES OF AMERICA

07 08 09 10 11 12 13 14 15 16 — 10 9 8 7 6 5 4 3 2 1

Library of Congress Cataloging-in-Publication Data is on file at the Library of Congress, Washington, D.C.

ISBN-13: 978-0-664-22812-5
ISBN-10: 0-664-22812-7

To Barbara

CONTENTS

PREFACE

First published in 1975, *Paul and the Anatomy of Apostolic Authority*, by John Howard Schütz, is a profound and important work. With literary, historical, hermeneutical, and theological finesse, it addresses a set of concerns that continue to bear great significance. What, for Paul and for emergent Christianity, are the meanings, functions, and interactions of gospel and tradition, authority and power—in relation to both the person of the apostle and the community called into being through the apostle's proclamation? Schütz presents a bold thesis: for Paul, the authority of the apostle is an interpretation of power—the power of the gospel. The apostle remains ever subordinate to this gospel, with its great reversal of power and weakness in the death and resurrection of Jesus, and embodies it in his own life and person. Because the gospel is dynamic and effective in the world, fashioning and continuing to shape communities of faith, the apostle's authority does not finally set him apart from, or over, those communities. Rather, they share this authority, this interpretation of power for which the gospel is the norm. It is a remarkable approach to power and authority, though not one that could long survive Paul's own apostolic ministry.

Schütz's argument is elegant and lucid, subtle and sophisticated. One finds in these pages close, perceptive exegesis of texts in the Pauline epistles; careful historical analysis; sharp critique of previous interpretations; and an extraordinary combination of theological insight and deft, critically discerning use of sociological analysis. We are delighted to make available once again, with a new introduction by Wayne A. Meeks, this classic work of biblical interpretation. May *Paul and the Anatomy of Apostolic Authority* continue to enlighten and challenge readers for another three decades!

THE EDITORS
THE NEW TESTAMENT LIBRARY

AUTHOR'S PREFACE

'His letters are constantly seeking to establish a basis for authority', Ernst Käsemann has said of Paul. This is an essay on the structure of that authority. I am not particularly concerned with whether, or how, Paul is to be called an 'apostle'. I am concerned with how he envisions his apostolic task and construes that authority which his letters seek to express.

Authority is very difficult to define, but something we comprehend all the time within a larger frame of reference, and within different vocabularies. The idiom may be professional or religious, social or political. Nevertheless, as Weber and others have taught us, behind the disparate vocabularies are basic and perduring conceptions of order, man's place in it and the values it seeks to express. I have tried to identify Paul's understanding of authority by locating it within the larger framework of order expressed by his vocabulary, a theological one.

There is no reason to assume that we intuitively know what authority is and how it functioned in a radically new venture like early Christianity. This new religious faith emerged as a challenge to an older sense of order and certainly had some new sense of authority. Those who sought to bear that authority needed new conceptualizations for their task. The need is not unique, but the conceptualizations may have been. Paul is only one who wrestled with this problem, but he is of peculiar importance. He belongs to the very first generation, and his literary legacy is rich. Moreover, he became, in time, an authority for subsequent generations even though his own understanding of authority was not destined to survive in anything like a pure form. Tracing how and why that was the case, and how early Christianity in general came to reshape man's view of authority, is another story. I have simply tried to show what Paul took to be 'the basis for authority'.

My interest in this question goes back several years, during which time I have accumulated not a few debts. Professor D. Ernst Käsemann did more to help me establish a set of controlling questions

XI

than I realized in the brief period I was privileged to study with him. Professor Paul Meyer, then of Yale, was instrumental in guiding my first attempt to provide some answers in a Ph.D. dissertation. Only portions of chapters 7 and 8 in this book survive as revised from that earlier study, though I hope that I have not wholly lost a sense of Paul Meyer's high standards of exegetical craftsmanship. The late Paul Schubert introduced me to early Christian history and literature, conveying an interest in its wider dimensions and a scholarly enthusiasm for which I shall always be grateful.

So many friends and colleagues have made their contribution in one way or another that I cannot mention them all. I would like to thank Professor Ruel Tyson for putting me in touch with some useful literature. Professor David Little has done much the same, helped me clarify my thinking at critical points, and kindly read a portion of the manuscript which is far better for his having done so. What remains unclear is not his fault. I can hardly thank Professor Hans Frei in any adequate way. He has listened, read and criticized, and done it all over again when asked. Above all, he has been a good friend.

A portion of chapter 4 appeared earlier as an article in *New Testament Studies* (15/4). I should like to thank Principal Matthew Black, editor of that journal and this series, for his interest and editorial help. Professor W. D. Davies carefully read the entire manuscript, providing very useful suggestions and welcome encouragement. He has saved me from several errors. For those that remain I must take full responsibility. I have had the help of good typists in Mrs Janet Taylor and Mrs Joyce Littlefield. The final version was typed by Mrs Judy Blumhagen when she could have declined the dubious honor. I appreciate her gracious and efficient efforts. The manuscript was completed in July 1972, and it has not been possible to take account of work published since that date.

This book is dedicated to my wife, without whom there would be no book. She understands many things better than I do, and surely patience and fortitude are among them.

Chapel Hill, North Carolina   JOHN HOWARD SCHÜTZ

INTRODUCTION TO THE WESTMINSTER
JOHN KNOX PRESS EDITION

There are two reasons to welcome the reissue of John Schütz's *Paul and the Anatomy of Apostolic Authority*. The first and most obvious is that it is a splendid piece of scholarship that still, more than three decades after its first publication, has many things to teach us. It deals with several of the key issues not only in our understanding of the first years of the Christian movement, but also in any attempt today to say what Christianity is or ought to be. The second reason is that the book stands as a landmark, too rarely recognized as such, in the recent history of New Testament interpretation. I begin with the latter.

In the early 1970s academic study of the New Testament in North America entered a period of ferment that continues to the present. For the quarter century before that the dominant understanding of the field's aims and its methods had been shaped by European models, principally either British or German. A number of the leading scholars in American graduate schools had either immigrated from Europe or studied there. From the end of World War II, more and more American students were drawn to the great Protestant theological faculties in Germany, where most of the chairs in New Testament were held by students of Rudolf Bultmann. All agreed that what the Germans called *die Sache*—that is, the subject matter whose elucidation was the purpose of the whole apparatus of exegetical and historical procedure—was theological. The aim of scientific investigation of the Bible was to produce a *biblical theology*. Biblical theology was construed by some in the mode of a theology of history, a *Heilsgeschichte*, as represented in some British and Swiss scholarship (notably Oscar Cullmann) and very widely adopted by theologians active in the ecumenical movement in this country and elsewhere. Others, however, followed Bultmann and his students in defining the purpose of a biblical theology as the evocation of the existential self-understanding implicit in a radical call to personal decision. That call to decision,

Bultmann argued, was the irreducible meaning of the New Testament proclamation, the *kerygma*, once the mythical language of the first century was appropriately translated for the modern, enlightened individual. The two schools were sharply critical of each other. The Bultmann disciples decried the *Heilsgeschichte* school for reducing the Christian proclamation to a kind of idealism or an abstract scheme of historical progressivism. The ecumenical theologians worried about the austere individualism implicit in the existentialist interpretation, which seemed to yield no basis for the sacraments, for life in community, or for a social ethic.

By 1970 it was apparent that biblical theology in both its reigning modes was "in crisis."[1] Theologians as well as New Testament scholars were becoming uneasy with the alliance between them. The business of the biblical scholars was making historical judgments—subject to continual correction by further evidence or alternative appropriation of the evidence—about the texts, their component parts, the prehistory of the traditions behind them, and the process of their composition. The business of the theologians was to find in those texts a coherent body of teaching that could provide guidance for the faith and life of present-day churches. The question of how one moved from one to the other was becoming increasingly fraught with doubts from both sides. Just what it meant to *interpret* the New Testament was no longer obvious. The strange word "hermeneutics" entered the vocabulary of many students previously innocent of the theoretical refinements it implied.

Questions about history and its meaning, about the interpretation of texts (or other systems of signs) and their appropriation, were not limited to biblical exegetes and theologians. Rather, these were questions that were disturbing the peace in all parts of American universities, particularly in the humanities at the outset, but soon also in the social sciences and even at the fringes of the natural sciences. Scholars were feeling the first shocks of a series of assaults on the foundations of those taken-for-granted forms of rationality that ruled academic discourse—shocks that in retrospect we may call the beginnings of postmodernism.

At the time when these questions were roiling the universities, New Testament scholars were finding themselves more engaged

---

[1] Brevard S. Childs, *Biblical Theology in Crisis* (Philadelphia: Westminster Press, 1970).

than formerly by such intellectual currents because of a shift in the working location of many of them. Academic study of the New Testament in Europe was conducted almost exclusively by professors in theological faculties of state universities, differentiated as Protestant or Catholic, depending on location. In the United States their counterparts worked predominantly in theological seminaries or in divinity schools or schools of theology attached to private universities that had for the most part some confessional parentage. In the 1960s the situation changed in this country, while the European scene remained largely the same. American state-supported universities, beginning immediately after World War II, were experiencing a period of expansion, making them the context for the post-high-school education of the majority of young Americans and the location of more and more of the advanced research done in the nation. The study of religion in most of those universities occurred, if at all, only informally or by ad hoc arrangements in the interstices of departmental structures. Could state universities, without violating the constitutional separation of church and state, properly establish departments of religion? Some groups, such as the Council on Religion in Higher Education (later the Society for Religion in Higher Education and then, more innocuously, the Society for Values in Higher Education) strongly advocated such a move, but until 1963 skittish administrators shied away from actions so likely to provoke controversy. In that year the Supreme Court declared, in its famous "school prayer" decision, *Abington School District v. Schempp*, that there was no constitutional obstacle to "study of the Bible or of religion, when presented objectively as part of a secular program of education." In short order, departments of religious studies were created in many state universities, and in several of the private universities older "religion" or "Bible" departments were reorganized in the secular spirit. The center of gravity of the academic study of religion rather quickly moved from a context in which the main interlocutors of biblical scholars were theologians to one in which they were either themselves members of humanities faculties or faced increasingly with questions from colleagues who were.

John Schütz and I experienced this shift immediately and directly. We had both been admitted to Yale's graduate school by an ad hoc Committee on Religion, composed almost entirely of members of the Divinity School faculty. When we received our doctorates, however—John in 1964, I a year later—they were awarded upon the recommendation of a Department of Religious Studies, which had been organized in 1963. After teaching in that new department for several years, John moved to the Department of Religion at the University of North Carolina—a longtime exception to the general rule that public universities lacked such departments—later to be reorganized on the new model as the Department of Religious Studies. I would soon be teaching in a brand-new Program in Religious Studies at Indiana University, organized in 1965, shortly to become a large and flourishing department. When I returned to Yale, succeeding John after he went to North Carolina, I joined a department quite different from the one in which I had been a student.

In this changing context, the ways in which the hermeneutical questions were asked were also bound to change. Driven on the one side by dissatisfaction with a previous generation's framing of the issues, stimulated on the other by different orders of discourse among colleagues in nontheological disciplines, students of the Bible groped toward new paradigms of interpretation. In the mid-1960s a small group of biblical scholars, theologians, and historians of religion gathered at Yale, meeting annually for several years to try out new approaches to the interpretive dilemmas we were facing. They included Brevard Childs, Hans Frei, Rowan Greer, David Kelsey, Wayne Meeks, Daniel Migliore, Thomas Ogletree, Willard Oxtoby, John Schütz, Ian Siggins, Freeman Sleeper, Eugene TeSelle, and Sibley Towner. Schütz was a very active participant. He had just completed his dissertation on "Soteriology and Apostolic Authority in the Pauline Homologoumena," but what he brought to the group's discussions was not so much the results established by that work as the profound questions that his exegesis evoked. What, after all, was authority? What made it different from power? How did it work or fail to work? How did one person gain authority over another? What shapes could the dialectic between a community and its leaders take? Schütz saw that if these questions were asked about the authority of an *apostle*, either as a personage in historical context or as speaking through apostolic Scripture to later generations, they ought to be treated as simultaneously theological and sociological questions. It was in papers read to the colleagues meeting in New Haven that he first articulated those questions in a way that would not only produce the present book, after he had wrestled with the issues for ten years, but also point the way for a significant turn in the direction of American New Testament scholarship.

Several members of the Yale group had begun to read and to converse with colleagues in the social sciences, inquiring whether those disciplines could help us to discover fresh tools for describing the communities of ancient Israel or early Christianity by whom and for whom the texts of the Bible had been written. Elsewhere in North America, others were beginning similar explorations. A few years later Leander Keck and I proposed a consultation at the American Academy of Religion meeting in Atlanta in 1971 on "The Ethos of the Early Christians."[2] A large number of interested scholars attended, and the following year a working group was established, under the joint auspices of the AAR and the Society of Biblical Literature, on "The Social World of Early Christianity." In various permutations this group and its offshoots and parallels have continued down to the present. Not surprisingly, John Schütz was a leader of that broadening effort. He was an early arrival at the table where a new dialogue between the social sciences and historical exegesis was beginning.

That new dialogue was in some ways distinctly American. Biblical scholars were exploring insights to be gleaned from several other disciplines, such as semiotics and the several waves of innovative literary theory that were sweeping across the Atlantic into American universities. Yet, more than any of these other interdisciplinary conversations, interaction with the social sciences tended to separate North American scholarship on the New Testament and ancient Christianity from the German schools with which it had previously been so closely allied and from which it had been partly derived. There seemed in the twentieth century some kind of preestablished harmony between the inquiring methods of the behavioral sciences and the mysteries hidden in the American national experience. We had had to invent our society, in the still-remembered fields newly cleared of forest, in the towns our grandparents had made, swelled to cities in recent memory by waves of new immigrants bringing with them languages and folkways that clashed and jarred in a cacophony of different ways of living. We

[2] See Leander E. Keck, "On the Ethos of Early Christians," *Journal of the American Academy of Religion* 42 (1974): 435–52.

had only lately confronted the scars of slavery and the deep guilt of racism in its multiple forms. We were a nation of tinkerers, of improvisers and inventive optimists who thought we could, somehow, make things work—even the great machinery of society, if we could but find its hidden pulleys and gears. Sociology, especially in its empiricist and pragmatic modes, seemed a natural for us. Indeed, "the only truly indigenous strand of American New Testament scholarship," the "Chicago School" that flourished from roughly 1920 until the 1940s, was marked by its sociological focus.[3]

German theologians looked with deep suspicion on the sociological investigation of Christianity's beginnings, in part because of the reductionism of which the Chicago School was often guilty, in part because of the excesses of some Marxist interpreters beginning with Karl Kautsky. Despite the key place occupied in the sociology of religion and the sociology of knowledge by such Germans as Max Weber, Ernst Troeltsch, Karl Mannheim, and Alfred Schutz, and despite the sociological dimension of early form criticism as practiced especially by Martin Dibelius, German New Testament scholarship in the mid-twentieth century turned self-consciously away from sociological forms of explanation. To theologians trained in the dialectical theology that was identified especially with Karl Barth and Rudolf Bultmann, those forms of explanation seemed naive. They seemed to belong to the failed modernist impulses of the late nineteenth century, implicitly blind to any transcendental reality and therefore lacking the crucial standpoint from which to criticize demonic forms of social progressivism like the imperialism that provoked the First World War, the nightmare of the Nazi state, or the totalitarian regime of the Stalinist USSR. In the 1950s and 1960s, a few scholars began to investigate some dimensions of early Christianity's social history, but their work at first stirred little resonance. One of the most creative of them was a young scholar named Gerd Theissen, whose work on the Pauline communities John Schütz translated and introduced to a wide English-speaking audience.[4] For many years after his doctorate in 1968 and his *Habilitation* in 1972, Theissen was unable to find a permanent professorship in Germany; only in 1980, after teaching in exile, as it were, in

[3] John Schütz, Introduction to *The Social Setting of Pauline Christianity: Essays on Corinth* by Gerd Theissen, ed. and trans. by John H. Schütz (Philadelphia: Fortress Press, 1982), 5.
[4] Ibid.

Copenhagen, was he invited to the chair of New Testament in Heidelberg, which he has filled with great distinction ever since. As late as 1978, when a paper on the social description of early Christian communities was delivered at the annual meeting of the *Studiorum Novi Testamenti Societas*, the leading international professional society of the discipline, one of the most eminent of German New Testament scholars, a disciple of Rudolf Bultmann, denounced the paper as "not worthy of our Society."

That same German scholar, the late Ernst Käsemann, is quoted in the first sentence of John Schütz's preface to the present book. Schütz had studied with him briefly, and the theological program inherited from Bultmann by his students, the "Old Marburgers," of whom Käsemann was perhaps the most articulate and certainly the most polemical representative, profoundly shaped Schütz's understanding of what the task of New Testament scholarship was. One of the remarkable things about *Paul and the Anatomy of Apostolic Authority* is that it undertakes to unite the theological with the sociological. It brings to that theologically motivated task, shaped especially by German Protestant theologians, a set of distinctively American social-scientific tools that those theologians abhorred.

Käsemann had written several essays about the problem of apostolic authority. One of the earliest, a study of the opposition to Paul underlying 2 Corinthians 10–13, was called "The Legitimacy of the Apostle."[5] Without engaging in overt polemics, Schütz quietly shows that this way of putting the question involves a simple category mistake—albeit one that Käsemann could hardly have avoided, given the habits of New Testament scholarship in his day. One must beware, Schütz warns, of the "dangers of too quickly equating legitimacy with authority" (271). Yet until recently both ordinary language and the specialized language of sociology had used the two terms more or less interchangeably. More careful analysis of the ways in which power is effectively exercised, however, suggested that one should reserve the concept of *legitimate* power for a particular social setting. "Legitimacy" enters into the discourse about power relationships only after an institutional structure capable of resolving conflicts has emerged. That refinement of the concept led to new insights into the history of apostolic authority, and thus dovetailed with some exegetical discoveries

---

[5] Ernst Käsemann, "Die Legitimität des Apostels," *ZNW* 41 (1942): 33–71.

Schütz had made in the Pauline letters. Thus he was able to escape from a legacy of post-Reformation polemics that was still affecting the general framework within which most twentieth-century New Testament scholarship operated. Schütz saw that to speak of legitimacy in those raw first years of the Christian movement, when many would-be centers of power competed for the ability to influence the shape of the new movement, is an anachronism. That anachronism was a serious flaw in the picture of earliest Christianity drawn by Käsemann and many of his contemporaries and students, notably in the sharp opposition they saw between purity of the apostolic gospel and the fall into "early catholicism." Moreover, the same category mistake, which was at its root a *sociological* error—however much the existentialist theologians wanted to deny that—was present from the beginning in some of the classic works of the sociology of religion, even in the master, Max Weber.

It was Weber, more than anyone before him, who defined the issue of authority and classified its various modes of effectiveness. Yet Weber himself fell into the trap of equating legitimacy with authority. And no wonder, for Weber drew much of the raw material for his sociological analysis of emerging authority in religious movements from his conversations with Protestant historians of early Christianity. Of particular importance was the famous debate between Adolf von Harnack and Rudolf Sohm, which gave to Weber his crucial distinction between charismatic authority and legal and traditional forms of authority. Among theologians, the Harnack–Sohm debate had defined the way Protestants saw the dichotomy between the early charismatic community of faith and incipient institutionalization, which the Bultmann school revived in the form of a conflict they perceived between the kerygma's demand for existential decision and the routinized forms of institutional power they called "early catholicism." Schütz, informed by more recent developments in the sociology of organizations, points out that, while Weber had taken the essential step of identifying charisma as a sociological rather than a psychological category, even he was insufficiently sociological in his analysis. Sociology borrowed the word "charisma" from Paul. It is the Greek term for the "spiritual gifts" that Paul treats so ambivalently in his Corinthian letters, and it enters sociological jargon and thence popular political talk through Weber's appropriation of Sohm's description of early Christian conflict. The irony, as Schütz wryly observes, is that by Weber's own definition, "Paul is not a charismatic" (267). Taking advantage of more recent interpreters of Weber as well as a more sophisticated reading of Paul's letters, Schütz here returns to the roots of a fundamental issue in the sociology of power.

The central point, which is the leading motif of this book, is that authority is best understood as the interpretation of power. That is, the authoritative person, in this case the apostle, calls upon the willing acceptance of his power by the followers by providing for them an interpretive framework, in the form of a master narrative or a pregnant constellation of metaphors, that makes sense of power that they themselves may experience or have experienced. In a sense, then, the interpretive process makes that power available to them. The interpretation of power is thus also an application of power. It is important to see that this judgment, when Schütz makes it about Paul and his communities, is first of all an exegetical observation and only secondarily a clarification on the basis of general sociological theory. Schütz does not begin with sociological theory, with supposed laws and models generalized across cultures and times, but with what we can know by observation from the only evidence we have, which, for ancient Christianity, is mostly textual. Nor, on the other extreme, does he base his readings on intuition or common sense, though he has plenty of both, for our intuition and our common sense are themselves formed by our own history and our own cultural setting and socialization. Rather we see at work here that dialectic between empirical observation and theoretical reflection that constitutes all proper science, and which Schütz would persuade us ought also to characterize exegesis and the writing of history.

Schütz is above all a fine close reader of texts, and the reader of this book, after working through one of Schütz's characteristically sharp analyses of a complex passage in Galatians or 1 Corinthians, will often say, "Aha! That is what Paul is really saying." It is what Paul is really saying—in the very special sense, to paraphrase J. L. Austin, of what Paul is *doing* with his words—that is the quarry of Schütz's hunt. The hunt begins with the observation that much of Paul's rhetoric is deployed for the purpose of securing his own authority in the communities for which he felt responsible. Many a reader has stumbled over this fact, and not a few have been put off by what they take to be Paul's arrogance and defensiveness. Schütz acknowledges that offense, but he presses through the superficial appearance to examine the precise claim that Paul himself is making: that the power he interprets, the power that is the substance of the authority he seeks to exercise, is not his own. It is rather the power of the gospel, another way of saying the power of God, made present to humans in the new community through the gospel. The chief merit of Schütz's work is to show that those theological statements, which so easily in our usage take flight into pious platitudes, represented specific forms of social relationships and specific experiences of empowerment in the communities Paul struggled to bring to life.

A number of essays and monographs have been written about Paul's use of the word "gospel" and its cognate verb. None is more cogent than Schütz's treatment of the question, which occupies a substantial part of this book. The gospel for Paul, Schütz argues, is neither to be identified with a doctrinal tradition, as it has been throughout most of church history and in such modern revisions as that of C. H. Dodd, nor with that punctiliar, individualist, nonobjectifiable *Ding-an-sich* of the Bultmann school's kerygma. Instead, gospel in Paul's discourse is *power*. That is the power that Paul interprets in his assertions of authority, which do not constitute a power grab for himself, but an attempt to enable the members of the community to experience that power and to live a life shaped in accord with its source. It is the gospel that authorizes its messenger—not the other way around, as in all later church tradition from the second century on. Moreover, the power that is thus interpreted is a most paradoxical kind of power, for it looks on the surface very much like weakness—a fact that Paul celebrates in his several catalogues of circumstances and in the flashes of autobiographical recollection like 1 Cor. 15 and Gal. 1–2, where Schütz discerns the "radical identification of the gospel and the apostolic agent" (135). A life lived by the power of the gospel must have a shape homologous to the paradox of the gospel, which tells of the crucified and resurrected Lord.

It becomes clear, then, that although Schütz critically and effectively deploys sociological theory throughout the book, his perspective remains in a strong sense theological. The focus is on Paul's own construal of the situation, not some theoretical portrayal of what the situation must have been like. So too, what the reader is likely to bring away from the book is not merely a satisfaction of curiosity about how Paul thought about his authority and how he used the rhetoric of authority in his letters. Rather, Schütz has retrieved, by means of a very refined analysis, an extraordinary vision of a special kind of authority, which has the potential not only of interesting the historian but also of inspiring the pastor or even the public servant or anyone else who wants to think seriously about the ways in which people of vision may motivate others to share that vision and the power which it engenders.

Many things have changed in research about early Christianity in the thirty-odd years since John Schütz wrote this book. Great labor has been poured into reconstructing the social history of institutions and movements in the Greco-Roman world, driven both by new methods and by new discoveries in archaeology, papyrology, and epigraphy. New research and new discoveries have utterly transformed our understanding of the variety of ways in which different communities of Jews maintained their identity while adapting to the larger culture of that world. Literary studies of Greco-Roman rhetoric and philosophy have brought new light to every page of the New Testament. The use of the methods of the social sciences, in which Schütz pioneered, has become routine, but has produced a multiplicity of approaches not infrequently preoccupied with internecine wars between the various academic camps. And the entire field has been churned by postmodern questioning of all the assumptions alike of modernist historiography and of the behavioral sciences themselves.

From that exciting but often bewildering scene, I return to Schütz's work with pleasure: how sophisticated this was—and is. To put it bluntly, how much more careful and illuminating and persuasive it is than so much that has been written since then at the border between the social sciences and the study of ancient Christianity and its texts. What I value about my reading of Schütz is that he makes me think. He pushes us to think along with him and with the texts he expounds, to pursue again the elusive rationale from which they spring. It is for this reason that I can invite a reader today to discover the treasures of this book appearing again after a third of a century. Not that it is an easy read: it is a scholarly monograph that makes no pretense of being popular. Yet its simple elegance, the directness and clarity of its arguments, touched by flashes of sardonic humor that every acquaintance of John Schütz will recognize, are immensely appealing.

How very much the field has missed that voice since 1985. In the autumn of that year a bicycle accident, never fully explained, left John in a coma, from which he awoke with his personality, his humor, and his capacity for human understanding intact, but with his short-term memory so impaired that he was forced to abandon teaching and research. The re-publication of his book here must inevitably reawaken our regret for what more he might have done in the years in between. Yet most of all it is a celebration of the huge contribution he did make and continues to make toward our understanding both of early Christian history and of the possibility of human flourishing.

ABBREVIATIONS

AThANT   Abhandlungen zur Theologie des Alten und Neuen Testaments

BAG   *A Greek-English Lexicon of the New Testament and Other Early Christian Literature,* by W. F. Arndt and F. W. Gingrich. A translation and adaptation of Walter Bauer's *Griechisch-Deutsches Wörterbuch zu den Schriften des Neuen Testaments und der übrigen urchristlichen Literatur.*

BDF   *A Greek Grammar of the New Testament and Other Early Christian Literature,* by F. Blass and A. Debrunner. A translation and revision of the nineteenth German edition incorporating supplementary notes of A. Debrunner, by Robert W. Funk.

BHT   Beiträge zur historischen Theologie

BJRL   *Bulletin of the John Rylands Library*

BSt   Biblische Studien

ES   *Economy and Society*

EvTh   *Evangelische Theologie*

FBK   *Introduction to the New Testament,* Founded by Paul Feine and Johannes Behm. Completely reedited by Werner-Georg Kümmel. Fourteenth Edition. Translated by A. J. Mattill, Jr.

FRLANT   Forschungen zur Religion und Literatur des Alten und Neuen Testaments

HNT   Handbuch zum Neuen Testament

HTR   *Harvard Theological Review*

ICC   International Critical Commentary

JBL   *Journal of Biblical Literature*

JTC   Journal for Theology and Church

KEK   Kritisch-Exegetischer Kommentar über das Neue Testament

KuD   *Kerygma und Dogma*

LCL   Loeb Classical Library

NTS   *New Testament Studies*

NTTS   New Testament Tools and Studies

RAC   *Reallexikon für Antike und Christentum*

RB   *Revue Biblique*

RGG   *Die Religion in der Geschichte und Gegenwart*

Str.-B.   *Kommentar zum Neuen Testament* von H. L. Strack und Paul Billerbeck

ST   Studia Theologica
TBA   Tübinger Beiträge zur Altertumswissenschaft
TDNT   Theological Dictionary of the New Testament
TF   Theologische Forschung
THNT   Theologische Handkommentar zum Neuen Testament
ThZ   Theologische Zeitschrift
TLZ   Theologische Literaturzeitung
TQ   Theologische Quartalschrift
TR   Theologische Rundschau
VuF   Verkündigung und Forschung
WF   Wege der Forschung
WMANT   Wissenschaftliche Monographien zum Alten und Neuen
   Testament
ZKT   Zeitschrift für Katholische Theologie
ZNW   Zeitschrift für die Neutestamentliche Wissenschaft
ZThK   Zeitschrift für Theologie und Kirche

CHAPTER I

AUTHORITY AND LEGITIMACY

INTRODUCTION

In the broadest sense this study is concerned with the problem of authority and holds that authority is an interpretation of power. While the essay itself is confined to an analysis of Paul's apostolic authority, it comes from and hopefully will say something about a wider concern.

For the student of the earliest Christian history and literature the problem of authority is very real even if its discussion must often be more oblique than direct. Renewed interest in such questions as the relationship of heresy to orthodoxy in the early Church is partial testimony to the centrality of this problem.[1] Similar historical problems cluster around the use of that convenient if imprecise term *Frühkatholizismus*, the perimeter of which we are still trying to define.[2] Nor is the question of heresy and orthodoxy merely a matter of historical interest. It has

[1] Symbolic of this interest is the reprinting of such standard works as A. Hilgenfeld, *Das Ketzergeschichte des Urchristentums* (Leipzig, 1884; repr. Darmstadt, 1963) and W. Bauer, *Rechtgläubigkeit und Ketzerei im ältesten Christentum* (Tübingen, 1934/1964[2]; BHT 10; E. t., Philadelphia, 1971). In the latter, the editor, G. Strecker, provides a useful survey of the reaction to Bauer's work which also gives some clue to the more recent discussion. Cf. also H. Koester's article 'Häretiker im Urchristentum', *RGG*[3] III, cols. 17–21; 'GNOMAI DIAPHOROI: The Origin and Nature of Diversification in the History of Early Christianity', *HTR* 58 (1965), 279–318; G. Bornkamm, 'Die Häresie des Kolosserbriefs', *Das Ende des Gesetzes* (München, 1958), pp. 139–56; E. Käsemann, 'Ketzer und Zeuge', *Exegetische Versuche und Besinnungen*, Vol. 1 (Göttingen, 1960), pp. 168–87; *The Testament of Jesus* (London, 1968).

[2] Cf. E. Käsemann, 'Aus der neutestamentlichen Arbeit der letzten Jahre', *VuF* (1947–8); 'Ephesians and Acts', *Studies in Luke-Acts* (ed. L. E. Keck and J. L. Martyn [Nashville, 1966]), pp. 288–97; 'Paul and Nascent Catholicism', *Distinctive Protestant and Catholic Themes Reconsidered* (New York, 1967; JTC 3), pp. 14–27; W. Marxsen, *Der Frühkatholizismus im Neuen Testament* (Neukirchen, 1964[2]; BSt 24); K. Beyschlag, *Clemens Romanus und der Frühkatholizismus* (Tübingen, 1966; BHT 35).

manifold theological implications which become clearer as rigidly dogmatic positions soften.[1] In fact, the theological questions raised by Christianity's development of a canon of scripture are even more difficult to solve than the historical questions. In this situation historians and literary critics find themselves aware of the accidental and occasional nature of canonical limits, unable to translate directly to their own work the canon's intended function of authority.

Certainly the matter of authority, even to limit our discussion to the Church, is not confined to scholarly interest. One need only glance at the mood of Roman Catholic thought to see that the oldest and most stable sector of the Christian community is in the process of rethinking the problem of authority. This has already come to expression in such tangible forms as Vatican II and its wake, and is exemplified in the recent controversy on birth control. Particularly in the case of the council, Catholic thought has raised questions which drive all Biblical scholars directly back to their sources.[2]

By no later than the middle of the second century the Christian Church had begun to sketch out the institutions of authority on which it would place particular reliance. Chief among these was the canon of scripture itself and the apostolic tradition which in its broadest sense was an appeal to the apostles as a designated group of authorized bearers of tradition. Although in retrospect this move toward the self-conscious explication of the framework of authority seems early enough, behind it lay a century of Christian thought, history and literature. In that century, which we can only dimly see, Paul played a central if not singular role. Whether the collection of his letters is testimony to his importance or more nearly the occasion of it for those who lacked immediate knowledge of the early days of the Church, that collection also thrust Paul into a position of authority for a later age. Thus, if one turned to scripture or the apostolic tradition, one could scarcely escape Paul.

For the period of Paul's activity the status of those developing criteria is uncertain. If he was useful for fighting heresy in a

[1] H. Küng, 'Der Frühkatholizismus im Neuen Testament als Kontroverstheologisches Problem', *TQ* 142 (1962), pp. 385–424.

[2] Cf. H. Küng, *Structures of the Church* (London, 1964), esp. ch. III, 'Council and Ecclesiastical Offices'.

later age, it nevertheless remains true that he struggled against opposition in one form or another in his own age without the benefit of such specific institutional forms of authority as later became available. And struggle he did. In an earlier age F. C. Baur could shock the theological world by suggesting the polarity of thought within early Christianity centering around the figures of Peter and Paul. Baur's rather simplistic scheme of development has long since been abandoned, while the idea of dissension and disagreement within earliest Christianity is hardly thought novel. Today, one is more likely to be shocked by the plethora of suggestions concerning Paul's 'opponents' in Galatia, Corinth, and elsewhere. If scholars have supplied more opponents than even Paul could have managed, the trend of this investigation is nevertheless clear and correct – Paul's letters are to be understood against the background of their specific occasion, and that occasion is more than a few times essentially polemical.

The effect of all of this is clear. When the Church made Paul a 'catholic' theologian and took him into its baseline of orthodoxy it incorporated him into the structures of ecclesiastical tradition and authority. Yet we must try to see the historical reality first and that reality is specific, occasional and, thus, anything but theologically catholic. In the process of re-historicizing Paul we have become increasingly aware of how he was engaged in controversy before the days of formalized institutions of authority, even before the days of 'heresy and orthodoxy'. How then, and why, did Paul proceed? What gave him his authority? How did he understand and exercise it?

A simple answer might be that Paul shows the embryonic forms of authority which were to develop more fully in later generations. That answer would be correct in some sense, but it suffers from being general and reducing the problem of authority in the first generations to its least common denominator.

No text can be read in an interpretive vacuum, and so it will be necessary to make plain the historical and conceptual presuppositions which put us at our starting point. That point, again, is the statement that authority is the interpretation of power.

I-2

APOSTOLIC AUTHORITY AND APOSTOLIC
LEGITIMACY

In more than a century of critical discussion, one vexing and intractable problem offered by the New Testament and other early Christian literature has been 'the name and office of the apostle', to use J. B. Lightfoot's phrase from an influential definition of the problem in his commentary on Galatians.[1] One might hope that a century would prove sufficient time for solving so specific a problem. It has not. Although in the history of scholarship there have been periods of general agreement on the nature of the problem and the directions in which a solution should be sought, not even that is true currently. From the manifold literature which has appeared on this subject just within the past few years it seems that there is agreement only in rejecting the last discernible consensus. Beyond that everything is fluid.

Both the persistence of the problem and the differences among proposed solutions are instructive. So central is the figure of the apostle to the missionary growth and the historical continuity of early Christianity that his identity remains a matter of primary importance for both the theologian and the historian.

In what may be called the first full flush of 'catholic' Christianity, at least one writer was quite clear about the origin and functions of apostles:

The Apostles received the Gospel for us from the Lord Jesus Christ, Jesus the Christ was sent from God. The Christ, therefore, is from God and the Apostles from Christ. In both ways, then, they were in accordance with the appointed order of God's will. Having, therefore, received their commands, and being fully assured by the resurrection of our Lord Jesus Christ, and with faith confirmed by the word of God, they went forth in the assurance of the Holy Spirit preaching the good news [εὐαγγελιζόμενοι] that the Kingdom of God is coming. They preached from district to district, and from city to city, and they appointed their first converts, testing them by the Spirit, to be bishops and deacons of the future believers. And this was no new method, for many years before had bishops and deacons

[1] J. B. Lightfoot, *The Epistle of Saint Paul to the Galatians* (London, 1865/ Grand Rapids, 1962), pp. 92–101.

4

been written of; for the scripture says thus in one place 'I will establish their bishops in righteousness, and their deacons in faith.'[1]

The author is Clement, bishop of Rome, writing to the Corinthian Christians at the end of the first century.[2] He locates the apostles not only in history as successors to Jesus' preaching mission, but also in what might be called salvation-history since 'they were in accordance with the appointed order of God's will'. They are those who received commands from Jesus and have been granted a resurrection appearance. They speak God's word and appear under the aegis of the Holy Spirit. Just as their relationship to Jesus is analogous to Jesus' relationship to God, so they are part of the divine economy as testified to by the concluding quotation from Isaiah 60: 17.[3]

Clement's genetic description is important not for its simplicity or for some apparent plausibility, but because it serves the central purposes of his letter. Here we have channel markings designed to establish the length and breadth of that pure stream of tradition and authority by which the Church proceeds and by which it is sustained. Fractious and insubordinate elements in the Corinthian community need reminding of this. One way of reminding them is to stress the historical connections and implications. Clement was himself quite well aware that he was heir to this apostolic tradition, as were those in Corinth whose hands he wished to uphold. Only in this way could legitimate leadership be recognized. But the breadth of the channel is even more important than its length. The question of authority is even more central, if also more implicit, than the question of legitimacy. The very fact that a bishop of Rome can presume the authority to write to the Corinthian Christians to admonish them for failure to heed their own duly constituted leaders shows how central is the whole question of authority in this appeal to the apostles. Furthermore, it is implicit in Clement's approach that authority is not merely a matter of historical continuity. It has a theological dimension as well.

[1] *I Clement* XLII; *The Apostolic Fathers*, Vol. I (London, 1952), tr. K. Lake, LCL.
[2] For a recent assessment of authorship and the evidence for dating, cf. J. A. Fischer, *Die Apostolischen Väter. Schriften des Urchristentums*, Vol. I (Darmstadt, 1964), pp. 16ff.
[3] On the peculiarities of the citation cf. Fischer, *Väter*, p. 79, n. 248.

In short, what Clement says about the authorized leaders of the Church, the bearers of its tradition, involves assumptions about both their authority and their legitimacy, though he does not make that distinction clear. On the contrary, the concepts of authority and legitimacy have been collapsed and equated. This is true not only of the apostles, figures from the past, but also of the bishops, their successors in the present. In both cases, authority is implicitly derived from the understanding of legitimacy. Such is the case where 'for the first time we find a clear and explicit declaration of the doctrine of apostolic succession'.[1] But what of an earlier stage where such succession cannot yet be presupposed? What is the relationship of apostolic authority to legitimacy when the scope and role of the apostolic 'office' is not yet so clearly defined?

Whatever the problems involved in Clement's view, its scheme has had a remarkably tight hold on the way in which even critical scholarship has addressed itself to the question of apostolic authority. Here too the matter of authority has not always been carefully enough distinguished from that of legitimacy. Perhaps this is because it was so long assumed that the apostles were to be identified with the Twelve. When Lightfoot opened up new paths by sharply distinguishing between these two groups, he began what has become a continuing search for two or more ideal types of the early 'apostle'. While recent study tends to see the role and status of the Twelve as problematical, most scholarship still seeks to reconcile what Lightfoot set asunder by insisting that the primary question of Pauline apostleship is the question of Paul's relationship to that group. So the key problems have long been those of relationship: of the Twelve to the 'apostles'; of the Twelve to the larger company of disciples; of Paul to the apostles in Acts, etc. In each case the common thread is the question of the appropriateness of the term 'apostle' to one or another group. Understandably, a great deal of attention has been focused on the linguistic problem of the derivation and original meaning of the term ἀπόστολος in hopes that clarity about its antecedent use might elucidate early Christian understanding of the office.

This raises a serious question with which we must be concerned at the outset. Is it clear that the sharp definition of an

---

[1] J. Quasten, *Patrology*, Vol. 1 (Westminster, Md., 1950), p. 45.

'office', the precise description of role and status, is the first question to be settled in coming to understand the role of the early Christian apostle? To find the coordinates by which an 'office' of the apostle might be located will help illuminate the matter of apostolic identity, but only from one direction. It helps us determine who is and who is not rightfully called an apostle. It approaches the question of identity exclusively through the category of legitimacy. But as we shall see, legitimacy and authority are not the same thing, and the primary question is not *who* is an apostle, or even *how* an apostle, but *why* an apostle and how does he lay hold on and exercise his authority.

In all of this the centrality of Paul is unmistakable. His unambiguous description of himself by the term 'apostle' and the very volume and style of his writings makes him the most accessible specimen to be found in the New Testament. But early foreclosure on the broad topic of Paul's understanding of his apostolic *authority*, by substituting for it the question of his legitimacy, has diminished rather than enhanced the possibility of reading the fullest possible apostolic configuration out of Paul's letters. Thus it is to this question that this book is directed.

Paul's authority is difficult to isolate for a number of reasons. The modern perception of authority is not necessarily the first century's perception. We can see this in even a very specialized case like that of ecclesiastical offices. To take one simple example of an important difference, Paul does not share the later notion of the Church as composed of clergy and laity, each with unique responsibilities. Where he distinguishes among various 'gifts' he also stresses the unity of the one Spirit; when he speaks of the variety of service he emphasizes the singularity of the one Lord (I Cor. 12: 4). It is true that God has appointed in the Church 'first apostles, second prophets, third teachers, then miracle workers, then healers, helpers, administrators, speakers in various kinds of tongues' (I Cor. 12: 28). But Paul does not elaborate on these functions, and his purpose again is to stress the unity of the Church within the plurality of its members and their gifts: 'Now you are the body of Christ and individually members of it' (I Cor. 12: 27).

Obviously we must be clear about what we mean by apostolic

7

authority. Paul's letters reflect a situation in which the Christian apostle is already something of an authority figure. When Paul feels called on to explain his claim to apostleship he implicitly justifies his claim to authority at the same time. In that sense, the position in I Clement is an accurate reflection of an earlier situation. Nevertheless, the primary problem with which Clement wrestles is authority as it has become embodied in legitimate forms. Would it therefore be more appropriate to try to distinguish Paul's quest for or defense of apostolic *legitimacy*? If he were only challenged on this point, the answer would be affirmative. The case for making some clear distinction between apostolic authority and legitimacy would seem to be set, in part, by the important and difficult material in II Cor. 10–13. This is a rich text for examining the problem of authority, but the material is found in a context where the issue of legitimacy is itself a primary fact. There we shall see that Paul's reply to one kind of attack on his credentials must turn to the root question of authority. By Paul's own testimony the two matters are closely related.

Yet not every reference to his apostolic status demands such a defensive interpretation. The problem is made even more complex by the fact that the whole question of the background and development of the apostolate is shrouded in sketchy sources. What we do know is that Paul thought himself to be within the limits of the apostolic circle, whatever its diameter. And we know that others were able to cast doubt on that claim.

These are the rough coordinates for our investigation. The problem is not simply to discover the answer to our question of apostolic authority, but to frame appropriately the question itself. What is the actual authority upon which Paul relies? Is it apostolic authority simply because Paul is an apostle, i.e., meets external criteria of legitimacy? Or is it the case that his authority is apostolic in the broader sense that Paul thinks that his own understanding is normative for all apostles?

There is the further matter of the existence of the letters themselves from the apostle's hands. The whole Pauline corpus[1] is testimony to the fact that Paul had something to say to 'his' communities and presumed both his right to say it and

---

[1] For the purposes of this essay the authentic corpus may be regarded as comprised of Rom.; I, II Cor.; Gal.; I Thess.; Phil.; Philem.

8

his effectiveness in doing so. In that sense authority is presumed. Only two of the seven undisputed letters are not addressed to Churches with which Paul has already had a sustained relationship (Romans and Philemon). In the others he discusses all manner of affairs and problems. This must presuppose some understanding of his right and ability to do so. But only at specific points does he defend his apostolic credentials; such a concern is not in itself the rationale for the custom of writing to these Churches. Nor is this extensive pattern of communication characteristic of the work of an apostle. The authority *behind* the letters is the authority *behind* Paul's apostolic claim. It is that authority about which we are inquiring.

Authority and legitimacy are twin motifs, integrally related even while they seem to demand sharper definition and distinction from one another. Our concern is primarily with the ingredients of the former. To plot its locus we must make some preliminary conceptual distinctions.

WHAT IS AUTHORITY?

Authority is different from its agents. There are people who are 'authorities' on gardening, polo or Egyptology because they possess acknowledged competence in these fields, but competence is not authority. As Bierstedt points out, our language sometimes plays tricks on us in this regard, as when we speak of the 'competent authorities'. But 'superior knowledge, superior skill, and superior competence need not be involved in the exercise of "competent" authority'.[1] The corporate officer who is 'competent' to sign executive orders is not competent because he is more skilled than others in the art of signing. What we mean by referring to 'competent' authorities is that they are *legitimate* occupants of positions of authority. Legitimacy, we shall see, is closely related to, but necessarily distinct from, authority.

Similarly, we should distinguish between leadership and authority. A leader functions as such so long as his followers will accede to his requests; but one in authority has a 'right' to require obedience. Some positions of authority may be closed

[1] R. Bierstedt, 'The Problem of Authority', p. 70, in M. Berger *et al.*, *Freedom and Control in Modern Society* (New York, 1954), pp. 67–81.

to those who lack sufficient capacity for leadership, but leadership and authority are two separate phenomena.

This distinction has sometimes been clouded, as in the very influential work of Max Weber concerning the role of the charismatic leader. Weber regards charisma as one of three types of legitimate authority, the other two being traditional and legal.[1] What stands out in Weber's analysis is the peculiar way in which the charismatic kind of authority rests not on a nexus of social relationships of shared assumptions, but in the person and even the personality of the agent, so that what Weber describes is less a kind of authority than a kind of person. We shall return to this matter in some detail later, as it is crucial for understanding Paul and some of his opponents.

If we concede that authority is not to be confused with its agents, or with leadership, how may we define and locate it more positively? It is, first of all, the *right* to power. 'Power is of itself not authority...Power alone has no legitimacy, no mandate, no office.'[2] Legitimacy, mandate and office are characteristic of authority and signify its 'right' to the power behind it. Second, 'authority is always a formation of social organisation'.[3] Just as it is 'impossible to conceive of a social aggregate...in which there is no organisation present',[4] so it is the case that 'where there is no organisation there is no authority'.[5] Thus we have a definition of authority as 'institutionalized power'[6] or perhaps better as 'formal power',[7] and a locus for it in the social aggregate. There remains the question of its source.

[1] M. Weber, *Economy and Society*, ed. G. Roth and C. Wittich, Vols. 1–3 (New York, 1968), 1: 3, 2 (pp. 215–16). All subsequent references to Weber's *Economy and Society* (*ES*) are to this translation and follow the editor's divisions into Parts (1, etc.), chapters and sections or subsections.

[2] R. M. MacIver, *The Web of Government* (New York, 1947), p. 83.

[3] Bierstedt, 'Authority', p. 72.

[4] R. Nisbet, *The Social Bond* (New York, 1970), p. 116.

[5] Bierstedt, 'Authority', p. 72.

[6] The phrase is Bierstedt's ('Authority', p. 80). 'Institutionalized power' is slightly different from MacIver's 'right to power', for MacIver thinks 'the accent is primarily on right, not power' (*Web*, p. 83), and the identification of authority with power is 'inept', p. 85. That is correct, but as Bierstedt shows, 'institutionalized power' is authority conceived as legitimacy, mandate and office, i.e., it fits McIver's criteria.

[7] H. D. Lasswell and A. Kaplan, *Power and Society* (New Haven, 1950), p. 133.

The question of source is somewhat more complex, and will require modifications in our definition. We must begin by distinguishing between an implicit source on the one hand and proximate and ultimate causes on the other. It is characteristic of much of contemporary writing in the social sciences that it is content to discuss the matter of authority in terms of an implicit source alone. This is the case where authority is thought to be basic to the fact of social organization itself. 'The reasons people submit to authority, in the larger focus, are the reasons which encourage them to obey the law, to practice the customs of their society, and to conform to the norms of the particular associations to which they belong.'[1] These reasons can be described collectively as social or associational preservation. Authority is 'supported, sanctioned and sustained by the association itself'.[2] Both the person who exercises authority and the one who subordinates himself by accepting it exemplify as a primary interest an acceptance of the group within which such status distinctions are found. From this Bierstedt draws the conclusion:

If we seek the rationale of authority...we find it in the very factors which induce men to form associations in the first place, to band together in organized groups, and to perpetuate these associations. It is the desire for stability and continuity which guarantees that the exercise of legitimate authority will be maintained in the statutes of the association, not as an underwriting of particular decisions, but as a bulwark behind the organization of the association itself. An individual who rejects this authority is jeopardizing the continued existence of the association. The ultimate answer therefore to the question of what sustains authority exercised in an association of any kind is that this authority is sustained by a majority of the association's own members.[3]

This is adequate as a description of the perduring tendency of social organizations and their members' acceptance of status difference and authority within them. Authority rests within the social organization and is constantly being underwritten

[1] Bierstedt, 'Authority', p. 76. 'Acceptance of authority is conceptually inseparable from participation in rule-governed activity', P. Winch, 'Authority' in *The Aristotelian Society*, Supplementary Volume XXXII (1958), p. 231.
[2] Bierstedt, 'Authority', p. 77.
[3] *Ibid.*

by those who command and those who obey, presumably because the goals of the social organization benefit, and are shared by, both. Moreover, those goals transcend personal relationships.

Nevertheless, the location of authority's source within this description is wanting. Bierstedt describes an implicit source, nothing more. The problem comes in asking how, in fact, social organizations come about which have this tendency toward endurance, this capacity to persuade toward obedience, this ability to provide *within the organization* the source of authority. It may be that 'the rationale of authority' is to be found in those 'very factors which induce men to form associations in the first place, to band together in organized groups, and to perpetuate these associations'. But if so, then the 'rationale' must somehow be available outside the group itself, i.e., before the group comes into existence. The source of authority, in other words, must be more than merely implicit.

What happens to call into existence those associations of the sort we are discussing? By definition the 'call' comes before there is a community which can respond, and its agency is the *auctor*:

The *auctor* is, in ordinary speech, creator of a work, father or ancestor, founder of a family or a city, the Creator of the universe. This is the crudest meaning; more subtle meanings have become incorporated in it. The *auctor* is the man whose advice is followed, to whom the actions of others must in reality be traced back; he instigates, he promotes. He inspires others with...his own purpose, which now becomes that of those others as well – the very principle of the actions which they freely do. In this way the notion of father and creator is illumined and amplified: he is the father of actions freely undertaken whose source is in him though their seat is in others.

But how can a man be the source of actions freely undertaken by others? By, in the first place, giving them the example – this is another meaning of the word *auctor* – but also by answering for the rightness of the action, for the certainty that it will yield good fruits to the man who undertakes it. The *auctor* is the guarantor, the man who vouches for the success of the enterprise... The root of the word denotes the idea of augmentation.[1]

[1] B. de Jouvenel, *Sovereignty: An Inquiry into the Political Good* (Chicago, 1957), p. 30.

The 'augmentation' supplied by the *auctor*[1] is the means by which power is directed toward specific goals and transformed from a natural to a social concept. Authority, in other words, is literally an interpretation of power or what we may call the hermeneutic of power. The *auctor* does not merely lay down his will, but augments it or elaborates it in such a way that the will seems appropriate and beneficial, perhaps even dangerous if disregarded.

There are at least two ways in which this can be done. The first is rational, and in fact turns on the notion of rationality itself as the source of authority. When an 'author', one who creates, seeks to gain obedience he is an authority to the extent that he *can* elaborate the reasons for his will, though he need not always do so. As Friedrich says, 'human reason can elaborate any utterance made, and it is the potentiality for such reasoned elaboration that lends authority to the utterance'.[2] For this to be a true description of authority requires that those who receive the communication recognize in it a relationship to knowledge they possess and values or beliefs they share. Thus as a 'quality of communication',[3] authority can exist prior to and apart from the community which may eventually be called into existence to recognize it, further its domain and help guarantee its perpetuation. Such a 'source' of authority is proximate rather than implicit in the social organization.

There is yet another way in which the will of authority may be elaborated, a way which is 'irrational' and more properly called ultimate. Antecedent to authority is power, and in this case authority itself interprets the power behind it so as to make that power available and effective for the purposes the authority has in mind. Here too it is a matter of communication, but it is a communication of power rather than reason which marks this view of authority. Authority not only has power behind it but can distribute and arrange the locus of power and, more im-

---

[1] Cf. Th. Mommsen, *Römisches Staatsrecht*, Vol. III, Pt. 2 (Leipzig, 1888), pp. 1033–4; K.-H. Lütke, '*Auctoritas*' *bei Augustin* (Stuttgart, 1968; TBA 44), pp. 13–46.

[2] C. J. Friedrich, *The Philosophy of Law in Historical Perspective* (Chicago, 1958), p. 203.

[3] C. J. Friedrich, 'Authority, Reason and Discretion' in *Authority*, ed. C. J. Friedrich (Cambridge, Mass., 1958; *Nomos* I), p. 36.

portantly, access to power.[1] That is to say, it can interpret
power so as to gain acceptance.

Force is not authority and not the use of power seen in this
way. It is an alternative to authority.[2] What distinguishes force
and authority is that force applies power to motivate those who
are less powerful and trades on a disequilibrium of power, while
authority distributes power or opens up access to it in order to
achieve the shared goals of those whose acceptance of authority
is crucial. If *reason* can augment will and create community on
the 'proximate' model, *power* can augment will and create the
community in which it continues to be accessible in this 'ultimate' model.

Leaving aside the implicit concept of authority with which
we began, we can describe two ways in which authority plays a
role in creating communities. In the instance of a proximate
source for authority, 'reason' augments will and creates
community. As the ultimate source of authority, power itself
augments will and creates the community in which power continues to be accessible as authority. Both models indicate that
authority need not be thought of wholly as implicit with existing
social organizations, and the second model shows power to be
reciprocally related to the concept of authority. We may thus
regard *authority* as the *interpretation of power*.

The relationship between power and authority can be both
confusing and illusive. Since they are so often found together,
they can appear to be equivalents, although they are not.
Power is always the ultimate source of authority, though there
may be more proximate sources and implicit causes. For that
reason it can be said that authority is, ultimately, the interpretation of power. This is not gainsaid by the very common occurrence, especially in liberal democratic political societies, of an
imbalance between power and authority. For example, a
national president may have considerably more authority
accorded him by the social aggregate than he has actual power,

---

[1] Here it is important to distinguish between power and access to it. In
political terms, power is never distributed equally, but equal distribution of
access to it is a goal of some types of political organization. Cf. Lasswell and
Kaplan, *Power and Society*, p. 226.

[2] Force is what Lasswell and Kaplan call 'naked power' and define as
'*nonauthoritative* power openly exercised', *ibid.*, p. 139 (italics added). Cf.
de Jouvenel, *Sovereignty*, p. 33.

should he need to display power to those who will *not* acquiesce, i.e., yield deference and hence grant authority. Or quite the opposite case may obtain. For example, many observers would say that in contemporary American politics presidential power exceeds executive authority while the legislative branch of government has authority it cannot use because it has suffered a diminution in power. This latter phenomenon, if true, does not precisely accord with our definition of authority because it interjects a new element, that of positive law, in this case a national constitution. Nevertheless, it is true that even in contemporary political analysis we must distinguish between the concepts of power and authority. For our purposes we do that by defining authority as the interpretation of power, i.e., the focus of power, its disposition and allocation, the opening of accessibility to power for members of social groups.

AUTHORITY AND LEGITIMACY

If authority should not be confused with power, neither can it be simply equated with *legitimacy*. The relationship between legitimacy and authority is rather like that between authority and power: close, complex and on occasion so reciprocal that in certain extensions of one or the other they may appear to be equivalents. But they are not.

We may illustrate the actual relationship by first distinguishing between 'legitimacy' and 'legality'. In our earlier analysis we spoke of authority when it is characteristic of and implicit in a social organization. Such organizations may develop positive law for their ordered life. What follows the mandates of that law is legal, but it is not thereby necessarily legitimate. Legitimacy belongs to the sense of rightness, justification and fitness which pervades the community and acts as part of its social cement. While we would normally expect a code of positive law to embody this sense of rightness, we can imagine cases to the contrary. Hitler's regime established positive law and then proceeded administratively in accord with that law. It was doubtless legal. Whether or not it was legitimate depends on whether or not the body of law accurately reflected the society's sense of fitness and rightness. To take another example, one can imagine specific laws which prove unenforceable even though the social unit is on the whole quite obedient to its laws in other instances. The Volstead Act, prohibiting the sale of alcoholic beverages in the United States, belongs in this class. The act was legal but not legitimate because it did not adequately express community norms.

Such a distinction between legitimacy and legality can be pressed too far, leaving the mistaken impression that legitimacy and authority are virtually indistinguishable, which is quite the opposite of our thesis. Legality is not other than legitimacy, but a particular mode of formalization, while formalization itself is a generic feature of legitimacy. Formalization is the development, in social aggregates, of status, role and deference.[1] One way to articulate the sense of authority implicit in social organization is to develop roles to be filled within the aggregate. These roles carry status of varying degrees, and the seriousness of the whole enterprise is underscored by the way differences of role and status are acknowledged through the use of deference. Legitimacy emerges where a pattern of roles, status and deference has developed. This development, or formalization, is itself an attempt to express the authority behind it, an authority implicitly lodged in the social aggregate, even if there be a more ultimate source. Thus *legitimacy* is an *interpretation of authority, i.e., an attempt to communicate authority and make it accessible – just as authority is an interpretation of power.*

Because of the close association between legitimacy and authority, the former is sometimes taken to be the latter, and phrases such as 'legitimate authority' make the matter only more confusing. The problem is particularly evident in the work of Max Weber. Since his terminology is somewhat different from ours it will help to clarify our analysis by paying some initial attention to both his vocabulary and the rudiments of his conceptual scheme.

SANCTITY, CHANGE AND SOCIAL ORDER

Of the three terms we have sought to distinguish, the most fundamental for Weber is 'legitimacy', or better, 'legitimate

[1] A good analysis of social aggregates and the place of role, status and authority within them, written for the non-specialist, is found in R. Nisbet, *The Social Bond*, chs. 5–8 (pp. 80–221).

order'. Belief in this order guides action, 'especially social action which involves a social relationship'.[1] Power (*Macht*), within a social relationship, 'is the probability that one actor...will be in a position to carry out his will despite resistance, regardless of the basis on which the probability rests'.[2] By contrast, domination (*Herrschaft*) 'is the probability that a command with a given specific content will be obeyed by a given group of persons.'[3] Hence for Weber domination is set within a context of legitimate order in such a way that some sense of that order is presupposed in the understanding of domination itself. The relationship between legitimate order and power is less clear, but power is defined wholly within the framework of social relationships, not as something external to those relationships. This makes it appear that legitimacy is the most primary term, something which can be confirmed elsewhere in Weber's analysis.

The term 'authority' corresponds to what Weber calls 'legitimate domination'.[4] By this he means those modes of domination which incorporate a sense of legitimate order rather than relying on mere force or power disequilibrium. Properly speaking there is no concept of authority except as it presupposes the ideas of both legitimacy and domination. Since legitimacy is, however, antecedent to domination, it is also logically prior to the idea of authority. Thus the three types of authority which Weber educes – rational (legal), traditional, and charismatic – presuppose the idea of legitimacy. This is underscored by the fashion in which Weber introduces the category of legitimacy as a fundamental sociological construct alongside those of social action and social relationship.

On what basis do persons ascribe legitimacy to a social order? 'The actors may ascribe legitimacy to a social order by virtue of: (a) *tradition*: valid is that which has always been; (b) *affectual*, especially emotional, *faith*: valid is that which is newly revealed or exemplary; (c) *value-rational* faith: valid is that which has been deduced as an absolute; (d) positive enactment which

---

[1] Weber, *ES*, 1: 1, 5 (p. 31).

[2] *Ibid.*, 1: 1, 16, A (p. 53).   [3] *Ibid.*

[4] On the problem of translation see Parsons' remarks in M. Weber, *The Theory of Social and Economic Organization*, tr. A. M. Henderson and T. Parsons (New York, 1964), p. 152, n. 83 and *ES*, p. 61, n. 31.

is believed to be *legal*.'[1] Weber goes on to explain that 'the validity of a social order by virtue of the sacredness of tradition is the...most universal type of legitimacy'.[2] This makes it clear that legitimate order is inherently contrary to change and may envelop itself in an aura which sanctifies the traditional. It also makes it clear that this 'sanctity' must be accounted for, that behind the diverse motives for ascribing legitimacy must be the source of legitimacy.

History is a process of change and we must be able to account for change in legitimate orders. Since there is more than one basis for ascribing legitimacy, we must ask if there is a single unifying concept behind the various motives, a source from which legitimacy itself comes. What is needed is not supplied by Weber's understanding of power, since that is defined only *within* social relationships while what we seek must lie outside any specific set of relationships and have the potential for creating them. Is there in Weber's scheme anything which constitutes an ultimate source beyond the social order and accounts for changes in it, something which corresponds to the idea of power developed above? Parsons has suggested that in fact the category 'charisma' plays just such a role and is 'the name in Weber's system for the source of legitimacy in general'.[3]

In isolating the charismatic phenomenon Weber is reaching back to early Christian vocabulary through R. Sohm's *Kirchenrecht* and K. Holl's *Enthusiasmus und Bußgewalt*. Charisma occupies a central role in Weber's sociology of religion, as we might expect. But it is also a basic category in the wider elaboration of the idea of legitimate order, without reference to specifically religious connotations. It is a category explaining social change. What then is the relationship of the phenomenon charisma to the category?

The main context is that of a break in a traditional order. Hence two of the most prominent aspects of the concept charisma – its association with antitraditionalism as its revolutionary character and its particularly close association with a specific person, a leader. The prophet is thus the leader who sets himself explicitly and consciously against the traditional order – or aspects of it – and who claims *moral* authority for his position, whatever the terms in which he ex-

---

[1] Weber, *ES*, 1: 1, 7 (p. 36).   [2] *Ibid.*, 1: 1, 7, 1 (p. 37).
[3] T. Parsons, *The Structure of Social Action* (New York, 1937/1968), p. 663.

presses it, such as divine will. It is men's duty to listen to him and follow his commands or his example. In this connection it is also important to note that the prophet is one who feels himself to be reborn. He is qualitatively different from other men in that he is in touch with or the instrument of a source of authority higher than any which is established or any to which obedience can be motivated by calculation of advantage.[1]

Here we have the two key elements: the *source* of authority which validates the *break* in the routine. Because charisma constitutes such a break, a change in the ordinary, Weber saw it primarily as a temporary phenomenon which had to be subsequently subsumed and embodied in the social structure. This question of the routinization of charisma is complex, but at heart it is the question of how *sanctity* is assigned to any social structure, i.e., legitimate order. For charisma is finally in touch with the sacred, 'a quality of things and persons by virtue of which they are specifically set apart from the ordinary, the every-day, the routine', where 'routine' means not that which is habitually performed, but that which is profane. In short, 'charismatic authority is a phase of moral authority'.[2] It now becomes clear that charisma is not merely one of three types of legitimate authority, but a constituent element in all legitimate order. If legitimacy is prior to authority in Weber's analysis, charisma is prior to legitimacy. 'There is no *legitimate* order without a charismatic element.'[3]

It is interesting to note that this fundamental and extensive concept has its genesis in the role of the prophet and is originally at home in a religious context. The sense of apartness which characterizes charisma belongs to man's propensity to recognize a world of spiritual entities, 'the ideological correlate of the attitude of respect'.[4] What Weber points to in this correlation is the role of the non-empirical in providing 'meaning' to the world, especially in a teleological sense. Such meaning is bound up with human interests and provides channels by which religious ideas, for example, can influence human action. For Weber these ideas are functionally equivalent to institutions, but they themselves exist apart from social relationships.

Man's religious ideas themselves are not empirical fact, but

[1] *Ibid.*
[2] *Ibid.*, p. 662, including n. 3.
[3] *Ibid.*, p. 665.
[4] *Ibid.*

that he has them, that he quests for 'meaning', is fact, according to Weber. Propensity to teleological views is not a metaphysical entity, though metaphysical entities may be involved in articulating the 'meaning' of the world. This distance between the religious idea and the role of meaning it supplies, and the action subsequently motivated, is precisely the span Weber intends to bridge in moving from the narrower, religious role of charisma to its more extensive role. We shall have occasion later to return to this problem and the whole matter of charisma. For the moment it is enough to see that charisma functions outside the bounds of social institutions in a way which makes it prior to the idea of legitimacy. It functions, in fact, as the equivalent of the concept 'power' in our own analysis. As Parson notes:

It is now possible to make a reinterpretation of charisma. It is the quality which attaches to men and things by virtue of their relations with the 'supernatural', that is, with the nonempirical aspects of reality in so far as they lend teleological 'meaning' to men's acts and the events of the world. Charisma is not a metaphysical entity but a strictly empirical observable quality of men and things in relation to human acts and attitudes.

Though its scope is broader than the religious in the usual sense there is inherent in the concept a religious reference. That is, men's ultimate-value interests are in the nature of the case inseparably linked to their conceptions of the supernatural, in this specific sense. It is hence through this religious reference that charisma may serve as the source of legitimacy. That is to say, there is an inherent solidarity between the things we respect (whether they be persons, or abstractions) and the moral rules governing intrinsic relations and actions. This solidarity is connected with the common reference of all these things to the supernatural and our conceptions of our own ultimate values and interests that are bound up with these conceptions of the supernatural. The distinction between legitimacy and charisma can be stated, in general terms, as follows: *Legitimacy is the narrower concept* in that it is a quality imputed only to the norms of an order, not to persons, things or 'imaginary' entities, and its reference is to the regulation of action, predominantly in its intrinsic aspects. *Legitimacy is thus the institutional application or embodiment of charisma.*[1]

[1] *Ibid.*, pp. 668–9 (italics added).

CONCLUSION

Power, authority and legitimacy, as we have defined and distinguished them, are the conceptual coordinates to be used in the analysis of Paul's understanding of apostolic authority. We can think of them as related in something of a logical sequence where power has priority (like Weber's charisma) and is followed by authority and legitimacy. In this relationship each concept is so closely linked to one or both of the others that there is a temptation to mistake very close associations for equivalence. But each is a separate category.

Power is the source of authority, and authority is a version of power as it interprets power and makes it accessible. Power may be an *implicit* source, as Bierstedt sees it, or it may be seen as more nearly *proximate*, or even *ultimate*. In any event, it is a source, and authority is its interpretation, its application. It is as an ultimate source that power functions in Paul's understanding of authority.

Legitimacy, on the other hand, is a formalization of authority in those circumstances where the shape and texture of the social aggregate allows or demands such formalization. From all the evidence available, for early Christianity such formalization comes only after Paul. The attempt to define a legitimate order is evident in the efforts of I Clement, for example. Success in the effort is marked by the emergence of nascent catholicism. But Paul comes before all this. Thus it is not with the concept of legitimacy that we should set out to understand Paul as an apostle, but with the concept of authority itself. As we shall see, that has not been the usual procedure.

CHAPTER 2

APOSTOLIC AUTHORITY IN RETROSPECT

How the term 'apostle' came into early Christian usage has been a long-standing problem. It says something about the intractability of this problem that those who approach it spend almost as much time rehearsing the positions of others as casting the outlines of their own solutions. This leaves us in the happy circumstance of possessing several good surveys of the scholarly status of the question[1] and makes more appropriate here a selective review which concerns itself particularly with the way in which the issues of 'legitimacy' and 'authority' are handled.

In 1865 J. B. Lightfoot published his commentary on Galatians which included an excursus on 'The Name and Office of An Apostle'.[2] The chief burden of Lightfoot's essay was to question the previously safe assumption that the office of apostle was coterminous with the institution of the Twelve by Jesus.

It is true that twelve is a typical number, but so is seven, also. And if the first creation of the diaconate was not intended to be final as regards numbers, neither is there any reason to assume this for the first creation of the apostolate... The extension of the Church to the Gentiles might be accompanied by an extension of the apostolate... the case of St. Paul clearly shows that the original number was broken in upon.[3]

Earlier there had arisen no real question about apostolic authority as such, for that authority was regarded as part of a

---

[1] For example, O. Linton, *Das Problem der Urkirche in der neueren Forschung* (Uppsala, 1932), pp. 69–101; E. M. Kredel, 'Der Apostelbegriff in der neueren Exegese', *ZKT* 78 (1956), 169–93 and 257–305; H. Mosbech, 'Apostolos in the New Testament', *ST* 2 (1948–9), 166–200, esp. 176–83; G. Klein, *Die zwölf Apostel* (Göttingen, 1961), pp. 20–65; J. Roloff, *Apostolat-Verkündigung-Kirche* (Gütersloh, 1965), pp. 9–37.

[2] Lightfoot, *Galatians*, pp. 92–101. This and succeeding references are to the reprinted edition (Grand Rapids, 1962).

[3] *Ibid.*, p. 95.

direct commissioning from Jesus. Lightfoot's theses, however, raised the problem of authority precisely where he distinguished between a fact common to all apostles, that they had seen the resurrected Lord, and one not shared by all, that this Lord had himself at one time or another commissioned them. Since the latter was not true of Matthias (Acts 1: 21ff.), there was no reason to regard it as constitutive of apostleship.

The effect of Lightfoot's observations was to open up the problem of apostolic authority by denying the necessity for a commission from Jesus. While he himself laid no heavy stress on the matter, his reading of the sources left the clear impression that (1) Paul's call to apostleship was generically like that of the Twelve, though from the risen Lord and not the earthly Jesus; and (2) that this commissioning was not itself the source of authority since other apostles, certainly Matthias at least, could not lay claim to it. Thus he found it impossible to establish with certainty the criteria of apostleship, for 'ancient writers for the most part allowed themselves very considerable latitude in the use of the title'.[1] In severing the apostolic office from that of the Twelve, Lightfoot isolated the question of authority.

By the close of the century Lightfoot's work had generated a lively discussion on the problem of the apostolate, including the work of E. Haupt.[2] In one sense Haupt's analysis was a regression, a maneuver to return discussion to a set of coordinates which would locate the apostolic title by reference to theological rather than historical and lexicographical principles. But only in one sense. In another, he was striving for a new comprehensiveness which would satisfy the various and conflicting pieces of evidence beginning to emerge so clearly from the literature; and he sought to pick up the threads of Lightfoot's work while turning aside the radical opinions of W. Seufert.

Haupt defended the essential historicity of the Twelve, but regarded their 'institution' as merely the larger framework, as it were, within which the characteristically Christian concept of apostle arose. The constituents of that concept were mission and charisma. From the Twelve and their efforts there spread a

[1] *Ibid.*, p. 101.
[2] E. Haupt, *Zum Verständnis des Apostolates im Neuen Testament* (Leipzig, 1895).

missionary force encompassing other notables, especially Paul. To the Jewish mission was added the Gentile; to the original apostles was added Paul, and eventually others such as the ἀπόστολοι ἐκκλησιῶν identified by Lightfoot and apparently confirmed by the then newly published (1883) Didache.

Secondly, Haupt regarded the apostolic role as a classical expression of charismatic endowment. In contrast to Lightfoot, the first to point carefully to the possibility of an *institution* of the apostle as derivative from Judaism, Haupt focused on the person of the apostle. Apostles are proven in their action, in their capacity to elicit obedience rather than in their right to compel it. We have here the quintessential characterization of the charismatic-apostle who has no 'office' as such. His claim is not one of legitimacy, but the expression of authority. The apostle is known by his actions and his 'success'. What is not clear in Haupt's study is how or why two or more such charismatics might disagree and what would provide an appropriate appeal to authority outside the person of the charismatic himself. Haupt could not account for the history of conflict in early Christianity.

Precisely this awareness of conflict lay at the core of W. Seufert's analysis.[1] It was Seufert's conviction that (1) *apostolos* was originally a general term for 'messenger', (2) the Twelve were an invention of the mid-first century and not rooted in the *historia Jesu*, but (3) designed to narrow the concept of apostle so as to exclude Paul in the wake of his controversy with Judaizers.

The availability of the Didache and its fundamental investigation shaped the developing theories of A. Harnack, who carried forward in a rather direct way Lightfoot's original observations.[2] The Twelve have their historical root in the ministry of Jesus, but are finally to be separated from the 'apostles'.[3] Yet they came to be identified with the apostles by none other than Paul, 'in his very effort to fix the value of his own apostleship'. Paul 'holds fast to the wider conception of the apostolate, but

[1] *Der Ursprung und die Bedeutung des Apostolates in der christlichen Kirche der ersten zwei Jahrhunderte* (Leiden, 1897).

[2] Cf. especially *The Mission and Expansion of Christianity*, Vol. 1 (London, 1908/New York, 1961), pp. 319–68.

[3] Matt. 10: 2, for example, is 'corrected' by Syr. Sin.

the twelve disciples form his view of its original nucleus'.[1] Unlike Lightfoot, Harnack does not think of the apostles as a simple extension of the Twelve, but of the Twelve as an example of authority used by Paul to articulate his authority as an apostle.

This raises problems about the significance of the derivation of ἀπόστολος from the Jewish practice of legal representation. Both Harnack and Lightfoot appealed to the practice of the Jewish patriarchate in sending its delegates through the diaspora, though both authors recognized that the custom can be secured textually only for the period after the destruction of Jerusalem.[2] For Lightfoot, the Jewish שָׁלִיחַ provides merely the terminology and basic model of ἀπόστολος, while apostolic authority is derived from the fact that Jesus himself first dispatched apostles in giving a mission to the Twelve. For Harnack, however, the Twelve come to dominate the apostolic picture only later. What then is the source of authority for the *apostolos*?

Harnack's treatment makes this a difficult question to answer. On the one hand there are visible in Paul certain *notae apostolicae*, including the primary element of a call of God, and charismatic provisions in the face of ecclesiastical needs, miracles and 'a work of its own' (I Cor. 9: 1–2).[3] These were apparently not self-authenticating, if Paul had to appeal to the Twelve as 'the pattern and standard of all subsequent apostles'. Thus, a calling by Jesus is of primary significance. But Paul does not surrender a wider view of apostleship either. It is this wider view which Harnack seems to derive ultimately from the Jewish שָׁלִיחַ, which 'afforded a sort of type for the Christian apostleship, great as were the differences between the two'.[4] How vexed the question of authority becomes here can be seen by the fact that Harnack takes as the red thread of the Jewish/Christian apostolate the collection of money common to Paul and the patriarchal apostles of Judaism who gather taxes from the diaspora for the Temple. But on these terms, Paul's apostleship would be signified primarily by Jerusalem Christianity's imposing on him the task of collecting money. It would have to be

[1] *Mission*, I, p. 323.
[2] Lightfoot, *Galatians*, p. 73; Harnack, *Mission*, I, pp. 327ff.
[3] *Mission*, I, p. 322.   [4] *Ibid.*, p. 330.

said, in such a case, that his authority rested with that Jerusalem center. Yet this has nothing to do with the 'marks' of the apostle found in Paul independently of any reference to the Twelve. For even if, as Harnack thought, Paul appeals to the Twelve as an example illustrating a concept of authority, the concept itself is independent of any relationship between them and him, and so independent of the model of the *Shaliach*.

To some extent K. H. Rengstorf's analysis of the term 'apostle'[1] can be regarded as an attempt to clarify these matters and provide a more compelling answer to the question of authority, grounding it both historically and phenomenologically. Rengstorf builds his predecessors' observations about the *Shaliach* into a coherent picture of an 'institution' of authority which serves as a general basis for the particular development in the early Church. The theory deserves attention because of its wide-spread influence on subsequent discussion.[2]

It cannot be denied that Rengstorf was interested in solving the emerging question of apostolic authority. Beginning with a review of the Greek antecedents to the New Testament, he showed that they yield insufficient evidence to serve as the background of the New Testament term. In classical Greek, *apostolos* means originally an expedition, by extension an emissary, one dispatched. Even in the extension the emphasis is primarily passive. A material connection with the New Testament term is somewhat more compelling than this formal connection and

[1] K. Rengstorf, 'ἀπόστολος', *Theological Dictionary of the New Testament* [*TDNT*] (Vol. I, Grand Rapids, 1965), pp. 407–47.

[2] Many of James Barr's strictures against the lexicographical approach inherent in *TDNT* could be applied here (J. Barr, *The Semantics of Biblical Language* [Oxford, 1961]). Given the very format of the article, it was necessary to find *a* 'meaning' for ἀπόστολος. Given the significance of the term it was necessary that this be *the* meaning. Given the wide variety of usage in early Christian literature such a least common denominator had to be sought elsewhere. Given the stinginess of sources, the only choice was to appeal anachronistically to a later institution. The logic of the format virtually determined the result. It is not necessary to subscribe to a wholesale indictment of the *Wörterbuch* enterprise to observe how the scheme skews the point of departure in investigation so that some kinds of questions become automatically screened out of the scholarly agenda. Rengstorf inherited the notion that apostolic authority was primarily a question of legitimacy, and went on to carve the dictum in stone.

at its closest in Epictetus' description of the Cynic κατάσκοπος.[1] Rengstorf's treatment of the term provides a clue to his approach. 'Internally, the need for religious assurance of [the Cynic missionary's] own authority [goes] beyond the mere fact of being sent. This was done by the adoption of the formula θεῖος ἄνθρωπος as a self-designation, especially by the Stoics.'[2] This sense of being divinely dispatched is found in another term, ἄγγελος, but for Rengstorf the multiplicity of terms denotes an unresolved problem concerning the relationship between divine initiative and human initiative. This problem the Cynic never solved. 'Hence the relationship of the messenger to the deity never has the character of an unconditional appointment to which he is subject; it is more like an agreement between two partners.'[3]

It is precisely this sense of unconditional appointment which Rengstorf finds in the *Shaliach* institution of later Judaism, which he regards as rooted in the culture at least since the exile. 'What characterizes the שְׁלוּחִים of all periods is their commissioning with distinctive tasks which take them greater or lesser distances away from the residence of the one who gives them. Thus the point of the designation is neither description of the fact of sending nor indication of the task involved but simply assertion of the form of sending, i.e., authorization.'[4] שְׁלוּחוֹ שֶׁל אָדָם כְּמוֹתוֹ (Ber. 5: 5): 'The one sent by a man is as the man himself.' Everything here turns on the *legal institution* and a corollary deduction, that 'the transaction could not be properly conducted without a resolute subordination of the will of the representative to that of the one who commissioned him'.[5]

The case against Rengstorf's argument is serious. It has been stated so frequently[6] that we need not rehearse more than its most essential features. There is first of all the fact, which Rengstorf himself recognizes, that the term is not used for missionaries or prophets, even by the Rabbis.[7] Furthermore, the

---

[1] Cf. Rengstorf's treatment, *TDNT*, I, pp. 409–13.
[2] *Ibid.*, p. 412. [3] *Ibid.*
[4] *Ibid.*, pp. 414–15. [5] *Ibid.*, p. 415.
[6] Cf. esp. W. Schmithals, *The Office of the Apostle in the Early Church* (Nashville, 1969), pp. 98–110; also, Klein, *Apostel*, pp. 26ff. who lists others p. 27, n. 99.
[7] There is some confusion on Rengstorf's part in describing the situation with regard to missionaries. There were 'quite a number in the time of

Rabbinic 'institution' is late. It cannot be dated before the first half of the second century A.D. and the term שָׁלִיחַ does not occur in Jewish texts prior to A.D. 140.[1] It must be remembered that the heart and core of the 'institution' is the patriarchial tribute collected by envoys dispatched throughout the diaspora *after* the destruction in A.D. 70 reduced the customary pilgrimages to Jerusalem and thus threatened to eliminate the means by which Jewish authorities there obtained revenue and communicated with the wider religious community. Yet it is this 'institutional' form on which Rengstorf's thesis depends. The more general legal principle of authorized representation, which clearly can be traced back to the Old Testament, is no novelty. The juridical ideal of authorized representation is not embodied just in the term *Shaliach* and cannot be subsumed in any single word. This, in fact, is part of the limit of the lexicographical approach. To discover the origin of the term *apostolos* requires something more than a concept of delegated authority.[2]

In short, Rengstorf has combined a particular institutional form of authorization which can be secured only from the second century A.D. with an earlier legal idea of representation, failing to notice that the question of the nature of authority depends very much on 'the fact of sending' and 'the task involved'. To say that the 'form of sending' or 'authorization' is all that matters is to transform the problem into one of legitimacy. Only now the focus of legitimacy has shifted from the institution of the Twelve to that of the *Shaliach*, a shift which will not work on historical grounds.

It can be seen from this brief review that Harnack's thesis represents a partial break with the pattern of isolating an 'institution' of authority, whether it be the Twelve or the *Shaliach*, both of which also figure in his historical analysis. This break turns on taking seriously the relative weight of the Pauline evi-

Jesus' but they are not שְׁלוּחִים, which is apparently what he means by saying later that 'there were no authorized missionaries in Judaism prior to 70 A.D.' But if 'even after 70 A.D. this was still essentially true', then 'authorized' missionary appears to be a fiction. It is this lack of clarity which elicits from Klein (*Apostel*, p. 27) objections which Roloff (*Apostolat*, p. 13, n. 28) appears unable to comprehend.

[1] A. A. T. Ehrhardt, *The Apostolic Succession in the First Two Centuries of the Church* (London, 1953), p. 17.
[2] On the particular difficulties, cf. Schmithals, *Office*, pp. 106ff.

dence. Paul and Luke alone offer the quantity of evidence sufficient for drawing a full picture. This view also takes seriously
the fact that Paul's view of apostleship may have been like no
other.[1] This last feature must be stated in guarded fashion, and
raises the serious problem of how central apostleship as such is
to Paul. Is it a basic concern and motif, or do modern interpreters succumb to the temptation to see more, and more
clearly, than Paul himself did?

Hans v. Campenhausen has suggested that the latter is precisely the problem, that for Paul 'Christ, the Gospel and the
meaning, necessity and glory of evangelical service are the departure point for his thought. From here he seeks to elicit the
determining factor in the conflict and struggles of his life, not in
recourse to his apostolic rank as such.'[2] Campenhausen goes on
to suggest that modern interpreters are frequently guilty of im-
porting to the text apostolic categories that do not belong there.
The admonition is well taken if 'apostolic' is defined by a rigid
understanding of some institution of apostleship, i.e., if Paul is
regarded as excessively concerned about the problem of
legitimacy. Such a view is not congenial to Campenhausen who,
like Harnack, underscores the variety of norms for an apostle in
the early literature and is particularly concerned to make de-
velopmental sense out of this variety.

Campenhausen's concern with authority as opposed to institution is nevertheless curiously flat and harmonizing. In an
attempt to show how the Lukan material successfully captures
the 'idea' of apostle and thus presents a picture in essential
unity with Paul and all other texts (except the aberrant attempts to continue the apostolic office beyond the first generation: Rev. 2: 2; Did. 11: 3–6; Hermas Sim. ix, 15, 4; Hom.
Clem. 11: 35)[3] Campenhausen reduces the concept of authority
to *authorization* alone. He thus drives a wedge between apostle

---

[1] Cf. the succinct statement of H. v. Campenhausen, *Ecclesiastical
Authority and Spiritual Power in the Church of the First Three Centuries*
(London, 1969), p. 29: 'On this subject there is only one apostle
whose thoughts we know with any degree of precision, and he – in this
respect as in every other – is to be regarded as an exception: the apostle
Paul.'

[2] H. v. Campenhausen, 'Die urchristliche Apostelbegriff', *ST* 1 (1948),
96–130.

[3] Cf. *Authority*, p. 23 and n. 59; 'Apostelbegriff', pp. 109ff.

APOSTOLIC AUTHORITY IN RETROSPECT

and missionary[1] though it is the missionary consciousness of Paul which, as he says, is the substance of the evidence. He also drives a wedge between apostle and church. 'The "apostles" are earlier than the Church, earlier even than the Church in the limited sense of a sociologically definable entity; and the later view of them in Church history and law is justified to the extent that theirs was an antecedent authority by which the Church itself was established and defined.'[2] For Campenhausen apostolic authority rests exclusively and without remainder in the shared, common experience of seeing the risen Lord.

This results in a certain historical reductionism and sociological naiveté. On the one hand, conflicts and controversies are admitted to be at the very core of Paul's missionary experience,[3] and to these Paul brings to bear his sense of service in the gospel. 'There is no need to idealize away the personal and practical conflicts which undoubtedly existed. We know from the Pauline Epistles how serious were the differences of opinion on particular questions, and how hard the men in authority found it to get along with one another.'[4] Yet the concept of authority is conceived of as something beyond and behind the differences, wholly other, impersonal, supernatural, unified. The apostles are 'authors' of nothing which manifests their authority. Even the churches they found are not an expression and manifestation of apostolic authority. Campenhausen's strict separation of missionary effort and apostolic existence takes its toll at this point, for authority is regarded as totally prior to the Church, as unconnected to the practice of 'authoring' specific communities, the missionary task itself. Thus, despite the practical and personal differences among apostles,

the decisive factor...was not one of the importance of particular offices or of the competence of ecclesiastical authority. That which in spite of everything held the primitive church and its 'apostles'

---

[1] *Authority*, p. 22: 'But the modern concept of a missionary is not wide enough to characterise fully the status and weight of apostolic authority. For the apostles are quite plainly vested with the direct power and dignity of their Lord himself.'

[2] *Authority*, pp. 14–15.   [3] Cf. above, p. 29, n. 2.

[4] *Authority*, p. 29.

APOSTOLIC AUTHORITY IN RETROSPECT

together was not the unity of an organized Church but the unity of their witness to Christ and their vocation. For this vocation and its authority a hierarchical or organizational basis was not of decisive importance.[1]

We shall see later that the 'unity of the Church' is a notion which creaks under the weight of Paul's particular perception of apostolic authority, while the problem of the unity of witness proves a bit more delicate. Campenhausen has correctly perceived the danger of reducing authority to the question of 'office', or what we prefer to call institution. It is not a matter of determining who may or may not belong within a defined pattern of office-holders. This reflects the larger intellectual background and history of a debate in which his work is a major contribution, the question of the relationship between charisma and office (*Amt*). With some Protestant biases seeping through, Campenhausen comes down squarely on the side of charisma, but he wishes charismatic authority to be understood as both specific and critical, i.e., with the inherent capacity to distinguish the right from the wrong representation of the truth of the gospel.

What is lacking, however, is any serious attention to the nature of authority as such and its explication. Authority simply exists and in that sense lies behind the apostolic endeavor, as Campenhausen sees it. In part it is this very distinction between charisma and office which tends to reduce the question of authority to overly simply choices, deeply rooted though the distinction is in the literature. This is particularly true in Campenhausen's case where the possible relationships between charisma and the individual charismatic personality, not to mention those between charisma and institution itself, remain unexplored. Between the sharp contrasts of charisma and office lies a whole territory of softer contours.

By ignoring this fact, Campenhausen has unwittingly shifted to charisma, and in this case its instrumentality – a resurrection appearance – a simple pattern of qualification or legitimacy. Despite the rich contribution of his broad, historical analysis, the earliest decades are once again viewed through the prism of legitimacy. Despite the strictures about organization and its discontents, the apostles represent an institution, a guild. The question of authority is collapsed into that of legitimacy.

[1] *Ibid.*

31

More recent investigations of apostleship in the earliest
Church have tended to remain within the framework of these
earlier studies, insofar as they have concentrated on the problem
of origins and development. G. Klein's analysis[1] of the idea of
the Twelve is a careful if not entirely persuasive[2] attempt to
show Luke responsible for their establishment as an apostolic
group. For that reason it focuses more obliquely than directly
on Paul, while W. Schmithals has sought to use the Pauline
material as a point of comparison for isolating the origins of
such an apostolic conception in Syrian gnostic circles. It is
characteristic of the present state of affairs that both essays assume the need of some external hypothesis to order the various
strands of New Testament evidence,[3] and see the Pauline version
of the apostle as sharply contrasting with the developed image
characteristic of later ecclesiastical thought. All of this betokens
a growing 'new consensus' of an essentially negative sort.

In this context Schmithals has taken seriously the problem of
authority, though he has not analyzed it in a systematic way.
He emphasizes the absolute nature of authority for Paul and its
genetic links to the proclamation of the gospel.[4] Schmithals
perceives the dangers of assuming too much for an apostolic
'office', but nevertheless he correctly stresses the importance of
apostolic self-consciousness in Paul.[5] If Paul himself only infrequently displays interest in the question of apostolic authority
per se, and then only in the face of a direct challenge, he nevertheless shows an interest in it that goes beyond defense of claims
to rank and office. Schmithals cites particularly Paul's references
to his ἐξουσία for 'building up', which he regards as distinct
from the authority of the gospel. It is a 'pneumatic' authority,
one shared with all true pneumatics, whereas the authority of
the gospel is one shared with all true preachers.[6] 'Evidently,
Paul knows a double authority.'[7]

[1] Klein, *Apostel*.
[2] Cf. the remarks of Schmithals, *Office*, pp. 265–72; E. Haenchen, *Die
Apostelgeschichte* (Göttingen, 1968[6]; KEK), pp. 675–9.
[3] 'In the comprehensive literature on our theme all the sources have been
investigated from every side; the viewpoints which have been brought forward are constantly repeated, without bringing an end of the discussion any
nearer. Only new sources, which are hardly to be expected, or essentially
new ideas offer any hope for real progress' (Schmithals, *Office*, p. 20).
[4] *Office*, p. 40.   [5] *Ibid.*, p. 41.   [6] *Ibid.*, p. 42.   [7] *Ibid.*

Schmithals' idea of two discrete dimensions of authority derives from his view of the 'gnostic apostle'. Unlike Paul, who is a representative of Christ, the gnostic apostle is not merely an envoy of Christ, but Christ himself.

In the gnostic apostle, indeed, Christ himself speaks. There is, therefore, no higher authority than the apostle, and no other apostolic authority than that of Christ himself...There is no question that such a radical claim had more convincing power for the gnostics, who bring Christ himself to expression, than for Paul, who can only assert that his message comes from Christ.[1]

Something of this anthropology of gnosticism, which is not accessible to Paul as representative of the proclaimed Christ, is, in Schmithals' view, evident in the matter of ἐξουσία. 'This grounding appears less disjointed when [Paul] refers to his ἐξουσία, in other words, to his *unmediated* authority as a pneumatic...He speaks in the traditional gnostic conceptualization, and if *we* can hardly recognize how he conceived of the practical application of his ἐξουσία, Paul himself may already have had the same difficulty.'[2]

On Schmithals' reading, the first kind of Pauline authority, that derived from the gospel, is 'unsuccessful' because not competitive with the gnostic claim. The second kind, however, associated with gnosticism, is opaque. Its practical consequences are not clear to us and were probably not clear to Paul. This leaves us in the embarrassing position of not knowing the value of Paul's gnostically derived sense of authority and not being able to see much value in the sense of authority more traditionally derived. We have reservations about Schmithals' whole genetic thesis,[3] and the idea of 'double' authority appears to be more a concession to that thesis than anything else. Schmithals *is* quite correct in pointing to *two foci* of Paul's understanding of authority, but they are integrally related.

[1] *Ibid.*, p. 215.　　　　[2] *Ibid.*, p. 216, italics his.

[3] In part, the matter at hand illustrates a general tendency of Schmithals' to divorce entirely 'gnosis' and 'church', itself a way of thinking which trades on the later division and reads it back uncritically into the earliest period. Other objections to Schmithals' work are summed up in Schweizer's comment that Schmithals has replaced one unknown quantity, the X of an apostle, with another, the Y of gnosticism (E. Schweizer, *TLZ* 87 (1962), cols. 837-40).

A study of recent secondary literature on the apostolic idea reveals clearly that no basic normative concept of the apostle was available in the time of Paul. We cannot make Luke the norm, nor can we take refuge in the *Shaliach* hypothesis. As it happens, we have only Paul himself as witness to one form of apostolic self-consciousness in his own time. Paul's sense of what it means to be an apostle is etched sharply enough in his letters to make it clear that apostles are something special. He belongs to a group of apostles, however ill-defined that group may be,[1] and his claims are intimately connected to his temporal primacy as one who establishes the communities through his missionary preaching activity. In light of this fact, it seems wise to isolate in investigation what in fact is isolated in our sources for the early decades of the church – the *Pauline* apostolic picture. Of course, Paul does not remain forever isolated. For reasons and in ways that are not entirely clear, he is gradually incorporated into a somewhat fuzzy picture of an earlier apostolate. Certainly one claim is being made for him in that regard, one feature is thought to bind him to other apostles: All alike are looked back upon as 'authorities' in the root meaning of that term. For that reason, the primary question to address to Paul's picture of the apostle is not the question of legitimacy, but that of authority.

[1] It is difficult to see how there could be any special apostolic claim or self-consciousness among gnostics, on Schmithals' view that to be a gnostic is by definition to be an apostle.

CHAPTER 3

THE GOSPEL, THE KERYGMA AND THE APOSTLE

THE APOSTLE AND THE GOSPEL

Terminology

When Paul discusses Paul, what he says often centers on or extends the term ἀπόστολος. It is impossible to move directly from the linguistic background of that term to a full description of its implications without paying particular attention to the context of Paul's use of the term. We can also observe characteristic associations when Paul speaks on the form or function of an apostle. These are no less important since they provide a necessary background for understanding what he says more specifically about his own apostolic status.[1] Finally, we shall need to observe the differences between Paul's introduction of the category 'apostle' when it is primarily illustrative and those occasions when he is responding to some challenge concerning his apostolic claim.

One term, one central concept stands out as inextricably tied to the purpose and the activity of the apostle. Nothing is more closely associated with the 'apostle' than the 'gospel'. Paul cannot separate his calling as apostle from its purpose – to serve the gospel. Thus in the opening words of the letter to Rome, where he is not yet personally known, Paul describes himself: '...a slave of Christ Jesus, called (κλητός) an apostle, set apart

[1] Disagreement about the breadth of Paul's apostolic self-consciousness explains in part the differences of opinion about its centrality. Like Campenhausen ('Apostelbegriff'), F. Neugebauer expresses reservations on this matter and warns against reading the idea of apostleship 'too quickly into the text' (*In Christus* [Göttingen, 1961], p. 115). Yet a bit later he suggests that the apostle's 'work and person' cannot be separated. If Paul's work is that of an apostle and this cannot be separated from his person, the force of the earlier remark remains a puzzle. On the other side, E. Güttgemanns, *Der leidende Apostel und sein Herr* (Göttingen, 1966; FRLANT 90), p. 12, n. 4 describes the apostolate as that place where the whole of Pauline theology comes to a focus.

35

2-2

for God's gospel (ἀφωρισμένος εἰς εὐαγγέλιον θεοῦ)...' (1: 1). This close association of apostolic calling with being set apart for the gospel is the heart of the apostolic autobiography, as can be seen from Gal. 1: 15f.: 'When he who had set me apart... and had called me (ὁ ἀφορίσας με...καὶ καλέσας) was pleased to reveal his Son to me, in order that I might preach him (ἵνα εὐαγγελίζωμαι αὐτόν)...'

The terms 'apostle' and 'gospel' are more than just intimately connected; they are functionally related. What precise forms that relationship assumes must be determined in part by a closer examination of the terms clustering around the Pauline references to 'gospel'.

Εὐαγγελίζεσθαι as Apostolic Activity

Nothing comes closer to suggesting the central, missionary nature of apostolic activity than the verb εὐαγγελίζεσθαι, 'to preach good news'. Paul uses the word nineteen times in the homologoumena (not counting the variant in Rom. 10: 15). In every instance he has in mind the missionary proclamation which is his task, but the range of that proclamation is broader than we might initially expect.[1]

This verb is used most specifically where it is found with its cognate noun εὐαγγέλιον as direct object:

I Cor. 15: 1: Now I would remind you, brethren, in what terms I *preached* to you the *gospel*...

II Cor. 11: 7: ...because I *preached* God's *gospel* to you without charge...

Gal. 1: 11: ...the *gospel preached* by me is not according to man...

In these passages we have broad contextual agreement for the technical use of the verb. Paul is referring to his own past action

---

[1] On the background and origin of the terms εὐαγγελίζεσθαι and εὐαγγέλιον cf. G. Friedrich, 'εὐαγγελίζομαι' etc., *TDNT*, II (Grand Rapids, 1964), pp. 707–37; J. Schniewind, *Die Begriffe Wort und Evangelium bei Paulus* (Bonn, 1910); *Euangelion: Ursprung und erste Gestalt des Begriffs Evangelium* (Gütersloh; Vol. I, 1927; Vol. II, 1931); E. Molland, *Das Paulinische Euangelion: Das Wort und die Sache* (Oslo, 1939); M. Burrows, 'The Origin of the Term "Gospel"', *JBL*, 44 (1925), 21–33; W. Schneemelcher, 'Gospel' in *New Testament Apocrypha*, Vol. I (ed. E. Hennecke and W. Schneemelcher, [Philadelphia, 1963]), pp. 71–5; P. Stuhlmacher, *Das paulinische Evangelium*, I (Göttingen, 1968; FRLANT, 95). Cf. also W. Marxsen, *Mark the Evangelist* (Nashville, 1969), pp. 117–50.

in the communities, a missionary activity about which he feels constrained, in the present polemical situation, to remind his hearers.

Even where the verb does not have εὐαγγέλιον as its object, its use can be equally specific. In Rom. 10: 15 Paul quotes Isa. 52: 7 with the words 'to preach good things'. In Isaiah the verb appears to have only a general sense, but Paul's use is more technical, as v. 16 shows. The same is true of the absolute use of the verb in II Cor. 10: 16 ('so that we may preach [the gospel] in lands beyond you') and Gal. 4: 13 ('...I preached [the gospel] to you at first...'). In similar fashion, Gal. 1: 8 uses the verb twice as the equivalent of the *constructio Graeca*. This is shown by the phrase ἕτερον εὐαγγέλιον of v. 6, which is explained and given its positive content in v. 8.[1] Closely parallel to II Cor. 10: 16 is Rom. 15: 20, where Paul is also speaking of the missionary task, i.e., of preaching the gospel where that has not already been done ('...thus making it my ambition to preach [the gospel]...'). That this same absolute use is to be found in Rom. 1: 15 (cf. v. 16) and I Cor. 9: 16–18 can be seen from the presence of the noun εὐαγγέλιον. Finally, in this catalogue of the absolute use of the verb, there remains I Cor. 1: 17 where the use of ἀποστέλλειν ('to send out') indicates that the verb 'to preach good news' has the same technical nuances that it does in other absolute occurrences.

A third category comprises a cluster of occurrences in Gal. 1: 9, 16 and 23. Here we find the verb used neither absolutely nor with the accusative of the cognate noun, but with three separate accusative objects:

Gal. 1: 9: ...if any one is preaching *you* [RSV: to you a gospel] contrary to what you received...

1: 16: ...that I might preach *him* [sc. the Son of God]...

1: 23: ...he is now preaching the *faith* he once destroyed...

Of the three, the first case is by far the most arresting, though we find it similarly in Luke 3: 18; Acts 8: 40; 14: 21; 16: 10; I Peter 1: 12. It seems roughly equivalent to the English term 'evangelize' and the passages cited indicate that by the end of

---

[1] It is possible that one should see here a greater emphasis on the establishment of an εὐαγγέλιον by the activity of 'preaching' than the ordinary *constructio Graeca* demands (so, Schniewind, *Wort*, p. 68).

THE GOSPEL, THE KERYGMA AND THE APOSTLE

the first century the verb had become established in the Church's glossary as the equivalent of the transitive verb 'to convert'. Paul's use, however, is dictated by the change from a hypothetical to an actual situation in Galatia, a change which he indicates in part by just this usage. And it is clear both from the substitution for εὐαγγελίζεσθαι with the dative in v. 8 and from the addition of the words 'contrary to that which you received' that the noun εὐαγγέλιον (v. 7) is still very much in the foreground.

The other accusative objects, in vv. 16 and 23, look like synonyms for or modifications of the object 'gospel'. This would mean that the 'gospel' can itself be thought of as 'his son' or '(the) faith'. If so, then their full significance will become clearer when we turn to analyze the noun.[1]

These passages are striking in one regard: In almost every one of them Paul's reference is personal. He does not talk of 'preaching the gospel' in general or abstract terms, but speaks of himself and his own work or of a very specific situation in which he also has a deep interest, as Gal. 1: 8–9. Sometimes the reference is to future activity and expresses what he hopes to do (Rom. 15: 20; II Cor. 10: 16). Sometimes it is clearly to past activity (I Cor. 15: 1–2; Gal. 4: 13 and II Cor. 11: 7). It should be noted that here Paul either defends what he did in the past or makes an attempt to call his past actions to the minds of his readers in order to suggest what the norm is by which he measures the present situation. Hence every passage is found in a polemical situation, and in each Paul seems to be recalling his own past work of 'preaching the gospel' as an authoritative deed. This is clearest in I Cor. 15: 1–2 but evident too in the other passages.

Thus it is no surprise to see that εὐαγγελίζεσθαι, when Paul uses it, is closely tied to his apostolic self-consciousness. The one who knows himself to be sent (*apostolos*) knows himself to be sent for the purpose of preaching the gospel. This is self-evident for Gal. 1: 11, 16, 23. But elsewhere, too, this close relationship is revealed through the concepts Paul uses in speaking of his task as being εὐαγγελίζεσθαι. The infinitive is used in I Cor. 1: 17 to express the purpose of Christ's sending of Paul: 'For Christ did not send me to baptize but to preach.'

[1] The noun is used by Paul with the genitives τῆς πίστεως and αὐτοῦ for τοῦ υἱοῦ αὐτοῦ.

38

In this connection between being sent and preaching lies the significance of Rom. 10: 15, although Paul's reference here is general and not personal. It is not the beautiful feet of those who 'preach good news' which interests the apostle, but the assurance which scripture yields that God has a plan which makes his message available to all men. If God's provision is to be executed, it is clear that those who preach must be sent, v. 15.[1]

Only a shade less direct in equating apostleship with the gospel's proclamation are those passages where Paul speaks of his *duty*. In the argument of I Cor. 9: 16–18 he characterizes himself as one on whom the necessity of preaching has been laid: 'Woe to me if I do not preach.' To avoid this charge would be to deny his very apostolic function, for he has been entrusted with a commission.[2] All of this comes in the context of a chaptei which begins with the words: 'Am I not free? Am I not an apostle?' Similarly, in Rom. 1: 14–15 he represents his 'eagerness' to preach to those who are in Rome as a natural extension or result (οὕτως, v. 15) of his being 'obligated' to Greeks as well as to barbarians, to the wise as well as to the foolish.

From these examples it is clear how central to his understanding of apostolic authority Paul makes the task of 'preaching good news'.[3] Yet in almost every instance the content of that preaching remains vague and ill-defined; in almost every instance the verb εὐαγγελίζεσθαι seems to presuppose the definition of its cognate noun.

[1] Paul may be closer to the Massoretic text than to LXX in his quotation from Isa. 52: 7 (O. Michel, *Der Brief an die Römer* [Göttingen, 1957[11]; KEK], p. 230, n. 2; C. K. Barrett, *A Commentary on the Epistle to the Romans* [New York, 1957], p. 204) but the peculiar plural τῶν εὐαγγελιζομένων is clear evidence of Paul's use here of Rabbinic tradition as in *Midr. Ps.* 147: 1 and *Pesikt. r.* 35 (161a). Cf. Friedrich, *TDNT*, II, pp. 715f. and Str.-B., III, 9.

[2] J. Weiss, *Der erste Korintherbrief* (Göttingen, 1925[11]; KEK), p. 241, takes the difficult v. 17 as misplaced, its proper position being after 18a. This makes the verse expressive of Paul's 'willingness' in preaching the gospel, and transforms the οἰκονομίαν πεπίστευμαι into a negative image of a slave who has obligations but no special rights. But the slavery image (if that is the best interpretation) is a positive one for Paul. This can be seen from the extensive use of δοῦλος in the letters, the explicit image of 'stewards' (οἰκονόμοι) in I Cor. 4: 1, 2 and the conjunction of δουλεύειν and εὐαγγέλιον in Phil. 2: 22. Cf. also Gal. 2: 7 and I Thess. 2: 4.

[3] '[Paul] can use εὐαγγελίζεσθαι to describe his whole activity as an apostle', Friedrich, *TDNT*, II, p. 719.

One passage, I Thess. 3: 6, is usually regarded as a clear exception to Paul's usual, technical use of the verb: 'But since Timothy has come to us from you and brought (this) good news (εὐαγγελισαμένου) to us: your faith and love, and the fact that you always remember us kindly longing to see us just as we are to see you...'[1] Whether or not the word is used technically here can only be determined from the scope of Paul's understanding of 'the gospel'. Is a report on the internal condition of a Christian community, and particularly its present relationship to its founder, somehow related to preaching?

The Apostle and the Εὐαγγέλιον

When in Rom. 1: 1 Paul describes himself as 'set apart for the gospel' he means that he is called to preach it. But this verbal nuance is not the whole of what is implied by the noun εὐαγγέλιον, for the subsequent relative clause stresses a substantive character as well. The 'preaching of the gospel' becomes almost imperceptibly transformed into the 'content' of the gospel,[2] for it must be the content 'which [God] promised beforehand through his prophets in the holy scriptures'.

From this starting point we can examine several passages where one or both of these ideas seem to be present in the use of the word. In *I Cor. 9: 14* we find this dual nature of the term: 'In the same way the Lord ordered those who proclaim (καταγγέλλουσιν) the gospel to live off the gospel' (ἐκ τοῦ εὐαγγελίου ζῆν; RSV: 'should get their living by the gospel'). If one is to get his living from the gospel, he is obviously to do so by his preaching. In this instance the noun has those qualities characteristic of the verb,[3] even while it appears a second time as the object of the verb 'to proclaim'.

At other times this metamorphosis of the noun into its verbal meaning is not so closely checked. In *Phil. 1: 12* Paul says that

---

[1] Friedrich (*ibid.*, p. 720), for example, regards this as a 'variation' from the usual use though he somehow seems to regard Paul as the one who ultimately brings good news 'from the field where he has been working as a missionary'.

[2] Cf. Molland, *Euangelion*, p. 48, 'The content of the message and its proclamation are not two distinct meanings of the word εὐαγγέλιον, only two sides of the one concept.'

[3] *Ibid.*, p. 40: 'ἐκ τοῦ εὐαγγελίου amounts to the same thing as ἐκ τοῦ εὐαγγελίζεσθαι'.

'the things which have happened to me have served to advance the gospel'. From the context it is clear that the delivery of the gospel is what is advanced. In 2: 22 Paul speaks of Timothy as one who, like a son with his father 'has served in the gospel', and the same meaning is intended as is clear also in 4: 15: '...in the beginning of the gospel...no church entered into partnership with me...except you alone.' II Cor. 2: 12 belongs in this same category[1] as do 8: 18, I Thess. 3: 2 and probably Philem. 13.

If εὐαγγέλιον can shade off into references to the delivery of the gospel, it is nevertheless true that it most characteristically and frequently refers to the object of preaching, the gospel thought of in terms of its content. Most notably this is the case in a number of passages with *verba dicendi*: κηρύσσειν, Gal. 2: 2; I Thess. 2: 9; καταγγέλλειν, I Cor. 9: 14; λαλεῖν, I Thess. 2: 2; and as we have already seen, εὐαγγελίζεσθαι itself, I Cor. 15: 1f.; II Cor. 11: 7; Gal. 1: 11.

In part because of this evidence interpreters have not hesitated to assume a high degree of specificity for the term 'gospel', and to assign to it a certain dogmatic flavor. Schniewind thinks that in just such passages the noun approaches the meaning of 'doctrine', that implicit in it is the idea of 'truth'.[2] He builds his case particularly on II Cor. 4: 3 and Gal. 1: 6f. There can be no doubt that in both instances the conception of the gospel encompasses a claim to truth, a claim specifically set over against what Paul regards as an unacceptable alternative. But does that of itself make appropriate the assumption that the gospel is *christliche Lehre*, as Schniewind supposes?

In these passages it is not a matter of setting one true, 'doctrinal' set of propositions over against another. The matter of the 'truth' of the gospel is considerably more ambiguous and even sophisticated than that. Furthermore, the need for caution is underscored by a peculiarity in Paul's linguistic conventions which may be of some importance. He never uses πιστεύειν, in

---

[1] Thus the phrase is difficult to translate accurately, as is the case in all these noun usages. But Molland (*Euangelion*, p. 48) properly rejects Windisch's view that the noun has become a pure *nomen actionis* here. Not only is that conclusion made questionable by the following genitive, but the ambiguity in I Cor. 9: 14 and Rom. 1: 11 dictates against it. Cf. H. Windisch, *Der zweite Korintherbrief* (Göttingen, 1924⁹; KEK), p. 94.

[2] *Wort*, p. 76.

41

the sense of 'believe', with εὐαγγέλιον as its object. Their close association is apparent in such places as Rom. 1: 16 ('the gospel is the power of God to all who believe' – but *not*, 'believe in it'); I Cor. 3: 5 (Paul and Apollos as missionaries are 'servants through whom you believed'); and 15: 4 ('whether then I or they, so we preached [κηρύσσειν] and so you believed'). However close Paul may come in associating the two terms, he avoids making 'the gospel' the object of faith. In I Cor. 15: 1–3, where one might think such a connection inevitable, Paul leaves πιστεύειν without a stated object. What stands in place of 'believing the gospel' is 'heeding' it. Similarly, in Rom. 10: 14–16 it is clear that a man cannot 'believe' what he has not heard and this hearing depends on there being somebody to preach the gospel. But when Paul must acknowledge that preaching the gospel does not guarantee this belief, he says 'but not all have *heeded* the gospel'. In I Cor. 9: 13 when he speaks of an 'acknowledgment' (ὁμολογία) of the gospel, he can call this a 'submission' (ὑποταγή) to it, obedience.

In this regard *I Cor. 15: 1ff.* is instructive. It indicates that there is some limiting factor in the objective, or content, character of the gospel even where this idea is undeniably present. The gospel which Paul preached is thought of here as a present reality in which the Corinthians can be said to 'stand' and 'through which' they *are being* saved. The focus is less on the gospel as *what* they *believed* than on the gospel as *where* they *are*. A similar emphasis is found in II Cor. 4: 3, where Paul speaks of 'our gospel' which may be veiled. The content of that gospel is significant because of its relationship to the *present situation* which Paul is addressing, a situation which is marked by some people's unbelief. The (our) gospel *is* veiled to those who *are being* destroyed. The periphrastic use of the perfect participle κεκαλυμμένον and the present participle ἀπολλύμενοι indicate that there is an on-going process here involving both the gospel and its hearers. The same is true of Gal. 1: 6f. and a number of other passages as well, so that we must conclude that even where Paul in some extended fashion considers εὐαγγέλιον as a body of content, there is a dynamic characteristic in the word which lies just below the surface and is essential for determining in what way the gospel is 'true'.

While the gospel certainly must have its content and the term can be used to intimate a more or less fixed body of material, its point of gravity can also lie somewhere outside the sum total of its content. The gospel is not simply and unambiguously the object of belief, and we shall see that very little attempt is made in the letters to spell out τὸ εὐαγγέλιον in propositional terms. So it is at least with some reservation that we should speak of this particular usage as the equivalent of 'doctrine'. Nevertheless, the connotations of the word as the fixed object of preaching, the thing preached rather than the preaching itself, is very clear.

Thus there are three categories of meaning. One is this fixed object of preaching, one is the act of preaching, and one is something rather more elusive, the gospel as an on-going entity 'in' which one can 'be' or 'stand'.

Such variety, and particularly the subtlety introduced by the last of these three categories, leads to what has been called the 'pregnant' usage of the noun. By pregnant we mean, with Schniewind, that use of the noun which exhibits its significance as an 'effective force'.[1]

In *Rom. 1: 16–17* Paul says: 'For I am not ashamed of the gospel; it is the power of God for salvation to every one who has faith...For in it the righteousness of God is being revealed.' Just what it means to call the gospel a 'power' is not entirely clear from this passage alone, but Paul does indicate why he refers to it in this way. It is power because God's righteousness is being revealed in it from faith to faith. 'Ἀποκαλύπτεται 'does not mean that the preached gospel expounds some teaching about righteousness, but that through it righteousness becomes a possibility (which in faith becomes reality) for the hearer of the gospel'.[2] This is the same meaning that the word has in 1: 18, from which we can see that the revelation is itself an event, whether or not it is so perceived by the man to whom it is directed. There appears to be no room in 1: 16–17 for understanding the gospel as a body of teaching, whatever it means to call it a 'power'. Rather, the gospel is the vehicle through which God brings about a possibility and a reality.

---

[1] '...the pregnant quality of the gospel concept resides primarily in the fact that the gospel is thought of as effective' (*Wort*, p. 78). Cf. Friedrich, *TDNT*, II, p. 731, '...proves itself to be living power'.

[2] R. Bultmann, *The Theology of the New Testament* (Vol. I, New York, 1951), pp. 274–5. Cf. Schniewind, *Wort*, pp. 82–3.

This gospel as power has a goal. It is directed εἰς σωτηρίαν, toward salvation. If 'righteousness' is an eschatological-forensic concept and refers to the declaration or pronouncement which is the 'right-wising' of man, righteousness is not quality but event.[1] To say, then, that God's righteousness *is being* revealed in the gospel is to say that God's activity of pronouncing righteous is made effective in the gospel. The passage does not allow us to determine any further what the nature of the gospel is which serves as this vehicle for revealing what God is doing. We have ruled out only that interpretation which would make εὐαγγέλιον the sum of instruction about God's righteousness. For such an interpretation is a misunderstanding of both terms, 'gospel' and 'righteousness of God'.[2] The gospel seems rather to be the 'field' in which God chooses to act.

In *Rom. 11: 28* the gospel is not so immediately linked with the idea of revelation, but it is clearly involved with God's plan for man's salvation. Paul is speaking of the Jews and their place vis-à-vis the Gentiles in God's design. More particularly, in this passage he is balancing two ideas: The rejection of the Jews is temporary, and for the benefit of the Gentiles; the Gentiles have no ground for boasting, no cause for complacency over against the Jews. Lest the Gentiles 'be wise in their own conceits' he insists on the full salvation of the Jews (vv. 25–7), quoting Isa. 59: 20–1. He continues in v. 28: κατὰ μὲν τὸ εὐαγγέλιον ἐχθροὶ δι᾽ ὑμᾶς, κατὰ δὲ τὴν ἐκλογὴν ἀγαπητοὶ διὰ τοὺς πατέρας. The two clauses are in parallel construction if we assume ἐχθροί is to

---

[1] Bultmann, *Theology*, I, pp. 270–4. On Bultmann's reading of the genitive in 'righteousness of God' as simply one of authorship (viz., Rom. 10: 3), cf. E. Käsemann, 'God's Righteousness in Paul', *The Bultmann School of Biblical Interpretation* (New York, 1965; JTC), pp. 100–10. Cf. also P. Stuhlmacher, *Gottes Gerechtigkeit bei Paulus* (Göttingen, 1965; FRLANT 87) and Bultmann's response to Käsemann, 'ΔΙΚΑΙΟΣΥΝΗ ΘΕΟΥ', *JBL* 83 (1964), 12–16.

[2] Käsemann underscores this point: 'The widespread view of God's righteousness as a divine attribute can now be rejected as misleading...it contradicts the basic Old Testament, Jewish understanding of righteousness as loyalty to the community; and it breaks down on the point that the conferral of a divine attribute on men cannot be convincingly made intelligent. Δικαιοσύνη θεοῦ is for Paul as well as for the Old Testament and Judaism a noun of action, which does not describe God as he is in himself but God as he reveals himself' ('Righteousness', p. 104).

be taken in the passive sense.[1] The Jews are 'hated' and 'loved' with regard to (κατά) the gospel and the election. Κατά τὸ εὐαγγέλιον cannot mean 'according to their attitude toward' the gospel, as Lietzmann and Michel would translate it,[2] for it must be parallel with κατά τὴν ἐκλογήν, and it makes no sense to say that the Jews are loved according to their attitude toward the election. To be loved is part of the evidence of their election; they are loved because they are elected. Paul can make the construction parallel because there is simultaneously an identity and a distinction between the two ways of God's working, represented by the gospel and by election. This equation is not fatuous. Paul intends that it be taken seriously, for the parallelism continues in the ensuing verses and at the same time dissolves into a unity expressed by the singular κλῆσις of v. 29 and the entirety of v. 32. If it is difficult to give precise definition to so plastic a term as 'gospel' when used in this way, we can only say that it is, for Gentiles, what the 'election' is for Jews – the disposition under which men, if they are faithful, can live out their lives.

Somewhat later, in *Rom. 15: 16*, Paul offers an example of 'gospel' used in some conscious analogy to Judaism, though neither the thought nor the structure exceeds the limit of an image or figure of speech. He speaks of himself as one who has been given grace by God 'to be a minister [λειτουργόν] of Christ Jesus to the Gentiles, serving the gospel of God as a priest [ἱερουργοῦντα τὸ εὐαγγέλιον τοῦ θεοῦ] in order that the offering [προσφορά] of the Gentiles may be acceptable, sanctified by the Holy Spirit'. The language is hieratic and even sacrificial,[3] as it is elsewhere in Paul (cf. Rom. 12: 1 and Phil. 2: 17, for example). Like any good metaphor this one resists being pressed too far. Paul is not really a priest and the Gentiles are not really a sacrifice. But the choice of such an image to

[1] Michel, *Römer*, p. 251; W. Sanday and A. C. Headlam, *A Critical and Exegetical Commentary on the Epistle to the Romans* (New York, 1902⁵/1958; ICC), p. 337. For evidence outside the NT for such a translation, cf. W. Arndt and F. W. Gingrich, *A Greek–English Lexicon of the New Testament and Other Early Christian Literature* (Cambridge, 1957), p. 331 (cited hereafter as B[auer] A[rndt] G[ingrich]).

[2] Michel, *Römer*, and H. Lietzmann, *An die Römer* (Tübingen, 1933⁴; HNT) *ad loc.*

[3] Cf. J. Roloff, *Apostolat*, p. 114.

express his apostolic self-consciousness (vv. 14, 15a) is suggestive. As Michel has pointed out, Paul here understands the gospel as the 'ordinance and the law in accordance with which the Gentiles are sacrificed'.[1] It is the ordinance under which are ranged proper functions of the apostle (priest) and the Gentiles (sacrifice). As in 11 : 28, the nuances of εὐαγγέλιον are fluid and more suggestive than specific. The gospel is not the law of the Temple. It is not election; it is not cultus. For the Gentiles it is what all these were for the Jews: the structure of man's life responsive to God's will.

In vv. 17–19 Paul explains how and why he 'boasts in Christ Jesus' of his work. He can do so because Christ has used him (δι' ἐμοῦ) to bring about the obedience of the Gentiles. Paul's use of ὑπακοή accounts for eleven of the fifteen occurrences in the New Testament. It is characteristic of his task as an apostle to bring about obedience (Rom. 1 : 15); it is characteristic of the Christian life to be obedient, or even to be 'a slave of obedience to righteousness' as opposed to a slave of sin to death (Rom. 6 : 16). In II Cor. 10 : 5–6 Paul's obligation to obedience is merged with the community's. In short, obedience is a goal toward which the Christian presses. Here in Rom. 15 : 18 Paul says that Christ has accomplished it through him 'by word and deed, by power of signs and wonders, by the power of the spirit'. Paul has not only preached a word; he has inaugurated a δύναμις even the δύναμις πνεύματος. We are led then to that *crux interpretum*, v. 19, where Paul concludes: '...(so that from Jerusalem and as far round as Illyricum) I have fully preached the gospel' [με...πεπληρωκέναι τὸ εὐαγγέλιον]. Paul could mean that he has 'finished' preaching the gospel in the East,[2] or he could mean that he has brought the gospel to its 'fulfill-ment', to its destiny among the Gentiles.[3] Although the former

[1] *Römer*, pp. 327–8.

[2] With varying nuances, P. Althaus, *Der Brief an die Römer* (Göttingen, 1954), p. 132; M.-J. Lagrange, Saint Paul; *Épître aux Romains* (Paris, 1950), p. 353; T. Zahn, *Der Brief des Paulus an die Römer* (Leipzig, 1910), p. 599, n. 33. Cf. also Michel, *Römer*, p. 330; BAG, p. 677; J. Knox, 'Romans 15 : 14–33 and Paul's Conception of his Apostolic Mission', *JBL* 83 (1964), 8–11.

[3] With varying nuances, R. Asting, *Die Verkündigung des Wortes im Urchristentum* (Stuttgart, 1939), p. 138; J. Jervell, 'Zur Frage der Traditions-grundlage der Apostelgeschichte', *ST* 16 (1962), 33–4; E. Lohmeyer, *Die Briefe an die Kolosser und an Philemon* (Göttingen, 1956[11]; KEK), p. 80.

is by far the preferred interpretation it represents both an un-usual use of the verb and a highly stylized manner of speaking.[1] Furthermore, v. 19b is introduced as a result clause (ὥστε) which is linked to the preceding 'what Christ has wrought through me'. This passage contains two separate ideas: (a) Christ's working through Paul to bring about the obedience of the Gentiles; and (b) the means by which this was done. So, too, v. 19b concerns itself with (a) the area of Paul's work, and (b) the fact that there he has 'fulfilled' the gospel of Christ. It would seem most straightforward to assume that Paul chooses πληροῦν to describe his relationship to these δυνάμεις of 18b and 19a, just as he chooses to make explicit which 'nations' he has served in. 'Fulfilling' the gospel is not having finished an assignment so much as having participated in the full inaugura-tion of those forces which Paul has mentioned as characteristic of the way Christ wins obedience from the nations, through him. The perfect tense, πεπληρωκέναι, seems to underscore the con-tinuing nature of these forces while describing at the same time Paul's past action. There can be no doubt that Paul goes on, in vv. 20 and 23 especially, to envision what new fields he can anticipate now that one phase of his ministry is ended.[2] Yet the term 'fulfill' does not describe the end of that labor, but rather the way in which Paul has executed his task: fully, in word and deed, with signs and wonders, etc. 'Preaching the gospel' im-plies setting in motion these forces.[3]

Like Rom. 15: 18, *I Thess. 1: 4–5* speaks of the gospel's being accompanied by 'power' and 'spirit'. 'For we know, brethren beloved by God, your election, because our gospel did not come to you [lit. 'happen among you'] in word only but also in

[1] Cf. Barrett, *Romans*, p. 276: 'It is evident...that when Paul says that in this region he has completed the gospel of Christ, he does not mean that he (or anyone else) has preached the gospel to every person in it, but that it has been covered in a representative way. The Gospel has been heard; more could not be expected before the *parousia*.'

[2] Verse 20 is particularly difficult to reconcile with 1: 15. For a recent suggestion cf. R. Funk, 'The Apostolic Parousia: Form and Significance' in *Christian History and Interpretation* (ed. W. R. Farmer *et al.*, Cambridge, 1967), pp. 249–68.

[3] F. Leenhardt, *The Epistle to the Romans* (London, 1961), *ad loc.*, takes πεπληρωκέναι to refer to both the scope and the manner of the preaching of the gospel. 'The gospel has been endowed with the two-fold richness of having been both very effective and universally recognized...'

47

power and in the Holy Spirit and in full conviction.' As in Rom. 11: 28, Paul can speak of the community's 'election'. Apparently the reason he knows them to be chosen is that the gospel has reached them with such accompaniment. The entire encomium of vv. 2–4a shows a parallelism which we should not overlook. While the causal clause of v. 5 conveys the ground for Paul's knowledge of the positive results of his preaching, he has already said in v. 3 that he, Silvanus and Timothy remember 'your work of faith and labor of love and steadfastness of hope...' Hence the fullness of the gospel, its power, the Holy Spirit and in this case also the 'full conviction', while not deduced from the actions of the Thessalonians, stand in a positive relation to those actions. Paul's conclusion from all of this is that his visit was not 'in vain' (οὐ κενή, 2: 1). The *power* of his *gospel* has become a *power* in the *community*.

Paul also mentions his remembrance of the community in his letter to Philippi, expressing thanks to God 'for your partnership in the gospel [ἐπὶ τῇ κοινωνίᾳ ὑμῶν εἰς τὸ εὐαγγέλιον] from the first day until now' (*Phil. 1: 5*). There is no real agreement on the proper interpretation of the phrase ἐπὶ...εὐαγγέλιον. Certainly it is grammatically noteworthy. We should expect either ἐπὶ τῇ κοινωνίᾳ ὑμῶν τῇ τοῦ εὐαγγελίου, or, if εἰς and the accusative are to stand, a personal reference like εἰς τοὺς ἁγίους (cf. II Cor. 1: 13) as is always found with κοινωνία and εἰς with the accusative. As Lohmeyer[1] points out, our expression is between the two. The first of these would actually be 'un-Pauline',[2] and the phrase εἰς τὸ εὐαγγέλιον seems to be Paul's substitution for it.[3] Thus the prepositional phrase does not demand that the term 'partnership' refer to some act of the Philippians so

[1] E. Lohmeyer, *Der Brief an die Philipper* (Göttingen, 1961¹²; KEK), p. 17.
[2] H. Seesemann, *Der Begriff* KOINωNIA *im Neuen Testament* (Giessen, 1933), p. 75, argues that Paul never repeats the article of a ruling noun in a genitive construction where the noun and the genitive are separated. Thus, while I Thess. 1: 8 (cf. also Rom. 7: 5; 8: 39; II Cor. 9: 3) offers us an example of correct usage (ἡ πίστις ὑμῶν ἡ πρὸς τὸν θεόν), it cannot be used to show that Phil. 1: 5 is to be interpreted like other passages using κοινωνία εἰς (viz., II Cor. 9: 13; Rom. 15: 26).
[3] It is true, of course, that εἰς can here be the equivalent of ἐν as it frequently is in hellenistic Greek. Cf. F. Blass and A. Debrunner, *A Greek Grammar of the New Testament and Other Early Christian Literature* (tr. R. W. Funk [Chicago, 1961]), par. 205 (cited hereafter as BDF).

specific as that of collecting money for Jerusalem (as in Rom. 15: 26 and II Cor. 9: 13).[1]

Such an interpretation is not demanded by the prepositional construction and does nothing to explain the unusual phrase. Moreover, it is contradictory to the tenor of the entire thanksgiving to tie it to this particular mundane transaction.[2] Paul thanks not the Philippians but God. It is not for some specific help they have rendered in conjunction with his apostolic activity that they elicit such a response, but for their participation *in the gospel* 'from the first day until now'. It is this reference to time, and a similar one in the next verse, which stamps the concept of 'partnership' in the gospel with its significance and shows its meaning. 'And I am certain of this, that he who began a good work in you will bring it to completion at (ἄχρι) the day of Christ Jesus' (v. 6). From the time when Paul first came to Philippi until now (ἄχρι τοῦ νῦν) they have had this fellowship in the gospel. For that he is thankful to God. Just so he is confident of their continuing until the day of Christ (ἄχρι ἡμέρας Χριστοῦ Ἰησοῦ). This eschatological note puts the otherwise superficially temporal notes of v. 5 into the proper perspective. From the 'first day' through 'now' to the Lord's day is no longer just a normal span of time. It is the time of salvation, the eschatological milieu of the Christian community which has a beginning and an end, but whose end is outside of history. The time from the first day until now is plain and visible, and for what the Philippians have been and done Paul can give thanks. The time from now until that final day is one about which he has a conviction, a persuasion. It is still a time invisible, in which only God can be said to be working in the community toward its goal. But just as the reference to the Lord's Day determines the eschatological nature of the whole, so the reference to God's 'beginning' and 'completing' a good work suggests that it is God who is the author of the participation εἰς τὸ εὐαγγέλιον of v. 5, as was already implied in the fact that the thanks are due to God.

Under the rubric 'partnership in the gospel' is ranged an understanding of the whole existence of the eschatological community. In conjunction with the 'first day', the term gospel has

---

[1] Asting, *Verkündigung*, p. 391.
[2] Lohmeyer, *Philipperbrief*, p. 17.

a specific referent, that which at a given time and place Paul preached in Philippi. But in conjunction with the subsequent thought of vv. 5 and 6 it moves out to mean a *force*, and even more than a force, that *source* of life to which the faithful community relates itself, a divine action.

The same understanding of εὐαγγέλιον lies behind *Phil. 1: 27*. Only the mood has changed, so that Paul can exhort the Philippians to do what, in 1: 5, he has expressed as God's will for them: '(Only) conduct yourselves in a manner worthy of the gospel of Christ [ἀξίως τοῦ εὐαγγελίου τοῦ Χριστοῦ πολιτεύεσθε] (so that whether I come and see you or am absent I may hear of you that you stand firm in one spirit), with one mind striving together for the faith of the gospel [μιᾷ ψυχῇ συναθλοῦντες τῇ πίστει τοῦ εὐαγγελίου]...' The exhortation to 'conduct yourselves in a manner worthy of the gospel' is reminiscent of I Thess. 2: 12. Whether πολιτεύεσθε is intended to convey the sense of unity which Loymeyer finds here[1] or is merely the equivalent of περιπατεῖν,[2] it indicates that the gospel establishes the norm of the Philippians' conduct.

'Striving together for the faith of the gospel' is more difficult. Are the Philippians to strive 'for the sake of' the gospel or is faith something 'alongside of' which they are to struggle?[3] If the latter is the case, it is apparently the 'opponents' of v. 28 against whom the struggle is waged. Despite Lohmeyer's objections, the verse seems to be couched in characteristic Pauline exhortation for unity and the reference to 'striving' seems in opposition to, rather than distinct from, the idea of 'standing' in one spirit. It is doubtful that this verse turns on some yoke of martyrdom shared by Paul and the Philippian community. But Lohmeyer's analysis of 'striving together for the faith of the gospel' does seem correct just because, as he points out, v. 28 introduces the note of the eschatological conflict of which this striving is the clear sign – either to destruction or to salvation. We shall see that frequently the 'gospel' occupies a central role when Paul thinks of the division between those perishing and those being saved. The exhortation in 1: 27 to strive together

[1] *Ibid.*, p. 74.
[2] M. Dibelius, *An die Thessalonicher I, II; An die Philipper* (Tübingen, 1937; HNT), p. 70.
[3] Cf. *ibid.*, and Lohmeyer, *Philipperbrief*, p. 74.

with the faith 'of the gospel' is essentially eschatological, just as standing 'in one spirit' is. The genitive τοῦ εὐαγγελίου is one of source.[1]

We may conclude this survey by looking at *I Cor. 9: 23*, where Paul states as his motive for the action described in vv.19–22: 'I do everything on account of the gospel, in order that I might jointly share in it [ἵνα συγκοινωνὸς αὐτοῦ γένωμαι].[2] This final clause, the last in a series of seven, points in a different direction from the six which precede it. In vv. 19–22 such clauses are distributed in alternating fashion, one in v. 19, two in v. 20, etc. They express Paul's own purpose in 'becoming what he is not', as one of winning men. To the Jews he became as a Jew in order to win Jews; to those outside the law he became as one outside the law, and so forth. Yet in v. 23 this last clause seems to express his purpose in doing all these things as related more directly to Paul's own interests.[3] For what can it mean to be συγκοινωνὸς τοῦ εὐαγγελίου except to share in either the promises of the gospel or the work of the gospel?

The critical context for this passage is the entire argument in I Cor. 9: 1–23, where Paul begins by saying that the Corinthian community is the seal of his apostleship (v. 2). They are themselves the visible sign of his rightful claim to be an apostle, even if that claim has been threatened. And he has other authenticating signs: 'Have I not seen Jesus our Lord?' 'Am I not free?' Paul then goes on to establish in principle his rightful claim to support from the community. Curiously enough, however, he subsequently rejects the use of this claim (v. 12b), lest somehow he place an obstacle in the path of the gospel of Christ. The argument of vv. 3–12a continues in vv. 13–14, and 15–18 are a repetition of his refusal to claim his 'right'. Again in v. 18 Paul states a reason for his refusal – that the gospel may be free of charge. Only now this has become a 'ground for boasting'. For necessity compels Paul to preach, and from that necessity he cannot appeal for a reward. Yet he will have a reward: 'What then is my reward? That in my preaching I may

---

[1] So Schniewind, *Wort*, p. 95, who notes that Paul never speaks of having faith in the gospel.
[2] RSV: '...that I might share in its blessings'. The translation here is that of BAG, p. 782. Cf. NEB, 'to bear my part in proclaiming it'.
[3] Cf. Weiss, *Korintherbrief*, p. 246.

present the gospel free of charge' [ἵνα εὐαγγελιζόμενος ἀδάπα-
νον θήσω τὸ εὐαγγέλιον] (v. 18a). To present the gospel free
of charge must be the equivalent of 'enduring anything', even
forgoing his apostolic right, in order to cause no hindrance to
the gospel (v. 12b), since the apostolic ἐξουσία in question
seems to be financial support from the community.

What does Paul understand by a 'gospel' which could be
'hindered'? He cannot be speaking about hindering the *content*
of the gospel. Nor can he mean that he will refrain from damaging his own *delivery* of it. To grasp the metaphors here we must
imagine the gospel as a force or agency able to accomplish
something, having a purpose toward which it proceeds. Paul
will do nothing to thwart that thrust of the gospel toward its
own goal. The renunciation of his apostolic 'right' seems to him
a small enough price to assure this.

Probably this same dynamic use of εὐαγγέλιον is found in
v. 18 as well as in v. 12b, for the two seem otherwise parallel.
In any case, vv. 19–23 continue the same theme of renunciation
of the apostolic right. 'For though I am free from all men',
v. 19, picks up the idea from v. 1 where this freedom is posited
as one of the marks of apostleship. But just this freedom Paul
has renounced. He has become a slave to all, that he might win
the more. After indicating in rather stylized, dialectical fashion
what he means in vv. 20–2 by his 'enslaving' himself to all,
Paul concludes that he did it that he might 'jointly share in the
gospel'. If vv. 19–23 repeat the same theme of renunciation as
is found in the preceding portion of ch. 9, then Paul must mean
that he has done all this to become participant in the dynamic
character of the gospel – to share in the gospel's *own* work. He is
commissioned to preach the gospel (v. 17), but his *reward* comes
in sharing in the effectiveness of the gospel, not hindering this
force. That is accomplished by disregarding 'apostolic' rights
and claims.

Hence there is no contradiction between the final clause of
v. 23 and those of vv. 19–22. 'To share in the gospel' and 'to
win men' are two ways of saying the same thing. And it is this
dynamic or 'pregnant' use of the gospel – the gospel as itself an
effective force or agent – with which Paul works here.[1]

[1] Many interpreters find it difficult to explain Paul's seeming desire to be
justified by his works. It is clear that he lays claim to a reward and that he

Summary

The apostle engages in the task denoted by the verb εὐαγγελίζεσθαι, and what he preaches is εὐαγγέλιον. Yet the noun
does not merely, certainly not always, mean the *content* of what
is proclaimed. In addition it can sometimes mean the *act* of the
proclamation itself, in which case the noun and the verb begin
to converge. More importantly, there is another nuance to the
noun which defies precise definition but may be called 'pregnant' or 'dynamic'. When this dimension is stressed the gospel
emerges as a continuing element in the life of the Christian
community.[1]

In this 'gospel' the Christian 'stands'. Alongside of it he may
be said to 'strive'. It is the field of God's activity as it touches
man's life. Sometimes it seems to be a force or agent thought of
as effective in its own right. Since the gospel construed this way
operates within history but works toward a goal beyond or outside the routinely historical, it must be thought of as an eschatological concept.

THE PROBLEM OF CONTENT

Introduction

Paul can refer to *the gospel* without further elaboration, suggesting that his meaning is obvious to his readers. The cognate
use of the noun εὐαγγέλιον and the verb εὐαγγελίζεσθαι conveys a similar sense of definition and precision. Furthermore,
Paul does not think Christian missionary preaching began with
him. He is aware of his indebtedness to earlier traditions (I Cor.

'boasts'. But the interpretation of v. 23 is what is crucial in deciding whether
or not Paul wants to be justified by his apostolic accomplishments. He does
not. If he may feel proud of his work it is nevertheless true that he has
behaved in this fashion for the sake of others – and the gospel, which is the
same thing. Yet of course he must also come within the sphere of this 'force'.

[1] Thus it approaches the significance we would ordinarily ascribe to
'pneuma' in Paul's letters; cf. W. D. Davies, *Paul and Rabbinic Judaism*
(London, 1955[2]), pp. 177–90. This has been graphically pointed out by
Schniewind (*Wort*, pp. 93–5) with reference to Phil. 1: 5. The point is not
that 'gospel' is the same as 'spirit' but that the gospel can be seen as more
than the original preaching or report, that it is itself a 'manifestation of
Spirit' (*ibid.*). Phil. 1: 5 views 'gospel' as the present action of God in the
life of the Christian community.

15: 1ff.; 11: 23) and he is quite clear about the existence of apostles before him whose work he can regard as parallel and directly related to his own (Gal. 1, 2). He is, as Rigaux says, 'the theologian of tradition'.[1]

Under these circumstances, is it not appropriate to regard 'the gospel' as primarily a matter of content,[2] and to look for its specific components in those passages where his use of tradition or his relationship to it, and to those who maintain it, is clearest? Paul does regard tradition as something which he shares with others and he does regard proclamation of the gospel as the quintessential apostolic task. Tradition is specific content. Is 'gospel' its synonym?

The Gospel as Tradition

Our concern here is not with the whole question of Paul's use of tradition,[3] but with the more specific question of the relation between tradition and gospel in Paul. We shall look at some representative and influential discussions of the role of tradition, or gospel, in Paul with this interest primarily in mind.

O. Cullmann[4] distinguishes between the tradition of the apostles and the rabbinic traditions 'of men' (Mark 7: 8). The New Testament speaks 'very positively of the former' but 'resolutely rejects the so-called explanatory tradition which the

[1] *Les Épîtres aux Thessaloniciens* (Paris, 1956), p. 656.

[2] ' "Gospel" can hardly mean anything but content', D. E. H. Whiteley, *The Theology of St. Paul* (Oxford, 1964), p. 11.

[3] For the question of terminological associations between early Christianity and Judaism see B. Gerhardsson, *Memory and Manuscript* (Uppsala, 1961), chs. 9, 10 and 15; J. Jeremias, *The Eucharistic Words of Jesus* (Oxford, 1955), p. 129. E. Norden, *Agnostos Theos* (Stuttgart, 1956⁴), p. 289 suggests a hellenistic origin for the terminology, an idea not entirely dismissed by W.-G. Kümmel, *Heilsgeschehen und Geschichte* (Marburg, 1965; originally in *ZNW* 33 [1934], 'Jesus und der jüdische Traditionsgedanke'), pp. 15–35, and L. Cerfaux, 'Die Tradition bei Paulus', *Catholica* 9 (1953), 94. In any event, the Rabbinic practice does have its hellenistic parallel. Cf. E. Bickermann, 'La Chaîne de la tradition pharisienne', *RB* 59 (1952), 44ff.

[4] O. Cullmann, 'The Tradition: The Exegetical, Historical and Theological Problem', *The Early Church* (New York, 1956), pp. 55–99. For bibliography on and useful typology of the treatment of tradition in Paul cf. K. Wegenast, *Das Verständnis der Tradition bei Paulus und in den Deuteropaulinen* (Neukirchen, 1962; WMANT, 8), pp. 9–23 and the wide-ranging discussion in W. D. Davies, *The Setting of the Sermon on the Mount* (Cambridge, 1964), pp. 341–66.

rabbis placed alongside and even above the Old Testament scriptures' (p. 59). Earliest Christian tradition was a summary of the kerygma (viz., I Cor. 15: 3ff.), but by Paul's time there had already been added words of Jesus (viz., I Cor. 7: 10; 9: 14) and narratives from his life (I Cor. 11: 23). In addition are to be found 'moral rules which, after the fashion of the *halakah*, concern the life of the faithful' (p. 64). Altogether this makes up the 'content' of the *paradosis*. 'All these are cases of traditions which the apostle has received from others and hands on, just as the rabbi received and handed on the traditions of the interpretation of the law. The authority with which the rabbi transmits tradition has here passed over to the apostle' (p. 65). Yet, unlike the Rabbinic scheme, here Jesus Christ as 'Lord' takes the place of all Jewish *paradosis*.

Cullmann notes a Pauline distinction between dependence on tradition, in such passages as I Cor. 15: 3ff., and the independence of his 'gospel' (Gal. 1: 12). Interpreters often explain this as a difference between fact and interpretation: For fact Paul relies upon tradition; controlling theological interpretation he calls 'gospel' and attributes to revelation. But Cullmann points out that Paul did not distinguish among different elements of the *paradosis*, so that 'gospel', while set alongside the other components, may not be regarded as separate. This is proven by I Cor. 15: 3ff., where we see the 'fact' of death 'interpreted' by the phrase 'for our sins'. Both fact and interpretation belong to the tradition. This is confirmed by I Cor. 11: 23. What Paul received 'from the Lord' (i.e., by revelation?) is not theological interpretation but 'a factual account of the last meal of Jesus'.

Cullmann's thesis turns on a proper understanding of what Paul means by the words 'for I received from the Lord what I also delivered to you' in I Cor. 11: 23:

The formula...refers to the Christ who is present, in that he stands behind the transmission of the tradition, that is, he works *in* it. The words ἀπὸ τοῦ κυρίου can quite well mean a direct communication from the Lord, without it being necessary to think of a vision or to exclude intermediaries through whom the Lord himself transmits the *paradosis*...The risen Christ is himself the author of the gospel, of which he is also the object (pp. 68–9).[1]

---

[1] Here Cullmann follows Schniewind and Molland, and refers to the subjective genitive εὐαγγέλιον Χριστοῦ, Rom. 15: 19.

From this understanding of tradition Cullmann concludes that Christ is the new law replacing that of Moses, although Paul only draws the conclusion somewhat obliquely. In II Cor. 3: 4f. Christ is implicitly set over against Moses (though explicitly it is Paul who in fact is contrasted). There the Spirit is contrasted with the letter, and the Holy Spirit which takes the place of the law is identical with the *kyrios*. But what Paul fails to carry out in detail can be traced in John's gospel (p. 71).

What, then, about the circle of intermediaries between this present Lord and the repetition of the tradition in (for example) Paul's letters? Since the apostles are not the sole recipients of the Holy Spirit, their role cannot be exclusive. For Paul that role is central, to be sure, because to them belongs 'an exceptional place...as the eye-witnesses commissioned directly by Christ' (p. 72). 'What distinguishes the paradosis of Christ from the rabbinic principle of tradition is this: firstly, the mediator of the tradition is not the teacher, the rabbi, but the apostles as direct witness; secondly, the principle of succession does not work mechanically as with the rabbis, but is bound to the Holy Spirit' (p. 72).

Because he is a direct witness, Paul can view his relationship to the gospel as direct and unmediated, as he does in Gal. 1. He has witnessed the resurrection, which is not theological interpretation, but fact (I Cor. 9: 1). Other apostles have witnessed other things, including the historical ministry of Jesus (Acts 1: 21-2).

Yet Cullmann cannot give any positive role to the Holy Spirit, the second major distinguishing characteristic which separates the early Christian understanding of tradition from its Jewish antecedents. Instead, he turns to the problem of Paul's relationship to those facts he has not witnessed. The role of the apostles is not singular and exclusive, but collective: '...every apostle is not able, as a direct eye-witness, to pass on information about all the facts. Paul himself cannot report, as an eye-witness, the events of the early life of Jesus...For the other events he must rely on the *eye-witness testimony of the other apostles*' (p. 72). So the term 'apostle' denotes two groups. A wider circle is composed of eye-witnesses to the resurrection, a narrower one comprises eye-witnesses to the whole ministry of Jesus. Together they share what they have witnessed and together they thus receive from the present Lord their traditions.

Transmission by the apostles is not effected by men, but by Christ the Lord himself who thereby imparts this revelation. All that the Church knows about words of Jesus, about stories of his life, or about their interpretation, comes from the apostles. One has received this revelation, another that. The apostle is essentially one who passes on what he has received by revelation. But since everything has not been revealed to each individual apostle, each one must first pass on his testimony to another (Gal. 1: 18; I Cor. 15: 11) and only the entire *paradosis*, to which all the apostles contribute, constitutes the *paradosis* of Christ (p. 73).

Cullmann's analysis raises more questions than it answers. One wonders about the propriety of equating Paul's 'vision' of the Lord (I Cor. 9: 1) with testimony to the *fact* of the resurrection, since in 9: 1 Paul is using the information to say something about himself, not about the Lord. Nor is it clear that the distinction between fact and interpretation (introduced into the discussion by Cullmann's predecessors) is applicable to the eucharistic tradition in I Cor. 11: 23. To the contrary, the words already carry clear interpretation of the deed described.

Much more important for our purposes, however, is Cullmann's twin view of paradosis and the apostolic circle, for it is on these two interpretations that the equation of gospel and tradition rests. On Cullmann's scheme the apostles share fragmented 'revelations'. One can certainly see what Paul could learn from the 'narrower' group of (twelve) apostles. But what could they learn from Paul? What is Paul's distinctive contribution to the paradosis understood in this way? And what is the evidence for the implied collegiality? In Galatians Paul is concerned to attract the image of Jerusalem apostles to his own, and stress a mutual profile and harmony. But he betrays no scheme of apostolic sharing save that concerning money. Otherwise, it is the division of separate but seemingly independent *spheres* of operation which he stresses.

The flaw in Cullmann's theory is inherent in his understanding of *paradosis*. He has idealized and projected that term into a concept which has no validity in these texts. He has converted it into paradosis as understood and defended by Clement: 'the rule of our tradition' (τῆς παραδόσεως ἡμῶν κανόνα). On the

57

only occasion when Paul himself even uses the term, I Cor. 11: 2, he does so in the plural, and for a very good reason. There is no *paradosis* which transcends the various traditions and incorporates them all, no ideal tradition beyond the constituent traditions to which Cullmann alludes. Some transcendent *paradosis*, composed of various traditions about Jesus but itself authored by Jesus, composed by various contributions derived from partial revelations of the separate apostles, is simply not to be found in the text. It is a product of scholarly imagination. Cullmann is correct in pointing to the variety of 'traditions' in existence at Paul's time, but there is no way conveniently to summarize and circumscribe these as he seeks to do, certainly no warrant for supposing some least common denominator behind them as itself *paradosis*.

L. Goppelt, in his investigation of 'tradition according to Paul',[1] also begins by noting the apparent inconsistency that Jesus rejected Jewish tradition while his followers at an early date engaged in the transmission of tradition. The difference between Jewish tradition and this Christian enterprise, however, he finds evident in the material itself. As the reference of Jesus' death 'for our sins' in I Cor. 15: 3 makes clear, there is an authority to this tradition which 'cannot be extended by human authority and cannot be appropriated by human resources' (p. 216). The contrast with Judaism is more material than formal, for in an event such as that described in this tradition the address or claim issues from above and the spirit rules over the formal proclamation. Tradition is like the Church: new and of a curious double nature. 'It is historical tradition, but at the same time it is of a kerygmatic-pneumatic kind' (p. 217). It is historical, but at the same time free of history and incorporated into the dynamic of eschatological proclamation. Like Cullmann, Goppelt wishes to guard against an artificial separation of 'event' and 'interpretation', but he does so primarily with reference to tradition as 'gospel' or 'preaching'. Just as tradition is simultaneously kerygmatic and historical (*historisch*), so it is the sole resource for preaching; and preaching is the sole means of sustaining the tradition (p. 218). Gospel and tradition are one.

But the traditions in Paul are manifold, to be typed according

[1] L. Goppelt, 'Tradition nach Paulus', *KuD* 4 (1958), 213–33.

to origin and content. From a primitive kerygma (*Urkerygma*) develops the gospel tradition and the confessional formulas. These are basic and constitutive. Paul regards them as coming 'from the Lord'. Something like exegesis of these (though normative exegesis) constitutes a second pair, dogmatic formulations and ethical rules.[1] Paul regards these as normative as they are adhered to 'in all the churches'. One group is apostolic, the other ecclesiastical.

It is the first group which concerns us here. A classic example is I Cor. 15: 3ff., a formula which Paul can *characterize as a statement of his gospel*. In origin this passage is not a confessional summary of the passion or Easter story of the gospels, but rather a confessional appropriation of the *Urkerygma* lying behind these stories. The gospel story is prefigured in the Petrine speeches in Acts,[2] the 'congregational confession is embodied in the confession traditions of the congregation' (!) (p. 220). But I Cor. 15: 3ff. is peculiar among these, being unusually closely related to the *Urkerygma*. Paul does not necessarily receive this tradition from the original apostles. It is simply community property, though clearly tradition. What he does with it shows the proper and actual relationship of apostles to the tradition. He authorizes it himself by including himself as a witness; and at the same time he depersonalizes this testimony by including it in the *gospel* (i.e., the tradition: 'he belongs as such in the tradition', p. 220). He also shows he is the faithful transmitter and guardian of the tradition.

Is Paul thereby a special transmitter and guardian of the tradition? Not really, for though he stands closer to the *Urkerygma*, and without such apostolic testimony no tradition can be handed down, other missionaries and all Christians receive and discern the tradition by means of the Spirit. The tradition is

---

[1] This distinction is widely observed and exploited in a fashion similar to Goppelt's. Cf. L. Cerfaux (above, p. 54, n. 3). B. Gerhardsson (*Memory*, p. 295), who regards early Christian tradition as formed and transmitted on Rabbinic principles, refers to the first set of traditions as 'Mishnah' and the second as 'Talmud'. Although he only intends the designations to be figurative, they are, as Davies has suggested, something short of useful in discussing the realities of the early Church's attitude toward tradition (*Setting*, pp. 478ff.).

[2] Following C. H. Dodd, *The Apostolic Preaching and its Development* (New York, 1951).

also kerygmatic-spiritual, not merely historical, as II Cor. 3: 1ff., 3ff. and 5: 16 make perfectly clear. Paul enjoys no particularly privileged position.

In Goppelt's view the term 'gospel' is to be used for Paul's formulation of the *Urkerygma* in the terms of an early community confession. Thus there can be no doubt about equating 'gospel' with 'tradition'. Gospel is nothing other than tradition. But three things remain unclear. What is the *Urkerygma* other than a logical construct to stand behind tradition, like Cullmann's hypothetical singular and unitary tradition? Further, what of Paul's use of the term 'gospel' in Gal. 1? Goppelt's definition of gospel could not apply to Paul's use of the term there. Finally, if Paul regards the derived gospel and confession traditions as coming from the Lord, how is that to be understood in reference to the tradition of I Cor. 15: 3ff.? Does not that come from the community?

The chief weakness in Goppelt's approach is not unlike that in Cullman's, and lies in his assumption of an ideal *Urkerygma* of which specific traditions – and Paul's 'gospel' – are merely the temporal embodiment. He gives no evidence for this *Urkerygma*. Furthermore, such an assumption puts Paul in the awkward position, in Gal. 1, of saying that he received by revelation the *form* of his expression for some primitive kerygma. How do we know that this is that form found in I Cor. 15? Might it not as well be the dogmatic or ethical traditions which Goppelt also sees operating in Paul? These are, after all, no less 'from the Lord'. In short, Goppelt has not equated a gospel with tradition, but some generic gospel with some kinds of tradition. No doubt I Cor. 15 seems to give license for that. But Gal. 1 must also be taken into account.

Jürgen Roloff[1] has recently sought to solve this problem by denying an identification of tradition with gospel. Gospel and tradition are overlapping but not coterminous (p. 85). Unlike a rabbi, Paul presupposes differences in tradition, and organizes the constituent elements (traditions) by the 'principle' of the gospel (p. 86). 'It is in this sense that the community confession of I Cor. 15: 3b–5 is received and handed on by Paul; because in all essential points it expresses the gospel, and not because he received it as an authoritative transmission from the original

---

[1] *Apostolat* (cf. above, p. 22, n. 1).

apostles' (p. 86). Thus Paul can be indifferent to the process of transmission itself, as we see in I Cor. 11 : 23 where he authorizes the tradition by reference back to its origin (ἀπὸ τοῦ κυρίου) and ignores the intervening chain of transmission.

Paul must do this, for the function of the apostle is to preach the gospel, not to pass on tradition. This preaching function is authorized at the time of Paul's call, when he is also provided the transmission of the *gospel* directly from the risen Lord (Gal. 1 : 12). The apostolic gospel, in turn, is the deployment of traditions (and scriptural interpretations, etc.) in such a way as to make concrete a public message which is the development of the original energizing word (*Tatwort*) which was the gospel as revealed to the apostle by the risen Lord. Here the sequence of Rom. 10 : 17 is paradigmatic: word of Christ – hearing – faith. But to provide the message which can be heard and then believed, the apostle must 'seek and use traditions in which the gospel can come to expression' (p. 90).

The cornerstone in Roloff's analysis is his treatment of Gal. 1 : 12. While it has often been observed that Paul's commissioning as an apostle and his conversion seem to be collapsed in this passage, Roloff goes farther in identifying as a unit three logically separate items: conversion, revelation of the gospel, commissioning as an apostle. Here, as an eye-witness of the risen Lord, Paul is provided with the gospel. His missionary activity is an attempt to interpret and flesh out this revelation so that others might hear and believe, and in this attempt he avails himself of traditions.[1] Thus there are really *two* senses of the term gospel, an original and a derived sense. How does one know that the derived sense (i.e., the use of traditions to speak the gospel) is authoritative? Since the 'unity of the gospel determines the unity of the normative traditions used in missionary preaching' (p. 92) and not vice versa, tradition itself cannot provide this authority. Instead, we must conclude that the apostle is self-evidently authoritative, that his authority rests in his own word *and in his unique position.*

For Paul this position is not some previously determined

---

[1] Just which traditions correspond to Paul's meaning in Gal. 1 : 12 is not clear. Roloff mentions those 'the content of which are the deeds and words of the one who became man and arose from the dead' (p. 87), but that definition has little to do with Gal. 1 : 12.

apostolate to which he justifiably aspires, but rather his own mission to the Gentiles. This mission is parallel to and derived from the same sources as Peter's mission to the Jews, as Gal. 1–2 intends to make clear. What distinguishes the two missions, however, is geography and not kerygma.[1] Although the risen Lord speaks through the apostle, the Lord's word is not the same as fixed kerygmatic word. Nor does the Lord speak only through the apostle. Wherever the Spirit is at work, there the Lord speaks, and the Spirit is at work apart from the apostles. But whereas the Spirit works ambiguously in the congregation, requiring the critical judgment of the gospel, in the apostles the Church encounters the Lord unambiguously. Thus there is nowhere to go behind the apostles' words, which means that the apostolic interpretation of the gospel is final and normative (pp. 93–8).

Can we then remain content with two gospels, an original gospel (of Jesus) and an apostolic gospel (about Jesus)? Roloff cannot, and finally capitulates in a now familiar fashion by speaking of an original kerygma (*Urkerygma*) which consists of 'the basic data about Jesus' death and resurrection, a canon of the Lord's words as well as in all probability a stock of Jesus stories' (p. 92). In this 'Christ himself is always the logical subject'. This kerygma becomes apostolic only insofar as it is *grounded in the eye-witness character of the apostles* and is actualized in his mission. That is going to go hard on Paul.

Roloff readily admits that Paul does not witness all the events of the tradition recited in I Cor. 15: 3ff., but instead includes himself at the end as witness to the risen Lord. Thus all Roloff can say is *that* paradosis and gospel are merged in this passage, which nobody will deny. The much more difficult question of how they are related or merged he leaves unanswered, contenting himself with pointing out that when Paul here calls the paradosis 'gospel' he does so only by extension, since the paradosis is not the gospel but only the words in which the Corinthians will be able to recollect what they must know about the gospel.

It might be said of this position that it shows a Catholic appetite and a Protestant taste. Roloff himself acknowledges that he wishes to steer a middle course between what he regards as

That is, the traditions are all the same. Cf. p. 92, particularly n. 169.

two extreme positions. One is represented in H. Schlier's collapse of kerygma into 'normative apostolic paradosis', a collapse which paves the way for viewing gospel in its entirety as nothing else but the sum of formulas and traditions which are generically on a par with, if antecedent to, the Church's dogmatic pronouncement. The other is kerygmatic theology such as R. Bultmann's or G. Ebeling's, in which tradition is confined to the naked *daß* of the Christ-event and eclipsed by the proclamation of kerygma. We might well conclude by looking more closely at these positions.

For H. Schlier,[1] *kerygma* is the central category absorbing both *gospel* and *tradition*. It is 'the proclamation of the events of the death and resurrection of Jesus Christ – events which have happened and continue to be operative'. It is the public announcement, encapsulated in a formula, of Jesus Christ as the Lord and of these events proving him as such, an announcement made through the apostles (p. 214). I Cor. 15: 1–11 provides us with more explicit information about the nature of the kerygma.

Its content is the event of God's raising Jesus from the dead. This is the foundation of the kerygma, without which it is 'empty'. The resurrection of Jesus Christ happened before witnesses, who comprise an exclusive and limited circle, though they represent the world. These witnesses to whom the resurrected one has 'witnessed himself' provide, in turn, a witness to this self-witnessing. So one must say that Jesus Christ's self-witnessing becomes a revelation in language and word, the language and word of his witnesses. By this means the original 'revelation of truth' comes to expression in tradition. 'The resurrection of Jesus from the dead, the appearance of the resurrected one before witnesses, and the testimony of the witnesses are really three modes of one revelation which inextricably depend on one another' (p. 215). Together they constitute a *revelation-logos*.

[1] H. Schlier, 'Kerygma und Sophia: Zur neutestamentlichen Grundlegung des Dogmas', in *Die Zeit der Kirche: Exegetische Aufsätze und Vorträge* (Freiburg, 1962), pp. 206–32. Cf. also his article in the same volume, 'Über das Hauptanliegen des 1. Briefes an die Korinther', pp. 147–59 and his commentary, *Der Brief an die Galater* (Göttingen, 1965[13]; KEK), pp. 36ff.

This revelation-logos shows certain proclivities. It tends toward unitary formulation because it is a unitary logos of manifold witnesses and testimonies. It also bears development, as the kerygma of I Cor. 15: 1–11 shows. But most important, the revelation-logos in its deployment as pregnant apostolic kerygma is a *normative* logos, normative for *both* the gospel and its proclamation *and* for faith which is bound to such a summary kerygma. The paradosis of I Cor. 15: 1–11 is *gospel* because it is the essential core of the gospel. Moreover it is the norm of the gospel. 'The kerygma in this sense and the symbol which proceeds from it is not a compressed and arid secondary abridgment of the living gospel; it is not, as frequently maintained, an extract of the gospel or the scripture...Kerygma as normative apostolic paradosis precedes the gospel as proclamation both in time and in substance' (p. 216).

Kerygma, gospel, paradosis – all collapse into one, even while they can be distinguished from one another. This is the heart of Schlier's analysis, an analysis deliberately set over against the use (and to his mind abuse) of the term 'kerygma' in Bultmann's theology. But at the same time the analysis grows out of his reading of I Cor. 1 and the problem of the relation of the kerygmatic word in the 'wisdom' prized by the Corinthians and rejected by Paul. Thus Schlier is able to move from this description back into the Corinthian situation, suggesting that the kerygmatic word is self-authenticating and incapable of proof – a word which demands faith as its proper response. It is an aboriginal word, behind which is nothing other than God; a word which in itself not only discloses a new world and a new reality, but actually creates it. Moving forward, Schlier sees this kerygmatic word encapsulated in paradosis which is not generically distinguishable from dogma itself. He is led to the conclusion that the church's dogmatic formulations are the self-disclosure which, again, allows no proof and suffers no authenticating, higher authority.

This movement back to I Cor. 1 and forward to a fully developed Catholic theory of dogma has been amply criticized.[1] As for the close identification of paradosis and gospel, every-

---

[1] H. Diem, *Dogmatics* (Edinburgh, 1959), pp. 41–52, 107–11, 179–81; G. Ebeling, *Theology and Proclamation* (Philadelphia, 1966), pp. 120–3 especially; U. Wilckens, 'Kreuz und Weisheit', *KuD* 3 (1957), 77–108.

thing in Schlier's position turns on the proper understanding of I Cor. 15, for which he provides insufficient exegesis. Yet some broader questions are in order.

Paradosis rests directly and essentially on Jesus' revelatory self-disclosure; it is not antithetical to revelation but demands it, which suggests the first and most obvious question. If 'tradition' for and in Paul has this most unique and other-worldly origin, why should Paul use the customary terminology for the process of 'human' traditioning? To put the matter another way, can we afford to use critical tools to isolate such traditions as that found in I Cor. 15: 3ff. only to throw away those tools in insisting that the origin is essentially revelatory? Without exegesis it is impossible to know why Schlier moves in this direction, but it is not transparently clear that I Cor. 15: 3ff. constitute the words of Jesus to Paul, and what Paul says in v. 8 about his vision he does not use to establish the origin of vv. 3ff.

Schlier senses that the ultimate problem regarding the relation of tradition to gospel is the problem of authority itself, and in this lies the strength of his analysis, so extreme yet so much more penetrating than others we have examined. His whole analysis of I Cor. 1, in the context of which he elaborates this relationship, is designed to isolate and answer this question of authority. Furthermore, he does not trade on any historically improbable picture of the apostolic office and thereby risk finding authority where it cannot be found. One may question his view of the exclusive nature of the apostolic circle. But it is not so much in the office as such that Schlier finds the authority as in the disclosure of Jesus to those who are, in fact, apostles. Yet here too problems arise. Paul does not regard Jesus as the author of his apostolic commissioning. He only suggests the simultaneity of God's revelation of his son and of his will for Paul's missionary endeavors (Gal. 1: 15f.).[1]

In short, Schlier's scheme raises serious questions precisely where it assumes the transfer from Jesus' revelatory word to the words of apostolic tradition. One suspects that, as often happens,

---

[1] Schlier can point to Gal. 1: 1 (ἀπόστολος...διὰ ᾽Ιησοῦ Χριστοῦ καὶ θεοῦ, *Galater*, pp. 26f.), but Gal. 1: 15–16 stands and is far less ambiguous regarding agency of revelation. Furthermore, as Wilckens, among others, points out, ἀποκαλύψεως ᾽Ιησοῦ Χριστοῦ in Gal. 1: 12 is in all likelihood objective, not subjective, genitive.

the term 'word' significantly changes content in the transition. The problem might not be insoluble in dealing with such passages as I Cor. 15: 3ff. But what about those traditions which are not expressions of community faith? What of the more cultically, paraenetically oriented 'words' of the apostolic paradosis? Will a close identification of Jesus' self-disclosure with tradition work for such traditions as I Cor. 11: 23ff.; I Thess. 4: 1ff., 15ff., etc.?

Schlier's failure to account for the wider strand of traditional materials is the result of his singular focus on the term *kerygma*, which to all intents and purposes he restricts to the historical preaching of the resurrection of Jesus. This focus, in turn, shows the heavy influence of R. Bultmann who was Schlier's teacher, who more than anyone else has raised the term *kerygma* to its central place in New Testament theology today, and over against whom Schlier was trying to construct a more 'traditional', Catholic alternative.

Bultmann begins his formal analysis of tradition in early Christianity by setting the phenomenon in the wider context of the history of religions.[1] Every religion requires the transmission of tradition. In the pagan background of the New Testament this process usually begins with traditions defining and locating cultic acts and liturgies; the etiological urge may result in traditions describing the origin of the cult. Finally, cosmogonic myths may enter the tradition, even displacing some of the older material, so that it is possible to speak of the retention of doctrine or theology in pagan transmission.

Judaism manifests all of this, and adds cultic ethical demands to the stream of transmission. But its characteristic feature is uniting such cultic traditions with the historical tradition which seeks to tell of the history of the people.

Out of this context emerges Christianity, following the same cultural pattern which stamps the content of tradition in paganism: I Cor. 11: 23–5 represents a tradition of cultic formula; I Cor. 14: 3f., a tradition corresponding to a cult myth. Furthermore, in line with the Jewish precedent, historical data are regularly incorporated into the scheme of tradition, especially in the wider context of christological formulas (Rom. 1: 3,

[1] R. Bultmann, *Theology of the New Testament* (Vol. ii, New York, 1955), par. 54 (pp. 119–27).

'under Pontius Pilate'; I Tim. 6: 13, etc.). 'That is, to the *paradosis* belongs history, an account about historical events' (p. 121).

Nevertheless, Christianity cannot be thought of as simply continuing the Jewish pattern of tradition, for

historical tradition could no longer have the meaning which it had ...in the Old Testament and Judaism...The 'new covenant', unlike the old, is not the founding event of a people's history, but, however much it arises from a historical event, the death of Jesus, it is nonetheless an eschatological event, and the 'People of God' with which this covenant is made is an entity not of world history but of eschatology (p. 122).

To continue Old Testament history in the Jewish mode of tradition would be to sacrifice this eschatological element. 'The tradition about Jesus, therefore, has this special character: that it speaks simultaneously of the eschatological occurrence and of an historical occurrence. The question is whether this paradoxical character was maintained' (p. 126).

For Bultmann this paradox would not be maintained with a one-dimensional concept of history but demands instead a distinction between two dimensions of history. *Historie* itself is *bruta facta*: the past arranged in chronicle and archival form, the past established by the historian's technical labor. It is of concern to those who wish to concern themselves with it, but it has no wider, existential significance. In contrast, *Geschichte* is the past as it expresses possibilities for human existence, as it has existential reference to the present for the one who understands his own possibilities for existence through perceiving the possibilities of which history speaks. The events which constitute history are the same in either dimension, but (1) the perception of these events differs, and (2) the proper form of expression for each is different. Only *Geschichte* can preserve the 'paradoxical character' of tradition in the New Testament by allowing the past to express its future which is of significance in the present.

Bultmann's position brings us back to the polarity of the word *gospel* which, in Paul's vocabulary, conceals its own tension between the past and openness toward the present or future. For Bultmann, however, Paul is not a reliable interpreter of the essence of early Christian tradition. He 'tries to guarantee the resurrection of Jesus by the enumeration of witnesses, as if it were an historically visible fact (I Cor. 15: 5–8)' (p. 127). Much more satisfactory is John, for whom 'the tradition is not historical transmission, which establishes the continuity of historical occurrence, but is the Church's preaching, in which Jesus is present in the Spirit'.

John and Paul together provide a good portion of the data for Bultmann's understanding of 'proclamation' and almost all the evidence for what he regards as a normative early Christian attitude toward tradition as 'eschatological' event. For Paul,

in the 'word'...the salvation-occurrence is present. For the proclaimed word is neither an enlightening *Weltanschauung* flowing out in general truths, nor a merely historical account which, like a reporter's story, reminds a public of important but by-gone facts. Rather, it is *kerygma* – herald's service – in the literal sense – authorized, plenipotent proclamation, edict from a sovereign. Its promulgation requires authorized messengers, 'heralds', 'apostles' (sent men) (Rom. 10: 13–17). So it is, by nature, personal address which accosts each individual, throwing the person himself into question by rendering his self-understanding problematic, and demanding a decision of him.[1]

The apostle, whose word is God's word, belongs to the eschatological occurrence.

Kerygma, rather than 'gospel' or 'tradition', is the controlling term. The apostolic task is proclamation, not the recitation of historical facts.[2] It might be said that kerygma is to tradition as *Geschichte* is to *Historie*; and perhaps Bultmann finds it a more acceptable term than 'gospel' in part because it has never been objectified in a corresponding literary genre.

Behind Bultmann's interpretation lies a consistent theological-philosophical position, the analysis of which would take us too far afield. We must be content with raising a specific exegetical question. It seems curious that what is new in the 'content' of

---

[1] *Theol.*, I, p. 307.

[2] It is interesting to note that discussing the technical term 'gospel' in the primitive (hellenistic) Christian community ('The Kerygma of the Hellenistic Church', *Theol.* I, par. 9–15, pp. 63–183), Bultmann provides content for εὐαγγέλιον only when he deals with it as a developing literary genre (cf. esp. p. 86). Otherwise (as on pp. 87ff.) he treats it as the equivalent of κήρυγμα and εὐαγγελίζεσθαι as the equivalent of κηρύσσειν.

68

Christian tradition, the eschatological dimension, should appear to be violated by Paul in I Cor. 15: 3ff. This is all the more unusual in light of Paul's meager use of the terms κήρυγμα and κηρύσσειν. We find the noun in I Cor. 15: 14, and only three times otherwise (Rom. 16: 25; I Cor. 1: 21; 2: 4). Though the verb appears in this technical sense more frequently,[1] its use in I Cor. 15: 11, 12 scarcely strengthens Bultmann's case for exempting this passage from *Paul's* understanding of the kerygma. It could be argued that Paul does not use the verb κηρύσσειν until I Cor. 15: 11f., i.e., after he has finished the *paradosis*. This would necessarily imply a distinction, at least in this passage, between εὐαγγελίζεσθαι and κηρύσσειν. However that may be, it does not accord with Bultmann's analysis of the technical terms as virtually indistinguishable. Yet Bultmann's sensibilities on that score are strengthened by a passage such as Gal. 2: 2.

We may put the matter another way. Bultmann says flatly that 'I cannot accept I Cor. 15: 3–8 as kerygma. I call that line of argument fatal because it tries to adduce a proof for the kerygma.'[2] But can he call it gospel? That is the key question. It seems strange to have to deny that I Cor. 15: 3 is gospel when Paul describes it as such. Yet Bultmann *equates* the *technical* terms 'gospel' and 'kerygma'.[3]

Our problem is how to understand the relationship between tradition and gospel. Behind these various approaches we have examined we can see emerging the controlling coordinates of that problem.

The first of these is *revelation vs. history*. Tradition is by definition an historical entity transmitted through historical processes and persons. Yet New Testament tradition points to a referent beyond itself, a referent which is more than historical. By nature, such a non-historical referent assumes priority of authority over

[1] Rom. 10: 8, 14, 15; I Cor. 1: 23; 9: 27; 15: 11, 12; II Cor. 1: 19; 4: 5; 11: 4; Gal. 2: 2; Phil. 1: 23. Rom. 2: 21 and Gal. 5: 11 are irrelevant here.

[2] H.-W. Bartsch (ed.), *Kerygma and Myth* (London, 1953), p. 112.

[3] It should be noted that Bultmann lays great stress on the fact that the terms are 'technical' only when used absolutely, and cites the absolute use of εὐαγγέλιον ('that is, used without any object of content to designate the Christian message, but simply implying its clearly defined content', *Theol.*, I, p. 87) as Paul's characteristic (and perhaps unprecedented) one.

historical tradition which is merely the language about the referent rather than the thing itself. The christological version of this problem was real for the earliest Christians. The production of literary 'gospels' testifies to the fact that even the 'words' of Jesus are an insufficient vehicle for his 'presence', i.e., his unmediated authority. That authority, presence or revelation, is to be found also, perhaps primarily, in his deeds. This is implicitly true in the beginning of the written gospel tradition with Mark, and explicitly a major theme of the end of that canonical tradition as found in John, for whom the deeds are 'signs' which render all observers, regardless of generation, equidistant from the revelation itself. It is no accident that the shape and course of historical tradition is so difficult to trace in the Fourth Gospel.

Texts such as I Cor. 15 and Gal. 1–2 pose the same problem, without seeming to offer clues to its solution. We have seen repeatedly in our survey that attempts to harmonize these texts require some bridge between revelation and history. The bridge may be called 'tradition' in an extended and idealized sense (Cullmann), *Urkerygma* (Goppelt, Roloff) or simply *kerygma* (Bultmann). But in each case the virtue of such a construct is also its vice. To serve as a transition from revelation to tradition the term must be essentially evacuated of all meaning which can be identified with *specific traditions* (Bultmann, less clearly Goppelt), or it must provide an additive which carries the essence, the Spirit, within all traditions and thereby enables them to transcend themselves (Cullmann).

A narrower focus on this very broad topic would lead to identifying the second coordinate: the *locus of authority*. Its value can be seen primarily with regard to Schlier. For Schlier there is no real transfer from the self-disclosure of the risen Lord to the apostolic testimony about this disclosure. There is no distinction, in fact, between these two 'events' and the 'event' of the resurrection itself. That is how the later events receive their authority. Of course, it is the apostles who bear this witness and bear this direct and unmediated authority – and the apostles who extend the tradition. But (1) how does the authority extend beyond the original apostles without an office in which it can be carried, and (2) how does the authority of those original apostles extend to traditions which generically are not of this testimonial sort, unless the apostles themselves are *by definition* authorities? Although Schlier does not appeal to a fixed apostolic office as a prerequisite to understanding Paul, the logic of his position demands one.

At heart, this matter of the locus of authority is a hermeneutical issue. It is the question of how to interpret tradition, whether it is tradition received by Paul (I Cor. 15) or from Paul (I Cor. 15). The problem can be solved only by observing how tradition is handled, how it is used, exploited, – how it is interpreted.

'My (Our) Gospel'

Perhaps what Paul 'received' was not, as has been assumed thus far, a denominator wholly common to all early Christian preachers. F. C. Baur long ago posited a split between two wings of the earliest Church, Pauline-hellenistic and Petrine-Jewish. Could it not be that there were also two gospels?

This is the way A. Fridrichsen reads the evidence in Gal. 1 and 2 where he finds two separate apostolates.[1] Since it is 'constitutive of the ministry of an *apostolos*...that he has been given a message to proclaim', a task central to his whole activity, 'we are now faced with the question whether Peter and Paul each had his own gospel, or, rather, his own form of the gospel'.[2] Fridrichsen breaks with the majority of modern interpreters in regarding Paul's statement of Gal. 2: 7 as indicating something more than a mere geographic distinction.[3] 'The gospel to the circumcised' is distinguished from that 'to the uncircumcised' in content as much as in locale. Confirmation is found in Paul's reference to 'my gospel' (Rom. 2: 16; 16: 25), 'our gospel' (II Cor. 4: 3; I Thess. 1: 5), 'the gospel preached by me' (Gal. 1: 11) and 'the gospel which I preach among the Gentiles' (Gal. 2: 2), phrases indicating 'that Paul had been entrusted with the gospel in a distinct form which was revealed and handed over to him personally through a special call...He

---

[1] A. Fridrichsen, *The Apostle and His Message* (Uppsala, 1947). Cf. p. 7: '...the apostolate in its full sense began with the calling of Peter...Some few years later the apostleship to the Gentiles was created by the calling of Saul from Tarsus.' [2] *Ibid.*, p. 8.

[3] Such an interpretation, however, is not peculiarly modern. Cf. Tertullian, *Praescr. haer.*, 23: *Inter se distributionem officii ordinaverunt, non ut separationem evangelii, nec ut aliud alter sed ut aliis alter praedicarent.*

was not called to preach the gospel in general, but to proclaim quite a peculiar and characteristic message of his own'.[1]

The problem raised by this apparent particularization of the gospel must go far back into the life of the early Church. Eusebius indicates that the Fathers thought Paul was referring to a specific writing, Luke's gospel: 'And they say that Paul was actually accustomed to quote from Luke's Gospel since when writing of some Gospel as his own he used to say, "According to my gospel".'[2] Unfortunately, that simple answer cannot be the correct one, and we must try to determine why Paul uses the phrase, and what significance it has.

At the outset it should be noted that of the four passages where Paul speaks of 'my gospel', only II Cor. 4: 3 is clearly polemical in both intent and content. To assume that the use of this phrase is always determined by Paul's desire to distinguish between 'his' gospel and some other gospel, or more especially a rival gospel, is not warranted by the evidence. Nevertheless, such an assumption seems attractive precisely because Paul's contribution to early Christian thought seems so distinctive and because there is clear evidence that it brought forth opposition and rival missionary activity. Therefore, Fridrichsen correctly includes the phrases in Gal. 1: 11 and 2: 2 as part of the larger picture. We shall delay consideration of II Cor. 4 and Gal. 1, 2 until we can deal with the whole problem of the 'opposition' which Paul engages there, and begin with an analysis of Paul's non-polemical use of the phrase 'my gospel' (Rom. 2: 16; 16: 25; I Thess. 1: 5).

In I Thessalonians Paul mentions the thanks he gives to God for their 'work of faith and labor of love and steadfastness of hope in our Lord Jesus Christ' (1: 3); and continues that he knows 'of your calling [τὴν ἐκλογὴν ὑμῶν, v. 4] for our gospel did not happen among you in word only [ὅτι τὸ εὐαγγέλιον ἡμῶν οὐκ ἐγενήθη εἰς ὑμᾶς ἐν λόγῳ μόνον] but also in power and in the Holy Spirit and with full conviction [ἀλλὰ καὶ ἐν δυνάμει καὶ ἐν πνεύματι ἁγίῳ καὶ (ἐν) πληροφορίᾳ πολλῇ], just as you know what kind of men we became among you for your sake' (v. 5).

[1] Apostle, p. 8. With slight modifications this interpretation is also adopted by J. Jeremias, 'Chiasmus in den Paulusbriefen', ZNW 49 (1958), 145ff.
[2] Eusebius, The Ecclesiastical History, iii, 4, 7 (ed. and tr. K. Lake [London, 1959]; LCL).

In this passage the gospel is delineated not by its content so much as by its mode of appearance in the community. It came not only *in word*, but also in power, in the Holy Spirit and with full conviction. If πληροφορία carries here the connotation of 'assurance', as it does elsewhere in the New Testament (cf. Col. 2: 2; Heb. 6: 11; 10: 22), it is perhaps possible to infer certainty or conviction about the future. In that case the term imparts an eschatological flavor to the passage. To say that the gospel comes 'in the Holy Spirit' can only mean that with it the Spirit is operative in the community to which the gospel is preached. What Paul means by 'power' is not transparent, but we note the similarity with I Cor. 2: 4.

Dibelius takes the trilogy of power, Spirit and conviction to point to an essentially supra-historical event as accompaniment to the preaching of the gospel. He sees the ὅτι clause of v. 5 providing the evidence for Paul's 'knowing' rather than for the Thessalonians' 'being chosen', since only in v. 6, when they have 'received the word in much affliction' is this election made manifest.[1] A rigid distinction between historical and supra-historical elements in the preaching of the gospel hardly seems warranted in this passage. It overlooks in particular the curious expression in v. 5b. Paul's reference to the kind of men he, Silvanus and Timothy 'proved to be among you for your sake' is a logical bridge between vv. 5a and 6. It suggests that if we are to locate the realm of such supra-historical phenomena we should look to the missionaries themselves. Moreover, it suggests that in and through the event of Paul's preaching something other than a mere historical consequence emerged, that Paul's own missionary activity involves God's action. For this reason the fitting manifestation of the Thessalonians' receiving the gospel is their becoming 'imitators' and receiving the word 'in much affliction, with joy inspired by the Holy Spirit'. That view is confirmed by vv. 7 and 8, where it becomes clear that as Paul 'became' something in his preaching of the word so the Thessalonians have become something and thus preached beyond their territory. We must conclude that vv. 5 and 6 are not set in distinction to one another, one couched in historical and

---

[1] M. Dibelius, *An die Thessalonicher I, II; An die Philipper* (Tübingen, 1925²; HNT), p. 4. But cf. A. Oepke, 'Die Briefe an die Thessalonicher' in *Die kleineren Briefe des Apostels Paulus* (Göttingen, 1962⁹), p. 159.

the other in trans-historical terms, but are intended by Paul to be coterminous. Hence, that which transcends the historical event of preaching the gospel, i.e., its manifestation in power, Spirit and conviction, is to be located in the apostle himself. It is 'his' gospel because it comes to expression not merely through, but in the Thessalonians.

Rom. 2: 16 offers a host of problems, unless, like Bultmann, we strike it as a gloss.[1] But it is difficult to know if the variant readings here attest to a confusion in the text or merely a text causing confusion. Because the theme of 2: 1–12 is highly eschatological throughout, it is vv. 13–15 which seem slightly out of joint with Paul's major concern, as if he had become side-tracked by the thought of v. 12.[2] The jump from v. 15 to v. 16 forces all commentators to an explanation. In v. 15 the Gentiles 'show forth' (ἐνδείκνυνται) the fact that what the law requires is written on their hearts. With this fact, in the same present tense, goes the thought of their conscience being co-witness (συμμαρτυρούσης) and their 'conflicting thoughts' which accuse or excuse them. But v. 16 refers to the future (regardless of whether we read κρίνει or κρινεῖ), as the cryptic reference to ἡμέρα indicates.[3]

One could bridge this gap by bracketing vv. (13) 14–15 as parenthetical remarks; by stressing the 'futuristic' sense of the present tense in ἐνδείκνυνται, by striking ἐν ᾗ ἡμέρᾳ (or ἡμέρᾳ ᾗ); by supposing that some phrase such as 'this hidden situation will come to light', or 'and they shall be right-wised'[4] is to be supplied between vv. 15 and 16;[5] or by reading κρίνει and sup-

---

[1] Bultmann, *Theol.*, I, p. 217. He presents a full discussion of the difficulties in 'Glossen im Römerbrief', *TLZ* 72 (1947), cols. 197–202, cf. 201f.

[2] Against this view cf. G. Bornkamm, 'Gesetz und Natur: Röm. 2: 14–16', in his *Studien zu Antike und Christentum* (München, 1959), pp. 93–118.

[3] Cf. v. 5; M. Pohlenz, 'Paulus und die Stoa', *ZNW* 42 (1949), 69–104, p. 79. A. Oepke, *Die Missionspredigt des Apostels Paulus* (Leipzig, 1920), p. 63: 'The reader who has read...v. 5 can only think in v. 16, with the word ἡμέρα, of the final judgment.'

[4] So Pohlenz, 'Stoa', p. 80.

[5] Bultmann dismisses this most frequently propounded solution ('Glossen', col. 201) as no small assumption. That is true, but neither is it a trivial matter to assume the text lacks integrity, an assumption perhaps too consistent with Bultmann's own theological propensities to be entirely persuasive. 'Bultmann's fascinating interpretation of Paul is governed by the fact that it resolutely makes the apostle's present eschatology the dominating

74

posing that it refers to some sort of present judgment, the dimensions of which would remain admittedly obscure. Which, if any, is the right solution?

Bultmann dismisses v. 16 as a gloss precisely because of the phrase τὸ εὐαγγέλιόν μου, a phrase he regards as redactional and based on I Cor. 4: 5. The motive for the gloss is not clear, however, and the job was remarkably awkward for something designed, as Bultmann assumes, to smooth interpretation.[1] Perhaps we should not banish the verse.

What is the connection between what Paul calls 'his' gospel and the eschatological-apocalyptic judgment he envisions? He could mean that the coming of this judgment is a constituent theme of his gospel, that judgment will follow just as he says it will. If so, the eschatological-apocalyptic motif is (part of) the content of 'gospel'. Or Paul could be suggesting that in some way his gospel will itself be involved in the judgment, not forgetting that the judgment also comes 'through Jesus Christ'.[2]

The first alternative suggests that the personal reference to the gospel is intended to indicate what Paul considers characteristic (of course, only in part) of his preaching. It is the content of the Pauline gospel. What content we should presuppose at any given occurrence of the term 'gospel' would still be an open question, though in this case the content is judgment. There can be no doubt that reference to a day of judgment and

center of his thought...What, however, from this standpoint is the meaning of the relics of apocalyptic theology which are indeed to be found everywhere in the Pauline epistles? Is it permissible to speak of relics at all if we do not shut our eyes to the fact that Paul's apostolic self-consciousness is comprehensible only in the light of his apocalyptic, and that the same is true of the method and goal of his mission?' (E. Käsemann, 'On the Topic of Primitive Christian Apocalyptic', *Apocalypticism*, JTC 6 [1969], 126).

[1] Bornkamm, 'Natur' (p. 117 and n. 69), assumes that the motive is to make explicit what is already manifest in the text without v. 16. Ultimately that would provide no motive at all, leaving a needlessly awkward addition.

[2] T. Zahn, *Römer*, p. 590, has proposed a third alternative, showing how difficult the matter has seemed and how extreme are the conclusions it has invited. Zahn suggests that ἀπολογουμένων (v. 15) indicates that the Gentiles lack the moral impulse characteristic of the Jews, requiring that God be more gracious in exercising judgment upon them. This note of graciousness is the characteristic feature of Paul's gospel and hence what gives rise here to an expression of its singularity. Yet in the text we see that it is wrath, not grace, which dominates the foreground.

specifically a day of the revelation of τὰ κρυπτά was part of that preaching (cf. I Cor. 4: 5; II Cor. 5: 10). Against this view, however, it must be said that Paul scarcely holds a copyright on the notion of a future judgment, a common part of general Christian preaching. What we know as peculiarly Pauline in the early Church's message is rather the idea of justification by faith, an idea which, if anything, seems to be one at odds with the notion of judgment expressed throughout ch. 2.[1] As a result, Lietzmann assumes that τὸ εὐαγγέλιόν μου is the totality of Paul's preaching, of which the first part, the wrath of God and judgment according to works, is being put forward. Lagrange[2] is convinced that some content which is peculiarly Pauline must be involved. It is not the idea of the judgment of secrets,[3] for that is common property; but it is the unusual notion that not only Jews, but also Gentiles are to be judged.[4] But was this not also common coin?[5]

Thus it seems more reasonable to press the second option. For Paul 'my gospel' refers to his *involvement* with the preaching and the *effect* of the gospel. Certain elements in I Thess. 1: 5 express this same connotation, suggesting the presence of an eschatological motif which springs from Paul's conviction that

[1] Lietzmann, *Römer*, p. 43. It cannot be said that some major discrepancy exists between ch. 2 and, let us say, 5: 1ff. Lietzmann's point is simply that in 2: 16 we should hardly expect a reference to a 'special' Pauline gospel.

[2] *Romains*, pp. 50–1.

[3] Barrett's solution, *Romans*, p. 54.

[4] Molland, *Euangelion*, pp. 73–5, 85, argues that 'according to my gospel' here refers only to the correspondence between what Paul says in his preaching and what he assures his readers will indeed happen. Molland is perfectly clear that there can be no 'special' gospel (*Sonderevangelium*), but only the one, true gospel. Thus he concludes that 'my' gospel does not refer to idiosyncratic content, but stems from Paul's acute apostolic self-consciousness (pp. 94–7). Yet elsewhere Molland seeks to lay bare the content of Paul's 'gospel', and assumes on the basis of Rom. 2: 16 that Paul preached judgment as part of it. Doubtless Paul did, but why is the gospel *his*? Molland's argument, that Paul's gospel is everybody's gospel, works against *any* attempt to equate 'my gospel' with particular content. Hence, to refer to the difference between *Christus iudex* and *Christus iudex omnium hominum* (p. 75) does not get us far unless we are willing to concede that only Paul in his generation thought of Christ as judge of all men, an idea Molland himself explicitly rejects (p. 85, in reference to Lagrange, above, n. 111) and implicitly denies by referring to Acts 10: 42 and 17: 31.

[5] Barrett, *Romans*, p. 54.

the apostle is involved not merely with a body of teaching or doctrine which demands a once and for all acceptance, *but with an on-going event or process that can be said to be 'effective' in the life of the community*. This 'pregnant' aspect of the term 'gospel' is brought out in these passages by Paul's reference to his own involvement with that aspect of the gospel. In Rom. 2: 16 this eschatological motif finds its sharpest and most conventional expression. But the very fact that the expression is so conventional suggests that the eschatological note *as such* is not the distinctive item. What is distinctive is its combination with τὸ εὐαγγέλιόν μου, which is Paul's 'gospel' insofar as he has a stake in that judgment himself. This involvement stems from Paul's obligation (1: 15; 10: 14–15); he is involved in making the judgment known and to that extent in preparing for it. Hence, God judges through Christ 'in accord with the gospel for which I bear responsibility' – i.e., in this instance, to Gentiles as well as Jews (cf. 1: 14). Κατά here serves a double purpose, expressing both the idea of the norm for truth which substantiates v. 16 and the norm or measure by which, through Christ, this judgment is executed (i.e., according to the norm of my gospel).[1] The nuances are difficult to express, but Rom. 16: 25, as we shall see, lends indirect weight to this conclusion. In any event, in 2: 16 *the personal pronoun refers to Paul's involvement with the gospel* and not to his awareness of having some particular or peculiar message identifiable with him exclusively. Since Rom. 16: 25 is almost certainly part of a longer non-Pauline interpolation,[2] it cannot count as evidence, although it could be shown to adhere faithfully to the sense of the pronoun we have now isolated.

As a result, none of the texts lends strength to Fridrichsen's interpretation of the phrase 'my gospel' as denoting some 'peculiar characteristic message of (Paul's) own'. The texts thus far suggest rather that whenever Paul refers to the gospel as *his* he is also thinking of the continuing life of the community in the gospel and his stake in the process which culminates in salva-

---

[1] Schniewind, *Wort*, pp. 78ff.

[2] Cf., in addition to the standard introductions, D. Lührmann, *Das Offenbarungsverständnis bei Paulus und in paulinischen Gemeinden* (Neukirchen, 1965; WMANT 16), pp. 122–4 and T. W. Manson, 'St. Paul's Letter to the Romans – and Others', *BJRL*, 31 (1948), 224–40, esp. p. 231.

tion. It is this sense of involvement which seems to be characterized by the pronoun.

Such involvement fits the pregnant dimension of the gospel seen as a force in history working toward a goal. If the gospel is eschatological in this sense, and the apostle is inextricably involved with the gospel, the apostle is himself tied to the gospel at beginning and end. In that sense it is 'his'. He and it are somehow alike, as we shall see.

APPENDIX

If form-criticism proves of only limited value in dealing with 'faith-formulas' such as I Cor. 15: 3ff., these formulations have nevertheless been influential in shaping form-critical assumptions. Dibelius,[1] for example, stresses their function within a setting of early Christian preaching and regards this particular text as a solid piece of evidence for that homiletical matrix to which he ascribes so much of the oral tradition behind the gospels.

Yet this obviously sociological interest in fitting the function of forms to the reality of the early Church has not developed apace with the rest of the form-critical task. It has often been remarked that Dibelius' interests are more 'synthetic' in this regard than Bultmann's.[2] It could be added that they are more synthetic than the concerns of most of the form-critics who have followed him. As a result, the sociological interest has remained underdeveloped and the wide net of 'preaching' which Dibelius suggested has appeared to many as too imprecise.[3]

An obvious response to this state of affairs is to ask more specifically how tradition was nurtured and transmitted in early Christianity. There have been some interesting attempts in this direction, none more noteworthy than K. Stendahl's *The School of St. Matthew*,[4] which draws much of its strength by subjecting a working hypothesis

[1] In *From Tradition to Gospel* (New York, 1965), pp. 18ff., Dibelius seems more certain of the function than the form of I Cor. 15: 3ff., a text which provides primary illustration of what he means by 'preaching'.

[2] R. Bultmann, *The History of the Synoptic Tradition* (New York, 1968²).

[3] Cf. G. Iber, 'Zur Formgeschichte der Evangelien', *TR* n.F. 24 (1959), 283–338, esp. pp. 308–20; and his supplementary essay 'Neuere Literatur zur Formgeschichte' in M. Dibelius, *Die Formgeschichte des Evangeliums* (Tübingen, 1959³), pp. 302–12.

[4] First American ed., with a new introduction by the author (Philadelphia, 1968), pp. 11–19.

about the school tradition treatment of Old Testament texts to a rigorous analysis of the relevant Matthean texts. Another attempt is found in B. Gerhardsson's *Memory and Manuscript*. Gerhardsson's work promises to be relevant to the problem of the relationship between apostolic authority and the authority of tradition, but it raises many questions.[1]

Gerhardsson plots the development of earliest Christianity with four basic coordinates. Jerusalem is the Holy City of the New Israel. Its cultic center is the Temple, long associated in Judaism with Torah activity and now representative of the same for Christians. Located in this center is a *collegium* charged by Jesus and recognized by the Church as the fountain of doctrinal authority. The 'product' of that collegium is the new Torah, the teaching of Christianity.

Whatever the merits of Gerhardsson's arguments on the first two points, the last two are attended by serious problems. In light of our earlier analysis of the development of the apostolic office and especially the role of the Twelve as apostles, a simple appeal to the fixed character and alleged authority of this group is not persuasive. More central to our purposes here, however, is a close examination of the gospel tradition as Torah, especially as Gerhardsson's treatment relates to Paul.

Gerhardsson finds a job description of the collegium of the Twelve in Acts 6: 4: ἡμεῖς...τῇ διακονίᾳ τοῦ λόγου προσκαρτερήσομεν. His analysis of this passage includes the following remarks.[2] 'The verb προσκαρτερεῖν means "to persist obstinately", or "to devote oneself to an occupation or an office". The nearest Hebrew equivalent would seem to be שקד. The word is used *inter alia* precisely to refer to concentrated, persistent occupation with the study of the Torah' (p. 241). 'By ὁ λόγος (6: 4) i.e., ὁ λόγος τοῦ θεοῦ (6: 2) Luke means *that word of God which, in the last days, proceeds from Jerusalem*. From the point of view of content, this logos has its focus in the suffering, death and resurrection of Christ, but nevertheless comprehends – as

[1] Gerhardsson's book has occasioned spirited discussion. Cf. M. Smith, 'A Comparison of Early Christian and Early Rabbinic Tradition', *JBL* 82 (1963), 169–76; W. D. Davies, 'Reflections on a Scandinavian Approach to the Gospel Tradition', *Neotestamentica et Patristica. Eine Freundesgabe Herrn Professor Dr. Oscar Cullmann zu seinem 60. Geburtstag Überreicht* (Leiden, 1962), pp. 14–24 (repr. in Davies' *The Setting of the Sermon on the Mount*, pp. 464–80); and G. Widengren, 'Tradition and Literature in Early Judaism and in the Early Church', *Numen* 10 (1963), 42–83. Gerhardsson replies to his critics, and especially to Smith, in *Tradition and Transmission in Early Christianity* (Lund, 1964).

[2] Cf. the entire section entitled Διακονία τοῦ λόγου, pp. 234–45.

Luke expresses clearly and decisively – all that Jesus did and taught from his baptism by John to the ascension. An important factor with regard to this logos is that it is particularly entrusted to the *Apostles'* (p. 243). 'During the first period of the Church they are a collegium, active in Jerusalem, acting as *witnesses* (μάρτυρες) to Christ and *teaching* (διδάσκειν) in the name of Jesus' (p. 244).

It thus becomes a cardinal point for Gerhardsson that to 'preach' the gospel or the word is not merely to proclaim it, but to *teach* it as well. Such teaching has two foci, scripture and the work/words of Jesus.

In regard to Paul, the concept of tradition 'is extremely complicated', and Gerhardsson limits himself to a 'cautious sketch'. This centers on the observation that

within the framework of the παράδοσις delivered by Paul and the authoritative διδαχή which he passed on, the core was provided by a corpus containing sayings of, and about, Christ. For the sake of simplicity we shall refer to this corpus as 'the gospel tradition'. It would be well to point out that ὁ λόγος, in common with הדבר, can denote the whole as well as each individual element. The gospel tradition is thus not to be regarded as a section within the tradition, but as a focus. We may make a comparison, though we do so fully aware of the dangers of using such a terminology, and say that this central corpus is the mishnah to which the rest of the Apostles' preaching, teaching and legislation is the talmud. At all events, this Christ-tradition seems to occupy a self-evident position as a basis, focus and point of departure for the work of the Apostle Paul...But he does not pass on this focal tradition in his epistles. He presupposes it constantly, since it has already been delivered, ἐν πρώτοις (p. 295).

On Gerhardsson's analysis, Paul has the 'authority' (of an apostle) to 'comment' on the tradition and extend it in that sense, something we often see him doing in the letters.[1] All of this illustrates 'the central role which the tradition from and about the Lord – i.e., the gospel tradition – played for Paul...' (p. 302). However, it also raises the question of the relationship of Paul's authority to that of the *collegium* of the Twelve in Jerusalem. According to Gerhardsson, from the latter Paul receives the λόγος τοῦ εὐαγγελίου of I Cor. 15: 3ff. Paul regards the Church as a unity with its center in Jerusalem and the Twelve as its highest doctrinal authority. 'It is from here that the word of God (ὁ λόγος τοῦ κυρίου) proceeds. Paul recognizes

---

[1] Cf. pp. 302ff.

this, and makes use of traditions originating from this Jerusalem doctrinal center' (p. 273).

How then are we to explain the fact that Paul does not receive this gospel from, or through, man (Gal. 1)?

The solution is to be found in the simple fact that 'the gospel' (τὸ εὐαγγέλιον) in its meaning of 'message of salvation' does not include everything that is called 'the word of God' (ὁ λόγος τοῦ θεοῦ). Or, if we may be allowed to use another pair of terms, which are also somewhat ambiguous: the *kerygma* (κήρυγμα, in its meaning of 'the elementary missionary message as it is proclaimed') and the *didache* do not coincide. Paul claimed to have received the former from the risen Lord direct (p. 273).

It is difficult to see how this analysis, involving an ill-defined *kerygma* as distinct from *didache*, squares with what Gerhardsson has just said about *paradosis* as *mishnah*. Of what would the *kerygma* consist other than what Paul 'presupposes...constantly, since it has already been delivered, ἐν πρώτοις'? To make the distinction possible, Gerhardsson must posit a fundamental distinction between 'the gospel' (which Paul receives from the Lord) and 'the word of the gospel' such as is referred to in I Cor. 15: 3ff., and which, of course, he has received from the Jerusalem teaching authority. Yet in his detailed analysis of I Cor. 15: 3ff. the author observes that it is arranged in the order of 'a series of *simanim*', i.e., 'each individual element functions as a siman for a passage from the *gospel tradition*' showing that Paul 'has gained access to a good proportion of that tradition (p. 300, italics mine). Thus I Cor. 15: 3ff. is 'unambiguous evidence that Paul had received an authoritative tradition about the death and resurrection of Christ'. One cannot help but wonder what would be the content of any *kerygma* which Paul might receive more directly from the risen Lord. In fact there seems to be no content with which to fill this term, and the term itself seems to be a loosely appended concession to Gal. 1, without which Gerhardsson's scheme would, thus far, be just as complete.

Yet Gal. 1 can hardly be ignored so easily, and Gerhardsson does not give up on his attempt to show a gospel beyond the boundaries of transmission from the Jerusalem *collegium*. Thus he picks up Fridrichsen's suggestion that Paul's gospel is different from Peter's, the former being commensurate with Paul's mission to the Gentiles, the latter with Peter's mission to the Jews.

According to Paul's account in Gal. 1–2, there are really two apostolates in early Christianity...Further, according to Paul's account *the original Christian message of salvation*, τὸ εὐαγγέλιον has been revealed in two forms, 'the gospel of circumcision' and 'the gospel of non-circumcision'...These all have their basic components in common (I Cor. 15: 2ff., cf. 1: 10ff.) but give rise to two somewhat different messages. One, the meaning of which was revealed to Peter, proclaims what the word of Christ means to the circumcised; the other, the meaning of which was revealed to Paul, proclaims what the word of Christ means to the uncircumcised. The term τὸ εὐαγγέλιον can be used in an absolute sense to refer to the message of salvation preached by all Christ's apostles (pp. 270–1, italics mine).

But what Gerhardsson calls 'the original Christian message of salvation...revealed in two forms' can, for Paul and his form, scarcely be distinguished from what he 'presupposes constantly, since it has already been delivered, ἐν πρώτοις'.

It is by now extremely difficult to know what τὸ εὐαγγέλιον does, in fact, refer to. Is it what is common to all apostles (i.e., is it ὁ λόγος τοῦ εὐαγγελίου)? Or is it what is revealed to each? If the latter, it does not precede *kerygma*, but complements it by suggesting implications and shaping apostolic activity, leaving the tradition as the root.

Nor does Gerhardsson find it possible to stay with an analysis of 'two apostolates', for the missionary division consummated in Acts 15 (Gal. 2), by which territory was divided, 'did not mean that two Churches had been set up side by side...The Church, *the apostolate* and *the gospel* were regarded as being one' (p. 279, italics mine). Paul's relationship to the Jerusalem *collegium* is not independent though fraternal, as an 'apostleship to the Gentiles' would suggest. Instead, 'his...relation to this *collegium* of the Apostles is rather like the relation between the single Rabbi and his colleagues ...The *collegium* has authority over against the single apostle' (p. 279). For evidence Gerhardsson refers to Gal. 2: 6, an expression which 'could only refer to a superior authority'.

The inconsistency of Gerhardsson's use of terminology and the confusion of his analysis are evident. In part this stems from the fact that the author does not choose to grapple exegetically with Gal. 1 and 2, preferring to concentrate instead on 'a question which we might express as follows: What are the positive aspects of the apostolate and the origins of the gospel which Paul *presupposes*, takes up in his argument, and relates himself and his gospel to?' (p. 263, author's italics). But there is no evidence that Paul *presupposes* the *authority* of a Jerusalem apostolic *collegium*, whatever the evidence might be that there was such a teaching office in the early Church. Although he wishes 'to examine the sources' to see if there is evidence showing 'that at least some branches of the early Church had leading *collegia*, similar to those in contemporary Pharisaism, the Qumran sect and possibly other groups as well',[1] the author never seriously questions Paul about where he sees apostolic authority to be located, assuming this instead from the outset. Thus Gerhardsson does not discover *collegia*, but a *collegium*.

[1] *Tradition and Transmission*, pp. 35–6.

CHAPTER 4

THE GOSPEL AND TRADITION: I COR. 15

Two texts are of central importance in coming to terms with Paul's understanding of apostolic authority: I Cor. 15 and Gal. 1 and 2. Because they are markedly different in their sensibilities, perhaps even contradictory, it will be best to analyze them in detail, starting with I Cor. 15.

What is the issue outstanding between Paul and the Corinthians? There appears to be no disagreement that Jesus rose from the dead.[1] Nor can we accept Schweitzer's thesis that the τινες of v. 12 represent an old line, Sadducean Christianity which denies the notion of the resurrection, believing that only those who remain at the Messiah's return will be vindicated. This fails to account for the practice of vicarious baptism (v. 29) which Paul makes clear is the custom of the Corinthian community.[2] It is unlikely that the Corinthians are platonizing Christians who shrink at the vulgarity of the Jewish-Christian

[1] U. Wilckens, 'Der Ursprung der Überlieferung der Erscheinungen des Auferstandenen', *Dogma und Denkstrukturen* (Göttingen, 1963), p. 61, n. 11. W. Schmithals, *Die Gnosis in Korinth* (Göttingen, 1965²; FRLANT 66) thinks the matter is in dispute. Schmithals' view is based less on evidence from ch. 15 than on the assumption that the opponents are gnostics. If the differences between Paul and the Corinthians go back to disagreement over the *facticity* of the resurrection, however, it is curious that Paul should fail to register that point. E. Güttgemanns, *Apostel*, pp. 67–72, seeks to sharpen Schmithals' observations by refining the christology and combining it with that of U. Wilckens, *Weisheit und Torheit* (Tübingen, 1959; BHT 26). For Güttgemanns the gnostic Corinthian denial marks a radical break between the dead, earthly Jesus and the risen Lord, so radical that those who are dead, whether Christ or the Christian, are incapable of resurrection (p. 65, n. 67).

[2] There are no grounds for supposing that the custom is limited to some group distinct from the τινες of v. 12; nor does Paul register any opinion about its propriety, perhaps because he is utilizing the example to his own advantage in this argument. In any event, that means that Paul identifies the practice with those against whom he argues. On the practice see M. Rissi, *Die Taufe für die Toten* (Zürich, 1962; AThANT 42).

notion of the resurrection of the body and hold instead a hope of the immortality of the soul.[1] Nothing in I Cor. 15 explicitly attributes this view to the Corinthians and nothing effectively counters it.

Like those named in II Tim. 2: 18, the Corinthians think the resurrection to have already taken place in the sense that they already experience the resurrection mode of existence.[2] It is quite apparent that between vv. 20 and 56 Paul does not argue simply to resurrection, but rather to the futurity of resurrection as a certainty. At the same time, the corollary of this future certainty is an emphasis on the presence and reality of death itself. If resurrection is a future certainty, death is a present certainty; only the future promises the destruction of death. The careful and graphic way in which Paul underlines the *present* reality of *death* and the *futurity* of *resurrection* makes it clear that he regards the inseparability of these two ideas to be the cutting edge of his argument and the burden of his opposition to the Corinthians.

This argument is hinted at in v. 6b, where the accent falls not on the fact that most of the 500 brethren are still alive, but on the fact that some have already died.[3] Its major development, however, begins in v. 20, where from the agreed upon premise that Christ is raised from the dead, Paul proceeds immediately to the heart of the distinction between the Corinthian position and his own: Christ, raised from the dead, is the 'first fruits of those who have fallen asleep'. To those who cannot believe in the future resurrection on any count, a distinction between the first fruits and the whole harvest is precious at best; but to Paul

---

[1] So A. Robertson and A. Plummer, *A Critical and Exegetical Commentary on the First Epistle of St. Paul to the Corinthians* (Edinburgh, 1914[2]), pp. 329ff., though they allow the possibility of an Epicurean view in Corinth.

[2] J. Schniewind, 'Die Leugner der Auferstehung in Korinth', *Nachgelassene Reden und Aufsätze* (Berlin, 1952), pp. 110–39. Cf. also H. von Soden, 'Sakrament und Ethik bei Paulus', *Urchristentum und Geschichte*, 1 (Tübingen, 1951), p. 259, n. 28; H. Conzelmann, 'Zur Analyse der Bekenntnisformel I Kor. 15, 3–5', *EvTh* 25 (1965), 10.

[3] K. Barth, *The Resurrection of the Dead* (London, 1933), p. 151; H. W. Bartsch, 'Die Argumentation des Paulus in I Cor. 15: 3–11', *ZNW* 55 (1964), p. 272. Otherwise, H. Grass, *Ostergeschehen und Osterberichte* (Göttingen, 1962[2]), p. 148. Cf. also H. v. Campenhausen, 'The Events of Easter and the Empty Tomb', *Tradition and Life in the Early Church* (Philadelphia, 1968), p. 48, n. 25.

the distinction represents a gulf which separates the apostle from a community which believes in resurrection not too little, but too much – or perhaps better, too soon. The Corinthians will not cavil when he says, 'For as by a man came death, by a man has come also the resurrection of the dead' (v. 21), but for Paul this means that 'as in Adam all die, so also in Christ *shall all be made alive*' (v. 22).

The distinctive and critical note is struck by the unusual reference to τάγμα in v. 23, where once again Christ is invoked as the first fruits: 'But each in his own order: Christ the first fruits, then at his coming those who belong to Christ.' Paul envisions the *regnum Christi* as temporal, coming to an end after the destruction of 'every rule and every authority and power', i.e., with the disposition of 'all enemies under his feet'. This unusual christology can only be explained as based on Paul's sense of the reality of death itself: 'The last enemy to be destroyed is death' (v. 27). From the perspective of Paul's counter argument, the Corinthian denial of the resurrection has two foci: proleptically it assumes the fullness of the eschaton which has not yet arrived; it denies the reality and power of death. Paul's equation of Christ's subjection of death with Christ's own subjugation to God illustrates both the centrality and the extremity of the issue. By this means the *regnum Christi* is redefined and preserved from being either a pious or a gnostic fiction.

Here it is important to underscore the complementary form assumed in Paul's argument. The resurrection is not yet; death abides. In 15: 1–11 the twin themes of death and resurrection are disproportionately treated, the emphasis falling on the latter. That imbalance is subsequently redressed in the rest of the chapter. More important, each element implies the other. Death and resurrection are indissoluble and inextricable.

It is no surprise, therefore, to find that the rhetorical question of v. 35, 'How are the dead raised?' is not the prelude to a description of the resurrection, but rather an introduction to a renewed emphasis on death as part of the resurrection itself. The imagery of v. 36 is not quite so curious as it is sometimes taken to be. Paul envisions not a process, horticultural or other-wise, but a relationship. 'What is sown is perishable, what is raised is imperishable.' What is sown is physical, what is raised, spiritual; but the physical must precede the spiritual. 'Flesh and blood cannot inherit the Kingdom of God.' Only in that Kingdom is death swallowed up in victory. In the meantime, death cannot be avoided, must not be evaded.

The reminder that flesh and blood cannot inherit the Kingdom of God makes it clear that the Corinthian objection has nothing to do with demurring in the face of some primitive, carnal notion of resurrection. The language of vv. 35–6 is not calculated to assure the reader that his worst fears about the bodily resurrection are unfounded. It is calculated to show that this life is perishable.

Curiously, in Paul's language death functions as something of a metaphor for life seen as fragile, contingent and limited. Such contingency itself is not to be despised; it is part of the sense of *order*, and may not be overlooked. Thus, though flesh and blood do not inherit *the Kingdom of God*, this contingency is necessarily a part of *the lordship of Christ*. As we shall see, this metaphorical nuance is not without its consequences for understanding the authority of gospel and tradition in Paul's argument.

Paul's argument is well calculated to meet the presumptions of hyperspiritualists who have drawn the eschaton into the present and, in Paul's terms, stripped life of its contingency, its inherent element of death. But what of the material in vv. 12–19 and 29–34? How do these passages really fit the argument above and what do they tell of the Corinthian position or Paul's understanding of it?

The argument in vv. 12–19 has a texture, a logic which runs from a present, general condition to a single consequence: If the dead are not raised, then Christ has not been raised (v.16). That this is the dominant movement of the thought is shown by the fact that its occurrence in v. 16b is merely a repetition of v. 13. To be sure, there is a more elaborate argument packed into vv. 13–15. Not only is a denial of Christ's resurrection derived from the initial premise concerning the resurrection of the dead, but further denials are derived from the first. This can be seen from the following scheme:

(*a*) εἰ δὲ ἀνάστασις νεκρῶν οὐκ ἔστιν
(*b*)   οὐδὲ Χριστὸς ἐγήγερται
(*c*)   εἰ δὲ Χριστὸς οὐκ ἐγήγερται
(*d*)   κενὸν ἄρα [καὶ] τὸ κήρυγμα ἡμῶν

(e)   κενὴ καὶ πίστις ὑμῶν
(d)   εὑρισκόμεθα δὲ καὶ ψευδομάρτυρες τοῦ θεοῦ
(c)   ὅτι ἐμαρτυρήσαμεν κατὰ τοῦ θεοῦ ὅτι ἤγειρεν τὸν Χριστὸν
(b)   ὃν οὐκ ἤγειρεν
(a)   εἴπερ ἄρα νεκροὶ οὐκ ἐγείρονται

Propositions about false kerygma, false witness and vain faith are completely surrounded by and anchored to the basic premise concerning the resurrection from the dead. Even where the central item (e) is picked up again ('Your faith is in vain', v. 17b) and paraphrased ('you are still in your sins', v. 17b), the initial premise is 'the dead are not raised'.

In light of this it appears that the truth or falsity of all propositions in vv. 13–17 (and v. 18, too, as we shall see) is derived from the truth or falsity of the general claim that the dead are not raised. That is the logic of the passage. It would be at best a singular mode of reasoning for Paul, who nowhere else argues from a general theory of the resurrection to Christ's.

Perhaps because the general line of argument here seems uncongenial, interpreters have often felt constrained to identify as the linchpin of the paragraph that portion which concerns the resurrection of Christ. Thus Weiss speaks of Paul's beginning in v. 13 to 'play with the logical law' that a negative proposition cannot be maintained in the face of one positive exception of it. But this is not the 'logical law' involved. Nowhere is it hinted that the positive particular instance ('Christ is raised') itself negates the negative general proposition ('the dead are not raised').[1] In the same vein, Bultmann has insisted on making

[1] He finally despairs of the logic he tries to identify: 'This argument *ad hominem* is in no sense of a logical nature.' J. Weiss, *Der erste Korintherbrief* (Göttingen, 1910⁹; KEK), p. 354. Wilckens, 'Ursprung', states the relationship between Christ's resurrection and the Christian's as fully reciprocal (pp. 61f.): To deny either is to deny the other. But this is not capable of proof here. It is true that the certainty of the Christian's resurrection depends on the certainty of Christ's. But the Christian's is only a certain *possibility*, and Wilcken's position would make the *fact* of Christ's resurrection dependent on the *possibility* of the Christian's. That is quite another matter. In short, we must attend to the question of the *relationship* of death and resurrection even in the tradition as *Paul understands it*. Is the resurrection, as Wilckens claims, at the very center of Paul's thought so that all logical lines feed out from it and return back to it? Or is it more nearly the case that for Paul death and resurrection form such a unity that they can scarcely any longer be separated? The latter is true for Paul as regards Jesus, and may be expected

primary the proposition concerning Christ's resurrection.[1] Bult-mann's emphasis on the phrase 'your faith is in vain', ignores the central movement, 'if there is no resurrection from the dead, Christ has not been raised'. The protasis and apodosis go together. The basic connection cannot be ignored by shifting the discussion to the relationship between Christ's resurrection and the Christian's faith, for this latter argument is caught within the confines of, and is dependent upon, the initial premise itself.[2]

Making Christ's resurrection the hub in vv. 12–19, from which radiate the spokes of the argument, rests on a prior decision that the direction of thought must be made to conform to the known Pauline proclivities and biases. Such an assumption, however, fails to take account of the most significant feature of the text: Paul's 'argument' does not actually look very Pauline.

Taking account of v. 29, Schmithals has suggested an alternative interpretation of vv. 12–19: Paul, on the basis of his slender information, has misunderstood the Corinthian position.[3] This is something of a court of last resort, as it invites us to construe the true Corinthian position from one portion of ch. 15, written by Paul, while construing from another portion Paul's failure to comprehend the situation he himself describes. The dangers are evident, and we find Schmithals prescribing radical surgery in vv. 45–7 to keep Paul from understanding

to hold as regards the Christian. Wilckens takes I Thess. 4: 14f. as evidence for the centrality of the resurrection of Jesus in Paul's thought. But there the tradition mentions both death and resurrection, and Paul's elucidation of the tradition can already presuppose the vivid reality of death for the Thessalonians.

[1] R. Bultmann, 'Karl Barth, "Die Auferstehung der Toten"', *Glauben und Verstehen*, Vol. 1 (Tübingen, 1958³), pp. 53–4. On this reading, vv. 12–19 show that where Christ is denied as a special category, faith really is in vain. To say that Christ is a special category is to say that the kerygma, and hence faith, rests on revelation, on miracle. Without this revelation there would be no basis for *faith*.

[2] Bultmann chooses this path because he concentrates solely on the nature of faith and wishes to insist that it is not the same as inferential knowledge. That is to say, the kerygma itself is not propositional and cannot be objectified, which we have already noted in reference to I Cor. 15 (cf. above, p. 69, n. 2).

[3] W. Schmithals, *Gnosis*², p. 147 (Paul mistakes the Corinthian sensibilities for those of Epicureans). Cf. also Bultmann, *Theol.*, 1, p. 169 and the note there on II Cor. 5: 1–5.

too much and too well the Corinthian scene.[1] Furthermore, he notes that 'some' who say there is no resurrection from the dead must be the same ones who practice the custom of vicarious baptism of the dead (v. 29). Schmithals thinks this negates the very plausibility of *Paul's version* of the Corinthian position, for if they thought there was no resurrection *at all* (ὅλως, v. 29) the custom would make no sense.[2] Surely there is another, and better, approach to vv. 12–19.

We must allow v. 29 to stand as *Paul's* question addressed to the Corinthians who say there is no resurrection *from the dead*, asking them how they can say so in the face of their own practice.[3] It is a rhetorical question which shows Paul to be as incredulous as his later interpreters about the harmony between the practice of vicarious baptism and the claim that there is no resurrection from the dead. But the question is only rhetorical, just as vv. 30–32a are, where there is no sufficient answer which can be made in defense to Paul. All alike are designed to show the inherent absurdity and impossibility of the Corinthian position that the *dead* are not raised. What remains is to ask how the Corinthians arrived at that position, and what they really meant by that slogan.

In this regard, v. 19 is central. From the position of μόνον, which most naturally would be taken with ἠλπικότες and not ζωῇ, it seems that the proper translation should read: 'If in this life we [who are] in Christ have *only hope*, we are of all men most to be pitied.'[4] On the basis of what we can glimpse of the Corinthian problem elsewhere in this chapter and its congruence with I Cor. 4: 8ff., this can be taken as an epitome of the Corinthian position. The Corinthians have far more than mere hope, they have a radically collapsed eschatology. Already they 'are filled', already they have 'become rich', *they* already reign (I, 4: 8) regardless of the status of the *regnum Christi*. Yet there is a particular way in which Paul can also espouse the sentiment

---

[1] *Gnosis*[2], p. 160, n. 2.

[2] So also Wegenast, *Verständnis*, p. 61. If these were the circumstances would Paul fail to suspect that his reading of the Corinthian position regarding resurrection must be wrong?

[3] Whatever the origin and meaning of the custom, it does not imply that death is considered the normal route to resurrection. It is Paul who seeks to make the custom and the claim appear mutually exclusive.

[4] As found in RSV.

of v. 19. In fact, the words are significant for both parties as both would agree that hope is not *all* that is to be had. Paul and the Corinthians are momentarily one on this point.[1] Yet the agreement is more formal than material. From Paul's point of view the decisive question is that of the τάγμα, the order in which the future will involve those who are in Christ. As vv. 20ff. show, he would reject the idea of a Christian's having only hope in this world by insisting simultaneously on the certainty and the futurity of the resurrection, the first fruits and the order. To do so he focuses on the peculiar status and importance of death, making it clear that this is where the Corinthians have erred. This gives to v. 19 a curious hypothetical quality. Both Paul and the Corinthians agree that the apodosis follows from the protasis, but both would agree (for different reasons) in denying the truth of the protasis. Thus, though it is not grammatically such, v. 19 functions as a condition contrary to fact. Since it also serves as the conclusion in an argument stretching from v. 13 and since in that argument there are no fewer than four parallel conditional sentences, there is reason to suspect that the whole of vv. 13–19 is similarly ordered.

In addition to the evident logic and movement of the argument, unattested elsewhere in Paul, two other features within the paragraph are unusual. Nowhere else does Paul refer to himself, or anyone else, as ψευδόμαρτυς (v. 15). In fact, the whole concept of preaching or proclamation as μαρτυρεῖν seems more Corinthian than Pauline. Only in 15: 16 is the verb used for this activity (κατὰ τοῦ θεοῦ). This is all the more striking in the face of the noun μαρτύριον in 1: 6. Far from setting any precedent for the Pauline use of the verb, μαρτύριον there reflects the characteristic usage *of the Corinthian community itself*, embedded as it is in the midst of Paul's sarcastic reflection of the Corinthians' self-understanding as 'enriched in all speech and knowledge...not lacking any spiritual gift'.[2] Thus the equation

[1] I am indebted to Paul W. Meyer for this and other suggestions made in an unpublished paper on the problem of NT tradition and its control.

[2] Μυστήριον is probably the correct reading in 2: 1, but even if μαρτύριον were preferred, the almost periphrastic construction with καταγγέλλειν and once again the barbed context ('testimony in lofty words or wisdom') would suggest a Corinthian milieu. Otherwise, μαρτύριον is not used for the gospel message in the undisputed Pauline letters (cf. II Thess. 1: 10).

of preaching with μαρτυρεῖν and what is preached with μαρτύριον appears to be part of the customary Corinthian vocabulary.[1]

By the same token, it is unusual to hear Paul speak of persons still 'being in' their sins (v. 17). That phrase is reminiscent of another, equally unusual, in 15: 3: 'Christ died for our sins.' Both depart from Paul's more customary generic singular ἁμαρτία. In the case of 15: 3 this can be explained by the fact that Paul is repeating an earlier tradition. Is he then in v. 17 influenced by that earlier paradosis? Such seems unlikely in the face of v. 56 where he reverts to his more usual style.

All these features yield the impression that behind vv. 13–19 we hear not Paul, but the Corinthian community, speaking. Paul is rehearsing a Corinthian argument[2] designed to reduce to absurdity any *denial* that the resurrection from the dead has already taken place. In v. 12 it is Paul himself who asks, 'How do some of you say there is no resurrection of the dead?' in the face of the fact that Christ is raised from the dead. He then goes on in vv. 13–19 to describe 'how', to paraphrase the Corinthian logic and argument. We might well expect Paul to ask instead, 'When Christ is preached as raised from the *dead*,[3] how do you say that the Christian now, having not yet died, enjoys the resurrection life?', for the real issue is 'death' and its proper interpretation. From the whole of ch. 15 we see that it is the definition of death and the role assigned to it which most fundamentally separates Paul from the Corinthians' position; the issue of resurrection is never divorced from this basic problem. In the discussion Paul is the realist over against the Corinthian spiritualism. The material in vv. 13–19 corroborates what we otherwise know about the Corinthians' collapsed

[1] As it is of the Pastorals (cf. I Tim. 2: 6 and II Tim. 1: 8), where the same problem of collapsed eschatology is evident, II Tim. 2: 18.

[2] The use of ἡμῶν/ὑμῶν (v. 14), εὑρισκόμεθα v. 15, and ὑμῶν (*bis*) v. 17, would make it appear that Paul is simply rehearsing the structure of the argument and drawing the obvious implications about himself and other Christian preachers. But nothing precludes the possibility that this is more nearly a direct quotation from preachers within Corinth.

[3] The specific testimony that Christ is raised ἐκ νεκρῶν is Paul's reading of the tradition, in which the words are conspicuously absent (cf. also v. 20). Again Paul makes it clear that 'death' and its role is the central item in his dispute with the Corinthians.

92

eschatology and shows how completely they have spiritualized the idea of death. It also shows their mode of argument and the nature of the appeal they make.

That appeal is startling. It makes explicit, direct contact with the tradition found in vv. 3ff. at two points: Christ's resurrection and man's sinful condition. It makes more general contact by means of its claim that preaching and faith can be 'vain', a point explicitly acknowledged by Paul in his introduction to the paradosis, v. 2. The Corinthians seek to sustain their point of view by making an appeal to the truth of the kerygma itself. They suggest that if their conclusion is wrong, the whole kerygma, in this case the paradosis of 15: 3ff., must be scuttled. If there is no resurrection from the dead (on and in their terms, i.e., 'resurrection' as deliverance from the 'death' of sin and transferral to the realm of the spirit), then Christ is not raised, preaching and faith are in vain, and Christians are 'still in their sins'. Point for point it is a *negative* appeal to the older tradition, designed to legitimate the view that there is now a 'resurrection'. It is the earliest example of such an appeal that we have in Christian literature, not the less significant for coming from errorists.[1] The phrase 'there is no resurrection from the dead' is not a crude Pauline misapprehension of the Corinthian position. The formulation stems from their trying to press an early paradosis into service as an appeal for the authority of their developing theological position.

Paul is not impressed with the Corinthian position. He is certainly not impressed with the Corinthian behavior, as vv. 29–34 make clear.[2] But the Corinthians have not tried to 'deny' their heritage, they have tried to use it to support a questionable

[1] The Corinthians execute a subtle step in erecting their theological scaffolding on this kerygmatic platform, forcing (intentionally?) the whole issue of warrants for the kerygma.

[2] The purpose of vv. 29–34 is to allow Paul to throw rhetorical questions at the Corinthians (vv. 29–32a) and show that he thinks bad conduct follows from poor theology (vv. 32b–34). This material cannot be used to show inconsistencies in Paul's understanding and evaluation of the Corinthians, but shows what he regards as inconsistent in them. Ironically, they are 'still in their sins', and Paul thinks that functionally there is not a dime's worth of difference between the Corinthian view on resurrection and a wholesale denial of resurrection. For details cf. J. Schütz, 'Apostolic Authority and the Control of Tradition: I Cor. xv', *NTS* 15 (1969), 447–8.

view. They would recruit tradition for their own theological purposes. Paul must find a way to govern a tradition which he thinks is improperly exploited. He must find the norm of authority for *tradition itself* by which tradition as norm can somehow be judged. To see how Paul does this we must first establish what is and is not the 'old tradition' in vv. 1–11, so that we may distinguish between the tradition and the sanctions Paul devises for it.

From the language of vv. 1–3a (παρελάβετε, παρέδωκα... παρέλαβον) it appears that Paul begins with v. 3b to cite the paradosis which he himself has carried to the Corinthians.[1] Where the paradosis ends is another, and more troublesome, matter. In part the problem is one of balancing stylistic matters with other kinds of observations. For example, from a purely stylistic point of view there are good grounds for confining the original paradosis to the following:

ὅτι Χριστὸς ἀπέθανεν	ὅτι ἐγήγερται
ὑπὲρ τῶν ἁμαρτιῶν ἡμῶν	τῇ ἡμέρᾳ τῇ τρίτῃ
κατὰ τὰς γραφάς,	κατὰ τὰς γραφάς,
καὶ ὅτι ἐτάφη	καὶ ὅτι ὤφθη

The parallelism between the two units would be exact and the function of each concluding ὅτι clause to underscore the claim lodged in the initial verb: That 'he was buried' confirms death

[1] This point is too well established and the literature too well known to require documentation. A good sampling of the discussion will be found in the citations in F. Hahn, *Christologische Hoheitstitel* (Göttingen, 1964²; FRLANT 83), pp. 197ff. (The E. t., *The Titles of Jesus in Christology* [London, 1969] has abbreviated notes; the original is cited here). Cf. also Conzelmann, 'Analyse', pp. 1–11. The long-standing debate between those who regard the original milieu as Hebraic, Jewish-Christian and those who regard it as Greek, hellenistic-Christian has not proven very fruitful. The former position is espoused by J. Jeremias, *Eucharistic*, pp. 129ff.; 'Artikelloses Χριστός: Zum Ursprache von I Cor. 15: 3b–5', *ZNW* 57 (1966), 211–15. Cf. also B. Klappert, 'Zur Frage des semitischen oder griechischen Urtextes von I Kor. xv: 3–5', *NTS* 13 (1967), 168–73. This position is challenged by, among others, P. Vielhauer, 'Ein Weg zur neutestamentlichen Christologie?', *EvTh* 25 (1965), 57ff.; H. Conzelmann, 'Analyse'; E. Schweizer, *Erniedrigung und Erhöhung bei Jesus und seinen Nachfolgern* (Zürich, 1962²; AThANT 28), p. 89, n. 352. The matter of the anarthrous use of Χριστός is directly relevant to this problem. In addition to the above cf. Güttgemanns, *Apostel*, pp. 53ff. and 'Χριστός in I Kor. 15: 3b – Titel oder Eigenname?', *EvTh* 28 (1968), 533–4; Stuhlmacher, *Evangelium*, pp. 272ff.

just as that 'he appeared' confirms resurrection. Over against this observation, however, must be set the fact that mentioning Cephas destroys such perfect parallelism even while it prepares the way for the catalogue of witnesses to the resurrection.[1] Yet the terms 'Cephas' and 'the Twelve' share with much of the rest of vv. 3bff. an un-Pauline flavor, and the impression we are left with is that what Paul received as tradition extends to the conclusion of v. 5.[2]

The situation is more complicated with regard to vv. 6 and 7. There is a stylistic unity in the series of independent clauses introduced by (ἔπ)εῖτα, indicating a sharp break with vv. 3b–5. Yet v. 6b is almost certainly Paul's own addition, whatever the origin of the rest. At the same time, v. 7b is extremely difficult to understand unless we regard it as a pre-Pauline, rather than a free Pauline, formulation. K. Holl thus held that the paradosis extends through v. 7.[3] That unitary view of vv. 3–7 today rightly has few proponents.[4] Where vv. 3–7 are thought to be of a piece, it is necessary to explain the relationship between (a) the recitation *of* the Easter events (vv. 3–5a) and (b) the recitation of the witnesses *to* those events (vv. 5b–7). Where it is assumed, however, that the paradosis ends at v. 5 (whether 5a or 5b is immaterial) and Paul is himself held responsible for vv. 6 and 7, this relationship becomes a matter of some importance.

Why accumulate a testimony to the resurrection? Having abandoned Holl's literary position, more recent exegesis might be expected to offer a real solution to this problem.[5] Instead,

---

[1] E. Bammel, 'Herkunft und Funktion der Traditionselemente in I Kor. 15: 1–11', *ThZ* 11 (1955), pp. 401–19.

[2] Hahn, *Hoheitstitel*, pp. 196f.; Wegenast, *Verständnis*, pp. 54f.

[3] K. Holl, 'Der Kirchenbegriff des Paulus in seinem Verhältnis zu dem der Urgemeinde', *Sitzungsberichte der Preußischen Akademie der Wissenschaften (Phil.-hist. Klasse)*, 1921, 920–47, most recently repr. in K. H. Rengstorf (Hrsg.), *Das Paulusbild in der neueren deutschen Forschung* (Darmstadt, 1964; WF XXIV), pp. 144–78.

[4] For these see E. L. Allen, 'The Lost Kerygma', *NTS* 3 (1957), p. 349 and the references in Wegenast, *Verständnis*, p. 54, n. 4, to which should be added E. Käsemann, 'Konsequente Traditionsgeschichte?', *ZThK* 62 (1965), 141ff.; Wilckens, 'Ursprung', pp. 63ff. and Stuhlmacher, *Evangelium*, p. 269. In the case of these last two, however, 'unitary' is not quite the correct term for the whole of vv. 3–7.

[5] There is a median stage represented by those who can, by positing rival traditions in vv. 5 and 7, account for some of the accumulation. But they

critical scholarship since Holl has usually not seen the problem clearly, often evading the basic question.

It is patently absurd to regard Paul's appeal to resurrection witnesses as bolstering the testimony itself.[1] That makes sense only if we assume Jesus' resurrection to be in dispute at Corinth. Nothing in I Cor. 15 indicates that it is, and v. 2 specifically contradicts such an assumption. Whatever the disagreement between Paul and the Corinthians, they have heard and believed that Jesus is raised from the dead, and that it is not a point at issue. In the midst of whatever is in dispute, Paul would scarcely seek to corroborate that on which there is already agreement.

If vv. 6 and 7 are detachable from what precedes them, we must still go on to distinguish between Paul's responsibility for their composition and his responsibility for their incorporation.[2] As regards composition, the evidence is mixed. Paul himself may have provided the description of the 500 brethren (v. 6b). It is far less likely that he composed the phrase 'to all the apostles' (v. 7b). As Paul's expression these words are jarring in two respects.

First, the appearance itself seems to be not of the same type

shed little light on v. 6, and thus evade the central matter. Cf. A. Harnack, 'Die Verklärungsgeschichte Jesu, der Bericht des Paulus (I Kor. 15, 3ff.) und die beiden Christusvisionen des Petrus', *Sitzungsberichte der Preußischen Akademie der Wissenschaft (Phil.-hist. Klasse)*, 1922, 63–4; G. Sass, *Apostelamt und Kirche* (München, 1939), pp. 97ff.; E. Bammel, 'Herkunft'.

[1] This assumption has almost canonical status in current interpretation. So, for example, Bultmann, *Glauben*, I, pp. 54–5, who finds this a vain effort on Paul's part; W.-G. Kümmel, *Kirchenbegriff und Geschichtsbewußtsein in der Urgemeinde und bei Jesus* (Uppsala, 1943), p. 4; Bammel, 'Herkunft', p. 403 (complete in a 'juridical' sense); Schmithals, *Office*, p. 73; Klein, *Apostel*, p. 43; Wilckens, 'Ursprung', p. 63 (though he knows that the resurrection is not in dispute, cf. p. 61); H. Lietzmann, *An die Korinther, I, II* (Tübingen, 1949⁴; erg. v. W.-G. Kümmel, HNT), p. 77. In his supplement, p. 192 (to p. 79, line 1) Kümmel modifies his earlier stance enough to explain how this testimony can be seen as referring to an event historically 'datable' but only eschatologically 'perceptible'.

[2] It is not their status as tradition but their function within vv. 1–11 which is central here. Regarded as traditional and pre-Pauline, they could reflect an original desire to warrant the unparalleled claim that Jesus was raised from the dead. They could also reflect the desire to warrant a different claim, the claim to a commission for those to whom the appearances were vouchsafed. The question is whether Paul uses vv. 6 and 7 for either purpose.

as the others. In the previous instance, we have reference to an appearance to either an individual or a well defined, distinctive group. Paul's understanding of the broad apostolate to be found throughout the Church lacks any definite perimeter; hence it seems unlikely that 'the appearance' is a singular event. If not, v. 7b stands alone in the lists as the only citation of witness not attached to a fixed datum, and one would certainly expect some qualifying reference such as καθεξῆς.[1]

Second, it is simply highly unlikely that this phrase, with its key term πᾶσιν,[2] can be attributed to Paul. Would Paul of his own accord refer to the apostles in such a way as to exclude himself? Since Paul could not agree that these apostles are 'all the apostles', surely he would choose some other mode of expression, if the choice were freely his.[3]

What seems certain in regard to v. 7b is at least possible in regard to vv. 6a and 7a – that Paul is relying here on previous formulations. It may well be that at an early date multiple allusions to the resurrection testimony were added to the basic paradosis. Such allusions could provide backing for the claims of resurrection, or they could license those commissioned to make such claims. It is not likely, however, that Paul is here interested in their ability to confirm or license.

Why should Paul use a phrase like τοῖς ἀποστόλοις πᾶσιν if he were really 'at pains emphatically to prove himself' a member of that group, as vv. 8–10 seem to show?[4] Klein assumes that vv. 8–10 constitute an 'excursus' and deviate from the central

---

[1] Schmithals' argument to the contrary misses the point (*Office*, pp. 76f.). The question is not whether the apostles were called singly or *en masse*, but why Paul of all people would give or leave the impression of a single event of this collective nature. When Schmithals goes on to argue that comparisons with εἶτα τοῖς δώδεκα are illegitimate because that is a *pre-Pauline* tradition, he fails to see that this is precisely the clue.

[2] Holl's thesis that 'all the apostles' is a cumulative reference to the previously mentioned twelve plus the immediately preceding James now appears an aberration in a persuasive line of interpretation stretching from Lightfoot, *Galatians* (pp. 92ff.), to Schmithals, *Office* (p. 77). On balance Klein's assessment of the problem is most judicious and satisfactory: 'It is certainly not excluded that the expression τοῖς ἀποστόλοις πᾶσιν implies the δώδεκα, but every proof constructed from this passage is purely and simply a *petitio principii*' (*Apostel*, p. 43).

[3] Cf. G. Klein, *Apostel*, p. 41.

[4] *Ibid.*, p. 40.

thrust of vv. 1–11, having as their goal Paul's apostolic defense.[1]
He refers to the 'polemic' of v. 10b as evidence for this
different concern. It is true that these verses seem an interruption in vv. 1–11, but the question of how much they
deviate from the heart of the argument is another, indeed the
central, issue.

This can be seen in U. Wilckens' detailed and suggestive
attempt to reconstruct the history of the traditions embedded
within I Cor. 15: 3–7.[2] Wilckens distinguishes between 'kerygmatic' pieces of tradition in vv. 3–4 and 'catechetical' pieces of
tradition in vv. 5–7. In the first category, v. 3b is an '(originally
liturgical?) formula' concerning the atoning death of Christ;
v. 4a mentions the entombment; v. 4b is a kerygmatic formula
from the primal missionary kerygma and the item on which
Paul lays the greatest stress given his argument with the Corinthians.[3] In the second category are found three items scarcely
to be thought of as added by Paul in an *ad hoc* fashion. Verse 5
is the oldest 'legitimation formula' of the primitive community
which testifies to Peter's primacy among the Twelve. Verse 6 is
a summary of an account of an appearance before 500, here
added by Paul but originating as a 'foundation legend' in the
early community. Verse 7 is a 'legitimation formula' of a later
time, self-consciously modeled on v. 5, denoting a shift in the
central leadership from Peter to James and a broadening of the
group to which an appearance was vouchsafed.

Perhaps the most intriguing part of Wilckens' analysis is his
argument that vv. 5 and 7 have undergone a functional shift in
the history of the tradition. Originally they were designed to
warrant the claim to leadership, first of Peter and the Twelve,
later of James and a wider group. In time, however, these traditions were pressed into missionary service to certify the factual-

[1] 'The excursive character of the statements in vv. 8ff. is a telling symp-
tom of the tendentiousness.' *Ibid.* Cf. Wilckens, 'Ursprung', p. 64.
[2] 'Ursprung', esp. pp. 63–81 and the tabular recapitulation at the top of
p. 81. Stuhlmacher, *Evangelium* (pp. 267–9), regards the 'tradition' as encompassing vv. 3b–7 with Pauline additions in vv. 6b and 8ff.
[3] Some of these distinctions are questionable. Verse 4a can scarcely be
considered 'tradition' of independent stature (cf. Güttgemanns, *Apostel*,
p. 61, n. 42). The difference between the 'primary missionary tradition' of
v. 4c and the loosely attached but somehow independent tradition of v. 3b
requires clarification.

ness of the Christian claim about the resurrection itself. In that stage they can be regarded as catechetical.

How is it then that Paul *uses* vv. 5 and 7? Wilckens suggests that for Paul the 'eschatological truth of the whole Christian tradition' depends on the fact that Christ was raised. Hence, Paul uses vv. 5 and 7 in their *secondary* function. As we have already seen, this view lacks a certain cogency, if, with Wilckens, we agree that Paul 'presupposes that the Corinthians are in complete accord on this matter'.[1] It would be far better to assume that whatever the history of these particular traditions may be, Paul is not necessarily bound to their older function.

The primary function of vv. 5 and 7, according to Wilckens, is legitimizing ecclesiastical leaders. He sees vv. 8–10 as Paul's polemical and excursive response to this covert function of the list of appearances. Although he wants to use the appearances primarily to buttress the claim about Jesus' resurrection, Paul is lured by the provocative wording of v. 7 ('all the apostles') to detour long enough to establish his own belated claim to apostleship, returning to the central argument only in v. 11.

Yet the whole theory of this primary functionality is questionable. On Wilckens' reading the apostolic mantle rests exclusively on those who have been given a resurrection appearance. This alone constitutes the whole of apostolic authority. 'There exists, therefore, an essential relationship between the apostolate and an appearance of the resurrected one.'[2] In vv. 5 and 7 the formula expresses an 'authoritative relationship which is grounded in specific appearances of the risen one'.[3] The appearance before 'all the apostles' is the sacral-juridical constitution of the apostolate.[4] This and this alone provides the apostle's ἱκανότης.[5] If that is true, and more importantly if that is reluctantly recognized by Paul as a truth against which he must struggle in the face of a closed apostolic circle, it is surprising that Paul specifically refuses to ground his ἱκανότης in the resurrection appearance given him. But v. 9b is unequivocal on this: οὐκ εἰμὶ ἱκανὸς καλεῖσθαι ἀπόστολος. Paul does not regard his sufficiency as grounded in a resurrection appearance at all, but in the surpassing 'grace' of God manifested in his missionary labors.

[1] 'Ursprung', p. 62.   [2] *Ibid.*, pp. 65f.   [3] *Ibid.*, p. 67.
[4] *Ibid.*, p. 69.   [5] *Ibid.*, p. 65.

4-2

Furthermore, Wilckens' theory of the primary function of vv. 5 and 7 lands him in inconsistencies, in part because he brings to the discussion indistinct images of authority and legitimacy. The comparison between Paul and James is instructive.

Paul must be polemical and apologetic in vv. 8–10, according to Wilckens, because he has certain impediments to overcome. Chief among these is the fact that he once persecuted the Church. The appearance thus came to him as one 'who very definitely did not bring with him the qualifications of an apostle. If the apostles before him were called as apostles, as disciples of Jesus before his death or at least as pre-eminent members of the community, he was called only as a fanatical persecutor of the Church.'[1] James, of course, does not fit Wilckens' criteria as either (1) a disciple of Jesus, or (2) a pre-eminent member of the community,[2] *prior* to receiving an appearance. 'It is to be supposed that the appearance brought James...into communion with the Jerusalem Church where, as a brother of Jesus and as himself legitimated through the appearance of Jesus, he understandably achieved pre-eminent significance...'[3] Somehow an appearance legitimates James better than Paul, as Wilckens understands it. But this is mere fancy. In fact, Wilckens' definition of the legitimizing function of the appearances has no inherent connection with the autobiography of the one granted an appearance. It is Paul who, in vv. 8–10, introduces the autobiographical note. What Wilckens has in mind is not legitimation but authorization, while an appearance as the sole criterion of authorization is not at all what Paul has in mind.

Schmithals comes by a different route to a conclusion similar to Wilckens', that Paul's stance here is apologetic and defensive.[4] Paul only *appears*, on this view, to deprecate his authority, just as he 'distanced himself in every way formally – but only for the sake of form at the same time – from the other apostles'.[5] But why, we might ask, the elaborate charade which makes Paul himself appear distinct from a group he wants to insist he be-

[1] *Ibid.*, p. 64.
[2] In fact, it is hard to know what (2) means if it is really distinct from (1).
[3] *Ibid.*, p. 69.   [4] *Office*, pp. 73–80.
[5] *Ibid.*, p. 76.

longs to, and of doubtful authority when he wants to stress his authority? Perhaps we should lay aside the assumption that Paul is defensive about his fragile apostolic authority at least long enough to inquire further into the nature and source of that authority. On that view vv. 8–10 play an integral role in the whole arrangement by which vv. 1–11 fit with the rest of ch. 15. They are not excursive. They are not defensive. Paul assumes an identification with a wider apostolic circle. What interests him, however, is the nature and function of the apostle, not the size of the circle.

Clearly v. 7b occupies a critical position, serving as the pivot on which the direction of thought in this paragraph turns. Only the reference to the apostles brings Paul to the point he wishes to make of the whole catena of resurrection testimonies. That point lies in the correspondence of vv. 1–2 with v. 11.

Despite a notable similarity between them, v. 11 does not simply repeat vv. 1–2 and Paul does not end this paragraph on the same note with which he opened it. The extent and nature of the shift can be noted in the way ἐπιστεύσατε (v. 2) is repeated in v. 11, while εὐηγγελισάμην becomes κηρύσσομεν. While in some respects κηρύσσειν seems to be a broader term than εὐαγγελίζεσθαι,[1] the fact that Paul can use either with the direct object 'gospel'[2] renders this distinction minimal. More important is his tendency to use the former in reference to the present activity of preaching.[3]

Such is the shift separating vv. 1–2 from v. 11. In the Corinthian situation, where faith in Jesus' resurrection is not the central issue, Paul uses an extension of the paradosis, perhaps originally designed to buttress that faith, for another purpose: to broaden the evidence for what is in fact preached in the

[1] In Gal. 5: 11, for example, κηρύσσειν could scarcely be replaced by εὐαγγελίζεσθαι.

[2] E.g., with κηρύσσειν, Gal. 2: 5; I Thess. 2: 9.

[3] In the indicative of the finite verb Paul uses the present tense of κηρύσσειν nine times and aorist twice. Since the aorist of II Cor. 11: 4 is intended to balance the present tense there, only I Thess. 2: 9 stands out from this general usage. On the other hand, εὐαγγελίζεσθαι is used far less frequently as a finite verb in the indicative, but four of the six occurrences are aorist. Again, there is a contrast built into the direct discourse of Gal. 1: 23. As a simple condition, Gal. 1: 9 scarcely constitutes a noteworthy exception; there the verb is used in its most technical sense, as the context indicates.

apostolic ministry.[1] This is the way 'we proclaim'. There is considerable difference between τίνι λόγῳ εὐηγγελισάμην ὑμῖν, v. 2, and οὕτως κηρύσσομεν, v. 11. The former is restrictive to Paul and tied temporally to a specific occasion in Corinth. The latter is broader. It covers an indefinite 'we' and describes how preaching is carried on by the Church as a whole – hence the present tense. Nevertheless, the two conceptualizations are alike since in both instances the Corinthians 'believed' this preaching. The net effect of the movement in vv. 1–11 is to broaden the spectrum of what constitutes authoritative preaching and still show that this expansion neither adds to nor subtracts from the tradition which the Corinthians first accepted and believed.

Once we have clear the order of priorities in vv. 1–11 and the relationship of issues there with the rest of ch. 15, we have the full form of Paul's argument with Corinth, but only the form. Paul wishes to control a tradition he regards as illegitimately exploited. To do so he must appeal to apostolic authority. But how can he substantiate *that* apostolic *authority* to which he appeals? He wishes to identify the paradosis with the apostles, including himself. Yet the authority he claims must be warranted outside the paradosis, for the Corinthians themselves have laid claim to the paradosis to warrant their own position. At this time the term 'apostle' has not yet undergone that connotational shift from meaning 'authorized' to meaning authoritative which was so significant a development in the whole later Church.

This is the context in which we see the purpose of Paul's self-references in vv. 8–10. These verses do not contain a serious and hidden polemic against other apostles. They are not an intra-apostolic defense, but an apostolic paradigm. By referring to himself Paul is able to expand on the nature of apostolic activity in concrete, illustrative ways. The effect of this transition from 'all the apostles' to himself as an apostolic example is subtle but crucial. Paul's desire here is twofold: To move (1) to an equation of general apostolic preaching with the paradosis, and (2) to an elaboration of apostolic activity in terms of his own experience. This accounts for the awkward shift from 'all

---

[1] This also explains the vagueness of ἐκεῖνοι, v. 11. While the most logical referent may be 'all the apostles' (Lietzmann-Kümmel, *Korinther*, p. 78), the very general nature of the pronoun suits Paul's purposes admirably.

the apostles' to 'last of all he appeared also to me...the least of the apostles'. Because Paul's claim to be an apostle is not an issue, the awkwardness can stand. It is precisely on the basis of this claim – that his experience is illustrative of generic apostolic activity – that he moves from 'all the apostles' to himself, the 'last' – in the first place, we might say. For Paul a description of apostolic activity is itself a statement of apostolic authority. That authority is so primary that it is nothing other than the expression of the authority of the gospel itself. The illustration of Paul's apostolic authority also serves as the final norm by which the paradosis itself is to be interpreted and the particular Corinthian appropriation of the paradosis is to be judged.

Such a description is provided *in nuce* in vv. 8–10. One of the chief features of this passage is the apparent tension between Paul's description of himself as 'least of the apostles...not sufficient to be called an apostle' and his claim that he nevertheless 'labored more abundantly than all of them'. Both claims underline a single and central feature of the Pauline concept of apostolic work: The apostle's sufficiency comes solely from God's grace, not from the apostle's own resources. His *calling and his authority* are not the product of his own natural gifts, but are attributable only to God. Thus if Paul did labor harder than all the others, it was still 'not I, but the grace of God which is with me'.

If this 'sufficiency' is not 'in vain', that means it has not failed to prove itself evident, that Paul *continually* attributes his sufficiency to God's grace. At the same time, his own personal 'insufficiency' is a necessary correlate of apostolic life. Like God's sufficiency, this human weakness and frailty is a continuing phenomenon. While the reference to his having persecuted the Church may stand as a decisive illustration of how the apostle himself was found wanting, it is not merely for the historical record. If the apostle is now what he is by the grace of God, his own inadequacies are only *exemplified* in his past persecution of the Church, not confined to that chapter of his personal life. This is confirmed by Paul's reference to himself as 'least of the apostles', a comparative, contemporary judgment, not a reference to his putative standing on the day he became an apostle. At the same time it is clear that to be the 'least' is to exhibit most abundantly the true essence and source of apostolic life – God's grace.

Similar observations can be made regarding the use of ἔκτρωμα. The term does not refer simply to the 'forced, abnormal, extraordinary' nature of Paul's calling, to the fact that he was not one of Jesus' disciples.[1] In fact the term refers not to the process of birth, but to its result.[2] Munck's analysis[3] suggests that only two possible meanings are significant for our text. Either the term refers to a monster and is reminiscent of such passages in LXX as Job 3: 16 and Eccles. 6: 3, or it refers to that which is embryonic and in need of formation. Munck, like Fridrichsen, assumes that the word must refer to Paul's Jewish past. That assumption seems challenged by the context, for throughout this passage Paul stresses the way God's grace complements his own insufficiency. Ἔκτρωμα is not necessarily abusive[4] and may be of Paul's own choosing. This becomes more probable when we realize that the two alternatives are not disparate. Though ἔκτρωμα in those passages cited means a stillborn child, Num. 12: 12 (LXX) preserves a peculiar nuance of the idea of death in the midst of life itself, or life in the midst of death. From this is derived the metaphorical use of the term. 'In all these passages the OT conception of life is revealed in the fact that a man in the depths of misery is compared to a stillborn child... "Like a stillborn child" is thus the strongest expression for human wretchedness.'[5]

At the same time, ἔκτρωμα can refer to that which is embryonic rather than stillborn, that which is incapable of sustaining life of its own volition, but requires (divine) intervention

---

[1] J. Schneider, art. 'ἔκτρωμα', *TDNT*, II, p. 466.

[2] A. Fridrichsen, 'Paulus Abortivus', *Symbolae Philologicae O. A. Danielsson octogenario dicatae* (Uppsala, 1932), pp. 78–85. For access to this and the article by Björck (below, n. 4) I am indebted to Nils A. Dahl.

[3] J. Munck, 'Paulus tanquam abortivus (I Cor. 15: 8)', *New Testament Essays, Studies in Memory of T. W. Manson 1893–1958* (Manchester, 1959), pp. 180–93. Cf. also T. Boman, 'Paulus Abortivus (I Kor. 15: 8)', *ST* 18 (1964), 46–50.

[4] The definite article need not indicate this. Cf. G. Björck, 'Nochmals Paulus Abortivus', *Coniectanea Neotestamentica* 3 (1939), 3–8. Güttgemanns (*Apostel*, pp. 88f.) follows Weiss (*Korintherbrief*, p. 352) and others in stressing the article. He regards ἔκτρωμα as a gnostic *Schimpfwort* and Paul's approach in vv. 3–11 as an effort to rally broad apostolic support to his claim that there is not only a temporal difference between Christ and the Christian, but also an essential difference which the gnostic Corinthians overlook.

[5] Björck, 'Abortivus', p. 184.

if it is to continue.¹ This is not vastly different from the meta-phorical usage mentioned already, underscoring an insufficiency to sustain life. Thus the word may well be Paul's own self-designation, and certainly need not be thought of as confined to his pre-Christian life. His apostolic life bears these same characteristic marks. An appearance of Jesus to Paul in this state cannot be distinguished from his apostolic calling, as Gal. 1 makes clear.

Ἔσχατον δὲ πάντων, coming as it does at the end of a serial list, could suggest that Paul is either the last of those to be granted such an appearance or the last of the apostles. If, how-ever, Paul is not interested in these appearances from a primarily historical perspective, and if the knotty problem of his relation-ship with the disciples is also not central in his statement, we should possibly look elsewhere for the force of ἔσχατον.

As we have seen, the thrust of vv. 8–10 describes the reality of apostolic life as something provided only by God's sufficiency, his grace. From the natural, human point of view the apostle is incapable of sustaining his own life. Moreover, Paul exploits this feature in calling himself the 'least' of the apostles, for to do so on his terms is actually to suggest he is the best example of what is quintessential in apostleship. So it may be with the phrase 'last of all' if it echoes the language of 4: 9ff.² There the apostles generically are described as ἐσχάτους, which is amplified by Paul's reference to their being ἐπιθανατίους, sentenced to death.

This concept of apostolic authority is not elaborately ex-pounded in ch. 15, but rather alluded to by means of pithy statements and self-characterizations. Paul's commerce with Corinth has already involved him in an explanation of his apostleship sufficient to allow him to presuppose here his basic frame of reference.³ In I Cor. 4 Paul describes what it means to be an apostle: 'Already you rule. And would that you did, that we might share rule with you.' The language is the language of exercising authority. The scorn reveals that same misplaced eschatological accent which is the root of the Corinthian mis-

¹ For texts and discussion cf. Munck, 'Abortivus', pp. 185–7.
² As assumed by G. Kittel, 'ἔσχατος', TDNT, II, p. 697.
³ I Cor. 4: 8ff. and 9: 1ff. are basic texts, but see also 2: 1ff.; 3: 5ff.; 4: 1ff. etc., and N. A. Dahl, 'Paul and the Church at Corinth According to I Cor. 1: 10 – 4: 21', Christian History and Interpretation, pp. 313–35.

construal of reality in ch. 15. Such is the foundation for Paul's sharp contrast of the predicates of apostolic and Corinthian life in ch. 4. There is no power of the resurrection without the accompanying weakness and ignominy of death; death is a reality of this world to be taken seriously. In that sense Paul the apostle is the living exemplification of the truth of the kerygma. It is precisely this conviction which allows him to interpret the kerygma by reference to himself in the face of the attempted Corinthian interpretation.

This same mode of argument emerges in 15: 31. Paul dies daily. The presence of death as part of the reality of life is also a part of the concrete reality of his own apostolic life. Moreover, this he swears 'by your confidence which I have in Christ Jesus our Lord'. With varying nuances Bultmann, Lietzmann and Weiss have all read ὑμετέραν as the equivalent of an objective genitive, describing Paul's boast which he has in the Corinthians.[1] Such a reference, however, is enigmatic and both unparalleled and unprepared for in the letter. While Paul speaks freely and frequently of his boast in the community in II Corinthians (7: 4, 14; 8: 24), such an attitude does not seem to mark this stage of his relationship with them. Instead, Paul is alluding to the Corinthians' own misplaced confidence (cf. I, 5: 6) and to the fact that theirs is actually dependent on his 'dying' while he himself has confidence in Christ.[2] Nor are the words τῷ κυρίῳ ἡμῶν mere liturgical embellishment. It is on the terms of that lordship, that *regnum Christi* which Paul has already described, that he places his confidence in Christ. That is what enables him to 'die daily' and even demands that he will.

In conclusion we may say that Paul identifies the message, the kerygma, with the apostle himself.[3] They are both based on

---

[1] R. Bultmann, 'καυχάομαι etc.', *TDNT*, III, p. 650, n. 43; 'By the renown I have won in you'. Similarly Lietzmann (-Kümmel), *Korinther*, p. 83. Weiss, *Korintherbrief*, p. 364, takes it as the pride which Paul has in the Corinthians.

[2] Neugebauer, *In Christus*, p. 123, correctly takes this as subjective genitive, but stressses insufficiently the contrast between Paul and the Corinthians.

[3] Bultmann says (*Theol.*, I, p. 129); 'Paul's discussion with his gnosticizing opponents in Corinth shows how one's understanding of "freedom" and "authorization" (ἐξουσία) leads to a particular way of living.' This is true for his opponents, but the situation is rather the reverse for Paul, for whom the apostolic mode of life is the given element from which is derived his definition of freedom and authority.

the same realities. They are reciprocally, even dialectically, related. Both are characterized by the reality of death as an inescapable part of Christian life, the necessary ingredient in an as yet unresolved eschatological hope. Paul is mounting an appeal. He does so to ascertain the correct meaning of the tradition and thus assess the propriety of the Corinthian extension of that tradition.

In all of this Paul has done nothing less than rely on his own construction of what it means to be an apostle, showing why the 'apostolic' testimony to the tradition is authoritative. He is moved to do so not merely by the substance, but also by the form, of the Corinthian denial. The Corinthians have not only failed to hear the gospel rightly the first time, but have sought, themselves, to invoke authoritative norms for their eccentric position. They have tried to make the kerygma authoritative. Paul's response cannot be limited to trading formulas, but must seek to establish the means by which the word itself is judged as rightly heard and proclaimed. To what norm can he turn?

Paul can only turn to the norm of the apostle. But to do even that he must ascertain what constitutes apostolic authority. What constitutes that authority is the evident fulfillment in the apostolic person of ideas which lie at the heart of the kerygma when it is correctly understood: eschatological reservation and hope, death as a constituent element of life, etc. We notice that Paul defines the apostle by his conformity with these ideas and his capacity to embody them, not by some appeal to his status. That is to say, Paul goes to the question of authority, not to the question of legitimacy.

As he must, Paul turns to the norm of apostolicity as he understands it from his own personal experience. This experience is a critical factor in his whole understanding of authority. Nevertheless, Paul also establishes an important precedent: appeal to an apostle as appeal to ultimate authority. When the apostolic circle finally becomes fixed, apostolic legitimacy as such can become a surrogate for apostolic authority. Ironically, this eventually happened to Paul himself, in whose name others later wrote letters. If they were successful it is because only the question of legitimacy was thought important, not the matter of authority.

Before leaving I Cor. 15 we must ask what it reveals about

another important issue: the relationship between tradition and gospel. The 'tradition' itself is not easy to delimit. We might call it porous. Wilckens and others have shown good reasons for regarding vv. 5 and 7 and perhaps also 6a as essentially pre-Pauline.[1] Certainly v. 7 looks stylized.[2] On the other hand, Wilckens' attempt to fragment vv. 3–5 is unsuccessful. The passage must be taken as a unit. Thus we have a texture in vv. 3–11 which starts with a firmly fixed unit, adds generous portions of less firmly identifiable (less unitary) material and finally includes what must be regarded as Pauline additions (vv. 6b, 8–10), all culminating in a return to the concept of apostolic preaching (v. 11) with which v. 1 began.

In this mixture, what is it Paul 'received' and 'handed on'? Certainly vv. 3b–5; perhaps also vv. 6a and 7; certainly not vv. 8ff. What is it that can be ascribed to τὸ εὐαγγέλιον ὃ εὐηγγελισάμην ὑμῖν, ὃ καὶ παρελάβετε? Is it only what can be ascribed with certainty to 'paradosis', i.e., strictly vv. 3b–5? Or does the less determinate status of vv. 6b and 7, the smooth transition between these elements and Paul's own addition suggest that the 'gospel' is something broader than the tradition more narrowly conceived?

These questions lead us directly to the dependent phrase τίνι λόγῳ εὐηγγελισάμην ὑμῖν (v. 2), which has been translated in a variety of ways and sometimes used as a wedge to separate 'tradition' from Paul's concept of 'gospel'. This is implicit in Lietzmann's arrangement and translation. He puts a stop after σώζεσθε and treats the next phrase as an independent interrogative: 'On what basis...?'[3] Kümmel's correction (the phrase is an indirect interrogative dependent on τὸ εὐαγγέλιον) and

---

[1] Of course, the term 'tradition' itself is rather porous, and this is part of the problem. Wegenast, *Verständnis* (p. 55, n. 3) rejects the idea of tradition in vv. 6f. because the material is not formulary. But the stylistic considerations already raised show the material to be as formulary (at least in v. 7) as anything in vv. 3–5, and Wegenast's own claim that Paul is referring to historical reports which he received 'through tradition' suggests that loose terminology.

[2] Stuhlmacher (*Evangelium*, p. 269) points out that v. 9 looks stylistically attracted to v. 6, as v. 7 does to v. 5. Obviously v. 8 cannot be pre-Pauline. The point then lies in seeing the careful way in which the paradosis, whatever its original scope, has been expanded – and asking why.

[3] *Korinther*, p. 76. For other efforts at translation see Lietzmann, and Wegenast, *Verständnis*, p. 57, n. 5.

translation ('in what words?') is better.[1] At least grammatically there is no distinction between the εὐαγγέλιον ὃ εὐηγγελισάμην ὑμῖν and τίνι λόγῳ εὐηγγελισάμην ὑμῖν. Does this mean that for Paul the gospel is the word of tradition? Is the paradosis the gospel?[2]

The answer must be both yes and no, because the form of the question is awkward. We have already noticed abundant evidence suggesting that Paul regards 'the gospel' as a pregnant entity, i.e., open, dynamic, eschatologically attuned. This is particularly clear where Paul speaks of 'my (our)' gospel, suggesting his own involvement in a dynamic and eschatological process. To this I Cor. 15: 3ff. now adds the clear evidence that the gospel is anchored in historical facts; and it cannot be denied that these facts are routinely reported in missionary proclamation. If the gospel has its future, it has its past as well.

Yet the gospel is reducible to neither its past nor its future. It is an embodiment of the tension between past and future, a tension which can be ignored only by refusing to stand in it (v. 1) but which is ignored to the threat of salvation itself ('through which you *are being saved*', v. 2). In short, the present dynamic aspect of the gospel is the product of its past and future orientations, but not the equivalent of either alone. When this point is missed, as it is by the Corinthians, it becomes necessary to ask about the nature and locus of the gospel's authority. Paul could not for a moment consider that this authority is to be found in the past report; the Corinthians do not find it necessary to deny the report of Jesus' death and resurrection. For Paul the authority rests in the *implications* of the historical report, and only the report so interpreted is genuinely 'the gospel'.

Something similar can be said about the resurrection appearance granted to Paul. In and of itself that appearance is not the source of his authority. Not everyone who saw the resurrected Jesus was an apostle.[3] Paul cannot persuade the Corinthians he is right by insisting that he is an apostle any more than he can by rehearsing the tradition. In both cases the question of meaning and significance, the matter of interpretation, remains.

[1] *Korinther*, p. 191. Similarly, Fridrichsen, *Apostel*, p. 19, n. 17 (to p. 9): '(stating) through which word I announced it (sc. τὸ εὐαγγέλιον) to you'.
[2] So Schlier, *Zeit*, p. 215.
[3] Cf. Klein, *Apostel*, pp. 43f.

He must persuade them that out of Christ's death comes the reality of a new life and the absolute certainty of the Christian's future. This is implicit in the *movement* of the paradosis but it cannot be reduced to the paradosis itself, for the theological argument is made up of two separate components.

The first of these involves the continuity of the crucified Jesus with the risen Lord, and in this particular context means, for Paul, that resurrection only follows death. The second component is the assumption that Jesus' fate in being raised involves the ultimate fate of every Christian, and in this particular context means, for Paul, that Jesus is the 'first fruits'. Neither of these two components is reducible to either the paradosis or the resurrection appearance to Paul. Both are merely implicit there. One set of implications, i.e., the continuity of Jesus crucified and buried with Jesus risen and living, and the continuity of Jesus' fate with the Christian's fate, leads to another, i.e., the precedence of death over resurrection, the precedence of Jesus' 'reign' over the consummation of all things when death is finally conquered.

Formally, the paradosis is only the occasion for two ranges of implications which Paul draws. The term 'gospel', as Paul uses it in v. 1 and implies it in v. 11, stands for this interpretation of the paradosis. The gospel is not identical with the paradosis but represents its effective interpretation. At least in the case of I Cor. 15 it must be said that the gospel represents for Paul the existential meaning, the anthropological appropriation, of the paradosis; and according to his lights, it should also for the Corinthians.

What is true of paradosis is also true of the appearance to Paul of the risen Lord. That is the same thing, in terms of content, as the paradosis. Thus we must ask what provides the needed interpretation of the appearance. The answer is to be found in vv. 9 and 10, which tell of a transition from death to life parallel to that of the paradosis, except that now it is part of the apostle's own autobiography ('I persecuted the Church of God, but by the grace of God I am [now] what I am'). Thus, to stay with the formal structural analysis a moment longer, the equivalent of 'gospel' is the apostle's personal experience and assessment of its meaning. Gospel is to 'paradosis' as apostolic experience is to the appearance of the risen Lord. At least in the context of this argument, *gospel and personal apostolic experience are read by Paul as equivalents.*[1] With this the γνωρίзω of v. 1 can come into its own with full force. Paul is making known something 'new' in his explication of the paradosis in the sense that the 'gospel' as the existential word to and about the situation of the one addressed (whether Paul in the vision or the Corinthians in the paradosis) is always dynamic and open, i.e., eschatological. That paradosis may refer to the past and the Christian's hope may be fixed in the future, but the gospel is the present manifestation and interpretation of this past and this future.

Again, the formal correspondence between this pregnant sense of 'gospel' and Paul's apostolic experience is stressed in the very phrasing of I Cor. 15: 1-11. The Corinthians 'stand' in the gospel and 'are being saved' through it (vv. 1-2) if they *have not* believed in vain; his labors have been productive and abundant because the grace of God which *came* to him *has* not *been* in vain; he is what he is by that grace. One can scarcely miss the echo in Rom. 5: 2, εἰς τὴν χάριν ἐν ᾗ ἑστήκαμεν, and the elaborate description which follows there of the basis for hope, hope produced ultimately out of present suffering.

It is not difficult to see in I Cor. 15: 1-11 why Paul moves along the chain of tradition to include his apostolic self-reference. The tradition cannot by itself be substituted for 'the gospel' and hence agreement on the tradition does not guarantee that

---

[1] Stuhlmacher (*Evangelium*, p. 275) is quite correct in pointing out that the effect of Paul's expansion of the tradition is to involve himself in the 'history of God's acts' to which the paradosis points. He is also correct in concluding that this incorporation into the Church's confession 'cast in a salvation-history scheme' (p. 277) moves the confession toward the didactic – even toward the later literary genre 'gospel' (cf. p. 277, n. 2). But in effect Stuhlmacher never asks why Paul is constrained to move the confession in this direction and makes mistaken assumptions about the context of I Cor. 15: 3ff. This is particularly true in his assumption that Paul's apostolic word had authority in the Corinthian community, a matter which Paul could scarcely presume under the circumstances. In short, one must ask not only why Paul expands on the tradition, but why he repeats it at all. The answer to both questions turns on the problem of authority. The addition of one more person to the list of witnesses to the risen Lord does not materially alter the content of the resurrection appearances, but rather for Paul elucidates the locus of authority (which does not reside in the tradition as such) and in that sense moves paradosis to gospel.

the word is rightly heard and understood. But neither can the 'apostolic' testimony for the tradition (at least as yet) provide the needed certification. In the last analysis Paul can only appeal to the form of the apostle and the circumstances of his labors as the equivalent of the gospel and in that indirect sense its certification. As has already been said, that may have established a very important precedent along lines Paul could not have envisioned, a precedent in which the apostolic word determines what one must or may believe, but it is clear that Paul does not draw that last conclusion himself.[1]

Paul does not regard the apostle as a guarantor of the tradition but as a manifestation or illustration of the truth of the gospel, a truth which cannot be regarded as frozen in propositional terms because its essential characteristic is power. The emphasis is on the dynamic. Although the idea of 'power' is never made explicit here (cf. vv. 24 and 43, however), it is implicit in the concept of κηρύσσειν which, as v. 11 shows, both comprehends and transcends the 'word' which is preached. We have already seen this evident in I Thess. 1: 4ff. Paul's missionary εὐαγγέλιον comes not ἐν λόγῳ μόνον but in power, in the Holy Spirit and 'with full conviction'. In short, his effort in Macedonia was not 'in vain' (2: 1). If the gospel had come in word alone, it would have failed to manifest the power Paul ascribes to it as its chief characteristic. That power is itself the evidence of 'missionary' activity (I Thess. 1: 7–8) on the part of the Thessalonians, for the word of the Lord has gone forth in their example (τύπος, v. 7). How close the concepts in I Thess. are to the understanding of the gospel in I Cor. 15 can be seen, finally, with reference to Paul's remarks in I Thess. 2: 8–14. He shares not only the gospel, but himself (v. 8) as a manifestation of that power (vv. 9–12) which the Thessalonians in turn manifest as proof that the word of God is something other than a human word, i.e., is something 'at work' (ἐνεργεῖται) among you who believe (v. 13).

Paul's use of παραλαβόντες λόγον ἀκοῆς…ἐδέξασθε (I Thess.

[1] We are reminded that Paul does not actually use εὐαγγέλιον as the direct object of πιστεύειν, for example. In I Cor. 15: 1–11 where he all but makes the connection (vv. 2, 11) the failure to do so becomes all the more noticeable.

2: 13) provides the final comment on the relationship of gospel and paradosis in I Cor. 15: 2. The word itself is transformed out of something other than human speech when it is accepted (δέχεσθαι), not merely received (παραλαμβάνειν). It then becomes ὁ λόγος θεοῦ ὃς ἐνεργεῖται. The λόγος characteristic of Paul's apostolic endeavor is marked by its power, by the transition from λόγος to ἔργον (Rom. 15: 18; II Cor. 10: 11).

CHAPTER 5

TRADITION, GOSPEL AND THE APOSTOLIC EGO: GAL. 1 AND 2

In Galatians, Paul's temper is noticeably warm, his tone un-usually cool. His relationship with these communities is severely strained, eliciting from the apostle a response which pushes everywhere against outer limits. One has the feeling that in a later generation Paul would have dismissed as simply heretical those against whom he struggles. There are few expressions of conciliation, little attempt to win by gentle persuasion, no com-promise. The outer limits of freedom and the gospel are not easily symbolized in Paul's time, however, and this becomes the problem with which he must wrestle. This is the central issue of the first two chapters. No other letter in the corpus better em-bodies the polemical form of theological argument which Paul learned to master. That means that for no other letter is it quite so important to be able to reconstruct both sides of the argument in order to understand adequately Paul's side.

THE PRESCRIPT, GAL. I: I–5

Polemic is scarcely veiled in the abrupt inscription and address with which the letter opens. Paul's description of himself as 'apostle' οὐκ ἀπ' ἀνθρώπων οὐδὲ δι' ἀνθρώπου ἀλλὰ διὰ 'Ιησοῦ Χριστοῦ καὶ πατρὸς κ.τ.λ. already suggests something more than an identification *pro forma* of the author's apostolic status. It signals an elaboration and exposition which, when developed, shows itself to be crucial to the larger purpose and argument of the letter. Complementing this unusual stress on his apostolic position is Paul's failure to dwell even for a moment on the status of those to whom he writes. They are not called 'be-loved of God' (Rom. 1: 3) or 'saints' (Phil. 1: 1; I Cor. 1: 2; Rom. 1: 7). Nor does Paul fill out a lean prescript by using such terminology in a subsequent thanksgiving period, as in I Thess.

The deliberate and grave tone of this opening paragraph is only enhanced by Paul's use of fixed christological formulations which also relate directly to the larger argument of the epistle. In v. 4 he incorporates a liturgical formula, τοῦ δόντος ἑαυτόν...[1] In v. 1 he uses a standard formulation[2] in his designation of God the Father as τοῦ ἐγείραντος αὐτόν [sc. Ἰησοῦν] ἐκ νεκρῶν.[3] The latter is reminiscent of a similar phrase in I Thess. 1: 10. There the reference to Jesus' being raised comes within a clear binary formula that unites repentance with the idea of apocalyptic salvation or rescue. The Thessalonians have turned to God who raised Jesus from the dead. They await Jesus, as God's son, from heaven; he will rescue them from the coming wrath.

In Gal. 1: 1–5, we see something different and more reminiscent of I Cor. 15, a movement toward soteriological eschatology. The resurrection of Jesus is separated from the apocalyptic (1: 1) and the apocalyptic (v. 4b) is brought into the closest relationship with the soteriology of v. 4a. Jesus does not save in the eschaton by virtue of his position in heaven, but by virtue of his sacrificial death. This represents a relativizing of the apocalyptic inasmuch as the final outcome of salvation is complemented by a change in the present circumstances of the Christian, a change which has nothing to do with the believer's intentions or will.[4] Paul's use of tradition in this address shows the growing importance of the concept of Jesus' death in the apostle's eschatological delineations, although the wedding of traditional phrases concerning death and resurrection into a soteriological eschatology is not complete.

[1] Cf. E. Käsemann, 'Formeln: II. Liturgische Formeln im NT', *RGG*[3], II, cols. 993ff.; Lührmann, *Offenbarungsverständnis*, p. 89.

[2] Cf. Rom. 4: 24; 8: 11; 10: 9; I Cor. 6: 14; II Cor. 4: 14; I Thess. 1: 10.

[3] Cf. W. Bousset, *Kyrios Christos* (Göttingen, 1926[3]; FRLANT 21), p. 102; W. Kramer, *Christ, Lord, Son of God* (London, 1966), p. 22; V. Neufeld, *The Earliest Christian Confessions* (Grand Rapids, 1963; NTTS, 5), pp. 48–9.

[4] Thus the motif of repentance, evident in I Thess. 1: 9f. and part of the early missionary proclamation, finds little room in this more developed pattern of Paul's thought.

THE NORMATIVE CHARACTER OF THE GOSPEL, GAL. 1: 6–9

In v. 4 we find the essential background against which vv. 6–9 must be read: Paul's reference to 'this present evil age' from which the Christian can be delivered. In taking up the contrast of this age and the coming age Paul avails himself of a familiar Jewish, apocalyptic distinction[1] of sharp contrasts. The category of 'this (evil) age' is common enough in Paul (cf. I Cor. 2: 6, 8; II Cor. 4: 4; Rom. 12: 2) and the verb ἐξελέσθαι indicates the manner in which this age holds man in its power. It is thus a sphere of power from which man must be delivered, and that is the effect of Christ's death 'for our sins'. Such is the soteriological description of the possibilities of human life: bound to this age through sin or freed from it through Christ's death. Characteristically, Paul uses these alternatives in such a way that they are not chronologically distinct or exclusive, but there is no denying that they are logically antithetical.

This same antithesis dominates his description of 'gospel' in vv. 6–9. Paul is astonished at the conduct of the Galatians, at their turning away (μετατίθεσθαι) *from* the one who has called them, *to* another gospel (εἰς ἕτερον εὐαγγέλιον). Though not described in soteriological terms, such apostasy reflects the same stark, alternative possibilities as vv. 4, 5. Turning from the one who calls in grace to another gospel means fleeing from the sphere wrought by Christ's death, from the sphere of grace itself. The parallelism of these distinctions in vv. 4 and 6 is confirmed in Rom. 5: 20ff. where sin and grace are set in sharp antithesis (and Christ is seen as intervening temporally) and where sin and grace represent 'powers' which are said to reign (βασιλεύειν).[2] Paul is fond of describing grace as power; as his power (II Cor. 1: 12; 12: 10; I Cor. 15: 10) but also as the sphere in which all Christians find themselves (Gal. 5: 4; Rom.

---

[1] הָעוֹלָם הַזֶּה and הָעוֹלָם הַבָּא; cf. IV Ezra 7: 50: ...*non fecit altissimus unum saeculum sed duo.*

[2] From Rom. 5: 20 – 6: 4 the actual nature of the alternatives becomes clearer. As general possibilities of existence they are parallel and simultaneous. But as specific possibilities of Christian life, they are, for Paul, mutually exclusive. Hence, their reign is both coterminous and disjunctive.

5: 2). It is the 'territory of the divine deed's sway' and 'a power that determines the life of the individual'.[1]

Thus the apostasy of 1: 6ff. is a *departure from power*, from that which marks the proper realm of Christian existence. Paul's language stresses the agency of God: τοῦ καλέσαντος ὑμᾶς ἐν χάριτι. The point is important primarily in the light of his apostolic autobiography which follows, when it becomes clear that the source of the calling has a capacity to subordinate all instruments of the call.[2] God calls ἐν χάριτι, where ἐν is less causal than instrumental, less instrumental than locative, indicating the place 'where' the Galatian Christians were called by God and in which they, as those called, stand.[3]

Yet the change in Galatia is not merely a turning away from something. It is also a turning to, εἰς ἕτερον εὐαγγέλιον. The introduction to the term 'gospel' at this point sounds somewhat harsh at first, for Paul has not yet mentioned preaching. He has, of course, referred to himself as 'an apostle not from men nor through a man', v. 1. So in vv. 11–12 he can speak of the gospel which 'is not of a human sort, for I did not receive it from man'. But the connection between the apostle and the gospel is made for the first time in vv. 6–9, and it is made indirectly. Paul is not the subject of discussion until v. 8 and there is no direct reference to his preaching the gospel in vv. 6 and 7. Nor is the apostasy in v. 6a referred to as a turning away from 'the gospel', as we might expect in order to make the connection with v. 6b clearer. What, then, is the connection between the desertion from God's grace and the allegiance to 'another gospel'? It must be that God's call through and to grace is identical with 'the gospel', so that apostasy from it is thought of as a turning to another proclamation. Schlier suggests that we presuppose here the

---

[1] Bultmann, *Theol.*, I, pp. 290–1.

[2] For Paul, the one who calls is always God (cf. Rom. 4: 12; 8: 30; 9: 12, 24; I Cor. 1: 9; 7: 15, 17 etc.). Only in one instance could the calling be directly connected with Christ, namely Rom. 1: 6, κλητοὶ Ἰησοῦ Χριστοῦ, though this is probably to be understood as a genitive of possession (so, BDF, par. 183).

[3] Schlier, *Galaterbrief*, p. 37. This is confirmed by Paul's use of καλεῖν ἐν in I Cor. 7: 15 and I Thess. 4: 7. The Χριστοῦ of some texts is omitted by Mcn., p46 among others, an omission which should be respected (cf. Schlier, *ibid.*, n. 2) since it probably is confirmed by the confusion displayed in other texts.

preaching of Paul as that which worked the beginning of life
'in grace',[1] even though Paul's share in the gospel is mentioned
only later. It is the 'calling act of God' which inaugurates the
life ἐν χάριτι. Here the argument does not move from defending
Paul's own claim of apostolic legitimacy to attacking those who
have attacked him. It does not move from an analysis of what
Paul has done to the present situation in Galatia. It moves from
an analysis of the situation in Galatia to a conclusion about the
truth (and singularity) of the gospel. Then to this conclusion
Paul subjects even himself or an angel from heaven. Turning
from God's calling is turning to another gospel, and so the calling
act of God is coincident with the gospel. This is why Paul prefers
to speak here of turning away from the one who called rather
than directly from grace. The defection is not from Paul who
preaches, but from God who calls.

How can there be 'another' gospel? The distinction between
ἕτερος and ἄλλος seems insignificant. When these two words are
differentiated, ἕτερος has a qualitative sense (i.e., *aliter*) while
ἄλλος has an enumerative sense (i.e., *alius*). But Paul usually
sees them as equivalents. Both are enumerative in I Cor. 12:
8ff.; both are qualitative in I Cor. 15: 39ff.[2] This means that
the context alone can suggest which is most suitable. Taking the
words in their usual distinctive sense, we would read 'You are
turning to a second gospel, which is not substantially different
at all'; or 'You are turning to a different gospel which is not a
second gospel...' If we press no distinction, then we can understand 'You are turning to a different gospel' (or 'another
gospel') 'which is not different' ('another'). In any case, ὅ
should probably be taken to refer neither to ὅτι...εὐαγγέλιον
nor simply to εὐαγγέλιον alone, but to ἕτερον εὐαγγέλιον.[3] Nor
is εἰ μή without its problems. We would usually translate it as

[1] *Ibid.*, p. 12.
[2] The evidence is not decisive, but just for that reason most commentators
seem to agree with BDF (par. 306: 4) that here they may be taken as used
'without distinction'. A. T. Robertson, *A Grammar of the Greek New Testament in the Light of Historical Research* (New York, 1919³), pp. 747ff., holds
out for a distinction, referring to I Cor. 15: 39–41 as an illustration.
[3] So Schlier, *Galaterbrief*, p. 13; A. Oepke, *Der Brief des Paulus an die
Galater* (Berlin, 1960²; THNT 9), p. 22 and virtually all modern commentators. If it were to refer to ὅτι...εὐαγγέλιον, we would expect ἅ (cf. 4: 24)
or τοῦτο γάρ ἐστιν.

THE NORMATIVE CHARACTER OF THE GOSPEL

exceptive, but it can stand as a simple adversative, as in I Cor. 7: 17.[1]

The crucial question, however, goes beyond grammar. How can there be more than one gospel, and if there is, in what way can we conceive of another? The problem is all the more difficult when we remember that there is virtually no evidence that Paul regards 'gospel' as coterminous with a body of information or propositions. If, as we have suggested in regard to I Cor. 15, Paul uses the term 'gospel' in a way that transcends the traditions and implies their proper, eschatological interpretation, how can there be 'another'? And what can Paul mean by saying that this other gospel is not another at all?[2] Paul would then be rejecting this idea because εὐαγγέλιον is not for him a general concept to be understood in a formal sense, but only the concrete message which he has preached. Yet it is doubtful that ἕτερον εὐαγγέλιον is a catchword of anti-Pauline elements in Galatia. Such a term would scarcely commend itself apologetically to those who preach in opposition to Paul.[3] If anything, they would probably accuse *him* of preaching a second, or different gospel. Hence the designation ἕτερον should probably be taken as Paul's own designation, and he himself is responsible for the equivocal phrase: '(You are turning) to another gospel, which is not another...' Schlier is correct in saying that the gospel is a concrete message which for Paul corresponds to what he has preached. The concluding verses, 8 and 9, make this particularly clear with their reliance on the terms εὐαγγε-λίζεσθαι and παραλαμβάνειν. But we have already seen that the term εὐαγγέλιον does not refer solely to the content of the message, to the exclusion of its effect, its result, its consequences.

It is from an analysis of the situation in Galatia that Paul moves out to the first part of his seemingly equivocal conclusion. It is from the failure of the Galatians to remain within the sphere of grace that he can say that they have turned to another gospel. In this sense they have, for they can no longer be said to be standing 'in the gospel' (cf. I Cor. 15: 1). But seen from the

[1] L. Radermacher, *Neutestamentliche Grammatik* (Tübingen, 1925²; HNT), pp. 13–14 (cf. p. 212) calls it an Attic nicety found in later writings.
[2] Schlier, *Galaterbrief*, p. 38.
[3] Oepke, *Galater*, p. 23.

point of view of its *content*, there is no other message, no second or alternative gospel.[1] Hence, ὃ οὐκ ἔστιν ἄλλο.

There is no other gospel in the sense of any other proclamation which can lay claim to the same status as the preaching the Galatians have already heard. But there is the specific problem in Galatia which negates the very essence of 'the gospel'. Hence Paul returns immediately to this problem which is now seen not from the viewpoint of the Galatians, whose very existence is threatened because of their turning away, but from the viewpoint of those who bear the responsibility for bringing about the situation (v. 7b). They are stirring up (ταράσσοντες) the community and seeking to pervert (θέλοντες μεταστρέψαι) the gospel of Christ.

Ταράσσειν is frequent in the New Testament for mental agitation (John 11: 33; Matt. 2: 3; 14: 26; Mark 6: 50, etc.). It conveys a combined sense of mental confusion and resulting community disorder, as in Acts 15: 24 and Gal. 5: 10. Μεταστρέφειν implies perversion, often in the sense of 'transforming something into its opposite'.[2]

There are two charges to be laid at the feet of the responsible parties. The gospel is perverted, its content transformed. No less serious is the disturbance of the community, an attempt to deny the necessary consequences or results of the gospel. So the gospel is thought of here in mutually exclusive terms – it either is or it is not – just as salvation (its result) is thought of in similar terms in 1: 4 and 6. Both together are indicated by the typical phrase 'the gospel of Christ'. In its usual sense, the characterization of the gospel as being 'of Christ' supplies the real criterion for its singularity and its exclusiveness. There is only one Christ (I Cor. 8: 6), and from that it follows that there is only one gospel, one calling. So also there is only one alternative.

The sharp statement of alternatives with which the passage is permeated reflects the same set of alternatives found in vv. 1–5. In fact, it is this antithetical frame of reference, eschatological/apocalyptic in its origin (αἰών), which explains Paul's distinction between 'the gospel of Christ' and 'another gospel'. In terms

[1] Cf. Schlier, *Galaterbrief*, p. 38: 'God does not put his gospel to a vote. In what he proclaims is expressed, in an unequivocal word, God's absolute judgment on men.'
[2] Cf. Deut. 23: 6 (LXX); Sirach 11: 31; Acts 2: 20.

of 'content' (in the broadest sense) nothing but 'the gospel of Christ' would or could be called gospel. But gospel is understood so thoroughly as an eschatological entity that Paul can treat it like an αἰών – in which case that which does not belong to it belongs to its opposite; another αἰών, another gospel.[1]

In vv. 8 and 9 Paul draws the necessary conclusions from this idea of the singularity of the gospel. Even if he himself[2] or an angel from heaven should preach something contrary to what he has preached, he should be accursed. The sentence is concessive, indicating an unmistakable degree of improbability.[3] Neither Paul nor an angel from heaven is likely to do this. But the rhetorical device itself points up the precedence of the gospel over the preacher. Even if such an extreme case as this were imaginable, the conclusion would not be in doubt – ἀνάθεμα ἔστω. In light of what has been said, the phrase παρ' ὃ εὐηγγελισάμεθα should be translated 'contrary to what we proclaimed', as Burton suggests.[4] Schlier, who sees the matter as centering on an *Ersatzevangelium*, prefers the translation 'in place of' for παρά.[5] But as we have noted, there are serious difficulties in understanding the concept of a counter-gospel as anything but antithetical, as merely competitive or alternative. It is exactly the sharp division, best expressed by the idea of contrariety, which dominates Paul's thought here. The gospel which is other than ὃ εὐηγγελισάμεθα is something clearer in its logical than its ontological status. Rom. 1:26 shows a similar use of παρά, where the idea of real antithesis is beyond dispute.

The just deserts for Paul's preaching a gospel contrary to the gospel he has preached, for proclaiming the gospel which is not really one, is a curse. Hence, the force of εὐηγγελισάμεθα is only to make concrete which gospel it is that Paul is speaking about. It is the one already known in Galatia. That Paul's own activity

[1] The αἰών scheme is something Paul uses more formally than materially. Hence he never describes the new age as αἰών and does not refer to the destruction of the old αἰών, but rather to one's rescue from it. This preference for the formal distinction, where the material counterpart is difficult to conceptualize, is quite as apparent in Paul's use of εὐαγγέλιον here. Formally, there must be the possibility of the opposite of 'gospel', but materially such 'another gospel' cannot be a gospel at all.

[2] The ἡμεῖς indicates plural of authorship; cf. Oepke, *Galater*, p. 24.

[3] Hence, ὑμῖν should probably be omitted in v. 8.

[4] *Galatians*, p. 27.   [5] Schlier, *Galaterbrief*, p. 40, n. 3.

brought it is entirely a secondary matter. The apostle himself is subordinated to the singularity of the gospel.

What is hypothetical in v. 8, however, becomes, in v. 9, specific and concrete. It is not Paul who is in danger of perverting the gospel and thus being anathematized. But this has happened in Galatia, and so the proper conclusion must be drawn. Ὡς προειρήκαμεν could refer simply to the preceding statement, or to Paul's having made this situation clear at an earlier time in the community (on the 'second visit', Acts 18: 23?). Προλέγειν is not itself decisive. The usage in II Cor. 7: 3 may refer to another place in the same letter (cf. II Cor. 6: 11), while the usage in I Thess. 4: 6 seems to refer to a more distant time. But the force of ἄρτι, in the phrase ἄρτι πάλιν λέγω, indicates that Paul is now repeating what he said some time earlier. Verse 9b is not a mere repetition of v. 8. Paul changes the hypothetical concessive clause into a present general condition, so that the condition may even be thought of as known to be fulfilled. Furthermore, εὐαγγελίζεσθαι is used transitively with ὑμᾶς, while the distinction between this false preaching and the actual gospel which the Galatians once endorsed is further emphasized by the phrase παρ' ὃ παρελάβετε.

The shift is complete. Paul is no longer talking about some hypothetical case in which he preaches a different gospel from the one he generally preaches. He is talking about the actual case in which somebody (τις, cf. τινες, v. 7) is preaching a different gospel from that which the Galatian community has already received. The conclusion is the same: ἀνάθεμα ἔστω.

Once this shift has taken place, 'the gospel of Christ' takes on a concreteness hitherto unknown. Paul suggests it has a discernible perimeter more visible than we have seen earlier. This is underscored by his use of παρ' ὃ παρελάβετε, v. 9. The phrase is surprising. We would have expected παρ' ὃ εὐηγγελισάμεθα in a construction parallel to v. 8. Why does Paul introduce technical terminology here?

We have noticed that there is no hard and fast distinction between παραδιδόναι–παραλαμβάνειν and εὐαγγελίζεσθαι, though there is a clear difference between gospel and paradosis. In I Cor. 15, Paul's capacity for, perhaps insistence on, blurring the lines between transmission of tradition and preaching of the gospel is born out of the immediate situation in which he must counteract an undue (and unusual) attention to the tradition process, where he thinks the very reliance on tradition threatens the gospel as a field of power in which the Corinthians stand. In Gal. 1: 1–8 Paul also makes an eschatological equation with the gospel. Is he here also fighting a concept of tradition at work among the Galatians who, he thinks, have erred? If so, the close conjunction of εὐαγγελίζεσθαι and παραλαμβάνειν in v. 9 would stand parallel to I Cor. 15: 1ff. and would be explained by Paul's ulterior polemical intent.

To determine this probability we must try to reconstruct, at least in a broad sketch, the Galatian 'heresy'. Before doing so, however, one other implication of vv. 6–9 needs to be noted. The theme of these verses is the singularity of the gospel, singularity here expressed as a function between Paul and his addressees. The gospel has been preached by Paul; it has been received by the community; it is identical with the Galatians' salvation. The larger theme of chs. 1–2 is also the singularity of the gospel, but it is expressed as a function between Paul and the Jerusalem leaders. With that in mind it is interesting to see what happens in vv. 6–9 when the idea of one gospel is the ruling concept. All figures in the historical transcript are subordinated *to it*. That includes both Paul and the community. As a result, not a word is said about the community's being directly subordinated *to Paul*. Again, this is emphasized by the shift from εὐαγγελίζεσθαι to παραλαμβάνειν in v. 9. Because the gospel is singular *and takes precedence*, both Paul and the community can be subordinated to it. Paul can preach only what he has already preached, and the community can receive only what it has already received. The gospel is thus a double-sided norm – for preaching and for receiving. It is a norm for faith and a norm for apostleship. By virtue of their common dependence on, and the need for their obedience to, the one gospel, faith and apostleship are brought into the closest possible relationship. Moreover, at the outset of a highly personal letter the person of Paul does not even directly enter the discussion. But when it does, a bit later, the context has already been set in a decisive fashion by these verses.

THE OPPONENTS IN THE GALATIAN CHURCHES

Insofar as there has been anything approaching a consensus about the origin and nature of the opposition Paul is countering with this letter, that agreement has focused on the Jewish nature of the opponents' interests. The second century Marcionite prologue to the letter states: 'The Galatians are Greeks. They first accepted the word of truth from the apostle but after his departure were tempted by false apostles to turn to law and circumcision. The apostle recalls them to the true faith, writing to them from Ephesus.'[1] Since there is no evidence that the opponents do not consider themselves Christians, it has been customary to identify them as Judaizers, 'emissaries of the Jerusalem Church, like the high-churchmen of Acts 15: 1...re-actionaries of James' party'.[2] Such a view, however, makes it difficult to account for a number of not characteristically Jewish concerns of these opponents.

As a result there have also been attempts to locate *two* fronts of opposition within the Galatian churches, one formed by Judaizers and another representing pneumatics of a more hellenistic stripe. The two groups could be seen at odds with one another and with Paul's understanding of the gospel.[3] This dual front theory has foundered primarily because the epistle gives no indication that Paul himself was aware of the divided nature of opposition to him and the gospel as he understood it.

More recent attempts to solve this puzzle have concentrated on the non-Jewish 'hellenistic' elements in the Galatian scene.[4] If these scarcely fit with a picture of Judaizers whose ultimate loyalty is to one or another wing of Jerusalem Christianity,

[1] Latin text in A. Souter, *The Text and Canon of the New Testament* (London, rev. ed., 1954), p. 188.

[2] J. Moffatt, *An Introduction to the Literature of the New Testament* (New York, 1918³), p. 85, second note; FBK: '...there exists some probability that the Galatian opponents were somehow connected with the primitive church in Jerusalem, certainly not with the "pillars", as 2: 6ff. shows, but with the "false brethren" mentioned in 2: 4, who in no case were still Jews...' (p. 195).

[3] W. Lütgert, *Gesetz und Geist* (Gütersloh, 1919); J. H. Ropes, *The Singular Problem of the Epistle to the Galatians* (Cambridge, Mass., 1929).

[4] J. Munck calls them 'Judaizing Gentile Christians'. Cf. his *Paul and the Salvation of Mankind* (Richmond, 1959), pp. 87ff.

might it not still be the case that the 'Jewish' concerns, especially the emphasis on law and circumcision, would fit with a more hellenistically or syncretistically oriented persuasion? Building on Lütgert's observations and reading Galatians as he does the whole of the authentic Pauline corpus, W. Schmithals regards the opponents as gnostics who have incorporated into their scheme certain aspects of Jewish Torah observance.[1] The term 'gnostic' in this context is more fluid and less precise than it might appear. Schmithals can scarcely account for the central concerns of chs. 3 and 4 by direct appeal to any known gnostic phenomenon, and certain indices of gnosticism seem missing throughout Galatians. Perhaps, in light of the fruitless earlier efforts to be specific in designating the opponents, it would be best to accept Schlier's strictures about equating the Galatian opposition with any known group as such and simply review the evidence as we have it.

Throughout the letter Paul suggests that law is central in the Galatian opposition, but this emphasis on Torah does not look like garden variety Pharisaism. Law is conceived by the opponents more in its cosmic than its casuistic sense, more as an element in universal salvation than as a component of Jewish piety. Advocates of the law (and circumcision) are not necessarily adherents of the law (3: 3; 6: 13). This cosmic and structural dimension of law can be seen in the opponents' claim that the law, given through the mediator Moses (3: 19), was nevertheless the substance of the other-worldly, the expression of the ineffable (3: 20 points up this distinction). From law they presume to derive Spirit (3: 2, 5) and so through law they make contact with that spiritual reality which controls the fate and destiny of the world. 'For them, law and the order of creation, law and fate, are one.'[2] There is an easy association of law with their deep concern for the elemental spirits of the world (4: 3, 8, 9) and with this are to be connected the astral, calendrical sensibilities referred to in 4: 10. Against this background the opponents understand Christ to be the most recent interpreter of the law. Whether or not they coined, and Paul sarcastically returns, the phrase 'the law of Christ' (6: 2) is unclear; but

[1] W. Schmithals, 'Die Häretiker in Galatien', ZNW 47 (1956), 25–67, repr. in revised form in *Paulus und die Gnostiker* (Hamburg, 1965; TF 24), pp. 9–46. [2] D. Georgi, *Theologische Existenz heute* 70 (1959), p. 211, n. 2.

they incorporate Christ into a history of revelation over against which Paul sets an alternative in 3: 6ff. and 4: 1ff. (cf. 4: 22ff.). Hence Paul's attitude toward Christ as the end of the law, as crucified under its curse, 3: 10ff., is the very antithesis of the opponents' christology. His anthropology (6: 15f.) is equally foreign. Using the dichotomy flesh/spirit, he rejects the cosmic-legal spiritualism of his opponents and highlights the radical individualism which results from their world view (5: 13ff.; 6: 13).

While we may see in this the seeds of a later gnosticism such as that testified to by Ignatius or even by Hippolytus[1] or Epiphanius,[2] its more immediate successor looks like the error in Colossae.[3] It is a fine blend of major religious and spiritual themes of the hellenistic Jewish experience. The opponents are hellenistic Jewish Christians.

This identification is central to discussing the whole problem of Paul's relationship to the Jerusalem Church. At the heart of the matter lies the question of what is polemical in Paul's letter and what is apologetic. This is a complex issue, as the treatment in recent secondary literature shows. To take one illustrative example, Schmithals begins his analysis of Galatians with the assumption that Paul is responding apologetically in chs. 1 and 2. The apostle has been accused of dependence on the Jerusalem apostles and seeks to separate himself from them, stressing his independent and equal status as one called to his mission and equipped with the gospel through direct revelation.[4] It is an 'apology', corresponding to the 'polemic' of 1: 1. From this reading Schmithals concludes that the opponents cannot have been Judaizers of Jerusalem-Christian sympathy, as often supposed, and identifies them as gnostics.

A key difficulty in Schmithals' reading is his exclusion of 3: 6 – 4: 7 and 4: 21–31 from the substantive issue dividing Paul and his opponents.[5] K. Wegenast, who also describes the op-

---

[1] *Ref.*, IX, 13ff.   [2] *Haer.*, 30, 17; 53, 1.

[3] Cf. Bornkamm, 'Häresie', and Koester, 'Häretiker'.

[4] Schmithals, 'Häretiker', pp. 13–22.

[5] Schmithals regards none of this as relevant to the Galatian scene since the opponents did not consider themselves followers of the law in a casuistic sense. Paul is merely using the *topoi* he uses in arguments with Jews, and doing so to make his point that any attention to or concern for the law is excluded in Christ. Georgi (above, p. 125, n. 2) rightly rejects such a radical exclusion of the very heart of the letter.

ponents as gnostics, has tried to correct this neglect by relocating the focus of argument. The opponents do not accuse Paul of dependence on Jerusalem, but blame him for not demanding the custom of circumcision and adherence to the law in his gospel.[1] Apart from the vexed question of whom we may and may not call a gnostic in Paul's letters, Wegenast is quite correct in construing the problem of 'tradition' to be a problem of the tradition represented *as Torah*. As we shall see, this puts Paul's argument in a quite different light and even alters the tone imputed to chs. 1 and 2.

Schmithals defends his reading[2] by appealing to a distinction between *polemics* and *apologetics*: The matter of circumcision is dealt with by Paul polemically, not apologetically; the matter of dependence apologetically, not polemically. The decision as to whether a Pauline passage is apologetic or polemical cannot be made on strictly formal grounds but involves a series of previous suppositions. In Schmithals' case, the chief of these is the gnostic identification itself, by which he excludes 3: 6 – 4: 7 and 4: 21–31 (although polemical, it is only understandable as polemic *against Jews*) and assumes that Gal. 1 and 2 *is* apologetic. Is this a workable and useful distinction?

It may be doubted that there is a single sustained apology in the whole of the letter. To begin with, Paul's treatment of his apostolic status in I Cor. 15: 3ff., a passage which finally must be brought into the discussion of Gal. 1 and 2, is not apologetic. He refers to that status to warrant an argument. Secondly, Paul has no apologetic stance for the gospel itself. The way of arguing the truth of the gospel is always through polemic. When we recognize the close association of apostolic authority and gospel authority, we see why, in cases like I Cor. 15: 3ff., we do not have apologetic: The apostolic claim rests in nothing less than gospel.

What is true in Corinth is true in Galatia, and Paul makes it clear in Gal. 1: 6–9. If he is to defend the gospel he will do so through polemic; but that means he will defend his apostolic status in the same manner. The polemic of 3: 6 – 4: 7 and 4: 21–31 cannot be excluded as irrelevant (unless one wishes to

---

[1] Wegenast, *Verständnis*, p. 39, n. 3.
[2] In the revised version of his essay (i.e., in *Gnostiker*) he replies to Wegenast, but not to Georgi.

assume Paul does not fully comprehend the Galatian scene and uses inappropriate weapons forged in other combat).[1] This means that the categories of polemic and apology are not primary means for determining the nature of Paul's opposition, as Schmithals' treatment of chs. 1 and 2, and reply to Wegenast, imply.

Hence it is safer to drop the presumption of apology in these first two chapters and view them instead as Pauline polemic, as aggressive explication rather than defensive response. As such they make perfectly good sense. Whether or not the opponents accused Paul of denigrating tradition and thus having an unanchored apostolic status[2] must remain an open question. Perhaps they did, but we cannot now determine that. For it is at least as likely, and less clumsy to assume, that Paul is on the offensive in attacking *their* attachment to tradition (i.e., the gospel as the law) and arguing over against this the case of the one gospel which is illustrated through the apostolic person. The oneness of the gospel is vividly emphasized in vv. 6–9 so as to exclude all others (i.e., the Galatian, heretical 'gospel') and its eschatological status is specifically referred to in vv. 1–5. Furthermore, Paul does not hesitate to subordinate to this one gospel himself and the very angels whom the Galatians revere as spiritual beings. The sarcastic reference to an angel in v. 8 is echoed in the use of παρ' ὃ παρελάβετε in v. 9. As in I Cor. 15: 3ff., Paul can regard the transmission of the gospel in terms of the traditioning process because he can also show clearly and unambiguously its origins and paths outside that process. If his opponents wish to equate gospel with tradition, he must show that it transcends tradition. To this he turns in 1: 10–2: 11. To do this he turns to himself.

GAL. I: 10–12

The idea that Paul seeks to persuade men (or God),[3] or to please men (v. 10), is one that he can reject out of hand. If the gospel is the primary eschatological datum of the Christian life,

---

[1] So W. Marxsen, *Introduction to the New Testament* (Philadelphia, 1968), pp. 45ff.

[2] D. Georgi, *Die Geschichte der Kollekte des Paulus für Jerusalem* (Hamburg, 1965; TF 38), p. 36, n. 113.

[3] The question is not disjunctive, but puts the emphasis on πείθω; Schmithals, 'Häretiker', p. 40.

Paul's motives are irrelevant. Certainly the anathema is neither pleasing nor rhetorically calculated to persuade. It is the pronouncement of a prophetic, eschatological, divine judgment without respect to persons.[1] If the Galatian heretics have sought to label Paul's attitude toward Torah as pandering to antinomian tastes, even here Paul responds with polemic rather than apology. Paul could hardly concede to opponents a more rigorous understanding of and respect for the law. In any event, it is likely that the phrase 'to please men' refers more generally to subordinating the gospel to human standards, as would be the case if Paul were an apostle ἀπ' ἀνθρώπων or δι' ἀνθρώπου. In that case the expression does not seek to defend Paul against an allegation from the opponents.

That this is the likely origin of v. 10 is confirmed by what Paul goes on to say in vv. 11–12. The connection between being a δοῦλος Χριστοῦ and his independence from human traditions is underscored by the linking γάρ of v. 12.[2] The gospel which he preaches is not a human gospel, nor did he receive it from a man nor was he taught it. It came through a revelation 'Ιησοῦ Χριστοῦ, which is why, and how, Paul is Christ's slave. The text invites us to regard the mode of gospel transmission and set over against the traditioning process (παρέλαβον, ἐδιδάχθην, v. 12) a wholly different *form* of communication and extension, the ἀποκάλυψις 'Ιησοῦ Χριστοῦ (v. 12). To do this we must know what Paul means by 'revelation', and how to read the genitive phrase 'of Jesus Christ'. Even more importantly, we must be clear about Paul's use of παρέλαβον.

Wegenast has suggested that in v. 12 Paul is not using παραλαμβάνειν as a traditioning term, but in a neutral sense. It is true that the complementary term παραδιδόναι is missing, but ἐδιδάχθην unequivocally suggests the scholastic, traditioning process in this context. Moreover, Paul has used παραλαμβάνειν (v. 9) in exactly the same close association with εὐαγγελίζεσθαι as that characteristic of I Cor. 15: 1ff., where the technical use

---

[1] Stuhlmacher, *Evangelium*, p. 69, regards it as a foundation of sacred law. Cf. G. Bornkamm, 'Zum Verständnis des Gottesdienstes bei Paulus, B: Das Anathema in der urchristlichen Abendmahlsliturgie' (*Das Ende des Gesetzes*, pp. 125–32, esp. p. 125). It should be pointed out, however, that the curse applies to one who *preaches* something different, not to one who believes incorrectly. It underlines the *unity* of preaching the one true gospel.

[2] Schlier, *Galaterbrief*, p. 43.

of these terms is undisputed. It is thus difficult to conclude that παρέλαβον in v. 12 is a casual reference to the 'reception of a revelation',[1] without regard to its more technical nuances.[2] We have seen that the most plausible way to account for the term in v. 9 is to assume Paul uses it because of the central role of tradition within the Galatian heresy – thus bringing this passage into close contact with I Cor. 15: 1ff., where the problem is not wholly dissimilar. Furthermore, it can be established that this viewpoint is central with those Galatians who have an undue regard for Torah.

This means that the problem of tradition is raised in Paul's mind, rightly or wrongly, in the context of an original Jewish attitude toward tradition. Primitive Christian tradition and its role in the Jerusalem Church is not the focal point of Paul's concern and not the ostensible occasion which educes argument from the Galatian heretics. It means, moreover, that the *mode* of Paul's receiving the gospel is only a consideration within a larger framework – that Paul regards form and content as indistinguishable, and if indistinguishable, also inseparable. We must understand this to understand how the gospel 'transcends tradition'. As Wegenast stresses, παρέλαβον is the single, controlling verb in v. 12 and hence cannot be used in a wholly negative way. But there is no ground for regarding its use as an aberration from the Pauline custom. The real contrast in our passage is not between 'received' (as tradition) and something else; one cannot even imagine an alternative to the idea of reception. The real contrast plays on the distinction between 'received from men' and 'received through a revelation of Jesus Christ'. Paul sees the alternatives as traditions embodied in entities like Torah and circumcision, set over against the one true gospel to which all men are subordinate. This is the polemic. The opponents have accused Paul of despising and ignoring tradition,[3] while he accuses them of having turned away from the very gospel itself, or having turned back by venerating

---

[1] Wegenast, *Verständnis*, p. 44.

[2] This is the central issue in reading Gal. 1, 2 and I Cor. 15: 1ff., as all interpreters recognize. It is curious that in a major exegetical treatment of this passage, Stuhlmacher (*Evangelium*, pp. 63–108) does not find it possible 'to discuss in detail the question, which emerges from Paul's alternatives, of the relation of the Pauline Gospel to (Christian) tradition', p. 70.

[3] Georgi, *Kollekte*, p. 36, n. 113.

Torah. In that argument, the problem of how early Christian tradition might be available or handled in Jerusalem is irrelevant.[1] It is important to underscore this fact which carries with it other implications. Within the compass of vv. 1-12 Paul has not yet raised a simple question of how the gospel is transmitted. The question of 'tradition' as it surfaces obliquely here in the terminology Paul uses is actually the question of whether or not there is more than one gospel, properly called. It is not a question of form over against content but one of form as content, an identification without which Galatians as a whole would make little sense.

'REVELATION'

In part, the casual assumption that Paul has turned his consideration away from the content of the gospel to its form results from his unusual introduction of the terms ἀποκάλυψις (1: 12; 2: 2) and ἀποκαλύπτειν (1: 16). Two recent discussions of this vocabulary and these passages point up the difficulties of interpretation.

D. Lührmann rejects the notion that for Paul ἀποκάλυψις means 'vision' in any passage other than II Cor. 12: 21.[2] More specifically, 'neither the use of the term ἀποκάλυψις nor the fact that Paul speaks here of his commission forces one to an interpretation of 1: 12 that sees Paul setting over against his opponents' understanding of tradition an origin of his gospel in an (ecstatic) vision'.[3] Paul means simply a disclosure of Jesus Christ (objective genitive). Because Paul is himself responsible for the introduction of these terms in 1: 12 and 16 we can only interpret the terminology with reference to other, related texts.

---

[1] Wegenast, against Schlier's interpretation of v. 12: '...in the compass of the verse nothing is said about the original apostles and nothing gives the apostle [i.e., Paul] reason to compare himself to a Jerusalem apostle. Paul compares himself with his opponents, not with the apostles' (*Verständnis*, p. 40, n. 2). Whether the opponents have somehow allied themselves with the Jerusalem apostles is another matter, not clear from this verse.

[2] Lührmann, *Offenbarungsverständnis*, pp. 40ff., 73f. Lührmann's argument rests on his reading of the noun in cognate literature and stresses the singular appearance of the word in Syr. Bar. 76: 1, which he interprets (following H. Schulte, *Der Begriff der Offenbarung im Neuen Testament* [München, 1949], p. 40) as referring not to a vision, but its interpretation (cf. Syr. Bar. 56: 1; 49: 6). Against this interpretation cf. Stuhlmacher, *Evangelium*, p. 76, n. 3.

[3] *Offenbarungsverständnis*, p. 74.

Lührmann concentrates on Gal. 4:4 and 3:27. Paul is working within a larger framework of Jewish apocalyptic and its two-aeon scheme, in order to portray to his opponents the radical break with the law inaugurated by the new aeon introduced by the sending (ἐξαποστέλλειν) of God's Son (4:4). That he does not speak here of the Son's revelation points up what is distinctive about ἀποκαλύπτειν in 1:16, where Paul is not referring to that event itself which separates the aeons but to its anthropological interpretation (cf. ἐν ἐμοί), i.e., to a parallel action of God which interprets the meaning of the sending.[1] Given the context, one in which Paul is arguing for the Gentile mission, this anthropological interpretation is not to be confined to its significance for Paul personally (as perhaps in Phil. 3: 2ff.). 'The apocalyptic two-aeon scheme is thus transcended by Paul by means of the anthropological connection; it would be completely wrong to understand this passage in the sense of apocalypticism's anticipatory relevation...'[2] This difference between 4:4 and 1:16 Lührmann sees confirmed by 3:23 where ἀποκαλύπτειν is also used and where again the two-aeon scheme is shattered in order for Paul to regard πίστις as the characterization of the anthropological appropriation and interpretation of the original salvation event.

P. Stuhlmacher has approached the problem of 'relevation' in Gal. 1 and 2 from a somewhat different direction,[3] beginning with a phenomenological account of Jewish apocalyptic which he finds repeated in Paul's usage. The foundation of apocalypticism is the notion of glimpsing proleptically the events of the end of time, which allows the visionary to disclose to this world the God who is coming at its close. On this foundation is built a dialectical pattern crucial for understanding the apocalyptic attitude toward revelation: the dialectic of hiddenness and disclosure, and its corollary, a high esteem of the word and message as events themselves. Because of this pattern, the apocalyptist can only offer his testimony to revelation as something hidden

---

[1] *Ibid.*, pp. 78f. and n. 3 on p. 79.

[2] *Ibid.*, p. 79.

[3] Stuhlmacher objects to isolating II Cor. 12:1 and seeing only there a use of ἀποκάλυψις as 'vision'. Instead, he regards Paul as rejecting in this passage not visions as such, but only their use to break open the 'mystery', the dialectic, inherent in the whole apocalyptic approach. Cf. *Evangelium*, pp. 76–81.

to some and revealed to others, i.e., he can only await the ultimate manifestation of its truth at the end of time. The message may be ultimate, but it is not transparent. The message and the messenger themselves remain, in part, a mystery capable of being misunderstood in human categories. For Paul this message is a spatial-temporal entity, an event combining the end-event with disclosure in the present. It is like an Old Testament theophany, and it guarantees Paul's equality with the other apostles because it is an epiphany of God's son.[1]

Lührmann's lexicographical approach seems a bit rigid, Stuhlmacher's phenomenology a bit loose. Their alternative views are not mutually exclusive but correspond to the two basic realities we have already isolated: An eschatological proclamation is embodied in its proclaimer. An exegesis of Gal. 1: 13ff. should clarify the relative weight of each of these elements and the true configuration of their relationship.

GAL. 1: 13–17

In vv. 13ff. Paul keeps squarely in focus the concept of tradition as a Jewish Pharisaic phenomenon. If the contrast to this is 'revelation' the field for this contrast must be the apostle's own life. But Paul does not confine his autobiographical remarks to a rehearsal of his zeal as a Jew. He also specifically mentions his zeal as a persecutor of the Church. Indeed, he mentions it as the primary instance in what we may call the *biography of reversal*. His reasons for doing so become clear in v. 16 where the antithetical parallel is his missionary commissioning by God. Paul has set up a direct contradiction to the present by viewing his past as itself a negative mission directed against, rather than for, the Church. In this contrast, the antithesis to his zeal as a 'follower' of tradition is his reception of a revelation of God's Son. The middle term binding both halves of the four-part antithesis is the experience of being set apart by God 'from my mother's womb'.

It is a strange way to picture one's biography, but ὁ ἀφορίσας με makes it clear that Paul regards both halves of the contrast to have been carried out under the sovereignty of and in loyalty to

---

[1] Hence, functionally at least, this vision is the same one Paul refers to in I Cor. 15: 8; 9: 1; Phil. 3: 8ff.

133

God.[1] This corresponds to his view of the relationship of law and grace and represents the very image of law with which he works in the rest of Galatians. Law is divinely ordained and operative until the dramatic break signalled by Jesus' death, interpreted as the provision of grace (Gal. 3: 19–25, where the operative term is faith, not grace). Thus there is a formal parallel between the autobiography and Paul's understanding of the nature of the gospel itself, a parallel underscored by the fact that however sharp the antitheses, both halves of the life, of Paul and of all men, are viewed as being under God's sovereignty. If we ask what is radically new on this side of the break, the answer is the manifestation of χάρις and the act of God's calling whom he has already set apart (v. 15). Being called into grace is being called into the εὐαγγέλιον; that is the presupposition of 1:6. Thus far, then, the autobiographical references are a paradigm not only of the apostle,[2] but of the Christian as such.

Yet the matter is also more complicated. Not only has Paul previously laid heavy stress on his apostolic status, he emphasizes here that God called him through his grace *to reveal* his Son *in order* that Paul might preach Him among the Gentiles (v. 16). While it may seem logically plausible that Paul's 'conversion' and his commissioning are separate items within the autobiography,[3] he does not treat them as separable. 'Conversion' and commission collapse into a single whole for which we scarcely have the proper term, unless it be 'call'. By collapsing these two ideas Paul does not just closely link his characteristic apostolic activity with the apostle as Christian. He identifies gospel with apostle. He makes the apostle the paradigm of the gospel he proclaims. Both the message and the messenger proclaim grace and both embody grace, grace as event.

This identification makes it necessary to hold together the two emphases of Paul's understanding of ἀποκαλύπτειν. 'Revelation' is the anthropologically oriented event (grace-event) which functions as interpretation and appropriation of

[1] On the prophetic background of Paul's call cf. G. Sass, *Apostelamt und Kirche* (München, 1939), pp. 40ff.; T. Holtz, 'Zum Selbstverständnis des Apostels Paulus', *TLZ* 91 (1966), cols. 321–30.

[2] Against A. M. Denis, 'L'investiture de la fonction apostolique par "apocalypse"', *RB* 64 (1957), 335–62; 492–515 (cf. specifically p. 339).

[3] Fridrichsen, *Apostle*, p. 13. But cf. U. Wilckens, 'Die Bekehrung des Paulus als religionsgeschichtliches Problem', *ZThK* 56 (1959), 273–93.

the 'sending' of the Son (4: 4). No less than this, it is also the substance of the 'gospel' itself, for the gospel is interpretation of the historical fact of the sending, as we have seen in I Cor. 15, an interpretation which itself is eschatological and constitutes a word which operates as a transcendent field of power within history.

Although it is more customary to stress the differences,[1] the similarities between Gal. 1 and I Cor. 15: 3ff. are rather striking. In both passages Paul's thought involves a radical identification of the gospel and the apostolic agent. Such an identification can lead to an explication of the 'gospel' (as interpretation of tradition) in terms of apostolic experience. This is the case in I Cor. 15 and it is the case here in Galatians thus far. It can also lead, however, to an explication of apostolic experience in terms of the truth of the gospel, as in Gal. 1: 18 – 2: 10. The essential unity of these two approaches is evident in 2: 11–21.

Before turning to these passages something must be said about continuity and discontinuity. Within Gal. 1, vv. 16 and 17 provide the most suggestive evidence that Paul contrasts not only Judaism with Christianity (i.e., Saul with Paul) but also himself as apostle with the Jerusalem Christians. Certainly this relationship becomes of primary importance in 1: 18ff. Yet we must remember that these contrasts are also coordinates: Saul *and* Paul. Thus in 1: 18ff., the undeniable distinction is arranged within a larger set of alternatives: Jerusalem *and* the Gentile mission. Paul enters into detailed comment on his commerce with Jerusalem, at the outset, to show his faithfulness to the calling in grace. While the implication of his independence from Jerusalem gains significance as Paul proceeds, the emphasis in vv. 16b–17 rests on the commission as a function of coming to believe. Told to preach beyond the bounds of Judaism, Paul immediately does so. If the emphasis comes to fall on discontinuity, it begins with continuity.

[1] Cf. J. Sanders, 'Paul's Autobiographical Statements in Gal. 1–2', *JBL* 85 (1966), 335–43; Wegenast, *Verständnis*, pp. 68f.; E. Dinkler, 'Korintherbrief', *RGG*[3] iv, cols. 17ff.

GAL. 1: 18 – 2: 10

Once firmly established in the autobiographical mode, Paul continues to relate his dealings with Jerusalem. The thrust of the first part of the narrative will be found in vv. 22–4: Paul is unknown by sight in Jerusalem, but well known by reputation. To stress this he uses again the antithetical parallelism of vv. 13ff. – νῦν εὐαγγελίζεται τὴν πίστιν ἥν ποτε ἐπόρθει (v. 23). 'The faith' Paul speaks of here is not simply the content of what is confessed, but the 'message of faith as objective power' like that described in 3: 23. As such it is the equivalent of εὐαγγέλιον.[1] Although they do not know Paul, the Jerusalem Christians, on the basis of what they hear, glorify God. They do so, Paul says, ἐν ἐμοί (v. 24), i.e., [they] 'found in me occasion and reason for praising God'.[2] The prepositional phrase is reminiscent of 1: 16, though there it functions in a somewhat different way. In 1: 16 it may put stress on the pronoun and underscore a sense of the unanticipated, though other interpretations are possible. Koine Greek knows the use of ἐν and the dative instead of a simple dative; or the construction could suggest some kind of inner, spatial reception, difficult to conceptualize.[3]

What could the two occurrences have in common? A primary clue is found in the sequential structure of 1: 16 and the characteristic Pauline collapse of 'conversion' and commission which it appears occasions the phrase in v. 16. 'St. Paul was not only the instrument in preaching the Gospel, but also in his own person bore the strongest testimony to its power.'[4] Paul places his person at the center of his understanding of gospel and apostle. Precisely the same thing is true in v. 24, where the phrase is equally unusual. The Jerusalem Christians do not just glorify God, but glorify God ἐν ἐμοί (cf. Isa. 49: 3, LXX). Yet the personal reference is oblique. As Chrysostom noted, Paul does not say that 'they marvelled at me, they praised me, they were struck with admiration of me, but he attributes all to

---

[1] Cf. R. Bultmann, 'Πιστεύω', *TDNT* vi, p. 213: 'The message itself, then, can be called πίστις.'

[2] E. Burton, *A Critical and Exegetical Commentary on the Epistle to the Galatians*, (New York, 1921), p. 65; cf. Schlier, *Galaterbrief*, p. 63.

[3] Cf. H.-J. Schoeps, *Paul* (Philadelphia, 1961), p. 54.

[4] Lightfoot, *Galatians*, p. 83.

grace'.[1] Once again the person of the apostle is isolated and underscored only to be subordinated to grace. As a result, Paul is not known as person, but as the occasion for preaching the gospel, as the manifestation of that grace which the apostle no less than the gospel represents.

Thus vv. 18–24 continue a dominant motif which has already (vv. 13–17) provided Paul with a context for his autobiographical remarks. Yet we notice that the tone has now shifted slightly, as indicated by Paul's emphasis on his brief introduction to the Jerusalem scene and by the seemingly gratuitous reference in v. 20. His effort to stress independence from Jerusalem here becomes unmistakable even if it should not be unduly emphasized. This new and understated accent on the independence of his person is set alongside that other major motif, the reality and power of his gospel which is capable of eliciting a doxology from those who do not even know him. The logic is subtle but tough. In Paul's terms this recognition of his gospel for what it really is[2] constitutes simultaneously a recognition of himself as an apostle. Why that would be a matter of moment will not become clear until the evidence from vv. 11–21 can be taken into account. For the present we must simply recall that the problem with which this is usually associated, the role of Christian tradition as normative in Jerusalem and Paul's access to or reliance upon it, does not seem to be an issue in the text.

Paul continues with his account of a meeting fraught with sociological as well as theological significance. With Barnabas and Titus he goes up to Jerusalem. He goes as an official representative of Antioch, a scene which Luke records in Acts 15. Luke is of limited value in reconstructing the actual events since he can be shown to have subordinated important details to a larger and literary and theological vision.[3] To what extent Paul's own account has itself been apologetically shaped remains to be seen, but thus far we have only a very slender basis for the common assumption that he is at pains to define his independence from the Jerusalem Christian community. And we have

[1] Lightfoot's translation, *Galatians*, p. 86.
[2] Cf. Lütgert, *Gesetz und Geist*, p. 57.
[3] Cf. esp. M. Dibelius, 'The Apostolic Council', *Studies in the Acts of the Apostles* (London, 1956), pp. 93–101; E. Haenchen, *Die Apostelgeschichte* (Göttingen, 1968[15]; KEK), pp. 405ff.

no evidence that he does so because the Galatian errorists have made this an explicit issue. The dominant themes in our story are different: (1) the singularity of the gospel; (2) its capacity to be 'recognized' even where the preacher is not; and (3) the firm identification of the preacher with the gospel to which he is subordinate.

Personalities play a major role at this point. Paul stresses the personal involvement of the central characters, giving little indication that he regards this meeting as bureaucratic in scope. It is no surprise therefore that the bureaucracy of early Christianity has largely remained hidden behind the narrative, despite interpreters' best efforts to trace its outline. For us the primary question will not be some table of organization but this matter of Paul's ruthlessly personal way of perceiving and narrating the story, and the problems that entails.

We encounter this personal style vividly in 2: 1–3. Paul and Barnabas go up to Jerusalem, 'taking along Titus'. Titus provides the best evidence of this meeting's true significance. That he was not circumcised suggests the meeting was called in response to the Gentile mission and resulted in its general acceptance. The source of potential hindrance to the mission, and its relationship to the Galatian problem, can now be only imperfectly perceived in the letter, but it is necessary to attempt a general reconstruction.

In the first instance, the inclusion of Barnabas suggests that, especially in light of events narrated in vv. 11ff., the Jerusalem meeting was not merely a personal accommodation to Paul. It was a formal negotiation between Antioch and Jerusalem, two independent centers of Christianity. If in coming to this meeting Antioch unilaterally included Titus in the entourage, the purpose could only have been to force a decision on the knotty problem of observing the law and its symbolic representation in circumcision. Under those circumstances, however, the 'false brethren' of v. 4 are not mere interlopers at the Jerusalem conference, but must be understood in a wider context as that group of Jewish Christians[1] who have 'spied' on the Gentile

---

[1] That they are to be regarded as Christians is probable from the designation ἀδελφοί. When Paul refers to Jews as such, they are brothers κατὰ σάρκα. Cf. Hahn, *Mission*, p. 78, n. 2; Wegenast, *Verständnis*, p. 47 against Schmithals, 'Häretiker', p. 10.

mission in an effort to exert pressure for conformity in law and circumcision.[1] Thus the fate of a gentile mission orchestrated from Antioch is at issue, and that means ultimately that the unity of the Church is also at issue. It scarcely seems possible that Antioch or Paul could have been unaware of the provocative implications of Titus' presence. Much more probably, such provocation was designed to precipitate a decision at Jerusalem.

The scene Paul portrays was in its nature official and ecclesiastical. Does it follow that Paul tacitly admits the superiority of Jerusalem over Antioch and himself? Verse 2 has often been taken as affirmative evidence. Paul is then seen stressing 'revelation' in order to counter Jerusalem's authority to call a meeting, although even he must admit Jerusalem has the power to determine whether or not his efforts have been in vain. 'Revelation'[2] however, is not necessarily a screen. Paul may simply wish to exclude *any* human motivations, including even his own. This seems likely from the conclusion of the verse in which he says he laid before them 'the gospel which I preach among the Gentiles but privately to those who were of repute, lest I run or had run in vain'. This obviously implies that Jerusalem could nullify Paul's efforts. Could Jerusalem nullify his gospel as well?

That seems incredible in the face of ch. 1 and improbable in the light of our earlier analysis of the phrase 'my gospel'. There we noted that Paul's reference turns not on the idea of some peculiar or idiosyncratic content, but on the eschatological accent of the gospel. Here Paul has in mind that same eschatological accent. Paul's 'running' reminds us of his frequent emphasis on the 'power' of the gospel in those contexts where he thinks of it as a durable force spanning time and reaching a goal. The durable gospel bears fruit, and by that fruit one knows his labors have not been in vain.

What Paul has in mind with particular reference to the δοκοῦντες is clear enough. They may challenge and even destroy the basic *unity* of the Church. The fruit of labor Paul has in mind is the building up of the one, single Church which he regards as the visible expression of the gospel. The threat which the

[1] Assuming we may rely on Acts 15: 1. Cf. Georgi, *Kollekte*, pp. 13–15.
[2] Probably with the consultation of a Christian prophet. Cf. Haenchen, *Apostelgeschichte*, p. 406; Lührmann, *Offenbarungsverständnis*, p. 41.

Antioch-Jerusalem conference seeks to avoid is the threat of a split in that Church. It is at least an open question whether from Jerusalem's point of view the Church's unity proceeds from the gospel's, or vice versa. For Paul, the gospel and Church are integrally related. Since they are, Jerusalem has something of a veto, the veto to abandon the gospel and claim another (which, from Paul's point of view, is no other). We sense in Paul something of a personal anxiety,[1] though the anxiety is certainly not indicative of an identity crisis which requires Paul's acceptance by Jerusalem. The element of the personal is rather more subtle and enmeshed in the fabric of Paul's thought.

The image of running reminds us of Phil. 2: 16, showing how Paul tends to personalize his concept of the gospel through a close identification of gospel with apostle and apostle with personal experience, Paul's own experience.[2] The effect of this on the narration in 2: 1ff. is noticeable. Paul has personalized a meeting of ecclesiastical, rather than merely personal, significance; he has made the dominant motif autobiographical, bringing it into harmony with ch. 1. He went up to Jerusalem (ἀνέβην) and took Titus along; he laid before those of repute the gospel which he preaches (ὃ κηρύσσω; he is not only personal, but also contemporary in language).[3] Titus, ὁ σὺν ἐμοί, does not need to be circumcised. Only the reference to Barnabas, whom Paul cannot say he 'took along', and the central clue provided by Titus' fate (cf. Acts 15: 1), destroy the illusion that Paul is negotiating on personal terms and suggest instead that he is an official representative of Antioch.

This same perspective dictates the way Paul describes the *dramatis personae* in Jerusalem. Not once does Paul use the term ἀπόστολος, though he did in 1: 19. Not once does he avail himself of any transparent term for identifying groups within Jerusalem. The ψευδάδελφοι are an evanescent group; the δοκοῦντες (vv. 2, 6) are the δοκοῦντες στῦλοι εἶναι (v. 9) but

[1] Schlier is essentially correct in pointing to Paul's concern about his efforts in building up the Church, *Galater*, p. 69.
[2] *Ibid.*, p. 68. Georgi objects (*Kollekte*, p. 18, n. 32) that this concentrates too much 'on the personal existence of the man of faith'. He misses a central element in Galatians as a whole, certainly the thrust of 1: 15f. – the peculiar identification of the apostle and the man of faith.
[3] Τρέχω, v. 3, is subjunctive. Cf. BDF par. 379: 2.

only properly identified[1] as James, Cephas and John.[2] The term στῦλοι itself is noteworthy. Not recognizable as a bureaucratic tag in the early Church,[3] it offers an interesting contrast to I Cor. 3: 10ff. and suggests the difference between Paul's vision of the apostle as an eschatological agent (I Cor. 3: 10ff., 16ff.) and another eschatological vision of the community as the new Temple in which apostles (rather than Jesus) are the supporting elements.[4] Such connections can scarcely be secured for this text; they are only possibilities. But to the extent that they are possibilities at all, they indicate that Paul is not using στῦλοι in any widely shared sense of the term currently fashionable in Jerusalem. Paul's terms show no concern with, and provide almost no insight into, a Jerusalem bureaucracy.

Paul's use of δοκοῦντες seems to point in the same direction. This certainly cannot be titular, as the qualifications εἶναί τι and στῦλοι εἶναι indicate.[5] Is it then sarcastic, or ironic, in Paul's mouth? Is he alluding to a contrast between appearance and reality, a contrast which would cast no particularly subtle aspersions on the Jerusalem apostles, aspersions which the Galatians could be expected to grasp? We cannot answer the question simply on the basis of δοκέω itself. The verb can be used to point the contrast between appearance and reality. Such use goes deep into Greek literature[6] and extends into LXX and Philo.[7] But the participle can also be used indifferently to

[1] That δοκοῦντες has the same reference throughout (vv. 2, 6, 9) seems the safest assumption. Schlier, *Galater*, p. 67, regards δοκοῦντες στῦλοι εἶναι to be a narrower group from the larger circle of vv. 2 and 6.

[2] How very much more Paul's mind runs to personal than to generic or group categories is evident in the vexing passage 1: 19. Cf. Schmithals, *Office*, p. 65: '…we can only conclude that this lack of clarity was intentional with Paul'; and p. 64: 'Gal. 1: 19 appears to be incurably ambiguous.'

[3] Nor as a title, *contra* C. K. Barrett, 'Paul and the "Pillar" Apostles', *Studia Paulina* (ed. J. N. Sevenster and W. C. van Unnik, Haarlem, 1953), pp. 1–19, see pp. 2, 4.

[4] On such an eschatological function for στῦλος cf. Barrett, *ibid.*

[5] Cf. D. Hay, 'Paul's Indifference to Authority', *JBL* 88 (1969), 36–44, here, p. 40.

[6] Passages which can be cited include Aeschylus, *Seven Against Thebes*, 592; Plato, *Gorgias*, 472A; *Euthydemus*, 303C; *Apology*, 21 *passim*, 41E; *Republic*, 11, 361B.

[7] LXX: Job 15: 21; 20: 7, 22. II, III Maccabees, *passim*. Philo, *Fug.*, 156; *Mos.*, i, 48 among others.

mean, simply and sincerely, 'nobility'.[1] In Paul, a majority of fourteen occurrences of the word seems to imply a contrast between appearance and reality (I Cor. 3: 18; 8: 2; 10: 12; II Cor. 10: 9; 11: 16; 12: 19; Phil. 3: 4). Gal. 6: 3 is perhaps the most obvious example. Yet none of these passages utilizes the participle, which lends itself so well to the more colorless meaning.

Some interpretive help comes from Paul's construction in v. 6: anacoluthon, parenthesis in 6b and emphasis on the pronoun in 6d. He begins by describing how, in the face of a threat posed by the 'false brethren', the Antiochenes did not yield for even a moment but persevered in (and hence preserved) the 'truth of the gospel'. Turning his attention to the δοκοῦντες, in contrast to the ψευδάδελφοι, he apparently intends to show how they sustained the Antiochene position, but he breaks off the sentence. Does Paul stop because there is implicit in this way of reporting things a certain supremacy attaching to the δοκοῦντες, a supremacy which he cannot admit without damaging his claim to independence? Hardly. Such supremacy would be known to the Galatian readers (or at least to the opponents) and there would be no reason to avoid mentioning it. But it is clear that Paul is vindicated, that nothing more is added, that the 'truth of the gospel' remains.

In the references to the δοκοῦντες we find again the contrast between authority of merely human agency and that of the gospel itself, a contrast Paul stresses in 1: 6ff., 1: 10ff., 1: 15ff. For Paul the importance of these people rests not in their office or rank, but in their obedience to the gospel expressed in their willingness to sustain Antioch's position. This is the significance of Paul's parenthesis. For him, and from his point of view for God as well, their position depends on their submission to the truth of the gospel and nothing else. Yet the very contrast implied here also suggests that for some, perhaps for the leaders themselves, position, or status, is critical.

One source of such status could be, and is often assumed to be, access these people once had to the earthly Jesus. Paul would

---

[1] Euripides, *Hecuba*, 294–5; *Daught. Troy*, 613; Plutarch, *Moralia*, 212B; Epictetus, *Enchiridion*, 33, 12; Josephus, *Ant.* 19, 307; *War*, 4, 141, 159. Nor do all interpreters agree on assigning meanings in the passages cited here. Cf. Barrett, 'Pillars', pp. 2–3, esp. p. 3, n. 1 (against Lietzmann, *Galater*, on 2: 2).

then be regarded as discounting the importance of such contact with Jesus, expressing his indifference to a relationship from which he is excluded by an accident of history. No doubt such contact was highly prized, but it is difficult to see its relevance in this discussion if the question of early Christian tradition and its exclusive care at the hands of the Jerusalem Christians is not an issue for Paul. Other motives for Paul's professed indifference have been suggested. The leaders were themselves deficient in some way before attaining their present rank.[1] Paul 'may have had in mind that they were unlearned, that they had left Jesus in the lurch, that James was unbelieving till he received a revelation from the risen Lord and that Peter had denied Jesus'.[2] Yet all this seems scarcely more relevant than the history of one's contact with the historical Jesus.

Nevertheless, the pattern is by now a familiar one. Previous human deficiencies are not a matter of moment in light of God's sufficiency supplied by grace. We may not be able to determine which particular items in others' biographies Paul might regard as 'deficiency', but if this is in fact the pattern he is using here, it has its origins in *his own* close association of the content of the gospel as the message of grace and the commissioning of the messenger as an act of grace. The leaders are construed along a pattern Paul supplies and derives primarily from his own experience. *They* conform to *his* pattern of 'apostolic' existence; he does not conform to theirs. More than that, this pattern of movement and attraction – they are made to join his 'apostolic circle' and are attracted to his profile of the apostle – is not a cunning and aggressive defense in the guise of an offense. It is the logical way for Paul to conceive of the problem of his relationship to the Jerusalem Church. The central agency is the gospel and its power both to subordinate and to re-create, to make sufficient what was deficient, to make new what is wanting – to shape a new creation (6: 15).[3]

In short, the more one stresses the connotation of deficiency among or within the Jerusalem circle as Paul describes it, the

[1] Cf. W. Foerster, 'Die δοκοῦντες Gal. 2', *ZNW* 36 (1937), 288.

[2] Munck, *Salvation*, p. 99.

[3] It is permissible to speak of the gospel's 'agency' here even though the re-creative energy is also construed as God's (cf. 2: 8; ἐνεργεῖν). This is part of the logical impact of Paul's equating 'conversion' and the commission to preach.

more he recognizes that pattern of contrast, that 'biography of reversal' which Paul considers the very essence of apostolic life. It is not some subtle Pauline expression of personal reservation, sarcasm or pique. Nor is it some coded way of accounting for a shift in power between the time of Paul's visit and the time of writing the letter, as G. Klein has attempted to construe it.[1] It must be remembered that the criteria expressed in the norm and creative power of the one true gospel can apply to others as well as to Paul. Indeed, they must apply. If Paul wishes to speak of and call attention to deficiencies he will have to honor them for others even as he does for himself. For this same reason, we doubt that there is any assumed distinction here between the 'visible office' of these men and some truer measure, 'their actual standing in the sight of God'.[2] It makes little sense to have Paul somehow magnanimously forbear in using negatively those features of biography which in fact are positive for him.

The key to understanding that criterion of judgment which is *not* a matter of indifference to Paul is to recognize that it is a criterion he claims is also not a matter of indifference for God. Since Paul does not claim for himself God's perception of the matter, where is the common denominator which serves to bridge the two ideas? It is the 'truth of the gospel'. Persons are subordinated to this and through this they come to be sufficient, even apostles. This Paul emphasizes as the single canon of authority in the letter. As D. Hay has suggested, Paul can use a phrase like πρόσωπον [ὁ] θεὸς ἀνθρώπου οὐ λαμβάνει to stress the pre-eminence of truth over human distinctions.[3] The bearing of this on the status of apostles is evident in II Cor. 5: 12 with its contrast of ἐν προσώπῳ and ἐν καρδίᾳ.[4] In the context of our letter it means that the action of the δοκοῦντες is significant and right not because they are of repute but because they uphold the gospel and its truth. It is from that, and not from

---

[1] G. Klein, 'Galater 2, 6–9 und die Geschichte der Jerusalemer Urgemeinde', *ZThK* 57 (1960), 275–95. He regards ἦσαν, by virtue of its tense, as masking the transfer of power from Peter to James and John who, at the time Paul is referring to, were not themselves leaders and hence were 'deficient'.

[2] M. Smith, 'Pauline Problems', *HTR* 50 (1957), 107–31, p. 121.

[3] I Esd. 4: 39; Sir. 4: 22, 27; 1 QH 14, 19–20. Cf. Hay, 'Indifference', pp. 41ff.

[4] Cf. also Gal. 6: 12.

some norm or concept of status, that their authority (which Paul nowhere contests but rather carefully locates and affirms) derives.[1]

This way of thinking is not only entirely consonant with Paul's view of his own apostolic status; it represents his consistent view of authority. He is not authoritative because he is an apostle, but is an apostle because he is the authoritative, i.e., faithful, commissioned preacher of the gospel. He exemplifies the gospel. In light of this, we can now see why Paul lays such heavy stress on the persons of this story, so light a stress on their office. Nowhere in ch. 2 are the δοκοῦντες referred to as apostles, though Peter is surely one. This may betoken the shifting status of Jerusalem authority and could indicate that the term apostle was somewhat insecure during the Pauline decades. But it scarcely seems warranted to conclude, as does Schmithals,[2] that the title 'apostle' is not at home in Jerusalem until Paul introduces it there in an effort to limit the circle of Jerusalem Christians to whom he is willing to owe responsibility. It seems far more evident that the very problem of authority itself is at stake and under discussion in Gal. 2. The problem cannot be discussed in terms of legitimacy of apostolic claims until the nature of apostolic authority is settled. For Paul that settlement is crucial in his argument with the Galatians themselves. Appeals to status would be premature in more than one respect.

This also explains why Paul breaks into the personal style so often in reporting the conference, why in particular he stresses his own personal involvement and construes the decision of the conference with an autobiographical thrust which is unmistakable in v. 6d: ἐμοὶ γὰρ οἱ δοκοῦντες οὐδὲν προσανέθεντο. Such personalization effects an equilibrium between Paul and the 'pillars'. Parity is achieved not by clarifying Paul's claim to apostolic status but by clarifying Jerusalem's subordination to the gospel's authority and hence the claim of those leaders to Paul's vision of apostolic authority. The Jerusalem leaders meet his standards. Legitimacy has nothing to do with it. Authority

---

[1] Schlier, *Galater*, pp. 75–6, sees that the fundamental matter here is that of authority and Paul will not question the authority of the Jerusalem pillars. But he fails to see that *their* authority for *him* lies not in their being 'Jerusalem apostles' but in their being faithful to the demands of the gospel.

[2] Cf. W. Schmithals, *Office*, pp. 82ff.

has everything to do with it. It is not surprising that Paul stresses that nothing was added to *him*.[1] He means that no restrictions were set to, no further and extraneous requirements laid upon, the fundamental proclamation of the gospel.

It is tempting to ask what further matters Paul might have in mind. While we have excluded the evidence from Acts 15 on general and procedural grounds, one item from that account may be relevant. At the conclusion of the conference in Acts we find the 'apostolic decree' (Acts 15: 9–21; 22–9). That decree does not fit gracefully within the structure supplied by Luke. It seems peripheral to the meeting's ostensible occasion, the problem of circumcision and its rationale within a gentile mission (Acts 15: 1–2). It plays little role in Paul's subsequent activities as portrayed by Luke. Finally, Luke repeats the decree in Acts 21: 25 as if to suggest it originated without Paul's participation or assent.[2] Assumptions about the origin and purpose of the decree are necessarily somewhat conjectural. Its provisions may be related to the Noachian commandments.[3] Schmithals conjectures that the origin of the decree is not to be sought in the Christian community but in diaspora Judaism where such demands were appropriate expectations laid by the Jews upon the 'God-fearers'.[4] This does not solve the problem of how and why such a decree became accepted by a gentile Christian mission. Although the matter is most uncertain, it is not as implausible as Schmithals thinks that these laws should have been viewed as useful in facilitating relations between Christians of gentile and those of Jewish origin within the same community. In all likelihood Paul is referring to such a demand which is insinuated at a later date into the gentile mission and which, if it did not originate in Jerusalem, may nevertheless have been pressed upon diaspora churches as a workable compromise.[5] For Paul

[1] For the probability of reading προσανατίθεσθαί τινι in this way cf. esp. Oepke, *Galater*, pp. 48f.

[2] On the decree, its possible origins and its significance within Acts, cf. Haenchen, *Apostelgeschichte*, pp. 410ff.

[3] On this cf. F. J. Foakes-Jackson and K. Lake, *The Beginnings of Christianity, Part I: The Acts of the Apostles* (Vol. 5, London, 1933), p. 208.

[4] *Paul and James* (London, 1965), p. 100. Cf. also K. T. Schäfer, 'Apostel-dekret', *RAC* I, cols. 555–8.

[5] Under the particular influence of Peter, after the Antioch split? Cf. Hahn, *Mission*, pp. 83f.

such an arrangement is a surcharge on the acceptance of the Antioch mission by Jerusalem. More than that, he regards it as a fundamental departure from the truth and singularity of the gospel.

The 'pillars' made no such demands. On the contrary (ἀλλὰ τοὐναντίον) they extend the right hand of fellowship to Paul and Barnabas who are free to pursue the Christian mission among the Gentiles. Here the tone and vocabulary suggest more the official and ecclesiastical than the personal dimensions of such recognition. Ἡμεῖς is Antioch, αὐτοί Jerusalem[1] and the extension of the hand of fellowship the signal of a joint missionary agreement involving one κοινωνία.[2]

It has been suggested that in vv. 7f. we have something of a verbatim report of the resolution of this conference,[3] but the arguments against this assumption[4] are stronger than those supporting it. Not only is the flavor of expression Pauline throughout, but the distinction between εἰς τὰ ἔθνη and εἰς τὴν περιτομήν does not lend itself to strict and legal interpretation, geographic or ethnographic. We should regard the alternatives as Paul's way of articulating a difference in major interests and responsibilities.[5] It is not the differences, of course, which Paul wants to emphasize here, but the common ἀποστολή. His use of this word is interesting, for Rom. 1: 5 makes it appear

---

[1] Georgi, *Kollekte*, p. 21.   [2] Schlier, *Galater*, p. 79.

[3] E. Dinkler made the suggestion in his review of Schlier's commentary (*Verkündigung und Forschung*, 1953–5, pp. 175–83). He has elaborated in *Signum Crucis* (Tübingen, 1967), pp. 270–82. His reconstruction of the text is found there, p. 280. (On this cf. Stuhlmacher, *Evangelium*, p. 93, n. 2.) Cf. also Dinkler's essay 'Die Petrus-Rom-Frage', *TR* 25 (1959), 189–230, and 'Petrus', *RGG³*, Vol. 5, col. 248. See also O. Cullman, 'Πέτρος, Κηφᾶς', *TDNT* VI, p. 100 and his *Peter: Disciple, Apostle, Martyr* (Philadelphia, 1958), p. 18.

[4] U. Wilckens, 'Ursprung', p. 272, n. 41, observes that the words bear a heavy Pauline stamp. Πεπίστευμαι with accusative is found only in Paul (I Thess. 2: 4; I Cor. 9: 17) and in the deutero-Pauline tradition (I Tim. 1: 11, Tit. 1: 3). The contrast ἀκροβυστία/περιτομή is almost exclusively confined to Paul in NT; ἀποστολή (Rom. 1: 5; I Cor. 9: 2) is found elsewhere only in Acts 1: 25. Ἐνεργεῖν is specifically Pauline. In addition, v. 7 is inextricably related, grammatically, with v. 6c.

[5] Cf. Hahn, *Mission*, p. 81; Haenchen, *Apostelgeschichte*, pp. 408f. Georgi, *Kollekte*, p. 18, takes εἰς to mean 'in the interest of', though it is not possible to establish precisely such a nuance elsewhere for Paul's use of the preposition. Cf. Stuhlmacher, *Evangelium*, p. 99, n. 1.

parallel to, but distinct from, χάρις. It is something alongside 'grace' which Paul has been given, as if 'grace' were an enabling presupposition. This corresponds well to the logical distinction between 'conversion' and commissioning inherent in Gal. 1: 15, so that we may suspect such a separation is more logically apparent than operative in Rom. 1: 4 also. Yet at the same time I Cor. 9: 2 shows that ἀποστολή can in fact be conceptually separated from the man of faith who is enabled and commissioned to it; the ἀποστολή is the act of fulfilling the commission, i.e., the establishment of Christian communities. In Gal. 2: 7ff. Paul connects his own ἀποστολή with that of Peter by its common thread, God's working power – something he apparently found Jerusalem could recognize and affirm. In light of this it would be hard to imagine that an εὐαγγέλιον τῆς περιτομῆς and one τῆς ἀκροβυστίας would be different *in substance*, since Paul regards the gospel as the matrix and form of God's work for men. Moreover, such an assumption would relativize Paul's whole emphasis on the unity of the gospel, made so vivid in these early chapters. And that would rob Paul of the only criterion he has for adjudicating the difficulties outstanding between Antioch and Jerusalem.

Paul says the Jerusalem decision also rests on another observation: the transparency of grace given to him. In a context where he has already appealed to grace (1: 6, 15) and identified it so closely with the gospel and his apostleship, this represents Paul's peculiar and idiosyncratic way of describing his credentials which have, in effect, been recognized. Here, most certainly, is the suture connecting the gospel with the apostle throughout Gal. 1 and 2. But implicit in what we have just observed from Rom. 1: 5 and I Cor. 9: 2 is this question: Does Paul identify ἀποστολή with χάρις or distinguish between them? The latter seems probable from the manner in which he segregates the two ideas into separate participial phrases: ἰδόντες (v. 7); γνόντες (v. 9). In this case, grace is conspicuously personal and individual. It is recognizable in Jerusalem, but not necessarily discerned as part of the common ἀποστολή. Recognizing that grace is the conceptual link to the one gospel, we can sense that this implied individuality may present a problem, for Paul should consistently conclude that *all* apostles manifest grace. With 'grace' is bound up the idea of the unity of the gospel; with ἀποστολή, the idea of the unity of the mission, i.e., the unity of the Church.

At this point we must consider, perhaps more explicitly than is customary, how very difficult are the implications of 2: 7–9 both in the context of the epistle as a whole and in the context of the life of the early Church. Jerusalem's recognition of the Antiochene mission was 'astounding',[1] but the scope and force of that recognition is put in immediate doubt by the events which Paul goes on to narrate from a later date in Antioch. We may assume that Paul is implicitly repudiating in v. 6 a later device to resolve a problem of table fellowship and general intercourse in mixed congregations. But it remains an unanswered question just how that problem could have gone unanticipated in such negotiations as Paul is apparently talking about. Could not the vital interests of Torah-free and Torah-true approaches to Christianity be expected to surface at precisely this point? We might expect that somebody would have anticipated the sociological dimensions of the idea of (one) 'gospel'. Is there really a singular gospel of the sort Paul is appealing to, a core which goes beyond the distinctions τῆς περιτομῆς, and τῆς ἀκροβυστίας, or is Paul deceived, or deceiving, in his supposition? To assume the latter would jeopardize, indeed shatter, Paul's underlying argument about the nature of apostolic authority.

Fridrichsen assumes that there really are two versions of the gospel, one characteristic of Peter's work among Jews and one characteristic of Paul's among Gentiles.[2] Peter's represents Jesus as the Jewish Messiah, Paul's as the savior of all mankind. The technical problem of 'one gospel' Fridrichsen solves by supposing a common core, paradosis, for both. But we have seen that while the paradosis may be common to both gospels, Paul would not consider the paradosis to be the gospel as such. This is too weak a peg on which to hang Paul's sense of the oneness of the gospel. Furthermore, Fridrichsen's reading of Gal. 1 and 2 would make no sense of Paul's implication that the meeting in Jerusalem had something to do with circumcision. A demand for circumcision has nothing to do with the paradosis, but for Paul it clearly has much to do with the gospel.

---

[1] Haenchen, *Apostelgeschichte*, p. 409.
[2] Cf. above, pp. 77f.

Finally, it is hard to see how Paul could be ignorant of certain implications in the working arrangement issuing from the Jerusalem meeting.

Within a Jewish sphere, circumcision was the token of the covenant and so the undisputed starting point. A different situation would arise if the Petrine gospel were to step over the Jewish boundary into the domain of the Gentiles, because there it could not but end with the demand that the Gentiles should become Jews if they wanted to partake in the New Covenant...In a Pauline congregation the Petrine gospel would of necessity appear as 'a different gospel', a false doctrine.[1]

But then would it not appear so to Paul also, and would it not have appeared to him that way already in Jerusalem? What is a 'different gospel' if it does not differentiate at this point?

GAL. 2: 11–21

We can only understand the situation and the appeal to authority implicit in Paul's remarks in 2: 1–10 by taking into account the crucial scene in 2: 11–21 and its probable historical background. At an unspecified time after the Jerusalem conference Peter was in Antioch along with Paul and Barnabas, enjoying full fellowship with the gentile Christians. Specifically, there was but one table, which may mean that the fellowship of the eucharist was being celebrated as part of a larger meal.[2] The common act of eating together denies any visible distinction between Jewish and gentile Christians, between those circumcised and those uncircumcised. When 'some men from James' come, however, Peter withdraws from this expression of common fellowship and 'separates himself' from the gentiles. Barnabas takes the same cue as do the 'rest of the Jews'.

Paul's displeasure is evident in vv. 14–21. Equally evident is the close connection of these verses to the larger body of the letter and especially to the christological argument in ch. 3. In 2: 11ff., Paul is moving from the Antioch scene to the purpose at hand in writing the letter. Nevertheless, vv. 14ff. also con-

[1] Fridrichsen, *Apostle*, p. 11.

[2] Cf. G. Bornkamm, 'Herrenmahl und Kirche bei Paulus', *Studien zu Antike und Urchristentum* (München, 1959), pp. 138–76.

stitute a reprise of themes introduced through chs. 1 and 2. Paul
will not set aside the grace of God (v. 21), the clear implication
being that Peter does. The break between a former and present
life, so sharply etched in 1 : 5ff., provides much of the theological
tenor of these verses. If one were to build up the very things he
has destroyed, he would prove himself a sinner (v. 18). Through
the law Paul has died to the law that he might live to God; he
has been crucified with Christ (v. 19). It is no longer he who
lives but Christ who lives in him (v. 20a).

All of this and more Paul educes in his reproach to Peter
whom, with the others, he accuses of not being 'on the right
road toward the truth of the gospel'.[1] But why? If Peter's
actions are a violation of the Jerusalem agreement, the agreement is astounding. Did both Jerusalem and Paul fail to foresee
at that time the implications of recognizing an independent missionary movement based in Antioch? If Jerusalem could foresee
such problems, was it acting in deception at the time of the
meeting? Why would Barnabas, the most visible member of the
Antioch missionary movement, succumb so quickly to Jerusalem's position if Jerusalem but reneged on an earlier agreement?[2]

Barnabas' action makes it almost impossible to construe the
Antioch affair as a simple act of bad faith on Jerusalem's part.
Certainly Barnabas does not regard it that way, and if Paul does,
then we must allow for the possibility that *Paul's* view of the
meaning and implications of the Jerusalem agreement was not
shared by Antioch. In point of fact it was not. Galatians 2: 11f.
stands as the memorial not only to Paul's break with Barnabas,
a rupture construed by Luke (Acts 15: 26–41) as purely personal,[3]

---

[1] G. D. Kilpatrick's translation of οὐκ ὀρθοποδοῦσιν πρὸς τὴν ἀλήθειαν
τοῦ εὐαγγελίου, 'Gal. 2: 14 ὀρθοποδοῦσιν', *Neutestamentliche Studien für
Rudolf Bultmann* (Berlin, 1957), pp. 269–74. Schmithals, *Paul and James*, p. 72,
suggests that the opposite of walking straight is 'limping with two different
opinions' (I Kings 18: 21).

[2] The phenomenon of Barnabas' turnabout is harder to deal with than
often thought. It certainly precludes seeing the Galatian opposition to Paul
as a bias toward Jerusalem and against Antioch as has, most recently,
Stuhlmacher, *Evangelium*, p. 67.

[3] Cf. Haenchen, *Apostelgeschichte*, pp. 414ff. Quite possibly Luke does not
know the origin of the rift between Paul and Barnabas, but if he makes of it
a personal rather than an official rupture, so does Paul in Gal. 2.

but to his emergence as a fully independent missionary with no ties to Antioch. It should not surprise us that Paul discusses all this in personal, rather than organizational, terms. For one thing, he identifies the apostolic 'status' almost exclusively in such terms. For another, there is no organization that well developed.

Jerusalem's reasons for extending its discipline into Antioch must have been pressing. To some at Antioch they obviously seemed valid. To Paul they did not. The net effect was his separation from Antioch in general and Barnabas in particular. This separation leaves Paul on his own as a missioner, and more importantly, it points up the distinction between apostolic authority and apostolic legitimacy. Whatever claims Barnabas and Peter might have to apostolic legitimacy are not touched by their behavior in Antioch, nor does Paul try to attack them on this ground. The point of attack is authority. They have not submitted themselves to the truth of the gospel. The charge of hypocrisy leveled at Peter accuses him of acting inconsistently, out of accord with an authority he himself means to recognize. This is clear from v. 15 where the ἡμεῖς addressed to Peter necessarily includes him – in fact, the Peter who again had begun to live Ἰουδαϊκῶς.[1]

Paul's argument with Peter from 2: 15 forward is so closely related to his argument with the Galatians that it is difficult to separate the two. It seems that Paul's rebuke focuses on the potentially disastrous effects of Peter's action in encouraging any positive move toward the law within the Christian communities. More than that, we can see a close parallelism between Peter's apparent outward acquiescence toward the force of Torah and his inner devotion to the gospel on the one hand, i.e., his 'hypocrisy', and the unnatural union of law and Christianity in Galatia on the other. It is not accidental that Paul introduces in 2: 19 the Christ who is crucified to law. Peter's actions, whatever their origin and intent, suggest some authority within the Christian community other than that of the gospel. Peter is an apostle, but for Paul no claim to apostolic legitimacy could resolve a dispute that centers on authority. Peter's real authority is something Peter must be self-conscious about and something the Galatians must be shown. To meet

---

[1] Schmithals, *Paul and James*, p. 73.

this problem Paul reverts to an identification of gospel and apostolic authority which is manifest in him personally. In doing so he is also restating his authority over the Galatian community.

In effect the Antioch rift isolates Paul in his understanding of apostolic authority precisely *because* he distinguishes between authority and legitimacy. Paul is perfectly consistent, even rigid, in his devotion to the 'truth of the gospel' as the gospel of grace. In that sense he seems far more authoritarian than Peter or Barnabas. This raises the question of whether they are responding to some countervailing claims of authority, as is tacitly assumed by suggesting that Jerusalem has broken its agreement. Peter and Barnabas would then be submitting to Jerusalem's arbitrary authority. If that were the case Paul could make an explicit charge and might be expected to accuse Jerusalem of bad faith, which he does not. Later he even fulfills his pledge to collect funds and nothing indicates that his separation from Jerusalem and Antioch is something he sees as a repudiation of the idea of the oneness of the Church, an idea for which he struggled in Jerusalem. For that matter, nothing in Gal. 2 indicates an arbitrary imposition of authority from Jerusalem. We might expect Barnabas to have resisted that quite as much as Paul if he too was a participant in an earlier working agreement now being scuttled.

On the contrary, it will be better to assume a distinction between τινας ἀπὸ 'Ιακώβου who come down and those ἐκ περιτομῆς whom Peter feared enough to warrant changing his habits.[1] While one can only conjecture about what is involved here, it seems plausible to assume that Jerusalem Christians are now under pressure from Jews who regard the fraternizing of Jewish and Gentile Christians in so urban a center as Antioch to be tantamount to Jewish-Christian surrender of the role of the Law. Judaean Christians had not dispensed with the claims of the Law, but according to Paul they have moved a wedge between the Jewish conception and the phenomenon of the Gentile mission by dispensing with the notion of the priority of circumcision. Now, under pressure from Jews without whose

[1] G. Dix, *Jew and Greek* (London, 1953), pp. 42ff. Paul (unlike Luke) never uses ἐκ περιτομῆς to refer to Jewish Christians, but to Jews as contrasted to Gentiles, as in 2: 7.

continued sufferance the Jewish-Christian position in Jerusalem would be untenable, the utility and significance of the original agreement appear in a different light. Jerusalem can portray the achievement as one threatened by Antioch's careless action. Both Peter and Barnabas might be responsive to this new claim. It is not merely their fear of the pressure which those ἐκ περι-τομῆς can exert on those 'from James'; it is the continued existence of the fragile Jerusalem agreement which is at stake. It is the hitherto carefully guarded unity of the Church, seemingly preserved at Jerusalem, which they now see hanging precariously in the balance.

This is a plausible interpretation which can explain what is *not* said in Gal. 2. It is apparent that Paul does not here make public his dissociation from other organized missionary enterprises, and does nothing to suggest a formal break which forces the reader to choose between Peter and Paul as two representatives of two gospels. On the contrary, what vexes Paul is the *inconsistency* of Peter's response and its potentially deleterious effects should others decide to take Peter himself as an authority.

In short, nowhere in Gal. 2 does Paul yield ground gained in his earlier, curious argument about the singularity of the gospel. Moreover, we can see that some of the controlling principles are still in force and operational *within* the dispute between Peter and Paul. If our reconstruction is sound, it will not do to regard the argument as a clash between expediency represented by Peter, and principle represented by Paul.[1] What is often called expediency is in fact a principle Paul himself had once subscribed to and struggled for in Jerusalem, the oneness of the new Church movement. It is difficult to believe that any consideration less significant would have occasioned Barnabas' otherwise seemingly abrupt shift in position. But in fact Barnabas did not perceive this as a shift; he perceived it as an extension of a singular principle in defense of which he had once been joined by Paul.

As a result we have not a distinction between principle and expedient considerations as a basis for action, but a potential conflict between two principles: the singularity of the gospel and the unity of the Church. Paul would not recognize the

[1] *Ibid.*

problem when stated this way, as is evident from the fact that in 2: 11ff., as throughout the letter, *he* derives the unity of the Church from the singularity of the *gospel*. But it is clear that others did not necessarily see things that way. If they had, the whole of the letter would be unwarranted and the events of 2: 11ff. would never have happened.

Paul himself must have at least glimpsed the problem we describe in these terms, for though he can rebuke both Peter and the Galatian errorists he nowhere can bring himself to assert a plurality of gospels, and he certainly cannot sever the unity of the Church by breaking off fellowship with it. That explains why, despite the very personal, indeed autobiographical, dimension in Paul's remarks in chs. 1 and 2, he does not recount how his independent missionary enterprise dates from this incident.[1] Paul is rehearsing a relationship with Jerusalem which began when he was formally associated with the Antioch mission and derived his 'authority' from that relationship. The relationship ended with this final separation from that missionary movement. He describes the change in associations obliquely, but the emergence of the true concept of apostolic authority as he now understands it is unmistakable.[2]

Paul's claims in chs. 1 and 2 have their primary rationale in two facts. First, there is no authoritative body of 'apostles' or other figures to which one might appeal to adjudicate two conflicting principles such as those held here, the singularity of the gospel and the unity of the Church. Were there such an authoritative body, there would be no potential conflict. This lacuna is documented by Paul's loose use of the term 'apostle' in 1: 19, by what we know of an apparent shift of Jerusalem leadership from Peter and the disciples to James and the elders and by the absence of any suitable bureaucratic model for the term 'apostle'. If one 'principle' is primary and the other derivative, the sanction for that does not repose in some exterior, bureaucra-

---

[1] We have seen the effect of this separation on Paul's 'memory' and style of narrative, as exemplified in the constant fluctuation between personal and ecclesiastical frames of reference. Paul, the independent missionary, is reflecting on events which led to his becoming independent, but occurred when he was more clearly an agent in a geographically centered, joint enterprise. For a sketch of the effect of this on his style, cf. Hahn, *Mission*, p. 80, n. 1.

[2] Cf. E. Haenchen, 'Petrus-Probleme', *NTS* 7 (1960–1), 187–97.

tic authority. None exists. Second, Paul construes his apostolic commissioning as derived from God, not man.[1]

Paul ranks his priorities at least implicitly if not explicitly. The gospel and its truth are first. This does not mean that he consciously sacrifices the unity of the Church, but rather that he construes it as a function of the one gospel.[2] In almost perfect parallelism he also construes his authority – and hence, the authority of an apostle – in the same terms and by the same device of subordination and derivation. That is, both the Church's unity and the apostle's authority are derived from, and subordinate to the gospel and its truth precisely because they are grounded in this gospel. Sociologically this is necessary, theologically it is plausible, historically it is fraught, like I Cor. 15, with consequences Paul could scarcely have envisioned. Most important, it allows Paul to assert his apostolic authority without having to deny, at least in principle, that of Peter or Barnabas. Peter and Barnabas are, in fact, not true to their calling because their action, like the Galatians' subsequent action, ignores God's grace and so nullifies the gospel. But Paul, we notice, does not say this. What he does say is that his apostleship constitutes an illustration of the gospel – a calling in grace – and not a human, flesh and blood authority. He also holds other apostles responsible to the same norm. Apparently he is more interested in *assuming* similar authority similarly derived than in *denying* it. Should others prove not to be illustrations of the truth of the gospel, Paul would have to deny their authority, and here he does seek to counteract their potential influence.

Gal. 1 and 2 should be seen not as Paul's attempt to open up the apostolic circle and admit himself. It is his attempt to pro-

[1] Though it is not clear that he thinks *any* apostle derives his commission from man rather than God. This is one of the chief problems of our text. It is not a question of whether Paul is successful in equating himself with other apostles. It is a question of whether he could, ultimately, include them under *his* criteria.

[2] Peter and Barnabas would rank the two principles in reverse order. Paul's scheme was destined to become dominant, from one point of view; but so was the alternative, from another. The needed resolution could only be achieved when authority could be embodied bureaucratically, so that one authority could define both the singularity of the gospel and the unity of the Church. Neither side in the Antioch conflict could do *both*.

vide a rationale for apostolic authority in the absence of a concept of apostolic legitimacy which is sufficiently well developed to include within itself an implicit appeal to authority. This argument is not Paul's attempt to defend his apostolic legitimacy, but his attempt to elaborate the idea of apostolic authority. The literary facts of life are these, that Gal. 1 and 2 prefaced another attempt by Paul to assert authority – in a style which, so far as we know, he initiated – in chs. 3–6. The very smooth transition which we have already noted in 2: 15ff. indicates how integrally connected are the two units of the letter. Apostolic authority elaborated in chs. 1 and 2 is applied, on the principles of its elaboration, in chs. 3–6.

Seen in this way, Paul's statements make it unnecessary to pretend that Barnabas is suddenly converted – or coerced – from a Gentile to a Jewish position. They make it equally apparent that the problem Paul is wrestling with transcends any simple geographic loyalties. It is not necessary to hypothesize about what claims have been lodged by the Galatians against Paul's apostolic legitimacy or authority. It is only necessary to see that from his point of view his authority has been disrespected rather than challenged by a competing alternative. The Galatian errorists despise Paul's break with Jewish traditions. Technically speaking, that is an argument over the truth of the gospel. It is Paul, not the errorists, who identifies the gospel with apostle in such a way that this becomes an argument about apostleship and its authority.

Hence we are relieved of one of the more problematical and unpromising hypotheses occasioned by this letter, concerning Paul's reference to himself as an apostle 'not from man nor through a man'.[1] As a tacit rejection of the Galatian position

[1] This had long been a difficult problem. Schmithals has effectively and exhaustively shown the illogic of assuming *both* that Paul is responding to a charge that he is merely dependent on the Jerusalem apostles *and* that the critics themselves are a Judaizing faction ('Häretiker', pp. 13–22). His own solution, that over against Paul the Galatian gnostics have set a pneumatic-apostle concept, depends on the general plausibility of that apostolic image in this time and place, and in this regard Schmithals is not persuasive. It could be assumed that the Galatians have appealed to Jerusalem apostles as representative of their position on Torah, in which case Paul is stressing all the more his separation from Jerusalem apostles and certainly not 'defending' himself. Moreover, this assumption does not minimize the Pauline contribution of coordinating the apostolic image with the gospel, as is done already in 1: 1f.

this simply says that tradition is human. As Paul's simultaneous assertion of apostolic status it says that the true gospel authorizes its messenger. It says nothing about a Galatian assumption that Paul's status is inferior to that of others. Such an interpretation proves extremely difficult and seems doubtful given the idiosyncratic nature of the Galatian error. That position is a curious blend of lopsided legalism and lopsided spiritualism which is difficult to associate intimately with any 'apostolic' circle we can identify. Paul's aggressive assertions of apostolic origin can scarcely be interpreted along these lines. They must be interpreted along the lines already suggested, as a creative union of the idea of the authority of the message with the profile of the messenger. The possibility of and impetus for doing this stem, in part, from the fluid and still expanding situation of the Church. As long as there are new frontiers to conquer, one can temporarily retreat from the strategic problem of the unity of the Church.[1] That question could not be ignored forever, of course. By the time it was resolved, Paul's own unambiguous and exalted claim to the authority of the gospel, which he documents so forcefully, had established the term 'apostle' as equally unambiguous and exalted, but with this cardinal difference: The apostle was no longer a manifestation of the gospel and hence truly subordinate to it (so that Peter could be made accountable to the gospel, reminded of the necessity of his subordination to it). He was now regarded as somehow prior to the gospel. The gospel no longer determined him, but he determined it, whether by protecting the stream of tradition and furthering it or by whatever means. Once that significant and un-Pauline shift takes place, the unity of the Church is guaranteed. It follows naturally from subordination to apostolic will. No longer can there be any discrepancy between such principles as the authority of the gospel and the unity of the Church. The apostle stands between these and represents both; he guarantees their harmony.

[1] The Christian mission had its own evolution, no doubt. Whatever may not be clear in detail about the development of the earliest Church in its various centers, the pattern of movement from pluralism to conformity, from greater to less differentiation in thought and practice, seems evident. What is also evident is that self-conscious 'institutions' of authority emerge with that development.

CHAPTER 6

THE NORMATIVE CHARACTER OF THE GOSPEL: PHILIPPIANS AND II CORINTHIANS

INTRODUCTION

In Galatians 2 we have observed a potential conflict of principles which goes unresolved. It is important to realize that Paul does not force the issue between himself and Peter to any ultimate conclusion. He does not try to invoke his authority over against Peter's. He tries only to establish the true nature of apostolic authority. That pattern of authority will claim Peter once again for Paul's position or it will fundamentally deny Peter's authority. We do not know which. The ambiguity and lack of resolution inherent in this picture is underscored by Paul's willingness to gather a collection from within his missionary sphere among the Gentiles. This is more than a casual reflection on his ultimate interest in the unity of the Church. Like his rebuke of Peter, it is based on a thoroughly consistent premise, as II Cor. 8 and 9 show.

Historically there is good reason for Paul's failure to press the issue to any ultimate conclusion. There is scarcely anything like one universal and organized Church in his time. The missionary enterprise still enjoys the luxury of an expanding horizon and a visible frontier. Fragmented and not yet bureaucratized, the structures of the 'Church' are immature in this period. 'It is especially important not to think of...heretics as organized sects – after all, there was scarcely an organized church-at-large at that time. The heresies in Paul's time are nothing but various and often *ad hoc* attempts arising within the Christian movement to solve the unavoidable internal problems of a syncretistic group (Early Christianity!), which emerged in the Hellenistic-Roman world.'[1] In the Galatian problem, for example, Paul does not invoke the organizational unity of the Church as an argument against Peter because there is no such unity to invoke.

[1] H. Koester, 'The Purpose of the Polemic of a Pauline Fragment (Philippians III)', *NTS* 8 (1961–2), 317–22, cf. 322.

Neither can this kind of pressure be used against Paul, though one might imagine Barnabas willing to try.

Such is the historical circumstance. Corresponding to it is one of Paul's persistent themes, that of eschatological reservation. Such reservation cuts in two directions. Its forward arc, evident in I Cor. 15, stresses the limits beyond which one may not go in appropriating the future to the present. Its backward arc can be seen in Galatians and Paul's insistence that one may not appropriate the past without radically revising one's understanding of oneself, and hence of the past itself. Between these poles, between the 'not yet' and the 'no longer', stretches the tightrope Paul walks, a dialectic in which men and events are neither what they were nor what they shall be. If the rope should break, according to one common view, we are left with the alternatives of gnosticism or early Catholicism.

While it is not our task to investigate that conclusion, it should be emphasized that the historical realities of the development of the Church encompass more than the differences between Peter and Paul.[1] Paul's eschatological reservation belongs within a movement of institution building. Acts and the Pastoral epistles make clear that his position was not well suited to more mature development. However we may choose to regard 'early Catholicism', the period signifies a tightening of institutional self-consciousness and a movement toward the resolution of earlier ambiguities.

In Paul's time the situation is still fragile. This accounts for the seeming inconclusiveness of the argument in Galatians about the gospel as norm, for Paul's refusal or failure to press that argument to its final consequences. Despite the unmistakable fashion in which he introduces his own person into the center of the discussion, Paul does not wish to reduce the matter of apostolic authority, or the norm of the gospel, to personal competition or argument. Precisely because the apostle is himself

---

[1] It is the merit of Munck (*Paul*) to have stressed how the idea of geographic expansion and physical frontier fit into the theology of Paul's mission to Gentiles mixing with those eschatological sensibilities which shaped his image of the apostle. But there comes a day, even if it is not Paul's day, when the frontiers are gone and history begins to call in the notes made out to it in formerly expectant, but now merely by-gone days. Cf. W. D. Davies, *Christian Origins and Judaism* (London, 1962), pp. 195ff.

subordinate to the gospel, the establishment of the norm of the gospel carries with *it* the establishment of the authority of the apostle.

This same arrangement is evident in Phil. 1: 15–18. The motives of the proclamation of the gospel are subordinated to the fact of its proclamation and then regarded as secondary:

Some indeed preach Christ from envy and rivalry, but others from good will. The latter do it out of love, knowing that I am put here for the defense of the gospel; the former proclaim Christ out of partisanship, not sincerely, but thinking to afflict me in my imprisonment. What then? Only that in every way, whether in pretense or in truth, Christ is proclaimed; and in that I rejoice. (RSV)

Here again we have an example of the over-riding supremacy of the message, a supremacy which serves as the norm for judging the action of apparently disparate groups of preachers. Unlike Gal. 1: 6–9, where the emphasis is negative, here it is positive. If it is not irenic, at least it is in keeping with the oft-repeated theme of the letter, 'rejoicing'.[1]

Paul distinguishes two groups of preachers by their motives: διὰ φθόνον καὶ ἔριν on the one hand; δι᾽ εὐδοκίαν on the other. Εὐδοκία must mean something like 'good will', or even a 'good desire' (cf. Rom. 10: 1).[2] 'Good will' can be directed not only to persons but also to objects such as the gospel. Φθόνος and ἔρις hardly have reference to the gospel, however, since they ordinarily indicate motives connected with either a person or a community. All these motives should be understood as directed to the same object, there being no specific indication to the contrary. Whether out of jealousy or strife on the one hand, or from good will on the other – and all in reference to either a person or a group of persons – the Christ is preached. Who is the object of the motives?

Paul virtually holds the copyright on the use of ἔρις in the

[1] The distinct possibility that Philippians is molded from three separate strands of correspondence (cf. FBK, pp. 235–7; Koester, 'Polemic') does not preclude the possibility of isolating this as a dominant theme.

[2] Cf. J. B. Lightfoot, *St. Paul's Epistle to the Philippians* (London, 1913/ Grand Rapids, 1965), p. 89.

NT.[1] Whenever he uses φθόνος it is found in either the same passage with ἔρις or very close at hand.[2] In Rom. 1: 29 the two words appear in the long catalog of sins which climaxes Paul's description of a disobedient world. In Gal. 5: 20–1 they occur within a chain of words indicating the world of flesh. This same association of ἔρις with flesh, and in the context of ethical exhortation, can be seen in Rom. 13: 13. It is impossible to know just how much weight may be laid on these individual terms, especially when they seem to occur in a somewhat fixed style. But in these passages a community is always in Paul's view. While φθόνος cannot be thought of as directed toward a community, in the passages cited no particular person is made the object. Rather, φθόνος and ἔρις seem to represent general dissonance within the group. So in II Cor. 12: 20 Paul can mention the latter in a succession of sins ending with ἀκαταστασίαι. Paul may himself be the object or the ostensible cause of some of the problems here, but he sees the attitude as one of general disorder, not as some specific disobedience or impertinence directed toward him. Even in I Cor. 1: 11 this general view predominates. As vv. 12f. indicate, ἔρις there has a very personal reference. Yet the entire letter shows that it is not party names which concern Paul, but the strife in general.[3]

The motives in Phil. 1: 15 are primarily cast in ethical terms. They are parallel, with both 'good will' and 'envy and rivalry' directed toward the entire community, or at least are not directed toward Paul as an individual. In vv. 16 and 17, however, the order is reversed and for the first time Paul makes specific application of these motives to his own situation. One group preaches[4] 'from love', knowing (εἰδότες) that the task of

[1] Rom. 1: 29; I Cor. 1: 11; 3: 3; II Cor. 12: 20; Gal. 5: 20. Otherwise, only I Tim. 6: 4 and Tit. 3: 9.

[2] Rom. 1: 29; Gal. 5: 21. Otherwise, Matt. 27: 18; Mark 15: 10; I Tim. 6: 4; Tit. 3: 3; James 4: 5 and I Peter 2: 1.

[3] This is confirmed by the one remaining occurrence of ἔρις, I Cor. 3: 3. Paul's treatment of the problem is dictated by a concern to show that the strife itself is ill-founded. He makes no attempt to weigh claims of various 'parties'.

[4] Κηρύσσειν goes with both ἐξ ἀγάπης and ἐξ ἐριθείας (Dibelius [Thessalonicher-Philipper], p. 66). Lohmeyer, Philipper, p. 45, n. 3 reads the two prepositional phrases as belonging to the subject and not the predicate. But certainly the sense of vv. 15 and 17 indicates that the two groups are preaching from two motives.

defending the gospel has been laid at Paul's feet. The other group preaches 'from partisanship', supposing (οἰόμενοι) that they are causing tribulation for him in his imprisonment. Both prepositional phrases could be taken in a general sense, without specific reference to Paul, but the participial phrases indicate a direct reference to him. We must start there in order to see what the relationship of the group is.

In 1: 7 Paul mentions both his chains and the defense of the gospel when he is speaking of the Philippian Church. The Church shares with him in grace, 'both in my imprisonment and in the defense and confirmation of the gospel'. Lohmeyer understands the peculiarly close relationship of Paul and the community to be based on their common fate: Together they are suffering persecution.[1] But Dibelius is correct in pointing out a definite contrast implied by the distinct genitives μου and τοῦ εὐαγγελίου.[2] Grace can be understood as the general rubric under which all three elements are arranged: Paul's imprisonment, the defense of the gospel and its confirmation. All three refer to the same situation, the situation in which Paul finds himself. Thus, in v. 12, he can specifically equate them. His imprisonment has come to 'advance the gospel'. From the perspective of grace, two ways of looking at what has happened to Paul (τὰ κατ᾽ ἐμέ, v. 12) coalesce. They are identical, not as historical events, but when viewed from their results.[3]

What distinguishes the two groups is this matter of perspective. Those who 'know' of Paul's responsibility for advancing the gospel interpret correctly his imprisonment. Those who 'suppose' that they are causing tribulation for him attribute to him their own viewpoint concerning his bondage. Thinking Paul frustrated, because his missionary effort is frustrated, they leap into the breach during his confinement. But whatever their motives and regardless of their desire to take advantage of his circumstances, they contribute to the same goal, and ultimately manifest the same grace which he does.

---

[1] Lohmeyer, *Philipper*, pp. 22–7, esp. p. 26.

[2] Dibelius, *Thessalonicher-Philipper*, p. 63.

[3] *Ibid.* 'In his imprisonment as in his service, Paul considers the Philippians to be his fellow participants – not in his suffering, however, but rather in his grace!'

6-2

Whether such phrases as 'from love', 'from self-seeking',[1] and 'not sincerely' refer specifically to Paul, as do their corollaries in the preceding verse, or refer to the community as a whole, makes little difference. The real distinction is that between viewing the whole matter as an act of God's grace and as an event involving only Paul's suffering. This fundamental distinction remains the same whether ἀγάπη and ἐριθεία are directed more toward Paul or more toward the community.

For whatever reason, 'whether in pretense or in truth', Christ is proclaimed (v. 18). This is the constant and binding factor which triumphs over envy and strife. Paul displays curious indifference about personal ill will directed toward him, as if the motives of a man in preaching were unimportant, as if in some way the end could justify the means. This indifference is really based on the conviction that the means are the same and beyond human manipulation, attributable only to 'grace', v. 7. Paul subordinates others to the gospel in vv. 15 and 18 just as he subordinates himself in vv. 7ff. and everywhere else. From this subordination stems the indifference about motives.

Dibelius suggests that Paul can be casual about these distinctions of motive because he is more missionary than church organizer,[2] as Rom. 15: 20 would indicate. On this view it is immaterial who preaches. Once the gospel is given expression it proceeds of its own accord and accomplishes its own purposes.

Such 'frontier' vision plays a role in Paul's thinking, but the matter is not simple. We have here a subordination to the gospel, perceived as the event of grace, markedly like that of Galatians. Yet the assertion of Paul's authority is the very stuff of Galatians. Here too, Paul specifically indicates a continuing interest in the affairs of the Philippian Christians (cf. 1: 9–11); and in such passages as 3: 18f. he asserts his, and the gospel's, authority in an undeniable and exclusive way, as we shall see. Moreover, next to Rom. 15: 20 must be placed Rom. 1: 15. It will not do to say that '...to a certain extent Paul wants only to kindle the fire'.[3] What is correct is to conclude from this passage

---

[1] 'Εριθεία is a difficult word. Before the NT it is found only in Aristotle and refers to self-seeking in regard to political office (cf. BAG, p. 309). If we assign here the meaning 'contentiousness', then the reference would seem to be more specifically directed toward the community.

[2] Dibelius, *Thessalonicher-Philipper*, p. 66.

[3] *Ibid.*

that Paul knows how to follow the logic of his own idea that the apostle, as a total manifestation of the grace which is the gospel, is subordinate to the gospel. His authority does not depend on his being liked.

Thus Phil. 1: 15–18 furthers our analysis of Paul's understanding of authority by showing how he can release his own, purely personal, interests to those of the wider horizon of the gospel. In doing so, Paul is no less personal or autobiographical than we have found him to be in other places, such as in the Galatian correspondence. The close relationship of his person to the needs and interests of the gospel is still evident. But the gospel is being served even by those who would not serve him. Thus the pattern holds. Their self-interest is necessarily subordinated to the gospel's, just as is his. There is a touch of irony in the scheme. Since his self-interest is subordinate to the gospel's, their efforts, which further the gospel while motivated by antagonism toward Paul, actually further 'his' interests.

Two further elements emerge quite clearly in this passage. One is Paul's considerable interest in the *result* of missionary activity. We have seen negative expressions of this in the disappointment registered in I Cor. 15: 1ff. and Gal. 1: 6ff. (cf. 3: 1). But here the result is positive, something which enables Paul to rejoice regardless of the motives of others. The other feature is the close relationship between the apostle and the community itself. This is a form of 'result' too, but of a slightly different sort. We shall see that the community and its actions constitute something of a norm for apostolic adequacy.

II COR. 2: 14 – 7: 4 AND CHS. 10–13

In sharp contrast to the casual tone of indifference in Phil. 1: 15ff. stands the embittered and embroiled rhetoric of much of II Corinthians. The letter includes a sustained polemic on chs. 10–13 and a spirited apostolic defense larded throughout 2: 14 – 7: 4. Paul's equanimity in Philippians is explained by his willingness to concentrate on the matter of ends rather than means. Paul can do that in part because of the integral relationship between means and ends and his overwhelming confidence in the results of even that preaching which springs from unworthy motives. In II Corinthians means and ends are also integrally related, but to Paul's despair the picture in Corinth, at some stages at least, is gloomy.[1]

Paul struggles against sharp attacks on his person and on his apostolic claim, attacks which he seeks to rebuff by counter-argument but which also lead him to anticipate a lively confrontation face to face one day (cf. 10: 2; 12: 14; 13: 1ff., 10). In such a confrontation Paul will face people who claim their own apostolic status, in part at his expense. They deny that he belongs to Christ (10: 7); they rebuke him because he does not draw financial support from the community (11: 7; 12: 1, 16); and they delight in contrasting his impression by letter with that he makes in person (10: 1, 10). All of this is apparently negative evidence for their identification if they are scorning Paul for lacking their own virtues or characteristics. More positive evidence about their identity is not abundant. Paul speaks of false

[1] The literary integrity of II Corinthians is a major problem. A century ago A. Hausrath isolated chs. 10–13 and suggested the 'four chapter hypothesis' (*Die Vierkapitelbrief an die Korinther* [Heidelberg, 1870]), building on the work of Semler. The tone of chs. 10–13 does not fit well coming after the calmer, more satisfied air of chs. 1–7. In chs. 8 and 9 Paul exhorts to generosity in the collection, but the mood of confident expectation is shattered by the corrosive quality of chs. 10–13, which would certainly prove counter-productive to Paul's intentions if they directly followed an appeal for money (D. Georgi, *Die Gegner des Paulus im 2. Korintherbrief* [Neukirchen, 1964; WMANT 11], p. 17). Attempts to save the letter's integrity and still account for this abrupt shift have not been persuasive (cf. A. Plummer, *A Critical and Exegetical Commentary on the Second Epistle of St. Paul to the Corinthians* [New York, 1915; ICC], p. xxxv; H. Windisch, *Der zweite Korintherbrief* [Göttingen, 1924⁹; KEK], pp. 15ff.). We are forced to conclude that chs. 10–13 come from another stage of correspondence (G. Bornkamm, *Die Vorgeschichte des sogennanten zweiten Korintherbriefs* [Heidelberg, 1961]). Since the issues which are burning in chs. 10–13 are dealt with in a calmer fashion elsewhere, it appears that chs. 10–13 represent a stage of correspondence earlier than much of the rest of the letter (cf. 1: 23 with 13: 2; 1: 24 with 13: 5; 2: 3 with 13: 10; 2: 9 with 10: 6 and 7: 16 with 10: 1. Cf. Plummer, p. xxxi).

Similarly, we can assume that 2: 14 – 6: 13 and 7: 2–4 is another fragment closely related to chs. 10–13 in theme, but different in tone. What remains after these divisions are chs. 8 and 9, two separate appeals from Paul for contribution to the collection, and 1: 1 – 2: 13; 7: 5–16 from the period of final reconciliation between Paul and the community. For the reconstruction of events and stages in the correspondence cf. Schmithals, *Gnosis*², pp. 94–106 and, better, Georgi, *Gegner*, pp. 25–9. Bornkamm, *Vorgeschichte* (pp. 24–36) seeks to provide a rationale for the present redactional arrangement.

apostles (11: 13) but also of superlative apostles (11: 5). With whom is he arguing? In 2: 14 – 7: 4 Paul must somehow 'commend himself' (5: 12; cf. 3: 1) because his relationship to the Corinthian community has been disturbed. The Corinthians are 'restricted' in their own 'affections' (6: 12). All of this has something to do with the opponents of chs. 10–13. Who are these 'apostles'?[1] F. C. Baur[2] saw them as representing the radical Jewish-Christian wing associated with Peter. Käsemann regards them as representatives of Palestinian Jewish-Christianity slyly laying claim to the authority of the Jerusalem apostles.[3] Kümmel thinks that they are Palestinian in origin but not necessarily connected with the authority of that center, intruders who make common cause with the more gnostic opponents found in I Corinthians, thus forcing Paul to fight on an expanded front.[4] Following W. Lütgert's earlier lead,[5] Bultmann[6] and Schmithals[7] have sought to locate the opponents in Jewish-gnostic spiritualism.

None of these attempts has proven wholly persuasive. In part that is because we have too little agreement on characteristics of the 'Jewish-Christian' and 'gnostic'. On balance, we prefer to follow Georgi's analysis of the background and location of Paul's opposition. He places the opponents within a diffuse tradition of wandering preachers having pagan and Jewish

[1] Georgi's analysis of the close relationship of 2: 14 – 7: 4 and 10–13 is persuasive (*Gegner*, pp. 16–25, 219–20), but we shall also want to mark a fairly clear difference. In the first unit Paul's concerns are directed less to the person of the apostles than to the need for explicating and thus restoring his relationship with the community. In the second, the community fades into the background as Paul takes on the task of delineating the norm of apostleship itself. The distinction is not wholesale and we call attention to it here primarily to show how each element involves or implies the other, something which itself distinguishes Paul's concept of apostleship from what we can determine of his opponents'.

[2] *Paulus*, 1 (1866²).

[3] E. Käsemann, 'Die Legitimität des Apostels', *ZNW* 41 (1942), 33–71. Cf. also T. W. Manson, 'St. Paul in Ephesus (3): The Corinthian Correspondence', *BJRL* 26 (1941–2), 101ff.

[4] In Lietzmann (-Kümmel), *Korinther*, p. 211. Cf. FBK, p. 209.

[5] W. Lütgert, *Freiheitspredigt und Schwarmgeister in Korinth* (Gütersloh, 1908).

[6] R. Bultmann, *Exegetische Probleme des zweiten Korintherbriefes* (Darmstadt, 1963²).

[7] *Gnosis*.

representatives throughout the hellenistic world. They are pneumatics who stand on a Jewish missionary tradition which has been appropriated by Christian circles. They wed a christology of the divine man to their apostolic self-consciousness. Georgi finds antecedents in the apologetic literature of hellenistic Judaism.[1] Their christology is based on the hellenistic-Jewish appropriation of Old Testament luminaries (especially Abraham and Moses) as divine men, while the apostolic self-consciousness rests on their understanding of themselves as wandering wonder-workers whose true identity is visibly confirmed in their capacity to manifest the spirit. In 2: 14 – 7: 4 and especially in chs. 10–13 we see Paul responding to these 'apostles' by rejecting their denigration of him and, at least in part, seeking to beat them at their own game. This latter fact is important.

Elsewhere in Paul's correspondence there is nothing quite comparable to the competitive and comparative posture he adopts here, which suggests he is on the defensive. The contrast to Phil. 1: 18 is particularly striking;[2] the distance from placid confidence expressed in texts such as I Cor. 3: 5, unmistakable. The issue in II Cor. 2: 14 – 7: 4 and 10–13 is personal in a way and to a degree it has not been heretofore. This can only mean that the propriety of Paul's self-designation as an 'apostle of Christ' has been called into question, and implies that his opponents use a set of criteria by which his apostolic claim is excluded. Are we thus, for the first time in our analysis, confronted with the issue of legitimacy rather than authority?

What would comprise this legitimacy? Käsemann sees the Jerusalem apostolate and a 'legitimation principle' lurking behind the dispute between the opponents and Paul. According to this view, Paul is confronted by spiritualists who 'commend themselves' and 'measure themselves by one another' (10: 12) with particular reference to their spirit-filled attainments, such as 'signs and wonders' (12: 12). On their terms, these constitute the public evidence of a true apostle. If this were all he faced, Paul might counter this hyper-pneumatic apostolic concept much as he argues against the excesses of spiritualism elsewhere. He does so when he refers to his opponents in such devastating terms as 'false apostles (ψευδαπόστολοι), deceitful workmen

---

[1] *Gegner*, p. 52, nn. 1 and 2.   [2] Cf. Bornkamm, *Vorgeschichte*, p. 11.

(ἐργάται δόλιοι) disguising themselves (μετασχηματιζόμενοι) as apostles of Christ' just as 'Satan disguises himself as an angel of light' (11: 13, 14). Nevertheless, taken in its entirety, Paul's polemic is equivocal. Why does he, who delights in taking a minor issue and moving its discussion back to fundamentals, settle here instead for arguing at the level his opponents have chosen, the level of personal assault and defense?

For Käsemann the symbol of this problem is the shift between 11: 4 ('For if someone comes and preaches another Jesus than the one we preached or if you receive a different Spirit from the one you received or if you accept a different gospel from the one you accepted, you submit to it readily enough') and 11: 5 ('I think that I am not in the least inferior to these superlative apostles'). Käsemann's solution is to distinguish between the false apostles (11: 13) and the superlative apostles (11: 5). The former are pneumatic opponents in Corinth, the latter the Jerusalem apostles whose authority the former subtly invoke on their own behalf.[1] The relationship between these two groups Käsemann finds confirmed in the 'letters of recommendation' (3: 1) which the opponents bear. Since Paul connects the matter of his κανών with that of 'recommendation' (10: 12ff.), it seems that these letters must have been of an official character, i.e., 'the opponents were a delegation with commissioned authority from a third party',[2] in this case the Jerusalem Church. But since that Church is run by a corporate body[3] of which the apostles themselves are but representative, and since we know of the animosity toward Paul of the παρείσακτοι ψευδάδελφοι of Gal. 2: 4, Käsemann concludes that this anti-Pauline wing has sought 'to press their special request raised against Paul, under the eyes and banner of the original apostles',[4] by influencing a group sent to Corinth by the larger bureaucracy

[1] 'Legitimität', pp. 42ff. Käsemann's historical reconstruction is not entirely satisfactory. Cf., in addition to Bultmann (*Probleme*, pp. 20–30), E. Schweizer, *Gemeinde und Gemeindeordnung im Neuen Testament* (Zürich, 1959; AThANT 35), p. 195, n. 836; Klein, *Apostel*, p. 58, n. 248. Nevertheless, it is still necessary to answer Käsemann's perfectly cogent question about how 11: 4 and 11: 5 can stand side by side. Much of the criticism directed against him does not do so.
[2] *Ibid.*, p. 45.
[3] I.e., the δοκοῦντες, Gal. 2, following Schlier, *Galater, ad loc.*
[4] 'Legitimität', p. 47.

for the specific task of inspection. As a result, Paul must encounter and refute his hostile opponents by means which will
leave the Jerusalem Church untouched. Hemmed in by this
necessity, he proceeds with a dialectical argument and a personal
polemic which only exaggerates his inability to transcend the
level of polemic originally directed against him.

With this set of coordinates Käsemann plots what he calls the
'principle of tradition' (*Traditionsprinzip*) which informs Paul's
opponents and establishes behind them the apostolic claim. It is
a principle against which Paul must make good his own apostolic
claim. Hence the appropriateness of speaking of 'legitimacy' in
II Cor. 10–13.[1] We prefer to translate Käsemann's term
Traditionsprinzip as 'the principle of traditional authority', for
what he has in mind is an element like one from Weber's well-
known tripartite scheme of legitimate authority: legal, traditional and charismatic.[2] The appeal to a 'traditional authority'
explains why Paul must take the challenge so seriously even
though his opponents have raised, specifically, only *ad hominem*
arguments against him.[3] For confirmation, Käsemann's thesis
requires that we agree with his reading of two central passages,
3: 1ff. and 10: 12ff.

In 10: 12ff. Paul says:

We do not dare to classify or compare ourselves with some of those
recommending themselves. Instead, we measure ourselves with
reference to ourselves and compare ourselves to ourselves. We shall
not boast beyond limits, but according to the measure of the
standard God apportioned to us as a measure, to reach even to you.[4]

It is difficult to decide whether Paul accuses his opponents of
boasting beyond limits[5] or they level the charge at him.[6] The
rebuke seems mutual.[7] The issue is not whether there should be

---

[1] And in 2: 14 – 7: 4 also, to which Käsemann makes only passing
reference.   [2] Cf. Weber, *ES* 1, 3 (pp. 212ff.).
[3] It is clear that the opponents represent not only an extrinsic authority,
but also an intrinsic one. This subtlety is what Käsemann's essay seeks to get
at. In Weber's terms (and not necessarily in Paul's) the intrinsic authority is
'charismatic'.
[4] This deliberately overly-literal translation omits (with D, G, it.,
Ambrst., etc.) the words οὐ συνιᾶσιν ἡμεῖς δέ. Cf. Käsemann, 'Legitimität',
p. 57; Bultmann, *Probleme*, p. 21; Windisch, *Korinther*, p. 309.
[5] Bultmann, *Probleme*, p. 21.
[6] Käsemann, 'Legitimität', pp. 56ff.   [7] Georgi, *Gegner*, p. 231, n. 1.

norms, but which norms are to be accepted. In this disagreement, indeed in these very verses, *the central element is the ἐγώ of
those who claim to be apostles*, whether Paul or his opponents.

Precisely for that reason it is impossible to accept the whole
of Käsemann's interpretation. Certainly there is at work for the
opponents some principle of tradition, as we shall see. It may
be perfectly satisfactory to describe it, as Käsemann does, as a
worldly, tangible, fleshly principle over against which Paul has
no appeal except to himself. But it is crucial to see that this
'principle' does not reside outside the opponents either. It has
no substance outside their person; it certainly is not tied to some
bureaucratic table of organization. The delicacy of the problem, and part of the reason Paul decides to meet his attackers
on 'their' ground, is that the ground is actually common. Their
κανών is no more detachable from their apostolic ἐγώ than is
his. The ἐγώ is quite different in the two cases, but the problem
of criteria is similar. The opponents do not represent or appeal
to 'objective marks of the apostolate which are subject to control'.[1] In fact, 'a *Traditionsprinzip* in a legal sense cannot be
found among the opponents'.[2] This is what makes the argument so elusive, yet important. Käsemann is quite right in insisting that we have a conflict between two very different
standards of apostolic authority, but it is doubtful that it is a
conflict over 'legitimacy', or between a sense of legitimacy and
a sense of authority. One is tempted to try to fit the situation
of II Corinthians into Weber's scheme. It does not fit entirely
comfortably because Weber, like Käsemann, presupposes the
idea of legitimacy. But clearly Käsemann's assessment of the
importance of *tradition* in the opponents' position is sound, and
Weber has taught us to regard that as only one mode of authority.

The 'letters of recommendation' in 3: 1ff. are scarcely
official, binding, authoritative documents.[3] Decisive against that
view is the fact that the opponents not only *bring* letters of recommendation *to* Corinth, but also *solicit* them *from* Corinth.[4]
These letters can scarcely be documents of authorization
guaranteeing legitimacy by appeal to established and recognized
authority (cf. Acts 9: 1ff., 22: 4). Nevertheless, the letters are

[1] 'Legitimität', p. 59.   [2] Georgi, *Gegner*, p. 229, n. 3.
[3] Bultmann, *Probleme*, p. 21.
[4] *Ibid.*, p. 22; Schmithals, *Gnosis*[2], p. 108, n. 2.

intended to authorize, and are a concrete form of commendation. Their true function, and the fact that such letters are
introduced by the opponents, is hinted at in the relationship of
parts (a) and (b) of 3: 1. The term συνιστάνειν, characteristic
of this stage of Paul's correspondence, indicates the repeated
posture of the opponents. But we have already seen in 10: 12,
where the term also occurs, that the charge of συνιστάνειν
ἑαυτόν is mutually used as a rebuke. Thus, while in 3: 1a Paul
might be either defending himself or accusing others, in 3: 1b
we see that the custom of the letters is directly related to his
opponents' habit of self-commendation. Why are they com-
mendable, and by whom? If we can answer this question per-
suasively, we shall be able to isolate and locate the apostolic
ἐγώ of the opponents, in contrast to Paul's. To do so, we must
look at the opposition in 2: 14 – 7: 4 and 10–13.

We may begin with this idea of self-recommendation which
seems so important in Paul's perception of these people. In
addition to 3: 1 Paul mentions this in 4: 2, suggesting that their
recommendation depends on adulterating God's word. The
centrality of the idea is underlined by references in 5: 12, 6: 4,
10: 12 and 12: 11. Closely tied to this is the notion of boasting,
10: 13 (cf. 10: 8; 11: 10ff.; 12: 1ff.). The fact that Paul boasts,
however uncomfortably, suggests he is merely meeting the
competition.

Georgi has shown that the fuss over Paul's refusal to take remuneration from Corinth (11: 7ff.; 12: 13ff.) is tied to a basic
item in the opponents' own sense of identity, and in an interesting, twofold manner. First, Paul's accusation that the opponents
are mere peddlers of God's word (καπηλεύοντες, 2: 17) suggests
that they expect to live from their missionary activity and are
able to do so. The term recalls Plato's distaste for the Sophists,
who, in his opinion, merchandized truth.[1] More important, this
remuneration is regarded by them as not merely a payment, but
a positive affirmation of their pneumatic endowment, so that
Paul's failure to participate in such a scheme becomes *prima facie*
evidence of his failure (ultimately, of course, his inability) to
share every spiritual gift with the Corinthians.[2] That is why it is

---

[1] (*Prot.*, 313 CD). Windisch, *Korinther*, p. 100, gives a list of passages
expressing the complaint that truth is debased by hawking it.
[2] Cf. Georgi, *Gegner*, pp. 234ff.

treated as a rupture of the proper relationship between Paul and the community.

Thus we are led to the general πνεῦμα doctrine of the opponents, the major issue which separates them from Paul. The opponents characterize themselves by reference to their performance under the spirit, such as in apostolic signs and wonders (12: 12). They claim that Christ speaks through them but not through Paul (13: 3). All this Paul summarizes and comprehends within one magnificent charge. They lay claim to 'another spirit' (11: 4).

It is a peculiar notion. While Paul may characterize his opponents as servants of Satan rather than, as they claim, servants of Christ,[1] this would constitute only a metaphorical πνεῦμα ἕτερον, as is shown by the fact that he nowhere attempts to elucidate a demonic spirit which is theirs. As we have seen, Paul's response elsewhere to hyperpneumatics is to stress the radically other nature of a future they ignore and emphasize the present reality of a contingency, a weakness and death, which they abhor. In other words, in these arguments Paul's eschatology comes to the fore.

Such is also the case in II Corinthians, especially in 3: 1ff., but with this telling difference. In I Corinthians the opponents were appealing to a future which they regarded as already present. In order to counteract this Paul must appeal to a past and appeals to *his* past to show the real, the contingent quality of the present. In II Corinthians Paul is confronted with opponents who themselves appeal to the past and seek to impose it on the present. In response, Paul's vision of the 'apostolic' present is constructed in large measure from a sharply eschatological, even faintly apocalyptic, image of the future.

This appeal from the opposition turns in part on their appropriation of a Moses typology, in part on their understanding of the Old Testament as the 'archive of the Spirit'.[2] In 3: 14–18 we have a capsule summary of the close connection these false apostles have drawn among several elements: (a) the principle of tradition as embodied in the Old Testament; (b) the figure of Moses, at once identical with the παλαιὰ διαθήκη[3] and him-

---

[1] *Ibid.*, pp. 244ff., 258ff.   [2] *Ibid.*, pp. 265–82.
[3] Cf. the parallelism of vv. 13 and 14, the presence of the Moses figure in vv. 15 and 16.

self a θεῖος ἀνήρ;[1] and (c) the Christian pneumatic who is being changed from one degree of glory into another and so is also θεῖος ἀνήρ. In this understanding of tradition and its relation to Spirit, the veil (κάλυμμα) mentioned in the Old Testament text (Exod. 34: 29ff.) is regarded negatively by Paul (v. 13b) but positively by the opponents, who see it as both the device which separates the true pneumatic (like Moses) from the people and the device which leads to spiritual attainment, where spiritual attainment is itself a repetition of the process of unveiling, turning to the Lord. This process is conversion. Specifically, it is conversion at the hands of the Christian pneumatic preacher.[2]

So radically different from Paul's is this understanding of the spirit that it is no surprise he attributes to his opponents 'another spirit'. We can also see why he charges them with having 'another gospel' in 11: 4. What this means concretely can be seen in reference to 4: 3, 'and even if our gospel is veiled, it is veiled only to those who are perishing'. The claim that Paul's gospel is veiled is not a charge levelled at him by the Corinthian opponents[3] and it does not anticipate the lament of II Peter 3: 16, as sometimes supposed.[4] The term 'veiled' has been introduced by the opponents' understanding of the Old Testament and Moses[5] and is in fact a positive term as much as it is a negative one. The claim that his gospel is veiled is Paul's own appropriation of his opponents' terminology. Opposite this stands what is described in 4: 2 as 'the open statement of the truth', which Paul also claims for himself in direct contrast to the opponents. Why, then, does he speak of 'his' gospel as 'veiled'?

We recall that when Paul speaks of 'my (our) gospel' he indicates that close identification of eschatology with the gospel itself, an identification which takes form in his own apostolic person and stresses the 'pregnant' nature of the gospel. Although here the polemic is sharper than in other passages where the phrase occurs, the essential meaning is the same. A basic eschatological note is struck in the phrase 'veiled only to those who are perishing', a phrase which alerts us to the entire

[1] Philo, *Mos.*, ii, 69f.
[3] Lietzmann, *Korinther*, p. 115.
[5] Windisch, *Korintherbrief*, p. 134.
[2] *Gegner*, pp. 270–1.
[4] Plummer, *Corinthians*, p. 113.

apocalyptic/eschatological matrix of Paul's remarks extending from 2: 15 ('those who are being saved...those who are perishing'). The 'other' gospel to which Paul refers, and to which he contrasts 'his' gospel, is thought of more in terms of consequences than content. The consequences of his opponents' gospel culminate in a *present* reality of spiritual perfection. The consequences of 'his' gospel culminate in a *future* judgment already inaugurated through his preaching in the present ('*are being* saved...destroyed'). Paul's opponents stress continuity with the past (Old Testament, Moses) and perfection in the present, while he stresses discontinuity with the past (Old Testament, Moses) and a culmination in the future. This is entirely consistent with Paul's understanding of the 'gospel' as we have found it thus far, and trades heavily on the gospel's capacity to define an historical sphere pointing toward a genuine historical future and climax.

While the images in 2: 14ff. are complex and the problem of identifying the strands of thought and catchwords with either Paul or his opponents makes the task of interpretation delicate, we should not lose sight of the fundamental consistency of II Corinthians with what we have been able to observe elsewhere about eschatology and its relationship to 'tradition' and 'gospel'. For Paul, the eschatological matrix turns 'tradition' into 'gospel'. It is not oversimplification to say that for his opponents, especially as revealed by a close analysis of 3: 7ff.,[1] 'tradition' turns 'gospel' into their spiritualistic, realized eschatology.

All of this impinges on our central problem, the identity of the opponents. We cannot lose sight of this, for the text which hovers in the background of our analysis, 11: 4, itself suggests (as Käsemann noted), by its continuation in 11: 5, that the matter of 'another gospel, another spirit' has something concrete to do with the apostolic claim behind the opponents. But what about 'another Jesus' in that trilogy of 11: 4? What does this say about the identity of the opponents and their 'apostolic' self-consciousness? The logical place to look for elucidation is 5: 16: Ὥστε ἡμεῖς ἀπὸ τοῦ νῦν οὐδένα οἴδαμεν κατὰ σάρκα· εἰ καὶ ἐγνώκαμεν κατὰ σάρκα Χριστόν, ἀλλὰ νῦν

---

[1] Cf. the efforts of Georgi, *Gegner*, pp. 274–82 and S. Schulz, 'Die Decke des Moses', *ZNW* 49 (1958), 1–30.

οὐκέτι γινώσκομεν. If Paul's opponents are hellenistic-Jewish missionaries, it is doubtful that this passage concerns the contrast between some direct connections which they have with the historical Jesus and Paul's distance from the historical Jesus.

In fact, 5: 16 is part of the emphasis on continuity and discontinuity which we have suggested is the crux of the argument between Paul and the opponents, as can be seen by a glance at its context.[1] Paul does not 'commend himself' and takes no pride in his position (vv. 12, 13). The love of Christ controls him (v. 14), a love expressed in Christ's death for all, which is itself all men's death (v. 14) to themselves that those living might live 'for him who for their sake died and was raised'. Here is the discontinuity signalled and symbolized by the 'death' of all men in Christ's death. We are reminded of Paul's references to 'conversion' in Galatians as a similar symbol of discontinuity couched in the event of Jesus' death and resurrection. And we have already seen that the moment of conversion for the opponents is symbolized by the 'veil' motif which stresses *continuity* with the old, in contrast to Paul's emphasis on *discontinuity*.

'Living to oneself', now precluded by death in Christ, Paul regards as 'commending oneself'. There is an unmistakable polemical tinge to 5: 16c: 'So that from now on we know no one κατὰ σάρκα'. Knowing someone κατὰ σάρκα is the equivalent of priding oneself on one's position, ἐν προσώπῳ καυχωμένων. In tandem with v. 16a, 16b is merely an illustrative, albeit extreme, example,[2] while the main thread of this thought continues in v. 17 with its contrast of καινή and ἀρχαῖα.[3] It is not necessary to assume, indeed it is impossible, that v. 16b reflects the actual christology of the opponents, if by that we mean that they lay a heavy stress on 'knowing Christ according to the flesh', i.e., prize the earthly, historical Jesus and their (or somebody's) earlier contact with him. But what of the possibility that κατὰ σάρκα is to be taken with Χριστόν and not the

---

[1] Schmithals regards 5: 16 as a gnostic gloss ('Zwei gnostische Glossen im zweiten Korintherbrief', *EvTh* 18 [1958], 552ff., now in the appendix to *Gnosis*², pp. 286–99). Cf. Güttgemanns, who takes 5: 16b as a gnostic gloss (*Apostel*, pp. 282ff., p. 294).

[2] Bultmann, *Probleme*, p. 17.   [3] Georgi, *Gegner*, p. 257.

verb, that it is objective rather than subjective, 'qualifying the view of the person who is estimated'?[1]

Georgi has pressed this view, seeing in the opponents a proclivity to glorify the earthly Jesus as a θεῖος ἀνήρ[2] and relating 5: 16b to the 'christology'.[3] The substance of this 'Jesus christology' is the attraction of the figure of Jesus to the pattern of Moses as divine man. Georgi concludes that 'Jesus' is the core term for the opposition, as seems evident in 11: 4 and in the frequency of the name in the polemical fragments where it occurs much more often than in the rest of Paul's letters. Confirmation is offered by 4: 5f., where Paul contrasts himself with the opponents. Paul does not preach himself but Χριστὸν Ἰησοῦν κύριον and himself as δοῦλος of the community. Paul misses in his opponents both a proper respect for Jesus and a sense of his lordship, stressed by the emphatic location of κύριον. In short, Ἰησοῦς, their term, is countered with κύριος, Paul's term.

What holds true for the relationship of gospel and apostle in II Corinthians as Paul understands them, also holds true for the relationship between christology and apostolic identity. Paul tries to tie firmly the knots between the apostle and these other ideas, and he does so by eschatological appeals. When we look closely at 5: 1 – 6: 10 as constituting the context of 5: 16f., we find that Paul not only stresses discontinuity with the past in 5: 16f., but that this theme is carried over to the idea of proclaiming the gospel, quite explicitly in 5: 30f., 6: 1ff. At the same time, a theme more familiar to us from I Corinthians, the discrete nature of a present which awaits fulfillment but can only be fulfilled in the future, shines through much of 5: 1–15. These two broad and compatible perceptions may be said to flank 5: 16–17, which stands as a watershed between them. Together, they provide the warp and woof of the fabric of Paul's eschatology. On the one hand Paul stresses the organic unity of the future fulfillment of the present, especially in the polemically tinged reference to the πνεῦμα as ἀρραβών (5: 5). On the other, the present is contrasted with the past as the time of reconciliation made possible by the event of Christ's 'recon-

[1] Plummer, *Corinthians*, p. 176. For the difficulty of choosing between objective and subjective, cf. Windisch, *Korintherbrief*, p. 187.
[2] *Gegner*, pp. 282ff.　　　　　　[3] *Ibid.*, pp. 290ff.

ciling the world to himself' (5: 19). Yet Paul's eschatology, always dialectical, takes on a color here to match the occasion of his quarrel. Thus in 5: 1–10 we are impressed also by the contrasts between present and future: 'naked...clothed' (vv. 3–4), 'faith...sight' (v. 7), 'away...at home' (vv. 6, 9). In 6: 1–10, similarly, discontinuity is modulated by the contact between past and present symbolized in the quotation from Isa. 49: 8.

To understand what this eschatological matrix has to do with the perception of the apostolic ἐγώ we must recall not only the role eschatology plays for Paul in transforming tradition into 'gospel', but also the fundamental way in which he yokes gospel and apostle – his particular 'identification' of the two. Frequently Paul appeals to himself and his own circumstances. Heretofore, he has done so in order to illustrate what he calls the truth of the gospel, not to defend the legitimacy of his apostolic claim. The apostle illustrates the gospel he seeks to uphold, confirm and defend against assaults and attempted perversions. He can do so because the authority of the gospel is the authority of the apostle.

Paul relies on quite the same network of associations in II Corinthians. Repeatedly, he links references to his ministry with illustrations of his form in the ministry, particularly to the circumstantial catalogs found in 4: 7–12 and 6: 4–10. How central the *peristasis* catalog is for Paul is confirmed by I Cor. 4: 8–13, but even more importantly by the way he slips into it in II Cor. 11: 23bff. It is, as v. 23 shows, his sign of being a διάκονος Χριστοῦ, a διάκονος θεοῦ (6: 4). What started as an ironic, even sarcastic 'boast', with Paul speaking as a 'fool' (11: 21b), soon becomes entirely serious. He will boast of things that display his weakness (11: 30).

In II Corinthians the term διάκονος emerges as a self-designation of the opponents, one which Paul will not deny to them but which he significantly reinterprets in reference to himself. This and the companion words διακονία, διακονεῖν play an obscure and varied role in early Christian literature. The root meaning of the stem suggests service, and the connotation of abasement is evident even in classical Greek literature.[1] Paul uses the terms in two quite different senses. One of these con-

---

[1] H. Beyer, 'διακονέω etc.', *TDNT*, II, pp. 81–93.

cerns the 'service' of the collection he gathers for Jerusalem (II Cor. 8: 4, 19, 20; 9: 1, 13).[1] The other refers to his ministry (II Cor. 3: 6; 4: 1; 5: 18; 6: 3f.). Passages such as I Cor. 3: 5 (Paul and Apollos) and Rom. 11: 13 make it clear that Paul could regard himself as a διάκονος, his work as διακονία. Used this way the terms scarcely have any technical flavor. But it is also the case that the *opponents* style *themselves* διάκονοι Χριστοῦ (11: 23). This may be as close as we come in II Corinthians to anything resembling a titular self-reference, though the opponents must have called themselves ἀπόστολοι as well in order to elicit Paul's sarcasm in 11: 13 (cf. 11: 5). The term ἀπόστολος is certainly fluid in Paul's use and II Corinthians provides no sharper definition. Instead, the close associations in 11: 13, 15 suggest that διάκονος is virtually its equivalent,[2] while 12: 12 assures us that the opponent laid claim to apostolic signs. If so, they must have laid claim to apostolic rank as well, while the phrase διάκονος Χριστοῦ was their preferred term.[3]

Whatever the origin of Paul's use of διακονία for 'ministry' and διάκονος for himself,[4] and whatever the penumbra around these terms when they are used in other contexts, in the setting of this argument Paul's use is instructive. He draws on the implications of submission inherent in the idea of service, stressing those tangible and concrete instances of his submission which are his 'sufferings' and the evidence of his 'weakness'. Paul actually co-opts the image of the 'worthless' or insufficient one who is made worthy only from without (by grace) and thereby sets his own apostolic image in diametrical opposition to that of his opponents. The stress on Paul's being quite other than, even opposite to, the superlative apostles should not obscure the fact that, as elsewhere in this section, here again Paul appears to take his cue from his opponents. He reacts; he appears to be on the defensive.

It seems puzzling that Paul would never provide the theoretical statement of his position, never move to the offensive and its higher ground which so characteristically he likes to command. But we do have important images in the Pauline position

---

[1] Cf. Rom. 15: 25, 31. [2] Plummer, *Corinthians*, p. 321.

[3] Georgi, *Gegner*, pp. 32–49.

[4] The notion of submission is persistent (cf. Rom. 13: 4 for a quite distinctive example) and more important than Georgi allows in his review. Cf. E. Schweizer, *Das Leben des Herrn in der Gemeinde und ihren Diensten* (Zürich, 1946; AThANT 8).

which tell a great deal. One of these is διάκονος. Paul implicitly transforms the definition of διάκονος in his collateral stress on the apostle as one who serves the community. His 'service' to the community was carried out at cost to others, but not to the Corinthians themselves (11: 8). This he specifically calls 'abasement' (v. 7) and contrasts with the Corinthians' own opportunity for exaltation. Mixing the metaphor only slightly, he is and shall be gladly spent (δαπανᾶσθαι) ὑπὲρ τῶν ψυχῶν ὑμῶν (12: 15). We see in 13: 9 how central are the reciprocal relationships between Paul's faith and that of the Corinthians and the contrast between their respective circumstances: 'We rejoice when we are weak but you are strong.'

Thus the catalogs of Paul's unhappy circumstances, the serial lists of his apparent weakness, are here pressed into service to elucidate the διακονία motif. We have already seen in I Cor. 4 and 15 the primacy of this apostolic profile and how closely tied it is to Paul's understanding and appropriation of Jesus' death. The apostle's circumstances make of him a living manifestation of grace, an idea finally linked to his whole autobiography in Gal. 1 and 2. What is different in II Corinthians is the way in which this profile is given a sharper polemical edge even while it remains anchored to the stylized form of the *peristasis* catalog and the theological idea of grace. This is evident enough in 6: 2ff. (cf. v. 11). Paul is a fellow worker with God, appealing that the Corinthians should not now prove to have accepted God's grace in vain – i.e., show they have stepped outside the sphere of the gospel. He ties his understanding of διακονία–διάκονος to this appeal in vv. 3 and 4 and shows that his ministry demands he be a servant in terms of the apostolic profile (vv. 4ff.). That his expression has a polemical edge (συνιστάνοντες ἑαυτοὺς ὡς θεοῦ διάκονοι, v. 4) is revealed by a glance at 10: 12. Thus he explicitly lays claim to this profile as a self-understanding which is alternative to that of his opponents. If there were any doubt about this it would be dispelled by the recognition that for Paul χάρις provides 'sufficiency' (I Cor. 15: 9), and the idea of sufficiency is itself a catch phrase among the self-sufficient superlative apostles.[1]

[1] Georgi (*Gegner*, pp. 220ff.) is more confident of the technical nuance of ἱκανός than the evidence warrants. Clearly Paul knew and liked the contrast of grace and insufficiency. This is explicit in I Cor. 15: 9, implicit through-

This polemical edge is further honed in 4: 5 where Paul accuses his opponents of preaching themselves and contrasts his preaching of Jesus Christ with himself as a servant. Here the word is even less ambiguous, δοῦλος. Again, the *peristasis* catalog follows close on the heels of this remark (4: 8–11). And again (4: 13) Paul stresses the second contrast, that with the community: 'Death is at work in us, but life in you.'

We have seen that it is difficult for Paul to rise above the terms set by his opposition. This double contrast, with its emphasis on the disparity between the exalted Corinthians and the humbled Paul, is an important feature in his attempt to transcend his opponents' terms. It is obvious that in manipulating the διακονία theme Paul contradicts his opponents' polemic. But he is also trying to open up an offensive operation and restructure the argument in terms he finds more congenial. His repeated references to the contrast between himself and the Corinthians, and the mode of his service to them, suggest the nature of this attack within a defense. The picture is further clarified by 5: 20 – 6: 2 and its relationship to 6: 3, which yields evidence of the theoretical distance between Paul and his opponents and the distinctive shape of his own assumptions about the apostolic form.

Paul's notion of reconciliation takes as its origin the death of Christ as an act of grace ('not reckoning to them their trespasses', 5: 19) but ties to this immediately the idea of a ministry of reconciliation, διακονία τῆς καταλλαγῆς (5: 18) which centers in a word of reconciliation, λόγος τῆς καταλλαγῆς (5: 19). As 5: 20 makes clear, Christ is thus extended through his ambassadors. Reconciliation, far from being confined to his death, is accomplished through the ministry by which God makes appeal.[1] In terms of our earlier analysis, the gospel is the extension of the Christ-event. For this reason Paul can speak of his working together with God (6: 1). How seriously he takes this idea is shown by his exegesis of the LXX passage he quotes,

out Gal. 1 and 2. Hence his opponents might have picked up casually at first an idea originally contributed by Paul, eventually to turn it to their own account.

[1] It should not be overlooked that 5: 21 provides the christological parallel and antecedent to the contrast between humiliation and exaltation which Paul applies to himself and the community. On the *imitatio* motif, cf. below, pp. 226ff.

Isa. 49: 8. The passage itself is poetic and constructed in typically parallel fashion: 'At the acceptable time I have listened to you' is rephrased in the second line: 'and helped you on the day of salvation'. The soteriological extension of this idea into the present Paul provides in 6: 2b. But more important, 6: 3 shows Paul interpreting Isa. 49: 8b as if it were independent of 49: 8a. *He* is the helper. This is his διακονία. In the wake of 5: 20ff., 6: 3ff. is not abrupt[1] except in a grammatical sense,[2] and there is no interruption in the train of thought.[3] Windisch is correct in pointing out the homiletical character of the quotation from Isaiah, which we may identify with missionary proclamation. It is important to notice the exploitation of a missionary motif in this setting. Paul is trading heavily on the eschatological character of 'gospel' as an entity which overcomes the contingency of Jesus (5: 16f.) and which dominates a sphere of existence in which there is no distinction between hearing the gospel for the first time and hearing it now. It is always to be heard anew because in it the Christian 'stands'. It is always to be heard lest grace be 'in vain'.

Out of this background Paul regards the Church not only as a missionary enterprise, to be called, but also as a pastoral enterprise, to be sustained and disciplined. The gospel's authority covers both the apostle's original responsibility and a continuing responsibility for the community. As a result, Paul can mix rather promiscuously the metaphor of himself as servant of God and servant of the Corinthian Church, as indeed he does throughout the polemical fragments. By this means Paul injects a new note and tries to move beyond a merely defensive position. Without dropping the polemical challenge he seeks to transcend it. He rearranges the argument by inserting a new dimension of apostolic *responsibility* to and for the community.[4] The ruling metaphor for this idea is 'building up', which we shall examine later in more detail.[5] For now it suffices to notice

[1] Lietzmann, *Korinther*, p. 127.

[2] Cf. Kümmel's remarks, Lietzmann (-Kümmel), *Korinther*, p. 205, and Bultmann, *Probleme*, p. 20.

[3] Windisch, *Korintherbrief* (pp. 201–3) supposes the text to have been disturbed.

[4] This, of course, always carries its corollary of community responsibility to and for the apostle, a matter which Paul treats in a highly dialectical way in II Cor.   [5] Cf. below, ch. 8.

that in appropriating the idea of διακονία to his apostolic profile Paul not only sharpens the polemic but extends the concept of the διάκονος. 'For we do not preach *ourselves*, but Jesus Christ as Lord and *ourselves* as *your servants* (δούλους) for Jesus' sake' (4: 5).

Despite Paul's eagerness and capacity for extending the range of terms apparently at home in his opponents' most intimate vocabulary, it must be said that the process of transforming the argument is of modest scope. He restructures the argument only with reference to the terms themselves. Otherwise, he remains within the boundaries supplied by his opponents' polemic. Why? Why, if Paul feels genuinely contemptuous in 11: 4, does he suddenly wish to become competitive in 11: 5? Käsemann's question deserves an answer.

Paul's thought moves in both directions along an axis represented by his use of the terms 'gospel' and 'apostle'. It is most characteristic of him to argue from the gospel to the apostle if he seeks to elucidate the significance of his being an apostle; from the apostle to the gospel if he seeks to confirm the truth of the gospel. In either case, he needs a firm conception of 'gospel' with which to work, whether it is supplied by himself or by another. This conception is precisely what he lacks for the opponents in II Cor. 2: 14 – 7: 4 and 10–13. *His* paradigmatic argument would run: The truth of the gospel warrants the apostle; their gospel is not true, therefore, they are 'false apostles'. But in contrast with Galatians, for example, where Paul has some sense of the shape of 'another' gospel, here he does not. He does not know the Corinthian polemicists' 'gospel'. As for *his* half of the argument, it must run from the apostle to the gospel, because his apostolic credentials are at stake. This Paul manages successfully enough. But he is never able to transfer the argument from one about apostles to one about gospels because he cannot isolate 'their' gospel as a foil over against 'his'.

The reason for this is not that Paul knew too little to identify their gospel. It is, rather, that their gospel is no way detachable from their claims about themselves; it is indistinguishable from them. Heretofore, Paul's own identification of gospel and apostle has seemed radical enough, but now we see that while the two terms are shaped by each other, and perhaps can be

183

considered extensions of one another, they are ultimately distinct. They are not collapsed for Paul. For his opponents they *are*.

This subtle difference is all-important for understanding the
shape of apostolic authority in the earliest Church. *This* is the
difference between legitimacy and authority, or more accurately, the difference between focusing on the question of
apostolic legitimacy and focusing on apostolic authority. For
Paul the gospel warrants apostolic authority. It does not define
apostolic legitimacy, and where he runs into that problem, as in
Galatians, he leaves it unresolved. But for his opponents the
beginning and end of the question is comprehended by the idea
of legitimacy itself. By their lights, the 'measure' of the apostle
is a legitimacy quotient cast in terms of external standards and
signs of belonging, cast in terms of 'legitimacy norms'.[1] Presence
of the signs indicates belonging to the group, but the group defines the terms. They deny finding the signs in Paul and hence
deny not *Paul's* claims, but Paul's *access* to *their* claims. That is
an awkward position to be put in and to argue against, and it is
no wonder that Paul finds it so difficult to get off the defensive.
Yet by attacking his 'legitimacy' they have raised for Paul the
problem of authority, for they have made themselves 'authors'
of the standards they proclaim. They 'measure' with no external
standards. But they can assume that measurement, while Paul
must first locate it, then argue it.

This marks in our text the profound difference between two
perceptions of the apostolic ἐγώ. At the surface they might appear to be alike. Certainly Paul, were he concerned with legitimacy, would have to say that all apostles exhibit his apostolic
profile. And indeed, this is what he is trenching on in his rebuke
to Peter. But Paul is not interested in the matter of legitimacy
per se. He is interested in the prior question of authority, i.e., the
question of who authorizes what is common to all legitimate
apostles and what is the substance of this authority. From the
point of view of legitimacy this is a matter of indifference,
strictly speaking, for the question has been pre-empted by the
question of legitimacy.

It would not have been necessary to rehearse the arguments
in II Corinthians merely to show that Paul's answer to his own

[1] T. Parsons, *The Structure of Social Action* (New York, 1937/1968),
pp. 658ff.

question of authority was the gospel, which we already knew. But the arguments here show that this is not true for the opponents, who can point to nothing beyond themselves. Paul cannot argue against their 'other gospel' because there really is none functioning as he thinks a gospel must. If it were otherwise, he could eschew the personal attacks he finds necessary. But he cannot because their person is their gospel. The 'other' gospel of 11 : 4 is, from Paul's perspective, a logical necessity. From the opponents' side, it is not. Their claims are entirely self-authenticating because they are entirely self-referential.

Thus Paul can show that they have no answer to the question of the role of the gospel, they have no conceptual link between themselves and anything external to themselves. Even the tradition they prize in 3: 7ff. only leads to the pneumatic apostle by arbitrary identifications: The Old Testament is Moses, Moses is θεῖος ἀνήρ, Jesus is θεῖος ἀνήρ, Jesus is Moses, they are θεῖοι ἄνδρες, they are Moses and Jesus. In opposition to this Paul sets the scheme now familiar to us. In it he underscores the idea of historical contingency in his autobiographical references, stressing that history is given shape and interpretation by the death of Jesus in the past and the resurrection of the Christian in the future.

The argument proceeds with incommensurate ideas from the two sides, and we might ask why Paul engages in it at all. He does so because they wish him to prove his legitimacy and if he were to do so, on his own grounds, he could only do so by the same principle they use, by reference to himself. He would have no other choice. But his conception of the apostolic self is entirely different from theirs. It is a 'controlled' self,[1] a self subordinated to something beyond it. It is the concept of a δοῦλος. As I Corinthians and Galatians show, that to which Paul's apostolic ἐγώ is subordinated is the gospel. Paul has only two choices when confronted with this kind of problem. He may let it go unopposed, which would mean sanctioning what is implicitly 'another gospel'. Or he may wrestle with the question of the apostolic self, which is in effect to play their game. This he does even while disowning the effort, for obvious reasons. This accounts for the derision and competition side by side, for the fact that he castigates his opponents even while he plays the

---

[1] II Cor. 5: 14.

'fool' they say he is. It accounts for the fact that immediately after 11: 4 comes 11: 5.

In his argument Paul has introduced the whole role of the community in the life of the apostle and the idea of apostolic authority as discipline as well as proclamation. He has spoken of his charge to 'build up'. He has suggested the very important role played by his concepts of history and the future, clearly part of the gospel as he understands it, in the apostolic task.

CHAPTER 7

THE CROSS AS A SYMBOL OF POWER: I COR. 1: 10 – 4: 21

As real as it is in human affairs, 'power' seems to slip through our fingers when we attempt an analysis of it. Except in its obvious physical manifestations, power resists our efforts to tease it into the open. Somehow it lurks behind its symbols, defying precise location and description. As a result, the quest for power often appears to be a quest for its symbols.

Certainly this is true of Paul's understanding of power, with this further qualification: Paul's sense of power is cast in terms of one dominant and very unusual image, the cross. This gives the whole understanding of power a thoroughly dialectical texture. Power appears as weakness and weakness as power. We are prepared for this by generous hints in Paul's autobiographical references. Although the apostle reveals the configuration of the power he interprets, the apostolic life style is scarcely an unambiguous display of power in the ordinary sense. To understand how the apostle assumes the shape of power manifested in the cross, and how the gospel is related to this central symbol, we have a rich and suggestive text in I Cor. 1: 10 – 4: 21.

In the first part of this letter Paul responds to the Corinthian situation as he has learned about it from 'Chloe's people' (1: 11). That situation is characterized by σχίσματα (1: 10) and ἔριδες (1: 11). 'What I mean is that each of you says "I belong to Paul", or "I belong to Apollos", or "I belong to Cephas", or "I belong to Christ" (1: 12).' The nature and status of these divisions is uncertain. In 3: 4 Paul reduces the list to two, himself and Apollos; in 3: 22 Cephas is again included. There Paul sets over against the claims of rivalry the contrasting phrase 'but you are of Christ' (ὑμεῖς δὲ Χριστοῦ) which may provide a clue to the 'Christ party' in 1: 12, Ἐγὼ δὲ Χριστοῦ. Were these words a gloss[1] we might suspect their

---

[1] With Weiss, *Korintherbrief*, p. xxxviii.

origin to lie in 3: 22, but there is no textual evidence for dismissing them this way. Dobschütz[1] has suggested that the phrase is Paul's rebuke to those who rally around the other three slogans. In any event, the 'Christ party' is extremely difficult to understand as a group.

It might be easier to decide about the phrase 'I belong to Christ' if we knew what motivated the other phrases. Reitzenstein has exercised considerable influence on modern interpretation with his notion that the mystery religions provide a model in which the initiate considers himself to belong to the 'father' of his initiation rite, the mystagogue.[2] But such a derivation leaves unexplained certain features of the text.

In the first instance, the connection between the parties and baptism, the Christian analogue to the mystery initiation on this scheme, is curious. Baptism is certainly a central motif in the letter. In 6: 11 Paul indicates that the Corinthians derive their particular charter of freedom from this source (cf. 6: 12ff.). The warning in 10: 1ff. suggests the same danger of misinterpretation and misappropriation. And the peculiar custom referred to in 15: 29, whatever else it shows, displays the centrality of baptism in the Corinthian thinking. But what of the disclaimer regarding Paul's own baptismal activity, 1: 14–17a? If he did so little of it in Corinth, it hardly seems likely that any sizeable group could claim an allegiance to Paul based on baptism. Yet there is a Paul party.

This leads to a second observation. The party spirit is interpreted by Paul as reflecting competing claims of authority. What kind of authority could be at stake? The evidence from the letter as a whole suggests a perception of freedom in Corinth which, (1) rightly or wrongly Paul attributes to the community as such and not to some specific leaders, and (2) is derived from a misinterpretation of the significance of baptism, one in which eschatology is collapsed. That raises a question about the kind of 'authority' which would be both consonant with this freedom

---

[1] E. v. Dobschütz, *Christian Life in the Primitive Church* (New York, 1904), p. 72.

[2] Cf. Reitzenstein, *Mysterienreligionen*, pp. 333ff.; *Poimandres* (Leipzig, 1904; Darmstadt, 1966), pp. 219f.; A. Dieterich, *Eine Mithrasliturgie* (Leipzig, 1923³; Darmstadt, 1966), pp. 52ff., 146ff. On some of the problems regarding Paul as a mystagogue cf. H.-D. Betz, *Nachfolge und Nachahmung Jesu Christi im Neuen Testament* (Tübingen, 1967; BHT 37), pp. 154ff.

and also characteristic of an apostle regarded as mystagogue. For the authority of one is obviously claimed against, in competition with, that of another. At least of Paul and Apollos this is true (3: 4ff.). Wilckens[1] senses this problem and notes that the Corinthian 'transeschatological' posture, making them 'already rich' (4: 8), means they no longer must take apostolic advice. From the eschatological vision in Corinth one can see no need for apostles.

This relates directly to another feature of the party spirit. Paul does not go on in the letter to address himself to a community in terms of its divisions, but treats the Church as a whole, even where he distinguishes τινες who hold certain opinions. He does not assign specific positions to rival factions. In fact, despite 1: 12f., the community does not seem to be 'divided' into rivalry. It seems to lack some more organic wholeness.

Specific dimensions of party strife in I Corinthians are beyond our grasp because of the way Paul approaches the community. Throughout the letter he makes clear his diagnosis. Corinth suffers from a collapsed eschatology and a misplaced sense of freedom. He has reduced the Corinthian problem to this central core, the origin of which lies in the Corinthian conception of baptism. Thus it is *Paul* who equates the party spirit with the baptism motif in 1: 12ff., thereby suggesting that a dispute about apostolic authority is tied to this pervasive Corinthian concern. As a corollary to this it must be emphasized that Paul drives a sharp wedge indeed between baptism and preaching in 1: 17. Commentators seem at pains to point out that he does not mean to denigrate baptism by this device, but that is true only in a certain sense. Elsewhere in the letters we find baptism a central motif, a rich and suggestive image for Paul. Nevertheless, we must not overlook the fact that in this discussion the Corinthian reading of baptism is rejected out of hand, and in 1: 17 set in sharp antithesis to εὐαγγελίζεσθαι.

Before examining the reasons for this, it should be pointed out that Paul's failure to provide more evidence concerning the party strife he has heard about is not unlike his treatment of the problem of apostolic authority in Galatians. There as here the 'unity' of the Church is at stake and quite possibly here as there are to be found authoritative sanctions (apostolic in regard to

[1] U. Wilckens, *Weisheit und Torheit* (Tübingen, 1959; BHT 26), p. 17.

Peter, in both letters) which come in conflict. Paul's treatment
of Apollos illustrates his approach. He remands others to the
authority of his own fellow workers (16: 16) of whom Apollos is
one (3: 9). By stressing the unity of the Church in terms of its
foundation in power, and by implication his own apostolic
authority, Paul sidesteps the issue of possibly competing claims
to authority. As in Galatians, here too the central idea is
'gospel'. The goal of that gospel he regards as the one Church,
as we shall see in a moment. In other words, the relationship
between gospel and Church, the two key elements in his vision
of apostolic authority, the beginning and end of that authority,
as it were, is the subject of I Cor. 1: 17 – 4: 21. It is no surprise
to find that the central term linking them is 'power'.

Strangely enough, Paul begins (1: 13) not by asserting his
authority but seemingly by denying it. 'Is Christ divided? Paul
wasn't crucified for you, was he? Or were you baptized in Paul's
name?' To see the problem we need only set over against this
4: 18ff., where Paul refers to the arrogant ones who suggest he
is not going to return and threatens to expose their true claim
to power when he comes. In 1: 10 – 4: 21 we have an elaborate
exposition of apostolic authority in preparation for its specific
application in 5: 1. Why, then, does Paul virtually begin by
rejecting the support of those who say ἐγὼ μέν εἰμι Παύλου?

If we cannot understand the claims of the rival factions, that
is because Paul has driven behind them to the Corinthian perception of baptism – i.e., he treats the fragmented Church as a
theological unity. We must begin by taking this seriously. Paul's
vision of the sociology of the Church is essentially a theological
vision in which the terms of membership and the terms of
apostleship are parallel. Because Paul does not deal with the
Corinthian problem as the specific claims of rival factions, what
he says by way of rejecting claims on his behalf must be seen as
part of his decision to regard not factions, but something else,
as the paramount problem. In fact, the only thing which makes
1: 10 – 4: 21 a coherent prelude to the later *assertion* of apostolic
authority[1] is that Paul starts afresh with an explication of that

[1] N. A. Dahl, 'Paul and the Church at Corinth', has also noticed this
intended function of 1: 10 – 4: 21. His informal reconstruction of the
problem of factions, however (p. 325) would not account for the peculiar
disclaimer of support for Paul as evidenced in 1: 13.

upon which authority is based. He is not interested in asserting *his* authority *over against* someone else's, but genuine, apostolic authority toward the Church. This authority, as the proper interpretation of power, is part of the gospel itself, is nothing less than the charter of the Church itself. As it happens, this is an authority to which the Corinthians can lay claim, and it is the *only* authority which they can claim. If they properly perceived power they would know that. Paul's rejection of some ascription of authority to him, at the outset, is but an extension of his rejection of the Corinthian understanding, or misunderstanding, of power (4: 1–5).

When Paul asks if Christ is divided,[1] he immediately questions the Corinthians about the origin of their baptism in such a way that we must assume he regards baptism as the entrance εἰς Χριστόν and Christ as the Church. As in 12: 12f. the figure of Christ is equated with the one body, so here the figure stands for the Church. Where the Church is, there is Christ.[2] A divided community is a divided Christ.

In Rom. 6, Christ's crucifixion is the Christian's point of entry into the story of Christ, the historicizing of the Christ-myth. Subsequently, in Rom. 8, Paul regards having the spirit as requisite to belonging to Christ (Rom. 8: 9b). Hence the origin of spirit-reception is participation through baptism in Christ's crucifixion. It requires no elaborate argument to see this logic in I Cor. 1: 13ff., where Paul takes the community back to its origin in the cross. He does so not by a rehearsal of the notion of baptism, however, but by reference to the gospel as λόγος τοῦ σταυροῦ. The reasons for this are not difficult to discern. From 5: 1 forward the concrete problems of the Church are before him and he addresses himself to them as one who has authority to do so. But the presupposition of that authority is the very thing which brought this community into being (3: 5ff.) and failure to attend to it has created the current crisis. The presupposition must be examined in order to re-establish the authority itself.

Ὁ λόγος τοῦ σταυροῦ of v. 18 is anaphoric. This word of the

---

[1] Not 'shared out', C. K. Barrett, *The First Epistle to the Corinthians* (New York, 1968), p. 46.

[2] Kümmel (Leitzmann-Kümmel, *Korinther*), p. 167. In Gal. 3: 28 it is εἷς, not ἕν.

cross is foolishness to those who are perishing, but God's power to those who are being saved. The parallel dative constructions express a relationship which is not entirely clear. Perhaps Paul means that the word appears to each of these two groups in such respective fashion, in which case it is μωρία and δύναμις because they are already either perishing or being saved. Or he may wish to express the sense of advantage and disadvantage:[1] The word of the cross is in some sense responsible for their respective fates. It seems wrong to exclude either nuance.[2] At any rate, those who are perishing cannot see the word of the cross for what it is, while those who are being saved can. Yet the latter are being saved by the power of God, the gospel (Rom. 1: 16), while those who are perishing are deprived of this power.

That is an unusual idea, but one closely related to v. 17, where it is said that the cross can be emptied or rendered void. Since the cross cannot be destroyed as historical fact, there are only two possible meanings of κενοῦν here. Either Paul means its essential meaning can be destroyed, or he means that it has an effect which can be rendered impotent. These two possibilities in v. 17 correspond to the two datives in v. 18. The δύναμις of the word of the cross may be an interpretation of the cross as expressive of God's power in the present moment without particular reference to a future result. Or it may be significant of God's power in a more extended, continuing sense that does include a future result.

The terms 'those who are being saved' and 'destroyed' are familiar to us from II Cor. 4: 3 where there is an intimate connection between the consequence of the gospel and the fact that some people are being destroyed. Such a close relationship is also envisioned here. The attitude of men to the word of the cross divides them, and this division corresponds to the division at judgment. The cross itself has an eschatological, critical function which, while it does not usurp God's final judgment in irrevocable fashion, anticipates and perhaps even determines it.[3] It is this critical function, this 'power' of the word of the cross, which is in danger of being vitiated, according to v. 17.

[1] So Robertson-Plummer, *Corinthians*, p. 18.

[2] Wilckens, *Weisheit*, p. 22.

[3] 'The λόγος τοῦ σταυροῦ thus has eschatological-"critical" power.' *Ibid.*, p. 23.

The polemical thrust of this idea touches on the 'judging' tendency in Corinth.

Paul is at pains to make the cross the very focus of the gospel in Corinth: 'I decided to know nothing among you except Jesus Christ and him crucified' (2: 2; cf. 1: 23). The phrase is not merely a casual designation of the Christian preaching in general, but is chosen to single out that element within the preaching on which Paul's argument with the Corinthians turns.[1]

With v. 19 Paul 'quotes' Isa. 29: 14 (cf. Psalm 32: 10) to show that God destroys the wisdom of wise men and the understanding of those who understand. If that is the case, then quite naturally one would have to ask: 'Where is the wise man? Has not God made foolish the wisdom of the world?' With this last phrase Paul introduces a note of universality which is confirmed both by the relationship of vv. 19 and 20 and by the individual elements within these verses. The Jewish αἰὼν οὗτος, differentiating between the present age and the coming messianic era, came in time to lose something of its purely temporal significance in proportion to the way in which the qualitative distinction between this age and the coming age was stressed. 'This age' is characterized by its enslavement to its ruler, one hostile to God; the coming age is both a symbol of what may be expected, and a cipher representing the rule and power of God.[2] So both κόσμος and αἰών express a universality, just as the 'making wisdom foolish' of v. 20 and 'destroying wisdom' of v. 19 are conceived in absolute terms.[3]

Κόσμος is not only the expression of spatial and temporal totality of mankind. It is also the creation of God (Rom. 1: 20) and the object of God's judgment (Rom. 3: 6) and reconciliation (II Cor. 5: 19). It is that with which God deals in his

[1] *Ibid.*, p. 25: 'The expression ὁ λόγος τοῦ σταυροῦ is not something like a formal description of Christian proclamation in general, but rather Paul characterizes it – and apparently in polemic with the Corinthians – in a quite particular way...'

[2] Cf. Weiss, *Korintherbrief*, p. 28.

[3] If it is true, as Wilckens suggests (*Weisheit*, pp. 27f.), that the γραμματεύς and συζητητής of v. 20 represent respectively the typical Jewish and Greek form of the σοφός, this universal note is only strengthened, and Weiss' suggestion (*Korintherbrief*, p. 38) that the phrase τοῦ αἰῶνος τούτου belongs in a real sense to all three nouns of v. 20 receives some support.

acting, acting which is the subject of v. 21b. Since the world did not know God in the wisdom of God, through his wisdom (21a), God saves those who believe through the foolishness of the kerygma. The two halves of this sentence set a theme which is carried out in vv. 22 and 23f. The world did not know God, v. 21a; the Jews ask for signs and the Greeks seek wisdom (v. 22). God chose to save through the foolishness of the κήρυγμα (21b); and we preach Christ crucified (v. 23a).

The aorist tenses in v. 21 present something of a problem. By themselves they seem to set the contrary action of God and all mankind, in v. 21, in the past. Yet vv. 22 and 23, as well as v. 18, clearly imply that the human situation is neither finished nor altered, but corresponds to the statement in v. 21. So too the decision of God to effect salvation by the foolishness of the kerygma has its consequence in the present: κηρύσσομεν. We must agree with Wilckens that in v. 21 the aorist (ἔγνω; εὐδόκησεν) is an historical expression only insofar as it includes the present. Why does v. 21 throw both the failure of man and the decision of God into the past? Because a turning point in the affairs of God and the *kosmos* came in the past. Thus Paul rather abruptly turns from man as the subject of 21a to God as the subject of 21b, and uses a causal introduction to explain why God was pleased to do what he did.[1]

This turning point is the establishment of a 'new' σοφία τοῦ θεοῦ, insofar as man has failed to recognize God in his 'wisdom'. Such 'new' wisdom can be described in more than one way. It is the 'foolishness of the kerygma' of v. 21; the 'making foolish this world's wisdom' of v. 20. But in its positive aspect how does this 'new' wisdom emerge? In v. 24 Paul speaks of the σοφία θεοῦ and the δύναμις θεοῦ which is grounded in the κήρυγμα of v. 21b. It is none other than what 'we preach', Christ crucified, v. 22. The turning point implied in v. 21 is then seen to be a specific event, the crucifixion of Christ. Paul does not speak of a *new* σοφία. But inasmuch as Christ crucified is mentioned as the wisdom of God for the first time in 1: 24, i.e., after v. 21 indicates that God has inaugurated a new way of salvation, this understanding seems to be the correct one.

Yet God's decision to offer salvation to an unacknowledging world can be called a μωρία (vv. 18, 21 and 23). This can only

[1] 'Επειδή is causal. Cf. BDF, par. 455: 1 and 456: 3.

be so from the point of view of the world's wisdom, v. 20. The most startling aspect of v. 21 is that from the causal clause the conclusion does not seem to follow. We should expect that God would meet the world's disobedience in an appropriately punitive fashion. Instead, through the foolishness of the kerygma, he chooses to save those who believe.[1] Everything points to the centrality of v. 21 and the need for properly understanding it. God does not give the world a new criterion so that it can judge correctly the wisdom it has failed to perceive. God makes foolish the wisdom of the world. He destroys it. Then, at the world's failure, he offers the foolishness of the cross. There is no simple transvaluation of wisdom and foolishness to accommodate man's inept seeking and searching.

Thus it is that when Christ crucified can be called God's wisdom in v. 24, it is still the same wisdom of v. 21. It is 'new' insofar as God does something new, inaugurating a κήρυγμα based on a crucified Jesus. If Paul can call this crucified Jesus the wisdom of God (v. 24), that only means that he is the wisdom of God when man's wisdom is really destroyed. Christ is not suddenly visible as God's wisdom because God's and man's wisdom have been interchanged, but because God has decided to make foolishness wisdom. In short, there can be no Christ the σοφία θεοῦ without there being *first* Christ the μωρία by this world's standards, and the μωρία κηρύγματος based on that. There is no more human wisdom.

Nothing is said in vv. 23 and 24 to indicate that those who are called 'experience' Christ in some practical sense as the wisdom and power of God, while the Jews and Greeks of v. 23 'experience' him as scandal and foolishness. In fact, such an interpretation[2] leads us astray. Paul does not establish in the foolishness-wisdom dialectic a new means of perception which marks a distinction between Christians and the rest of the world. Insofar as they are distinguished, *it is through an action that they are what they are*. Hence, the adjective κλητός of v. 24 refers to the same act as v. 21. Yet there must be, at the same time, a dis-

---

[1] As the context makes clear, this group is not thought of as closed. It is as universal as the conjunction of 'Ιουδαῖοι καὶ Ἕλληνες (v. 22), 'Ιουδαίοις and ἔθνεσιν (v. 23) and 'Ιουδαίοις καὶ Ἕλλησιν (v. 24). Paul does not concentrate on the ἡμεῖς of v. 23, but on αὐτοῖς δὲ τοῖς κλητοῖς of v. 24.

[2] Weiss, *Korintherbrief*, p. 33.

7-2

tinction between the act of God in the cross and his calling of men, for it is said in v. 21 that by the former he intends to accomplish the latter.

This differentiation is made explicit by the word κηρύσσομεν in v. 23. The proclamation of the cross is the bridge from the deed itself to those who are called, for whom Christ is the power and wisdom of God. All the predicates of Christ in v. 24, while they may be only in loose apposition to Χριστὸν ἐσταυρωμένον,[1] represent Christ preached. It is not that Paul preaches Christ as foolishness to the Gentiles and as a stumbling block to the Jews, while to the 'called' he preaches Christ as power and wisdom; but it is nonetheless as *preached* that Christ is all these things. It is no accident that only after Paul has twice mentioned the proclamation, both in its origin in God's will (v. 21) and in its existence in the apostolic activity (v. 23), does he call Christ σοφία.

We should have expected such a designation in v. 18, where the parallelism of the sentence is interrupted by Paul's use of δύναμις in the place of σοφία. By referring to δύναμις instead, Paul does more than prepare for v. 24 (δύναμις καὶ σοφία). He avoids risking a serious misunderstanding of what 'wisdom' means for him.[2] At the same time he underlines the intimate bond between the preaching and its role as power. In v. 18 the word *is* power; in v. 24 the preached Christ is power. The 'called' who know Christ as power and wisdom cannot continue to be dependent on the preaching for such an acknowledgment, because as 'called' they continue to need the original message. The reason that some men can know Christ as σοφία is not that their previous inability to perceive foolishness and wisdom in their true shape has been corrected. There is no anthropological counterpart to God's 'new' σοφία. There is no new human

[1] Lietzmann (-Kümmel), *Korinther*, p. 10.

[2] Wilckens, *Weisheit*, argues that the significance of σοφία in these verses is to be ascribed to a christological heresy in Corinth. Over against this heresy Paul sets the orthodoxy of the cross, that element in a christological heresy which is omitted in Corinth, enabling them to make σοφία their catchword. By not mentioning it until v. 24 Paul avoids possible misunderstanding. First he must set the gospel of Christ crucified squarely in the forefront of the discussion. It is not necessary to agree with Wilckens' derivation of the problem through the history of religion (on this cf. H. Koester's review, *Gnomon*, 33 [1961], 591) to agree that the wisdom of this passage presents a specific contour, a Corinthian alternative which Paul rejects by emphasizing the cross.

THE CROSS AS A SYMBOL OF POWER

wisdom to correspond to the new situation described by v. 21. The change is tied up not with man's faculties but with 'power' and 'preaching'.

Verses 26–31 offer something of a proof. It is important that Paul keys this proof to the Corinthians' own experience. In v. 25 he can urge them to consider their own κλῆσις.[1] But at the same time this word recalls the κλητοί of v. 24 and deals with God's act in that aspect which manifests itself in the Christian community. It is characteristic of this act of God in v. 21 that it has two aspects: God's decision with respect to Christ, and God's decision with respect to those who believe. What Paul says about the latter in vv. 26–31, however, is also significant for the former, as is made clear by the fact that the christological predicates of the preceding verses are now shown to be soteriological predicates as regards the Corinthian community. We see once again the close connection between these two facets of a single act. From the anthropological condition God decides to act, and his acting has consequences without altering the basic inability or weakness of man. Strictly speaking, the consequences are not anthropological. When man rejects God's σοφία, God does not concede to him the power to use his (man's) own. God acts to create a new possibility and destroys man's wisdom; but he does not make man σοφός.

This is brought to light in vv. 26–31 by Paul's statement that God chooses those who are not wise κατὰ σάρκα (= σοφία τοῦ κόσμου of v. 21). What God does with them is expressed in two characteristic ways. He chooses them (v. 27) and makes Christ wisdom for them (v. 30).[2] He is wisdom 'for' men, not 'of' men, because God, not man, is the agent. As it is with wisdom, so it is with strength and nobility of birth. These too were lacking in Corinth, yet just those who lacked such attributes were the objects of God's choosing.

---

[1] Both Wilckens (*Weisheit*, p. 42) and Weiss (*Korintherbrief*, p. 35) take κλῆσις as referring to the act of God's calling (as in Rom. 11: 29) and not the condition of being called (as in I Cor. 7: 20). Taken this way it does fit better with v. 21, which act of God the reference here is supposed to illuminate. The verb ἐξελέξατο of vv. 27 and 28 leads to this same interpretation of God's past act and the present consequences, as we note in the aorist verbs in v. 21 and as v. 30 makes clear. So we should avoid too rigid a distinction. The same is true of the adjective κλητοῖς of v. 24.

[2] Not 'our (ἡμῶν) wisdom' as RSV, but 'wisdom for us (ἡμῖν)'.

This action also carries with it an inevitable negative consequence. It is the destruction of what is this world's wisdom (vv. 19, 20). A corollary to each of the three expressions of God's choosing is the expression of God's rejecting. God chooses the foolish not just to save them, but ἵνα καταισχύνῃ τοὺς σοφούς. He chooses the weak not just for their own sake, but ἵνα καταισχύνῃ τὰ ἰσχυρά. And so he chooses the ignoble and despised, indeed, τὰ μὴ ὄντα, ἵνα τὰ ὄντα καταργήσῃ. The last phrase erases any lingering doubt about man's contribution. God chooses what is not, in order to destroy what is. Paul draws from this the conclusion that all flesh is deprived of its ground of boasting before God (v. 29, cf. v. 31).

Just beneath the surface is an allusion to God's creative function. In choosing, God does not settle with what opposes his will, but creates what is not there. By implication the Corinthians are now wise and strong and noble because they are, *who* were not, and so are *what* they were not. But Paul does not say this. This new creation is ἐν Χριστῷ 'Ιησοῦ,[1] and Christ is, in this new creation, the σοφία for them.

Elsewhere Paul refers to this creative function of God and its implication of man's total dependence. Creation and choosing are combined in Rom. 4: 17. When God chooses Abraham he gives life to the dead and 'calls into existence the things which do not exist'. Even more striking parallels to our text are to be found in Gal. 6: 14–15. 'May it never be true for me that I boast except in the cross of our Lord Jesus Christ, by which the world has been crucified to me and I have been crucified to the world. For neither circumcision counts for anything, nor uncircumcision, *but a new creation*.' Here the totality of all that is implied by the abolition of boasting, the cross of Christ and the destruction of the world (its crucifixion) is summed up by the idea of a καινὴ κτίσις (cf. II Cor. 5: 17).

The calling act is God's creative act. What he has brought into existence can be described as being in Christ. In the last analysis it is not possible to distinguish between the κλῆσις as a past event and as a present condition in v. 26. The former implies the latter as much as the latter is dependent upon the

---

[1] Emphasizing the ἐστε of v. 30, along with Lietzmann (*Korinther*, p. 11) and Weiss (*Korintherbrief*, p. 39) against Kümmel (Lietzmann-Kümmel, *Korinther*, p. 169) and Wilckens (*Weisheit*, p. 43, n. 3).

former. Since ἐν Χριστῷ in v. 30 is now set over against the ἐν σοφίᾳ of v. 21, it is justifiable to speak of Christ as a 'new' wisdom over against that of v. 21. The phrases ἐν τῇ σοφίᾳ and ἐν τῷ Χριστῷ are, if not exclusively, at least significantly temporal and represent the distinction between two spheres of time separated by God's act of making Christ σοφία ἡμῖν. To be ἐν τῷ Χριστῷ is to be ἐν τῇ σοφίᾳ and God's original purpose, which appeared thwarted in v. 21a, is accomplished (v. 30).[1] That purpose was expressed in v. 21 as God's good pleasure 'to save'.

Paul has elaborated on one of two important aspects of vv. 18–25. There he spoke of God's acting in the face of men's failure to acknowledge God, and at the same time he linked this act closely with its proclamation. The first of these has been the subject of the discussion in vv. 26–31. The second is the subject of 2: 1–5. Yet as 1: 21 makes clear, the two cannot ultimately be separated, so that it might be better to say that Paul views God's act from the Corinthians' personal involvement in vv. 26–31 and from his own personal involvement in 2: 1–5.

Paul begins autobiographically by describing the way in which he came proclaiming the 'mystery' of God.[2] It was not by the criterion of the abundance of λόγος or σοφία. At first glance it would seem that Paul is now referring to the rhetorical accompaniment of his proclamation. But σοφία and λόγος in 1: 17 set the stage for a discussion not of dialectical skill but of the basic opposition between the cross and wisdom as a principle. In v. 2

---

[1] It is admittedly difficult to know how best to translate ἐν of v. 21a. Wilckens has a lengthy discussion (pp. 32–4) in which he rejects the temporal meaning (cf. Lietzmann, *Korinther*, p. 9) which would be analogous to Rom. 3: 26 ἐν τῇ ἀνοχῇ. He chooses a 'basic locative meaning' in which ἐν σοφίᾳ represents the 'world's realm of existence' (p. 33). But by the time we reach v. 30 it seems very clear that Paul envisions the act in v. 21 as separating two worlds. This means that the ἐν passages of vv. 21 and 30 are at least as significant temporally as they are spatially. Furthermore, the very parallelism between the two phrases which Wilckens sees does not really hold if Christ is to be thought of as the *Existenzraum* of the Christian in any purely spatial sense. Cf. W. Grundmann, *Der Begriff der Kraft in der neutestamentlichen Gedankenwelt* (Stuttgart, 1932), p. 112, n. 5 and Neugebauer, *In Christus*, p. 100.

[2] The text offers both μαρτύριον and μυστήριον. This occurrence of the latter in p46 might seem to strengthen its claim, but from the context either is suitable, μαρτύριον being found in 1: 6 and μυστήριον in 2: 7 and 4: 1. Textual witness is discussed in Lietzmann-Kümmel, *Korinther*, p. 11. Also cf. above, ch. 4, p. 91, n. 2.

the opposite of the negative expression of v. 1 is the 'decision' to know nothing but Christ and him crucified. That is what Paul preaches (cf. 1: 23) and that is, 1: 18–25, the opposite of the wisdom which plays so important a role in Corinth.

Yet once again in vv. 3 and 4 the simplest understanding of Paul's distinctions is one which turns on the *way* he came and preached, not on the content. Is it possible, then, that he has here shifted the focus of his concern from the latter to the former? When Paul goes on to say that he came to Corinth 'in weakness, in fear and in much trembling', when he says that his 'word' and his 'kerygma' were not in 'persuasive words of wisdom' but in 'the demonstration of Spirit and power', does this not all refer to the manner of his coming rather than to the content of his preaching?

Paul himself apparently does not think so, for he states as his purpose, 'that your faith might not be in men's wisdom, but in God's power'. The faith of the Corinthians is at stake in his 'weakness', his 'fear and trembling', etc. The Corinthians' faith would be most intimately linked to what Paul says and not to how he says it.

It is noteworthy that Paul does not cast the alternatives of faith in v. 5 in such a way that σοφία is ranged over against Christ crucified, the subject matter of his preaching. Instead, the alternative to man's wisdom is God's δύναμις. It is this word which provides the key to this passage, and, as we shall see, a good bit of the adhesive which holds together all of the discussion from 1: 17 forward. The δύναμις θεοῦ and the σοφία θεοῦ are one and the same (2: 4) and indeed are actually Χριστὸς ἐσταυρωμένος. Over against these stand the single alternative of σοφία, whether of this world (1: 20) or of men (2: 5). So when Paul makes δύναμις and σοφία the alternatives of v. 5, these are none other than the alternatives of Christ and wisdom. But he chose δύναμις in 2: 5 for a particular reason, and that reason is important in discovering the seeming change of subject matter in 2: 1–5.

How is Christ the 'power' of God? He is the focus of God's act in 1: 21, and this entire act is the revelation of his power. But this act includes the establishment of the kerygma (1: 21), and indeed the proclamation of the kerygma, ὁ λόγος τοῦ σταυροῦ, is itself the 'power of God'. Paul, as the apostle who came to the Corinthians, is responsible for the proclamation. When in 2: 1–5 he discusses this apostolic mission, he can refer to his 'word' and his kerygma as being ἐν ἀποδείξει δυνάμεως and not ἐν πειθοῖς σοφίας λόγοις. The δύναμις is not just confined to the past historical act of God in Christ. It is 'revealed' or demonstrated in the work of the apostle.[1] But the apostle's work is not in and of itself a δύναμις. He lacks all the outward signs and accoutrements of one who works wonders himself. He is the vehicle through which God's power is demonstrated, insofar as he acts responsibly as an apostle.

Thus it is that Paul couples together in 2: 1–5 the two ideas of what he does and how he does it. Insofar as he decides to know only one thing, Jesus Christ and him crucified, his responsibility is exercised toward the 'what' of the kerygma, over against which stands σοφία. Insofar as he comes 'in weakness, and in fear and much trembling', his responsibility is exercised toward the 'how' of the proclamation, over against which stands the ὑπεροχὴ λόγου ἢ σοφίας. Ultimately both are an obedience to one and the same thing, the δύναμις θεοῦ; and this δύναμις is, in both of its aspects, the opposite of σοφία. Paul can refer both the 'how' and the 'what' of preaching to the δύναμις θεοῦ. Were he to confine his remarks here to the method of his work, his argument could not conclude as it does. He has not prepared for the idea that the method of proclamation is going to determine the results he offers as alternatives in the purpose clause of 2: 5. By the same token, were he to confine himself to a discussion of the rivalry between 'Christ crucified' and 'wisdom', then he could not follow up his discussion of the 'calling' of the Corinthians with any parallel account of his participation in that calling, for all would have been said that could be said.

This leads us to ask why Paul wants to elaborate in 2: 1–5 on that portion of 1: 21 which concerns the foolishness of the kerygma. Why does he feel he must look at the central facts not only in such a way as to bring home to the Corinthians their involvement in God's act, but also in such a way as to bring home to them *his* involvement?

In the apostolic labor to which Paul refers, God is thought of as still acting. Indeed, as we have already said, 1: 26–31 and

---

[1] The variant, ἀποκαλύψει (v. 4) in the sixth cent. ms. Claromontanus is indicative of this same understanding of the present reality of δύναμις.

2: 1–5 are two ways of looking at the same central act. If the Corinthians must be reminded *that* God 'chose what is foolish', etc., then they must also be reminded of *how* he did so. He did so through the preaching of Paul, which is itself the very demonstration of God's power. The dialectic between the 'how' and the 'what' of the kerygma in 2: 1–5 is, in the final analysis, not just a dialectic of Paul's activity; it is also, even preeminently, a dialectic of God's acting.

This is brought out in the terms Paul uses. Not only are wisdom and foolishness once again set in contrast as they were in 1: 18ff., but Paul picks up the term ἀσθένεια from 1: 27. There Paul reminded his readers that God chose what was weak in the world in order to put to shame the strong. In the Corinthian biography this is the proof of v. 25. From the perspective of Paul's autobiography, this same relationship holds good. Weakness is the proper sphere of God's acting, which is itself power. Weakness is what God uses, the indispensable starting point of his acting. It is not simply a human quality, the niggling but all-important human contribution to a divine action. Just as God's 'foolishness' is really foolish insofar as it involves God's entry into the world (and is, therefore, not just apparent foolishness), so too, his weakness is real. 1: 25 makes this clear by combining the two thoughts.

What Paul does when he comes to Corinth and how he does it are inseparable. In this, and behind it, we see what God does and how he does it. Paul's weakness is the corollary of his knowing only Christ crucified. But both are, as God's acting, the expression of the δύναμις θεοῦ. Just as we could say that the same power which marked God's act in Christ (1: 21) was to be seen in the calling of 1: 26–31, so we can say that the same power is to be seen in 2: 1–5. It is not confined to some past event, Christ crucified. It is demonstrated in the very calling of the Corinthians and the preaching of Paul. Power is the key element in 1: 17ff.

We now know what it means to empty the cross of power. It means robbing it of its eschatological capacity, a capacity located in the λόγος τοῦ σταυροῦ which creates through κλῆσις. What is created is the Church, 1: 30, 'your life in Christ Jesus'. In the specific Corinthian setting this emptying is a denial of the ultimate eschatological goal or orientation which

Paul always attaches so closely to the idea of 'gospel'. The Church is 'eschatological' not in the sense that it precludes or renders meaningless a final judgment, but only in the sense that it adheres to the 'authority' which interprets this power. The power itself is interpreted in a highly dialectical way, since over against this stands one of Paul's infrequent references to the Kingdom of God (4: 20) as power. When the gospel has reached its conclusion, in the eschaton, power will no longer be conceived dialectically through weakness.

Thus it is no surprise to find in 3: 5–15 and 4: 5 the emergence of a sharp eschatological reservation, and in 4: 8ff. the contrast between the collapsed eschatology of the Corinthians ('power now') and the apostolic form cast in a *peristasis* catalog. The apostle who embodies the gospel not only builds the community under the sign of the end, but embodies power in the only way it can be appropriated before the end. This is his interpretation of power, the charter of his authority.

But is not the Church also an eschatological community? Doesn't the gospel also have the Church as its goal, its orientation? It does, but power is no more available to the Church apart from its manifestation in weakness than is wisdom apart from foolishness. The Church is an everyday reality within history, not something beyond it. It follows that the apostolic paradigm is not merely an embodiment of the gospel ('the word of the cross') but a model for the Church. As we shall see, this is made explicit in much of the rhetoric of apostolic authority.

All of this is immediately relevant to the hyper-spiritualism of the Corinthian ethos. Insofar as they judge before the day of judgment and think of themselves as powerful or wise, Paul can remind them of their former state and strike the parallel of his own initial appearance among them (1: 26–31; 2: 1–5), in order that their faith 'might rest in God's power'. The Corinthians are called to remember the way in which they first experienced the power of the gospel so that they might now remain faithful to that pattern. Hence the *peristasis* catalog of 4: 11ff., and its long prefatory introduction, is really designed not as apostolic defense but as apostolic warning. In this consists the only form of power short of the kingdom of God, power Paul will not hesitate to use when he comes again.

203

CHAPTER 8

THE RHETORIC OF APOSTOLIC AUTHORITY

We have tried to demonstrate that there is a central structure to apostolic authority as Paul understands it, an authority which he consistently refuses to subvert by erecting a canon of legitimacy. If we ask about Paul's authority there emerges a picture of an apostle whose very existence is like that of every other man in Christ and is somehow dependent upon his capacity to educe from others that awareness of shared power. It is a picture not unlike de Jouvenel's description of the *auctor*: the father and adviser whose primary function is to augment the power at his disposal by seeing that it is diffused through those over whom he exercises authority, all the while guaranteeing the ultimate rightness and fitness of their actions so long as these are grounded in that power which he exhibits.[1] It is a restricted view of authority which calls upon the *auctor* to assert not himself and his authority, but the primary source of power. When others perceive this power correctly and act accordingly, they share in the same power with Paul and are themselves authoritative. When they misperceive, he exercises power over them.

It comes as no surprise that inside the letters the vocabulary of authority is not a technical one. Not only κλητός and χάρις, but εὐαγγελίζεσθαι and even οἰκοδομή, while they may cluster around Paul's descriptions of his apostolic person, cannot be confined to that. All have their counterpart in the common responsibility of all Christians.[2] So dominant is the missionary milieu out of which Paul's customary vocabulary comes that this vocabulary is made to serve the needs of apostolic

---

[1] Cf. above, pp. 12f.

[2] Schmithals attempts to isolate something like an apostolic vocabulary (*Office*, pp. 24ff.). But the language Paul uses is striking simply because it draws so heavily on the common stock of his missionary preaching and is so intertwined with the basic themes of that preaching.

identification too. Rhetoric is, among other things, the specialized use of linguistic images. There is a rhetoric of apostolic authority.

THE APOSTOLIC TASK

THE APOSTLE AND CHRIST

An Apostle through Christ

II Cor. 5: 18ff. shows that while the apostle is the instrument of God's acting, just as Christ was, the relationship of the apostle to God is *through* Christ. This means something more than that the apostle has been vouchsafed an appearance of the risen Christ. In Gal. 1: 1 Paul refers to his apostleship as coming 'through Jesus Christ and God the Father who raised him from the dead'. In Rom. 1: 5 he speaks of receiving 'grace and apostleship' through 'Jesus Christ our Lord'. In this latter passage the designation 'Jesus Christ our Lord' is a summing up of the christology of vv. 3 and 4, where it is the resurrection which inaugurates the sonship in power. Gal. 1 and Rom. 1 together enable us to see the relationship of God and Christ in the apostolic calling. *Through* Christ for Paul means that God calls him through the soteriological event, here designated in both instances by reference to the resurrection. The common activity of God in Christ and in the apostle, as expressed in II Cor. 5: 18ff., makes such a deep impression on Paul that he can go on in II Cor. 6: 1 to speak of himself as 'working together with Christ'. Paul, who so frequently styles himself a 'slave' of Christ, has no illusions about standing on an equal footing with Christ. But as the vehicle of God's activity, he does stand in a common relationship. The common expression is *through* Christ, giving scope to the idea that God acts in Christ and in the apostle without making Christ and Paul coordinate in any other way.

Does the idea of Paul's apostleship coming διὰ Χριστοῦ also give scope to the idea that God and Christ together act in Paul? G. Sass, in his treatment of II Cor. 5: 20, speaks of Paul as one who continues the work of Christ.[1] Is that a proper description of the relationship of Paul's work to Christ's?

---

[1] 'Since God's founding of the "office of reconciliation" the apostle can speak "in place of Christ". V. 20a states the fact: The apostle is one sent "for Christ". In v. 20b Paul exercises his representative office in asking the

Sass' understanding of II Cor. 5: 20 is part and parcel of his whole view of Paul's mission as itself a conscious extension of Christ's activity. In II Cor. 1: 6 and 4: 12 he sees Paul as a servant whose vicarious suffering is reminiscent of only two other figures: Jesus and the Suffering Servant of Isa. 53. This interpretation he finds confirmed in Phil. 2: 16 and II Cor. 12: 15. Paul comes to terms with his own suffering by seeing himself suffering on behalf of the Christian community.

The problem with the general theory is that suffering is not something of which Paul has a monopoly. While he often refers to his tribulation, θλῖψις is the common experience of many Christians (Rom. 5: 3; 8: 35; 12: 12; I Cor. 7: 28; II Cor. 1: 4, 5; 8: 2). Indeed, Christians are even said to share voluntarily Paul's sufferings (Phil. 4: 14; I Thess. 1: 6). Moreover, Christ's death and resurrection are not called 'sufferings' except when Paul is comparing his own to Christ's fate. The image is secondary in Paul's mind, and it is doubtful that he intended any such direct connection as Sass finds. Not only does Paul's language of soteriology fail to establish this hypothesis; his view of soteriology will not sustain it. Christ's death is ἐφάπαξ (Rom. 6: 10). The unrepeatable founding event is reflected in the new creation it inaugurates; but it is not repeated in this constitutive sense. Paul does not *repeat* what Christ has done. He *reflects* what Christ has done. In him the account of that action is made manifest.

An Apostle of Christ

In 16 of the 24 occurrences of ἀπόστολος in the undisputed letters, the noun stands without an accompanying genitive.[1] In seven other occurrences which have a genitive complement, four use the title 'Christ'[2] and the others no christological title at all.[3] The remaining passage speaks of the ἀπόστολος διὰ

believers to be reconciled with God. Thus the apostle stands, on God's behalf, where Christ stood earlier, as one who continues the work of Christ' (*Apostelamt*, p. 81).

[1] Rom. 1: 1; 16: 17; I Cor. 4: 9; 9: 1, 2, 5; 12: 28, 29; 15: 7, 9 (*bis*); II Cor. 11: 15; 12: 11, 12; Gal. 1: 17, 19.

[2] II Cor. 11: 13; I Thess. 2: 7 (ἀπόστολος Χριστοῦ) and I Cor. 1: 1 (ἀπόστολος Χριστοῦ 'Ιησοῦ).

[3] Rom. 11: 23 (ἐθνῶν ἀπόστολος); II Cor. 8: 23 (ἀπόστολος ἐκκλησιῶν) and Phil. 2: 25 (ὑμῶν ἀπόστολος).

Ἰησοῦ Χριστοῦ. Paul never speaks of an apostle 'of the Lord' or 'of the Son of God', but only of an apostle 'of Christ (Jesus)'. On the basis of the close relationship of the title Χριστός with the salvation events themselves, the preference for this title would seem to indicate a close relationship in Paul's mind between apostleship and the actual events constituting salvation. Such use of Χριστοῦ only confirms what we have already found to be the case.[1]

An Apostle in Christ[2]

The phrase 'in Christ' sums up for Paul the new life which belongs to the Christian. Standing 'in Christ' the Christian experiences the events of Christ's death and resurrection as his own death to an old age and entrance into a new possibility of

[1] It makes little difference whether the description of the apostle as Χριστοῦ is original with Paul or represents an earlier understanding. We are inclined to agree with Kramer that the phrase ἀπόστολος Χριστοῦ (Ἰησοῦ) is Paul's own (*Christ, Lord, Son of God*, par. 13). But Kramer's formal analysis of the terminology is not itself very persuasive in this paragraph. The evidence is scarcely as obvious and as unilateral as he supposes it to be. More persuasive in identifying the idea as Pauline is the whole relationship of Paul to the events of Christ's death and resurrection, as we shall see. But, of course, even this is not decisive. For the view that the phrase arose among Paul's opponents (in II Cor. 10–13) cf. Käsemann, 'Legitimität', p. 37 and Klein, *Apostel*, p. 57, n. 24.

Kramer comes closer to the mark when he asks why Paul might coin such a phrase. 'There could be two reasons why it is just this title and not that of Lord or Son of God which Paul uses: Either Paul saw in that one who appeared to him before Damascus the dead and risen figure which the hellenistic church called "Christ", or he understood his call to become the apostle to the Gentiles in such proximity with the content of the message which he was given to preach that he inserted "Christ", which characterises this content, even where it is a matter of characterising his apostleship.' Because Kramer understands the genitive Χριστοῦ to be one of authorship, he chooses the former. But this is a questionable criterion, as is evidenced by the fact that Paul's 'revelation' subsumes both the appearance of 'Christ' and the delivery of the gospel which tells of 'Christ'. It is more probable that the identification of the apostle as 'of Christ' reflects the close association of the apostle with both the gospel and the Christ preached in it. This preference of Paul's is shown in the phrase δοῦλος Χριστοῦ (Rom. 1: 1; 7: 23). Though we might expect the very natural metaphor δοῦλος Κυρίου, it never occurs (cf. I Cor. 7: 22, 23).

[2] For a general discussion of the relationship between the idea of apostleship and the phrase 'in Christ', cf. Neugebauer, *In Christus*, pp. 119–30.

life. This newness of life so bears the contours of Christ's death and resurrection that it is never to be understood in isolation from those events. When one is in Christ, he lives in that particular confluence of past, present and future which unites the this-worldly life with an already fulfilled eschatological promise of new life, both now dependent upon and reflecting the particular events which themselves make this new life eschatological existence.

It is no surprise that Paul's apostolic self-consciousness shows there to be a most intimate connection between his being an apostle and his being in Christ. Yet we cannot expect to find here an exclusive quality of apostleship. All Christians are 'in Christ' and the members of the Church are the members of the body of Christ. What Paul says about his apostleship 'in Christ' does not show what is distinctive about apostleship; it shows what is the norm for Paul's own understanding of his apostleship. This is illustrated by Rom. 16: 3, 7, 9, 10. Some notable Christians are singled out here for greetings at the conclusion of Paul's letter. Among these are Apelles, 'approved in Christ' (v. 10); Urbanus, 'our fellow worker in Christ' (v. 9) and, of course, Prisca and Aquila, 'my fellow workers in Christ' (v. 3). None of these is an apostle, and all are 'in Christ'. But Andronicus and Junias, 'my kinsmen and fellow prisoners...are men of note among the apostles, and they were in Christ before me' (v. 7).[1] Being 'in Christ' is not limited to apostles, though apostles are in Christ (cf. Philemon 23).

More illuminating are a number of passages where Paul uses the phrase ἐν Χριστῷ to describe some aspect of *action*.

'Begetting' in Christ, I Cor. 4: 15ff.[2]

Because Paul has preached the gospel to the Corinthians, he can style himself their 'father in Christ Jesus'. The figure, echoed in Gal. 4: 19 (cf. Philemon 10), establishes Paul's continuing concern for and authority over the Corinthian community. While it is an authority which extends beyond preaching the gospel, the relationship depends upon the fact that Paul has preached

[1] This use of the phrase ἐν Χριστῷ is scarcely more than a periphrasis for the as yet non-existent adjective 'Christian'. Cf. Bultmann, *Theol.* I, p. 311.

[2] Cf. O. Betz, 'Die Geburt der Gemeinde durch den Lehrer', *NTS* 3 (1957), 314–26.

in Corinth (διὰ τοῦ εὐαγγελίου). Ἐν Χριστῷ complements γεννᾶν; the apostle as one whose call itself comes διὰ Χριστοῦ and who preaches the gospel τοῦ Χριστοῦ is the one who begot the Corinthians. The ἐν Χριστῷ formula, however, serves no less as the complement to ὑμᾶς. The Corinthians have been born into that newness of life which is Christ.

The sense of authority conveyed by Paul's language here is heightened by his reference to παιδαγωγός (v. 15). The term has an overtone of derision, suggesting the household slave employed to teach manners and poise.[1] Paul's obligation is not to tutor the Corinthians in the niceties of their new life. It is to bring them into that life and assume the responsibility for their behavior as a father does for a child. Thus the context shows Paul urging his imitation. To this end he is sending Timothy to 'remind' the Corinthians of his 'ways in Christ', just as he teaches them everywhere in every church. The ὁδοί of Paul can scarcely be his travel plans. The New Testament use of the word, outside of the gospels, is always figurative[2] and reflects the use of the LXX. Paul's 'ways' could be his 'teachings' or 'rules', as the word διδάσκειν in v. 17 suggests.[3] What these teachings would be we do not know. Paul nowhere describes himself as a teacher. His rule about women keeping silence in the church (14: 33) is for 'all the churches'; but his reference in 7: 17 to a rule valid in all the churches refers more broadly to general conduct like that in 4: 9–13. It is not impossible that his 'ways' are both taught and illustrated by his life. At least v. 14, serving as a transition from his description of his own behavior (vv. 9–13) to his admonition to his 'children', implies that it is not for nothing that Paul describes his 'weakness' in contrast to their 'strength'. So we should probably connect ὁδοί with vv. 9–13 and assume that his example there is also what he 'teaches'. Since Paul's ways are not his own free creation, but are themselves anchored 'in Christ', they have a normative quality for his 'children in Christ'.

[1] Cf. the detailed description and bibliography in Oepke, *Galater*, pp. 86–8.

[2] Neugebauer, *In Christus*, p. 121.

[3] W. Michaelis, 'ὁδός etc.', *TDNT*, v (Grand Rapids, 1967), pp. 87f. Michaelis dismisses perhaps too easily the possibly Rabbinic flavor of the term. Cf. D. Daube, *The New Testament and Rabbinic Judaism* (London, 1956), pp. 87ff.

Here we see Paul describing his work as an apostle by reference to its beginning in Corinth διὰ τοῦ εὐαγγελίου. Beyond this beginning, however, the Corinthians and Paul share together the life in Christ. His ways in Christ are to be their ways in Christ. All of this begins with the gospel but goes far beyond missionary preaching.

Paul's continuing concern and responsibility is not made explicit in the revelation which calls him to preach the gospel. This concern and responsibility is, however, implicit in that revelation when the gospel which he is commissioned to preach is understood in its pregnant sense.

Speaking in Christ: II Cor. 2: 14, 17; 12: 19b; Rom. 9: 1

In three places Paul uses the phrase 'speaking in Christ' (λαλεῖν ἐν Χριστῷ). Is this merely a periphrasis for 'preaching', or does he mean that in a more extended sense all that he says is shaped by his being in Christ?[1]

II Cor. 2: 17 stands in a context where the 'gospel' is the point at issue. Λαλεῖν ἐν Χριστῷ could easily be taken as an alternative expression for εὐαγγελίζεσθαι. Paul's speaking in Christ is set in opposition to the 'peddlers of God's word'. His reference to his 'speaking' is introduced by v. 16b: 'Who is sufficient for these things'? This sufficiency is the theme of 3: 4ff. where it is said that 'our sufficiency is from God who has made us sufficient to be ministers of a new covenant' (vv. 5b, 6), the gospel, contrasted to the covenant of Moses.[2] Thus in 4: 2 when Paul states his refusal to 'tamper with God's word', he means that he does not subvert the gospel. The phrase echoes 'peddlers of God's word' in 2: 17.

Other aspects of the context in which we find 2: 17 indicate its close connection with preaching. In 2: 14 Paul uses the unusual verb θριαμβεύειν with ἐν Χριστῷ. God leads the apostle in triumph in Christ. The verb is here best translated without any reference to its possible derisive overtones.[3] It is not set in antithesis to φανεροῦν of the same verse. The latter complements the former. Taking ἐν Χριστῷ in its adverbial sense, with

---

[1] Neugebauer, In Christus, p. 119 suggests that ἐν Χριστῷ, with λαλεῖν, should be taken adverbially, similarly to λαλεῖν ἐν ἀληθείᾳ, ἐν ἀφροσύνῃ etc. It is impossible to render this precise nuance in graceful English.

[2] Above, ch. 6.   [3] Cf. Lietzmann, Korinther, p. 108.

θριαμβεύειν, we see that Paul is describing God's acting in Christ by making the focus of that activity the life of the apostle himself. In the apostle is the manifestation of God's acting. God acts by spreading the 'fragrance of the knowledge of Christ' everywhere through the apostle. Verses 15 and 16a show that Paul is working with the idea of the gospel uppermost in his mind.[1] Thus both phrases with 'in Christ' are closely associated with the idea of preaching.

Our analysis of II Cor. 3: 7ff. has shown, however, that here the gospel implies for Paul much more than a single message delivered once and for all, a missionary preaching for conversion. We have seen that the reference in 4: 3 to 'our gospel' is only made clear in the larger context of chs. 2 and 3, and shows how Paul thinks of the gospel as a continuing force in the life of the Christian. From this perspective, 'speaking in Christ' in 2: 17 must at least be given the latitude implied by Paul's own 'pregnant' understanding of the gospel in this context.

Just how great this latitude must be is shown by the word εἰλικρίνεια in 2: 17. Not only does Paul speak 'in Christ', he also speaks 'out of God and before God'. The phrase ἐκ θεοῦ indicates the source of Paul's speaking;[2] the phrase κατέναντι θεοῦ his awareness that God scrutinizes what he says. Both stand parallel to and clarify ὡς ἐξ εἰλικρινείας.

Εἰλικρίνεια (I Cor. 5: 8; II Cor. 1: 12) and εἰλικρινής (Phil. 1: 10) always characterize moral integrity.[3] Paul betrays here an understanding of his 'speaking in Christ' which goes beyond his role as preacher to suggest a characterization of his whole behavior.

The breadth of this characterization is confirmed by II Cor. 12: 19b. Here Paul is referring to a speaking which is not directly connected with preaching. The context shows clearly that Paul means by λαλοῦμεν what he has just been saying in his own defense. This is not an 'apology' in his own behalf. He is not defending himself by any human standard (cf. 10: 12). Instead, he is speaking in Christ before God. The passage varies

---

[1] Cf. T. W. Manson, '2 Cor. 2: 14–17: Suggestions Towards an Exegesis', *Studia Paulina*, pp. 155–62.

[2] For Paul this characteristically expresses God as the actor. Cf. Rom. 2: 29; I Cor. 2: 12; 7: 7; 11: 12, etc.

[3] F. Büchsel, 'εἰλικρινής etc.', *TDNT*, ii, pp. 397f.

from 2: 17 only in omitting the words ἐκ θεοῦ. Paul's purpose is not to enhance himself, but to 'build up' the community. Here Paul wants the Corinthians to know that his personal defense is not intended to redound in his own credit, but to their stability in faith. His very act of 'defending' himself is, in fact, a 'speaking in Christ', and in speaking in Christ he is laboring in their behalf.

In Rom. 9: 1 Paul says he is 'speaking the truth in Christ', he is not lying when he tells of his great sorrow and unceasing anguish over the Jews' rejection of God's gift. There is nothing discernibly 'apostolic' here about what Paul says or how he says it. He could not speak in Christ were he not in Christ (8: 1), but that alone does not distinguish Paul from others.

Nevertheless, Paul means something more. He speaks ἀλήθειαν ἐν Χριστῷ. Truth is, for Paul, always a predicate of God (Rom. 1: 18; 3: 7; 15: 8) or of Christ (II Cor. 11: 10) who became a servant ὑπὲρ ἀληθείας θεοῦ. Man's truthfulness is false, for he has 'exchanged the truth of God for a lie', Rom. 1: 25. God's truth is found in the 'truth of the gospel' (Gal. 2: 5, 14); through the gospel man has access to it. Life in this gospel is a life in obedience to the truth (Gal. 5: 7).

Boasting in Christ: Rom. 15: 17; I Cor. 15: 31; Phil. 1: 25f.

Nowhere does the phrase ἐν Χριστῷ better serve to bind a narrower understanding of apostolic labor with a broader one than where Paul speaks of his 'boasting' in Christ. This is particularly clear in Rom. 15: 17: 'Therefore, I have a boasting[1] in Christ Jesus before God.'[2] As Neugebauer remarks, 'Rom. 15: 16 and 15: 18 show unmistakably how "boasting" is meant to be taken, namely, that Paul boasts only insofar as he is a servant of Christ and dares not speak of anything Christ does not do through him'.[3]

Verse 17 serves as a transition between vv. 15–16 and vv. 18–20. Paul boasts, but his boasting is not self-adulation. It is ἐν Χριστῷ. Thus he is not to be misunderstood in vv. 15–16. His

---

[1] "Ἡ καύχησις is first of all the act of boasting (Rom. 3: 27; II Cor. 11: 10, 17), by extension the object or basis of boasting (II Cor. 1: 12)' Michel, *Römer*, p. 328, n. 4.

[2] Taking τὰ πρὸς τὸν θεόν adverbially. Cf. BDF par. 160.

[3] *In Christus*, p. 123.

boldness is no personal quality. Nor is he to be misunderstood in vv. 18–20, for he only 'dares' to speak of what Christ has done through him, for the purpose of 'winning obedience from the Gentiles' (εἰς ὑπακοὴν ἐθνῶν). 'Obedience' stresses the on-going responsibility of the Christian. This is no less Paul's own responsibility than is missionary preaching. It is part of the on-going nature of the gospel that it demands this obedience from the Gentiles; it is part of that same on-going quality that it demands Paul's own continued responsibility. Thus 'in the priestly service of the Gospel of God' Paul is a λειτουργὸς Ἰησοῦ Χριστοῦ (i.e., ἀπόστολος Ἰησοῦ Χριστοῦ). He renders priestly service '*in order that* the offering of the Gentiles may be acceptable' (v. 16). Both vv. 16 and 18 describe Paul's function in terms of his continuing concern for the Gentile mission.

Because this concern is his and is part of what it means to stand in the priestly service of the gospel, Paul can take it upon himself to 'remind' the Roman community. Here we have a classic example of the pregnant dimension of the gospel, the key to understanding πεπληρωκέναι τὸ εὐαγγέλιον in v. 20. In preaching the gospel Paul has inaugurated its power, not exhausted its possibilities. The powers of v. 19 are actually those of Christ working through him. This sense of the on-going gospel is what enables Paul to assume the authority to remind the Romans of those things he mentions. Verse 15 is strikingly parallel to I Cor. 4: 17, where Paul can remind the community of his 'ways in the Lord' because he has begotten them ἐν Χριστῷ. This same sense of authority and responsibility is evident in Rom. 15: 15ff. Even though Paul did not establish the church at Rome, he has written to it 'very boldly by way of reminder'.

He does so because of the grace given him by God, defined in v. 16 in terms of his on-going responsibility for the Gentiles. That he has carried out this responsibility is his boast in Christ (v. 17). But no less than that, he boasts because Christ is working in and through him in bringing the Gentiles to obedience (v. 18), through the power which is characteristic of the gospel, power which Paul has inaugurated. All of this is καύχησις ἐν Χριστῷ. It is a boasting about what Paul has accomplished and is accomplishing. But it is ἐν Χριστῷ because Christ himself is acting in Paul's work. It is objective, because Paul can see the tangible evidence of his ministry. It is not subjective because Paul relies on God's grace and Christ works through him. By itself, 'boasting in Christ' does not show the formulary meaning of ἐν Χριστῷ, but Paul's whole ministry is very much shaped by Christ's death and resurrection, and it is not improper to give the formula here the broadest possible scope, as does Michel when he suggests that ἐν Χριστῷ means for Paul that his ministry is conducted in intimate relationship with Christ, that Paul is himself responsible to Christ and that his own boasting finds both a criterion and a limit in Christ.[1]

Phil. 1: 26 connects the community's boast in Paul with its boast in Christ. Paul proposes to come again to Philippi; and he 'will remain and continue' with them (v. 25) so that their boast 'in him' may abound 'in Christ'. Again, the boast in Christ serves for Paul as a means of designating his own relationship to Christ, his own limitation. The community may have confidence in him, but what he does to encourage this actually increases their boasting ἐν Χριστῷ.

Weakness in Christ: II Cor. 13: 4b; Phil. 4: 13

Paul speaks of his 'weakness in Christ' (II Cor. 13: 4b), which is based on Christ's crucifixion in weakness. But as Christ lives out of the power of God, so Paul will deal with the Corinthians by living with Christ out of that power. II Cor. 10–13 is one single, sustained attempt on Paul's part to explain his authority as an apostle. 'Weakness and power' is the dominant theme in those chapters. In 13: 4b Paul connects his weakness and power with the death and resurrection life of Christ. Being himself in Christ, he is weak. But his being in Christ means that he himself is shaped by the totality of the Christ event, weakness and power. We expect Paul to go on to say that he is 'powerful in

---

[1] Cf. Michel, *Römer*, pp. 328f. Neugebauer's objections to this diffuse interpretation of the phrase (*In Christus*, p. 123, n. 22) are not persuasive. He objects that the relationship of three such meanings cannot be shown. His own interpretation of the passage merely stresses that the Christ proclaimed is the Christ working in the proclamation: 'In the proclamation occurs salvation' (p. 123). But that is not an interpretation of καύχησις ἐν Χριστῷ of v. 17; it is an interpretation of v. 18. That Paul *boasts* in Christ suggests (1) that in Christ Paul's work has been done and (2) a very real limit to Paul's own personal claim to fame. In short, it suggests how seriously Paul takes his understanding of 'power'.

214

Christ', but he does not. Instead he says that he shall live with Christ out of God's power.

The future tense, ʒήσομεν, is a clue to a very important aspect of this passage. We have been reviewing Paul's use of ἐν Χριστῷ, where the phrase is connected with his function as an apostle. But it is not only apostles who are in Christ, and this emphasis keeps him within the bounds of the common Christian experience. He does not, at least in these passages, appeal to a special 'apostolic existence' to explain his work.[1] Yet being in Christ has significance for Paul's apostleship. It shows the limit, the source, the true agent in what at first glance might appear to be only the apostle's own accomplishment. It is no exaggeration to say that being in Christ is a criterion, and a limiting criterion, of the apostle's self-understanding. All those who are in Christ are not necessarily apostles; but all who are apostles are necessarily in Christ. They recognize their apostleship as conforming to this criterion (assuming that what Paul says about himself he takes to be normative for all genuine apostolic self-understanding). In II Cor. 13: 4b Paul might mean that as a Christian he is weak in Christ but shall live with him out of God's power. In that case, ʒήσομεν would have to be taken either as a 'logical' future[2] or as a reference to the resurrection from the dead as a living with Christ out of God's power. If a logical future, it would mean only that as Christ died and was raised, so the apostle has been crucified in weakness and now understands his existence from the resurrection. But ʒήσομεν can and should be taken as a simple future tense referring to what Paul will do in the very near future. Paul means that he 'will live' not just generally as a Christian (he already does that) but as an apostle in Corinth. Here is where the power he speaks of will become evident. This will occur when he makes his impending third visit (13: 1). For this reason Paul specifically says he will be powerful εἰς ὑμᾶς.[3] Thus the weakness-power theme in II Cor. 13: 4 is given a specific apostolic reference. Paul is speaking as an apostle, not just as a Christian.

---

[1] This is emphasized by Paul's understanding of the apostle as a member of the Christian community.

[2] Windisch, *Korintherbrief*, p. 419.

[3] The mss. which omit these words (B, D) take ʒήσομεν in its more soteriological sense.

We have seen that the weakness-power theme, based on Christ's death and resurrection, permeates Paul's understanding of the whole of Christian existence. Like the terse phrase 'in Christ' which serves as a summary for it, this theme applies to the new life of all men who are 'of Christ'. It is therefore impossible to conclude that in 13:4 Paul is giving the grounds for his claim to apostolic *legitimacy*. He is only giving his understanding of life in Christ. But since *his* being weak and powerful here refers to his apostolic life, we must conclude that he is saying something about apostolic *authority*.

This is confirmed by v. 3: 'since you desire proof that Christ is speaking in me'. The Corinthians miss in Paul some indication of pneumatic immediacy, which they themselves have been taught to prize highly as an apostolic credential. Paul's opponents are pneumatics who accuse him of weakness (11:21), and being ἰδιώτης τῷ λόγῳ, 11:6. Reitzenstein has connected this latter charge with Paul's lacking πνεῦμα. Such a failure would manifest itself in his inability to improvise and speak 'freely'.[1] In response to their objection Paul says that when he returns to Corinth he will not spare those who have sinned, and this will be his δοκιμή.

It is possible that Paul's answer would be unsatisfactory from the Corinthians' point of view because it does not meet the challenge they have raised. If in questioning whether Christ speaks in him they are asking about his legitimacy as an apostle, then Paul's answer is not entirely to the point. For he does not defend himself by saying that he is a πνευματικός. The gap between the Corinthians' concern and Paul's is illustrated by 13:3b: '(Christ) who is not weak in dealing with you but powerful in you'. As Windisch points out, this sentence is the more remarkable because it expresses a truth to which both Paul and the Corinthians could assent.[2] For Paul this would mean only that Christ crucified is the power of God (I Cor. 1:24). From Paul's point of view v. 3b is true when understood in the light of v. 4. It is difficult to be certain of the origin of this assertion. Since both Paul and the Corinthians could assent to such a statement, it could originate with either. Yet the evidence points toward an origin in the Corinthian community. That Christ is powerful in them and not weak over against (εἰς, as in

---

[1] *Mysterienreligionen*, pp. 362f.   [2] *Korintherbrief*, p. 418.

v. 4)[1] them seems to be a slur on Paul, who is weak. How does Paul pick up the challenge?

The relative clause ὅς εἰς ὑμᾶς οὐκ κ.τ.λ. may be a direct continuation of the Corinthian position stated in the question about Christ's speaking in Paul: 'Since you seek proof of Christ's speaking in me, Christ who is not weak...' Or, Paul may already connect the power of Christ in Corinth with what he promises will be evident on his arrival. This latter is the interpretation of Schmithals, who prefers it because only then does v. 4 have a meaningful connection with what precedes it.[2] We prefer the former, for only then does the specific question about Christ's speaking in Paul relate to the whole discussion of weakness and power. The Corinthian community thinks of Christ as powerful in it, in its individual members. Paul stands over against them as weak. Does this not show that Paul lacks the power of Christ in him? He is weak εἰς Corinth, Christ is powerful ἐν Corinth. The preposition εἰς denotes Paul's relationship to Corinth as one who does not belong to the community but assumes some authority to deal with it. If Christ were really speaking 'in' Paul, then as he stands εἰς the community he would be known to be powerful, just as Christ himself is powerful 'in' that community.

Paul's reply simply turns the Corinthian scale of values upside down. Christ is not in *him*,[3] *he* is in *Christ*. Being in Christ is being stamped by the death and resurrection of Christ. So v. 4 begins: '*For even* Christ was crucified...' The words καὶ γάρ refer back to v. 2[4] and begin to establish Paul's rationale for his own apostolic power. In his very weakness is the power which is his from being in Christ. Because Paul is ἐν Χριστῷ he will be powerful εἰς Corinth when next he visits.

Understanding 'being in Christ' as referring to an existence which bears the shape of Christ's own death and resurrection,

---

[1] *Ibid.*, p. 419.   [2] *Korinth*, p. 159.

[3] That Christ is 'in Paul' is also true, but only in a way that already knows of the Christian's sharing Christ's crucifixion. Cf. Gal. 2: 19.

[4] If we read εἰ καὶ γάρ with A, Koine and others, as does BDF, par. 457, then v. 4 is a continuation of the Corinthian objection cast in a concessive clause. This should be rejected because it is the easier reading, and because v. 4b (καὶ γάρ) is consciously parallel to v. 4a. Paul is illustrating his own weakness and power from Christ's. The 'weakness' in v. 4a should not be dismissed in a concessive clause.

his own weakness and power, is crucial for Paul's understanding and defense of his apostleship. Paul makes this understanding, normative for all Christians,[1] normative for himself as an apostle. That means he does not really discuss the question of whether he deserves to be called an apostle; he assumes his claim to apostleship and tries to show how his way of discharging his responsibilities is determined by his being in Christ.

In Phil. 4: 13 Paul says that he is able to do 'all things in him who empowers me'.[2] In the light of II Cor. 13: 4b there is no need to inquire about what Paul means by power. It is clear that the death and resurrection of Christ (the latter being God's empowering of Christ) are the source of Paul's power. The passage, however, shows Paul can connect his own personal condition, the physical state of life, with the theme of Christ's own weakness, his death and resurrection. We shall see that this condition becomes an important element in Paul's apostolic self-consciousness when he specifically refers to his apostolic labors.

Sufferings in Christ: Phil. 3: 10

In Phil. 3: 8ff. Paul speaks of his burning desire to 'gain Christ' and be found 'in him'. To gain Christ Paul has suffered the loss of all things, indeed he has counted as loss all that he once thought gain.

The thought of these verses is closely structured. Paul begins (v. 8a) by saying that he counted everything as loss because of the surpassing worth of knowing Christ Jesus his Lord. Verse 8b merely repeats this thought, although the change from ζημίαν to the passive verb ἐζημιώθην, and the shift from ἡγοῦμαι ζημίαν to ἡγοῦμαι σκύβαλα, may reflect an awareness that he alone did not 'decide' his way to Christ.[3] He experienced the loss of

---

[1] Since Paul's criterion of apostleship is also a criterion of Christian existence in general, his rejection of the Corinthians' contempt is at the same time a rejection of their false self-understanding. Christ is no more 'in them' in the unbalanced way they suppose than he is 'in Paul'.

[2] The v.l. Χριστῷ (Koine) makes this a reference to being in Christ. Without it, the antecedent to ἐν τῷ ἐνδυναμοῦντι would be κύριος of v. 10. Even if the former is the preferred reading, we do not have an example of the exact formula ἐν Χριστῷ because of the intervening participle. Cf. Neugebauer, In Christus, p. 128.

[3] P. Bonnard, L'épître de Saint Paul aux Philippiens (Neuchâtel, 1950), p. 64.

218

all[1] *in order that* he might gain Christ, be found in him (v. 9) and know him (v. 10). These three expressions are not consecutive or essentially distinct. They are mutually interpretive, three alternative expressions of one purpose.

Being found in Christ is elaborated in the participial clause beginning with μὴ ἔχων. Paul is found in Christ when he no longer has his own[2] righteousness, based on law, but God's righteousness which comes through faith in Christ. The third purpose clause, 'to know Christ', is extended by the phrase καὶ τὴν δύναμιν τῆς ἀναστάσεως αὐτοῦ καὶ τὴν κοινωνίαν παθημάτων αὐτοῦ. Like the second, it finds elaboration in a subsequent participial clause.

Since Reitzenstein,[3] it has been common to see in this passage evidence for Paul's 'mystical' experience of and attitude toward life in Christ.[4] This seems an especially fruitful line of interpretation in the face of the unusual expressions τὸ ὑπερέχον τῆς γνώσεως Χριστοῦ Ἰησοῦ τοῦ κυρίου μου (v. 8) and τοῦ γνῶναι αὐτόν (v. 10).[5] Yet it is difficult to know how the 'mystical' relationship is to fit with the obvious historical realities to which Paul refers. At least from v. 8 on the language refers to Paul's actual historical existence. Suffering the loss of all things is suffering the loss of those advantages listed in vv. 4b–6. Similarly, vv. 12ff. are perhaps the clearest expression we have in the whole Pauline corpus of the Christian's looking to the future to keep before him the ultimate goal which determines his life in the present, the time of knowing Christ.

Even more important is the definition Paul gives of τοῦ γνῶναι αὐτόν in v. 10. By knowing Christ Paul means 'knowing the power of his resurrection and the fellowship of his sufferings'. The conjunction καί following αὐτόν should be taken as epexegetic, explicating αὐτόν.[6] The relationship of the epexegetic

[1] The term τὰ πάντα is radical (cf. Rom. 11: 36; Gal. 3: 22, etc.). Lohmeyer rightly equates the statement with Gal. 6: 14 (*Philipper*, p. 134).
[2] Note the emphatic ἐμήν.   [3] *Mysterienreligionen*, pp. 258ff.
[4] As recently as F. W. Beare, *A Commentary on the Epistle to the Philippians* (New York, 1959), pp. 122ff. So also Seesemann, ΚΟΙΝΩΝΙΑ, p. 84 and Dibelius, *Philipper*, p. 80.
[5] 'We encounter "my lord" nowhere else in the Pauline letters…The phrase "knowledge of Christ" is unique not only in Paul, but in the whole NT (with the exception of II Pet. 3: 18)' (Lohmeyer, *Philipper*, p. 133).
[6] BDF, par. 442: 9.

clause to the pronoun is parallel to the epexegetic καί in I Cor. 2: 2[1] where Paul speaks of deciding to 'know' only one thing: 'Jesus Christ and him crucified'.

The absence of the article before κοινωνίαν[2] in v. 10 suggests that καί binds τὴν δύναμιν τῆς ἀναστάσεως αὐτοῦ with κοινωνίαν παθημάτων αὐτοῦ into a single explanation of what it means to 'know Christ'. It is important to notice here that Paul entertains no thought of a temporal distinction between these two ideas. To know Christ now (i.e., to be found in Christ) is to know the power of his resurrection and the fellowship of his sufferings. This union of Christ's death and resurrection as a (temporally) single experience is similar to what Paul says in II Cor. 13: 4f. That the power of the resurrection comes first in the pair only underscores the present significance of this idea.

Like v. 9b, the participial clause of v. 10b is an explication of Paul's thought. In that sense it too is epexegetic. But within vv. 10–11 the two descriptive passages are arranged in chiasmus, and the terminology Paul chooses in the second differs from that of the first. Paul speaks not of Christ's sufferings but of his death (θάνατος) and explains that what he has been speaking of is a transformation to the death of Christ, εἴ πως he may attain to the resurrection. The chiastic arrangement indicates that there is no substantial difference between the two clauses. Both alike speak of death and resurrection. The distinction in language, however, conveys a subtle and important distinction in Paul's perspective on this death and resurrection.

Paul hopes to attain to the resurrection from the dead as the climactic event of Christian life. The change from ἀνάστασις in v. 10a to ἐξανάστασις in v. 11 reveals two different perspectives. In the former, the resurrection contributes to the present reality of Christian existence; in the latter it is the final event of the Christian's life, his own resurrection.[3] This distinction is underlined by the words εἴ πως καταντήσω,[4] showing Paul's unwillingness to consider the final goal as something already assured. In similar fashion, the distinction between δύναμις τῆς

---

[1] *Ibid.*

[2] It is more likely that the v.l. with τήν is designed to balance the second phrase with the first, than that an original article has been removed.

[3] Dibelius, *Thessalonicher-Philipper*, p. 90.

[4] On the use of εἰ cf. BDF, par. 375.

ἀναστάσεως in v. 10a and the ἐξανάστασις itself in v. 11 is not casual. It is precisely the power of Christ which is now available. The present reality of this power, however, does not exhaust the future significance of the resurrection.[1]

We find a parallel distinction in Paul's expression of the reality of Christ's death. Verse 10a speaks of sharing Christ's sufferings, v. 10b of being transformed to his death. Since Paul never speaks of Christ's death as a πάσχειν, it might appear that he has in mind some sufferings of Christ which are not those of his death. The chiastic arrangement of this verse makes this unlikely, however. Moreover, Paul never speaks of Christ's sufferings at all except in contexts where he either links his own sufferings to Christ's or indicates that these are the equivalent of Christ's death.

We have in Phil. 3: 8ff. a clear description of life in Christ as the experience of knowing the power of Christ's resurrection and the fellowship of his sufferings. Not only is ἐν Χριστῷ shown here literally to mean being shaped by Christ's death and resurrection; it also is clear that being so shaped, being ἐν Χριστῷ, is interpreted by Paul as experiencing power and suffering in the same indissoluble unity that characterizes Christ's death and resurrection as salvation events.

Again it should be pointed out that what Paul says is not exclusively a description of apostleship. Personal as this passage appears to be, it describes the common Christian experience.[2] The entire context, and especially the paraenetic tone of vv. 2 and 3, makes this clear.[3]

Boldness in Christ: Philem. 8

In a curious little verse in Philemon, Paul parades a theoretical apostolic authority unmatched elsewhere in his letters. We say theoretical because Paul mentions what he *could* do, but he does

---

[1] As already implied, Phil. 3: 8ff. is virtually a companion piece to Rom. 6: 1–10. Lohmeyer's objections to this stem from his incorrect insistence that the leading idea in Rom. 6 is sacramental, i.e., baptism (*Philipper*, p. 139, n. 2).

[2] Against W. Michaelis, 'πάσχειν etc.', *TDNT*, v, p. 932.

[3] This paraenetic tone is resumed in the climax of v. 14, εἰς τὸ βραβεῖον τῆς ἄνω κλήσεως τοῦ θεοῦ ἐν Χριστῷ Ἰησοῦ. These words illustrate how very close in Paul's mind stand the ideas of his calling and the Christian's, as we have seen in I Cor. 1: 26 – 2: 5.

not do it: 'Wherefore, although I am bold enough in Christ to command you to do what is required (v. 8), yet for love's sake I prefer to appeal to you...' (v. 9).

Paul appeals to Philemon for the acceptance of his runaway slave Onesimus, who is returning. Apparently Paul wishes to set his request in the framework of the mutual relationship between himself and Philemon which he mentions in vv. 6 and 7. Sharing Philemon's faith and love, Paul hopes Philemon will share his regard for the returning slave.[1]

It is therefore all the more surprising to find such a strong statement following διό in v. 8. With a concessive participle (ἔχων) Paul claims for himself a broad authority.[2] 'In Christ' Paul has more than the requisite boldness to command what is required. 'Ανῆκον presumes a binding authority, whether political or religious, to which one is obligated.[3] What is required here, of course, is the proper treatment of the slave.

The verb ἐπιτάσσειν occurs nowhere else in Paul's letters. He uses the noun ἐπιταγή in I Cor. 7: 6, 25 to refer to an authoritative command, as also in II Cor. 8: 8. In these passages it is noteworthy that Paul does not 'have a command' to offer, and offers instead an opinion, a concession or an exhortation. Paul never uses the term in a positive way to refer to some authoritative statement of his own.[4] 'Επιτάσσειν is not infrequent in the New Testament for Jesus' commands (Mark 1: 17; 9: 25, etc.). It is also used of other figures such as Herod (Mark 6: 27) and Ananias (Acts 23: 2). As in the LXX, the verb is confined to situations involving undisputed religious or political authority[5] and carries with it an implied demand for obedience that transcends volition.

Just how Paul has jurisdiction over the affairs of Philemon is not clear. 'What is required' of the slave-owner must be a moral

---

[1] In Knox' view, Paul literally hopes Philemon (or better, Archippus, v. 2) will share Onesimus. Cf. J. Knox, *Philemon Among the Letters of Paul* (New York, 1959).

[2] This authority is all the more remarkable, coming as it does in a letter traditionally interpreted as written from a Roman prison.

[3] Cf. E. Lohmeyer, *Die Briefe an die Kolosser und an Philemon* (Göttingen, 1956[11]; KEK), p. 183.

[4] In Rom. 16: 26 he refers to an ἐπιταγή of the eternal God.

[5] Lohmeyer, *Philemon*, p. 183, n. 2.

obligation; it can scarcely be a legal one. Perhaps this fact itself explains Paul's reference to having πολλὴν ἐν Χριστῷ παρρησίαν. If Paul means that he has the requisite 'boldness, audacity' to command Philemon, he may be indicating that he himself knows the intervention to be unprecedented.

The context itself lends to the word the sense of 'authority'.[1] Yet it is not an unmitigated authority. It is authority 'in Christ'. The position of ἐν Χριστῷ, intervening between the noun and its modifier, indicates that Paul wishes to explain what kind of (as well as how much) authority he has.[2] It seems reasonable to assume that Paul has in mind the παρρησία which he mentions in II Cor. 3: 12, 7: 4, and in Phil. 1: 20. In II Cor. 3 παρρησία stands over against the idea of 'veiling', which implies shame. The hope engendered by the new covenant makes bold, and this boldness is freedom (3: 17). Paul specifically connects παρρησία with the opposite idea of shame (αἰσχύνεσθαι) in Phil. 1: 20, a passage which shows the sharp eschatological flavor which both words can have in Paul's vocabulary. II Cor. 7: 4 may be part of this same pattern. Paul's παρρησία in the Corinthian community is nothing other than his boast about them. Verse 4 is the positive expression of the *apologia* in v. 2.[3] 'Boasting' in its positive sense is also an eschatological idea in Paul (cf. Rom. 3: 27; 5: 7; I Cor. 4: 7).[4]

These uses of παρρησία are not homogeneous. There is no single English word which translates all of them with equal success. But together they present a picture of religious, eschatological freedom, not legal or divine right. Thus while the concept of authority is clearly present in Philem. 8, Paul is referring to eschatological freedom grounded in the new covenant.

Thus it is no surprise that for the sake of love Paul prefers to appeal, rather than command. His authority is not grounded in such fashion as to exclude all others. Though he is a πρεσβύτης

---

[1] Cf. H. Schlier, 'παρρησία etc.', *TDNT*, v, pp. 871–86: 'In Philem. 8, ...we have an instance of παρρησία in much the same sense as ἐξουσία' (p. 883).

[2] The emphasis is not, as Neugebauer supposes, on Paul's *having* παρρησία in Christ, though the distinction is admittedly subtle.

[3] Cf. Windisch, *Korintherbrief*, p. 221.

[4] Rom. 5: 2, 'we *boast* in the *hope* of the *glory* of God', echoes the 'hope' and 'glory' of II Cor. 3: 11–12.

and δέσμιος Χριστοῦ, his boldness is in Christ, and all Christians are in Christ.[1]

The appeal to love as the proper motive for and limit to exercising one's will is a firm part of Paul's exhortation to the communities. 'Knowledge puffs up, but love builds up' (I Cor. 8: 1). We shall see that where Paul speaks directly of his own ἐξουσία, its purpose also is οἰκοδομεῖν.

BUILDING UP

In II Cor. 10: 8 and 13: 10 Paul mentions an authority he has to 'build up and not tear down'. The word ἐξουσία is striking. In reference to apostolic authority Paul uses it only here and in I Cor. 9, where it represents a 'right' which he renounces.

Schmithals has interpreted Paul to mean here that he has an authority exclusive of that of the preacher of God's word, a pneumatic authority which remains hidden to us. This is not the case. The conjunction of 'building up' and 'destroying' is frequent in the Old Testament: Isa. 49: 17; Jer. 24: 6; 31: 28; 42: 10; 45: 41; Ezek. 36: 36; Psalms 28: 5; Job 12: 14; Prov. 14: 1. In respect to God's dealing with the people of Israel, building is what he does with grace, destroying what he does with judgment. God's grace and judgment correspond to Israel's obedience and disobedience.[2]

It is not only God who builds and destroys. In his prophet God is himself speaking and acting, so that God can say to Jeremiah: 'Behold, I have put my words in your mouth. See, I have set you this day over nations and over kingdoms, to pluck up and break down, to destroy and overthrow, to build and to plant' (Jeremiah 1: 9b–10). The same eschatological self-consciousness which informs the use of this image in the Old Testament is in Paul's mind when he uses it of his ἐξουσία. This is confirmed by the fact that Paul does not think of authority as anything other than the authority granted him in his commission to preach the gospel.

---

[1] Neugebauer, *In Christus*, p. 120: 'Authority in Christ is an authority over brethren which receives its definition and derives from the merciful redeemer. Hence "in Christ" denotes the apostle's authority as a derived one, founded on a calling. That is the indicative of the apostolate from which, in our passage, the imperative, in the proper sense of the word, follows.'

[2] Cf. P. Vielhauer, *Oikodome* (Karlsruhe-Durlach, 1939), pp. 11–12.

The idea of 'building up' plays a role in Rom. 15: 20 and I Cor. 3: 10–15. In both instances it relates specifically to apostolic authority. We have already seen that the passage in Romans comes in the context of Paul's explaining the fullness of his work in the gospel, which is to be accounted for by Christ's working in him.[1] Paul says that if he preaches where Christ has already been named, he builds on another foundation (ἐπ' ἀλλότριον θεμέλιον οἰκοδομῶ). Despite the fact that v. 21 interprets this preaching as missionary preaching, vv. 15–20 show Paul to be thinking of 'preaching the gospel' in the broader sense of inaugurating the powers of the gospel. 'Building' is simply a metaphor Paul uses to express his sustained interest in and responsibility for the gospel understood in its durative dimension, with reference to the community.

The image shifts slightly in I Cor. 3: 10–15. Now the roles of laying the foundation and building are more sharply differentiated. According to the grace given him, Paul has laid a foundation in Corinth, and another (Apollos) is building on it. But the foundation which Paul has laid is none other than Jesus Christ himself. Since Paul specifically refers to the grace given him by which he accomplishes this, he must mean here that he has preached the gospel; and apparently he means he preached it when Corinth was virgin territory. Apollos' role is now to build on that foundation.

What is noteworthy in these two passages is the way in which it is assumed that beyond the preaching of the gospel there is a continuing responsibility for the life of the community. This 'building up', like missionary preaching, is traced back to God's own activity. Paul compares his work with Apollos' in order to show that there can be no division in Corinth centering around these two personalities. Both are 'servants *through whom you believed*, as the Lord gave to each' (v. 5). If Paul planted and Apollos watered, it was God who gave the growth (v. 6).

When, therefore, Paul says his ἐξουσία is οἰκοδομεῖν, he is claiming for himself the same authority which inheres in his commission to preach the gospel. The center of gravity of this figure is the activity of God, continuous and continuing in the life of the community.

[1] Cf. above, pp. 213f.

THE IMITATION OF PAUL AND OF CHRIST[1]

Because Paul's life as an apostle itself reflects the power of God made manifest in the gospel, the apostle becomes a 'norm' for Christians much as the gospel is a norm for apostolic behavior. This is expressed by Paul's exhortations to the imitation of himself. I Thess. 1: 6; Phil. 3: 17; I Cor. 4: 16; 11: 1 (cf. I Thess. 2: 14).

An exception to Paul's appeal for others to imitate him is I Thess. 2: 14, where he speaks of the Thessalonians' having become imitators 'of the churches of God in Christ Jesus which are in Judaea'. This unusual verse suggests that imitation for Paul is not a matter of disciples following a master. It is not merely Paul who can be imitated. The Thessalonians have become imitators of the Judaean churches because like the Judaeans they have suffered for their faith. The context here is not exhortative. Paul is not asking that this be the case; he is stating that this is indeed what has happened. Its significance is found in v. 13. When the Thessalonians heard Paul preach God's word, they accepted it for what it was. It was not man's word but God's word at work (ἐνεργεῖται) in them. That they accepted it as God's word working in them is shown by the fact that they have now become imitators of the Judaean Christians. Their persecution has become the index, the credential which authenticates their reception of it as λόγος θεοῦ.

As has been noticed by many interpreters, 'imitation' has here a predominantly passive quality about it.[2] This is due not solely to the use of ἐγενήθητε[3] with the noun μιμητής, but also to the connection which exists between vv. 13 and 14. Paul does not say that the Thessalonians have sought to imitate others. He

---

[1] Cf. W. Michaelis, 'μιμέομαι etc.', *TDNT*, IV, pp. 659–74; D. M. Stanley, '"Become Imitators of Me", Apostolic Tradition in Paul', *Biblica* 40 (1958), pp. 859–77 (cf. his *The Apostolic Church in the New Testament* [Westminster, Md., 1965], pp. 371–89); E. J. Tinsley, *The Imitation of God in Christ* (London, 1960); W. P. de Boer, *The Imitation of Paul* (Kampen, 1962); E. Larsson, *Christus als Vorbild* (Uppsala, 1962); A. Schulz, *Nachfolgen und Nachahmen* (München, 1962); Betz, *Nachahmung*, pp. 137–89.

[2] Cf. for example, Stanley, 'Imitators' (*Biblica*, pp. 865, 867); Michaelis, *TDNT* p. 670; C. Masson, *Les deux épîtres de saint Paul aux Thessaloniciens* (1959), p. 21.

[3] Masson, *Thessaloniciens*, p. 21: 'It is certain that the agent of the passive verb is God.'

is remarking that the word of God has become an effective force in their midst, the proof of which is their 'imitation'. The passive tone is then reinforced by the verb πάσχειν with ὑπό in v. 14.[1] The active, voluntary aspect of what has happened in Thessalonica is the Thessalonians' 'acceptance' (δέχεσθαι) of the word of God from Paul as they 'received' (παραλαμβάνειν) it. Since they have 'accepted' it as an 'active word', Paul gives thanks. He knows they have done so because he sees in them the same steadfast faith in the face of suffering that he sees elsewhere.

It is not insignificant that this 'acceptance' of God's word for which Paul gives thanks is itself the occasion of a former thanksgiving in 1: 4ff. Paul knows that God has 'chosen' the Thessalonians, 'for our gospel came to you not only in word, but also in power and in the Holy Spirit and with full abundance'. In the same breath Paul adds: 'Just as you know what kind of men we became among you on your account.' What Paul proved to be personally was nothing different from what 'his' gospel showed itself to be. By the same token, the Thessalonians became imitators of Paul and of the Lord (μιμηταὶ ἡμῶν ἐγενήθητε καὶ τοῦ κυρίου) with the result that they themselves became an example (τύπον) to all who believed in Macedonia and Achaia. This example of theirs means that they have shared in preaching the word of the Lord.

As in ch. 2, so here also Paul's thankfulness is called forth by what he knows of the force of the gospel in this community. It came in power, with the Holy Spirit, in full abundance (v. 5a). This mode of appearance is in fact nothing different from the way in which the apostle himself appeared (v. 5b). Then, in becoming imitators, the Thessalonians 'accepted' (δεξάμενοι) the word in much affliction with the joy of the Holy Spirit (v. 6). There would be no continuity in Paul's thought unless the affliction of the apostle which they imitate can be equated with the power in which he appeared in coming to them, i.e., unless the powerful apostle is also the weak and suffering one.

---

[1] W. P. de Boer, *Imitation*, tries to soften this passive tone. The dependent ἐγενήθην is certainly not militantly passive. Πάσχειν ὑπό he finds more difficult. That Paul does not preclude all possibility of the Thessalonians' having decided to do as others have done is beside the point. It is the word at work in them which is held responsible for what Paul chooses to call here 'imitation'.

Then, in becoming his imitators, the Thessalonians themselves become the means of transmitting the word of the Lord, as Paul has done.

Thus the Thessalonians have manifested the power of God in their own weakness, which is what Paul also says in 2: 14. Between these two passages there is a sustained defense of Paul's apostolic behavior (2: 1–12) intended to remind them that his visit was not 'in vain' (2: 1). It was not in vain despite the odds Paul faced and the manner in which he subordinated himself to the necessities of the situation. It was not in vain because the power of the gospel was brought precisely in and through Paul's preaching of the word.

Before leaving I Thessalonians we should notice that while imitation here is an accomplished fact, there is an imperative note introduced by Paul in 2: 10–12. Behaving himself with holiness, righteousness and blamelessness, Paul exhorted and besought the Thessalonians to live ἀξίως τοῦ θεοῦ τοῦ καλοῦντος ὑμᾶς εἰς τὴν βασιλείαν καὶ δόξαν. God's calling is thought of here as a continuing act, and Paul's behavior was ὑμῖν τοῖς πιστεύουσιν (v. 10). The apostle behaves as one worthy of the calling of God in order to urge others to that same worthiness.

In I Cor. 4: 16 the reference to imitation is in the form of an imperative. Paul is not reminiscing over what has already happened. As Paul's 'children' in Thessalonica have become imitators of him, so he urges his children here to do the same. Because of Paul's reference to 'teaching', v. 17, Michaelis interprets Paul here as demanding obedience to his precepts.[1] The difficulty with this interpretation is that what Paul teaches is not clear. Nor does Paul elsewhere demand this kind of obedience. The Christian is obedient to the gospel, not to the apostle or the apostle's rules. When, as in II Cor. 10, the Christian is thought of as necessarily obedient to the apostle, it is because the apostle himself manifests the same power visible in the gospel.

Paul's 'teaching', as we have seen, could well be his behavior as he catalogs it in 4: 9ff. This is the more likely in the absence of any direct reference to διδάσκειν, and in light of 4: 6. Paul concludes a paragraph (vv. 1–5) in which he rejects the Corinthian disease of 'judging' with the claim that God will

---

[1] *TDNT* IV, p. 668.

give the final commendation. He has 'applied all this to Apollos' and himself (v. 6) for the benefit of the Corinthians, ἵνα ἐν ἡμῖν μάθητε τὸ μὴ ὑπὲρ ἃ γέγραπται, ἵνα μὴ εἷς ὑπὲρ τοῦ ἑνὸς φυσιοῦσθε κατὰ τοῦ ἑτέρου. What the Corinthians should 'learn' from Paul is what he 'teaches' everywhere, his 'ways in Christ'. These are described in vv. 10–13 in terms of weakness. But when Paul comes he will find out what power the arrogant ones have, for the Kingdom of God consists of power (v. 20). Because Paul's weakness itself is power, what he urges is that the Corinthians become powerful through this same weakness. This is what they are to imitate.

Paul urges on the Corinthians something more specific than just a posture of humility. His awareness that his whole life reflects the weakness-power dialectic of Christ and the word of the cross is an awareness of being continually obedient and subservient to the gospel. It is, in fact, an expression of Paul's awareness of his role in the on-going gospel. This comes to expression in I Cor. 11 : 1 in Paul's request: μιμηταί μου γίνεσθε, καθὼς κἀγὼ Χριστοῦ. The imitation Paul calls for is exemplified in 10: 33. He is one μὴ ζητῶν τὸ (ἑαυτοῦ) συμφέρον ἀλλὰ τὸ τῶν πολλῶν. In commending this attitude to others, Paul is merely repeating what he has said in 10: 24, 'Let no one seek his own good, but the good of the other one.' That verse, in turn, is an elaboration of 10: 23: 'All things are lawful but not all things are helpful. All things are lawful, but not all things build up.' We have seen that the idea of 'building up' is but another way in which Paul envisions the continuing work of God in the life of his people. It is a norm not only for the apostle, but the congregation as well (I Cor. 8: 1; 14: 5, 12, 17, 26). In that sense the community participates in the activity of God, which is the on-going activity of the gospel. Thus while Paul urges himself on the community as an example to be followed, what he is urging is not obedience to his own commands, but obedience to the gospel itself as it actively sustains and should inform the life of the community. He can do so because he understands himself as one who has become transparent to the gospel.

This is what Paul also reflects in his imitation of Christ. There is no reference in the immediately preceding verses to anything Christ has done. Only σωθῶσιν of 10: 33 echoes Christ's own work of saving. But is it likely that Paul means that as Christ saved, so he, Paul, saves? Is this how he imitates Christ? That this is not the most reasonable interpretation is suggested by several factors.

In the first place, Paul urges the Corinthians to imitate him *just as* (καθώς) he imitates Christ. Yet what he urges them to do is 'build up'. They are not urged to 'save others' as Christ saved. In the same way, there is no reason to think of Paul's equating his work with Christ's, so that both alike 'save'. Paul 'continues' the work of Christ only in the more passive and oblique sense of reflecting the power and activity of God in his life; he does this precisely by being weak.[1] This is not a decisive action like Christ's saving man through his death and resurrection. The work of Christ is constitutive; the work of Paul is reflective. It reflects the same power, God's power, which informs the deeds of Christ. But those founding events of death and resurrection are irretrievably ἐφάπαξ. So even in Rom. 15: 1–3 the 'continuation' of Christ's work is not itself constitutive, but dependent on that work. It builds up. There is no reference in I Cor. 11: 1 to what, in fact, Paul imitates when he imitates Christ. Nor do his letters at all suggest any qualities or attributes of Christ which are normative, except the quality of weakness in which power is manifested. It must, therefore, be in this way that Paul imitates Christ and the Corinthians are to imitate Paul.

This is a highly qualified understanding of imitation. At every turn Paul's own references to himself as bearing the weakness and the power of Christ's cross show that while this weakness and power are understood in their personal manifestation in Paul's life, Paul does not think of himself as the agent. It is God's weakness and power which is evident in his life. It is God who is acting through Paul. The apostle is not so much the agent as the vessel of the one whose power really does shine through weakness. In short, Paul is of himself insufficient; his sufficiency comes from God. Thus the charge to imitate this 'pattern' cannot be thought of exclusively, or even primarily, in terms of man's own power. To imitate the weakness and

[1] Cf. Betz, *Nachahmung*, p. 159: 'Quite clearly, through such a μίμησις τοῦ Παύλου the Corinthians should be led into the δύναμις τοῦ σταυροῦ τοῦ Χριστοῦ.' Stanley, 'Imitators', understands Paul's imitation of the Lord (I Thess. 1: 6) and of Christ (I Cor. 1: 11) as Paul's becoming himself a suffering servant.

power of Christ is to become the recipient of God's power in one's own weakness. This alone explains the passive sense of imitation in I Thess. 1 and 2. There imitation is simply what is seen of the work of the powerful gospel, the powerful word, at work in the community. To 'imitate' Paul or Christ, or another church in its suffering, is to be receptive to the fullness of God's power which never is to be separated from weakness and suffering.

Phil. 3: 17 is the only other passage in which Paul calls for imitation of himself. There he uses the unusual noun συμμι-μηταί.[1] Paul means that the Philippians should join with him in imitation. The exhortation follows Paul's demand: 'Let us hold true to what we have attained' (v. 16), where what has been attained is the present situation of sharing Christ's sufferings and the power of his resurrection (v. 10). In this posture the Christian at once 'knows Christ' or is found in Christ, and at the same time presses on to the ultimate goal (vv. 12ff.).

Here as clearly as anywhere we see the unique implications of 'imitation'. One cannot merely decide to appropriate Christ's weakness and power.[2] Being shaped by the death and resurrection of Christ depends on the power of that death and resurrection being operative in the whole of life. This is God's power, not man's. The Christian does not mime the events of Christ; he reflects them. But this reflection depends on his willingness to receive the word as God's own word, not merely man's (I Thess. 1: 16; 2: 13). It is no accident that Paul counsels the imitation of himself. His whole apostolic self-consciousness is shot through with this awareness of his personal service in weakness which is at the same time God's power in him. Such a relationship to the gospel is not reserved for the apostle alone, any more than the demand for οἰκοδομεῖν is exclusively his. What Paul reflects as an apostle is only a facet of the possibility, the demand of the new life in Christ. The imita-

[1] The συν- compound of this noun is rare and difficult to interpret. It may be redundant, not affecting μιμηταί; it could indicate that Paul wants his readers to join in being imitators as he is one; or it could mean that the Philippians are to unite their internal divisions by their common act of imitating. For a full discussion of the problems and possibilities cf. de Boer, *Imitation*, pp. 177ff.

[2] Cf. our interpretation of v. 10 above, and especially the significance of the passive verb ἐζημιώθην in v. 8.

tion of Paul is an imperative that has its only source in the indicative of this new life, so that its acceptance itself becomes the reaffirmation of the indicative (cf. I Thess. 1: 7ff.).

CONCLUSIONS

Paul's consistent reference to the apostle's being 'in Christ' is part of the whole christological, soteriological rationale for apostolic activity denoted by the phrases 'of Christ', 'through Christ' and 'in Christ'. None of these shows why Paul should be an apostle and some other Christian should not. But all show that apostleship has its clear limit in God's working in the apostle by and on the basis of what he did in Christ. This may also be stated as Christ's working in the apostle.

There is a central point at which the work of God in Christ and Christ's own work merge: the gospel. Thus it is that the specifically *apostolic* quality of Paul's self-consciousness focuses on his charge to preach the gospel. All Christians are men τοῦ Χριστοῦ and ἐν Χριστῷ. Less general and more distinctively apostolic is the claim that because he is in Christ and of Christ, the apostle is himself the vessel of God's work through Christ. For Paul we have seen that this close connection to the gospel, the source and norm of apostolic activity, is made possible by the nature of the gospel as an on-going force, the continuation of God's action. Paul's service in the gospel transforms the christological-soteriological hallmarks of the apostle.

Paul appropriates to his *entire* ministry this close relationship to the gospel. In a sense all that Paul does is a reflection of what the gospel does; all that he is, is a reflection of what the gospel is. As the gospel is the manifestation of God's acting, so is the apostle.

THE SHAPE OF APOSTOLIC AUTHORITY

It is interesting to note that many of the themes which Paul connects with the apostle's being 'in Christ' are such an important part of his apostolic self-awareness that they are repeatedly mentioned, even when this qualifying phrase is absent. This is especially true of his boasting and his references to weakness, power and suffering.

232

PAUL'S APOSTOLIC BOAST

As all men who boast should boast 'of the Lord', so does the apostle himself. Boasting of the Lord is boasting in the new creation where there is experienced the calling, creative activity of God (I Cor. 1: 31). The whole meaning of 'boasting' turns on the distinction between man's own accomplishments and God's action. Thus we have seen Paul boasting in his labors, yet boasting 'in Christ' because Christ himself is active in the apostle's labors (Rom. 15: 17).

This boast becomes pride in the Christian communities. It is striking to see the eschatological dimension of the term καυ-χᾶσθαι carried over into the figurative sense of II Cor. 7: 14: ὅτι εἴ τι αὐτῷ ὑπὲρ ὑμῶν κεκαύχημαι, οὐ κατῃσχύνθην...οὕτως καὶ ἡ καύχησις ἡμῶν ἐπὶ Τίτου ἀλήθεια ἐγενήθη. Sometimes it is a pride which must be sustained by concrete action on their part (II Cor. 8: 24; 9: 2, 3).

Paul's pride may be that of the parent in those whom he has begotten (I Cor. 4: 15), but the life he has opened to them is eschatological life in Christ. Thus, too, his boasting is the genuine 'eschatological' boasting of one who knows his work can be and will be judged one day. In I Thess. 2: 19 Paul speaks of the Thessalonians themselves as the hope, joy and crown of his καύχησις 'before our Lord Jesus in his coming'. Thus in Phil. 2: 16 Paul is hopeful of having not 'run in vain or labored in vain'. These terms are characteristically used by Paul in the context of the on-going work of the gospel itself (I Cor. 1: 17; Gal. 2: 2; I Cor. 15: 14, 17), as we have already seen. If the Philippians 'hold fast to the word of life', Paul will have a boast in the day of the Lord. His boast, which depends on his not having labored in vain, ultimately depends on the gospel's not having been emptied of its power. So the boast is derivative in one sense. It depends not alone on what Paul does, not even alone on what the Philippians do, but on what the gospel, which he preaches and they hold fast to, accomplishes. Still, to be able to boast at all, he must labor in the gospel and they must hold fast to it. In *this* sense Paul's pride is parental pride in those whom he has begotten and who now stand in the gospel. Again, boasting denotes not Paul's pride in himself or in his own work, but his sense of responsibility for his own role in God's work in which he has been commissioned to participate.

From the future eschatological 'boast' Paul can move into the present, not only in the figurative sense of II Cor. 7: 14, but in a genuinely eschatological sense. II Cor. 7: 4 explains Paul's confidence (παρρησία) and pride (καύχησις) as his being 'filled with comfort'. In his affliction he is overjoyed. 'Affliction' and 'comfort' are the present manifestations of the death and resurrection of Christ which the Christian shares (II Cor. 1: 3ff.). Thus he and the Corinthians 'live together' and 'die together'. These unusual terms (συναποθανεῖν, συзῆν) seem to refer to more than just dying and living with Christ. Συναποθανεῖν is not found elsewhere in Paul, though συзήσομεν is used in Rom. 6: 5 for sharing Christ's life. Here the terms reflect the union of Paul and the Corinthians in the soteriological event of Christ's death and resurrection. Paul's pride in the Corinthians is based on his knowledge that he and they together share the death and resurrection of Christ. Again we see the peculiarly ambivalent meaning of such pride. It is personal pride for Paul as an apostle whose preaching brought to Corinth the 'word of the cross', the message of Christ's own death and resurrection. But in that word, and thus in Paul's whole labor, God himself is acting. Paul and the Corinthians are alike the beneficiaries of that activity.

This close relationship of the apostle to the community is one in which the apostle shares the experience of the community because both together share something which originates beyond them. For this reason Paul's pride can be mutually enjoyed by the church: 'I hope...that you can be proud of us as we can of you, on the day of the Lord Jesus' (II Cor. 1: 14; cf. 5: 12; Phil. 1: 26).

Since Paul's boast covers all that has been accomplished through him, he may also boast of how he has behaved in his ministry. His behavior is marked by 'holiness and godly sincerity' (II Cor. 1: 12). Yet this boast too is in something other than himself, for he has done so 'not with earthly wisdom, but by the grace of God'.

In summary, the idea of boasting shows more the limit of Paul's activity than his own personal contribution. Despite the fact that the term is inevitably personal, Paul uses it to point beyond what is seen and heard in him to the real agent whose hand is visible in all of Paul's own accomplishments. Yet the personal dimension of boasting is not to be surrendered. Paul does not hesitate to point to himself since in doing so he points beyond himself.

In I Cor. 9 Paul rejects a 'rightful claim' which he might make upon the community. He does not accept financial support, in order that he may put no hindrance in the path of the gospel (v. 12). His 'ground for boasting' is also his service to the fullness of the gospel – even if this means rejecting an apostolic right. The same theme arises in II Cor. 11: 10, and must be understood in the same way. Only now Paul has achieved a clear distinction between himself and those who insidiously move into his apostolic labors. In their 'boasted mission' (ἐν ᾧ καυχῶνται) they have failed to see the peculiarly subordinating quality of Paul's own boast in this manner.

This problem of Paul's rejection of an apostolic 'right' is important, as its prominence in the Corinthian correspondence indicates. It is important for us, because it gives an insight into Paul's understanding of authority. It is clear that he knows he has the right to claim support from Corinth (I Cor. 9: 3–12). This is an apostolic right. But Paul's rejection of it is based on a higher authority than apostolic privilege; it is based on the demands made on him by the fullness of the gospel in Corinth. His 'boast' becomes, once again, his claim to have subordinated himself to this gospel. In Corinth he has done so in the particular way such subordination was demanded under the circumstances.[1] That his failure to make use of his right could be interpreted by his opponents in Corinth as a sign of his lacking apostolic status shows that their criteria of apostolic authority were not his. At this point Paul refuses to invoke an authority which is rightfully his in order to submit himself to a greater authority, the demand of the gospel.

Our interpretation of II Cor. 10–13[2] is substantiated further by Paul's references to boasting in 11: 10 – 12: 9. He asks that he too be allowed to boast 'a little' (11: 16). This can only mean that his opponents also boast, and Paul wishes to make

[1] Paul's decision not to accept support in Corinth is not a consistent feature of his apostolic behavior (II Cor. 11: 7f.; Phil. 4: 10).
[2] Above, ch. 6.

his reply to their vaunting claims on their own behalf. Nowhere do we see more clearly the subtleties of the 'boasting' terminology than in these verses. Here the full force of Paul's estimate of his 'personal qualities' as an apostle come to the fore. He speaks in personal terms but manages to ground his boast outside of his own personal achievements. The very necessity of making the separation between himself and the source of his strength, however, is distasteful. It might be misconstrued as a purely personal *apologia* (as indeed it is, in one sense), despite what it shows Paul's position actually to be. Hence, he speaks not κατὰ κύριον, but ὡς ἐν ἀφροσύνῃ (v. 17),[1] for he will now boast 'since many boast κατὰ σάρκα'.

Apparently Paul means in v. 18 that he too will boast 'according to the flesh'. He prepares for the proper understanding of this in v. 21 with a reference to his own weakness. There follows in vv. 21b–29 a catalog of what Paul has suffered in the flesh, beginning with an argument designed to show that he is the equal of his opponents (v. 22). But in v. 23 he is no longer content to be equal; he is superior. He is a better servant of Christ. This is substantiated in vv. 22–9 exclusively by reference to what he has suffered, and reaches its climax in v. 30: 'If it is necessary to boast, I will boast of what shows my weakness.'

In this context 12: 1–4 constitutes a striking departure from what Paul has been saying. He 'will go on to visions and revelations of the Lord', and does so by referring to a vision he himself had fourteen years ago. Such a vision is scarcely a sign of weakness. What is important for Paul, however, is the relative uselessness of this particular boast. He must boast (δεῖ); he is driven to it. But what he now says will gain nothing, οὐ συμφέρον.[2]

Paul uses συμφέρω and the adjective σύμφορος to describe the individual good of the Christian and the common good of the Christian community. The fact that all occurrences fall within the confines of our two Corinthian letters suggests that there is some cohesion among them. In I Cor. 6: 12 Paul counters the argument of those who would interpret their freedom in Christ

[1] Or, Paul speaks 'as a fool' inasmuch as what he will boast about will not appear worthy of boasting (Bultmann, *Probleme*, p. 27).

[2] For a defense of the text of B, G, p46 and others, cf. Lietzmann, *Korinther*, p. 152.

as meaning 'all things are lawful for me' with the reminder that 'not all things are helpful' (οὐ πάντα συμφέρει). This is interpreted further in I Cor. 10: 23: 'All things are lawful, but not all things are helpful' (οὐ πάντα συμφέρει); 'all things are lawful, but not all things build up' (οὐ πάντα οἰκοδομεῖ). The addition of οἰκοδομεῖν in I Cor. 10 makes Paul's position clear as regards the whole community, just as in 6: 12, where he is dealing with an individual position (πάντα μοι ἔξεστιν), he elaborates by saying: 'I shall not be enslaved to anything.' This individual good and the common good merge in I Cor. 10: 33 when Paul speaks of his own behavior: 'Just as I try to please all men in everything, not seeking my own advantage, but that of many in order that they may be saved.' The apostle's concern for the common good is also indicated by σύμφορος in I Cor. 7: 35 and συμφέρω in II Cor. 8: 10. All this is merely a reflection of the fact that the Spirit which the community possesses in various forms is itself intended for the common good (I Cor. 12: 7).

When Paul says in II Cor. 12: 1 of the vision he is about to relate that οὐ συμφέρον, he does not mean merely that there is nothing to be gained for his argument by this particular boasting. He means that the boasting itself makes no contribution to the common good that he, as an apostle, must bear in mind. In these cryptic verses Paul distinguishes between his personal claim to grace and his apostolic claim to grace (vv. 6–10).[1] Thus he moves on quickly in vv. 6ff. to reiterate what he has already made clear, that he will boast in weakness.

[1] Relating this passage to II Cor. 5: 13–14 and the problem of glossolalia in I Cor. 14, Käsemann ('Legitimität', p. 17) has provided a careful analysis of the way Paul distinguishes between manifestation of the Spirit in his personal life and in his apostolic διακονία. On this view, while we cannot distinguish between 'sarkic' Paul and pneumatic Paul here, we can and should distinguish between Paul's private life and his apostolic ministry. Paul does so to show that the private gifts (as is true with glossolalia) are limited in their application, but as χαρίσματα are marks of the one χάρις which is also the force in his apostolic life. Käsemann's interpretation would have been better grounded had he noticed the distinctive συμφέρον in v. 1 instead of tying the distinction to ἐν σώματι/ἐκτὸς τοῦ σώματος (v. 2). The latter has nothing to do with some putative distinction between personal and apostolic standing in grace.

In fact, the distinction is unacceptable in these terms. It should by now be clear that Paul does not separate his claim to apostolic authority from what he sees in himself and others should see in him. He thrusts himself into

The vision is of no account in Paul's own defense because it does not correspond to what is seen and heard in him (v. 6). In his ministry Paul is not an ecstatic, pneumatic creature. He is Paul of the thorn in the flesh (v. 7). The curious style of the third person in vv. 1–5 and Paul's transition in v. 5 show that Paul wishes both to identify himself with the man of the vision and distance himself from that man. In order to accomplish the latter he need only return to his boasting in weakness. He does so in vv. 7–10 in such fashion as to lay claim to the whole dialectic of weakness and power.

What Paul says of boasting in II Cor. 12: 1ff. is paradigmatic of the peculiar usefulness the term has for him everywhere. In boasting he turns attention to his own person, and his own work. But Paul is not in any unqualified sense an initiatory agent of the gospel. He is a 'passive agent', the recipient of power which enables him to do his work, which, in fact, works through him.

THE APOSTLE'S WEAKNESS AND POWER

There is no reason to think more of Paul than what is seen in, and heard from, him. Yet one sees in Paul the suffering, weak apostle of II Cor. 11: 23–9, and one hears from him the sounds of a man 'unskilled in speaking' (11: 6, cf. 10: 10). If this is to be recognizably Paul of the unparalleled vision of the third heaven, then his weakness must visibly become an asset and cease to be a liability. It is no accident that Paul juxtaposes the vision of vv. 1–4 with his boast of weakness in vv. 7–11. By doing so he underlines the continuity of the one gift, the one recipient, the one source.

Lest Paul's revelations serve to make him think too highly of himself (ὑπεραίρομαι, cf. II Thess. 2: 4), he is humbled by his thorn in the flesh,[1] a veritable messenger from Satan. But when

the very center of the discussion and in doing so he also insists upon his own subordination to a power beyond himself; for he is not responsible, as it were, for who he is. Thus he can actually boast of a vision (which all would say was 'powerful') in a negative (and cryptic) fashion, thereby making the claim that his own weakness (which nobody would agree was 'powerful') represents the same source of strength and grace.

[1] On the possibilities for understanding the σκόλοψ τῇ σαρκί cf. the extended notes in Lietzmann, *Korinther*, pp. 156ff.

he beseeches the Lord that it might leave him, the Lord says to Paul: 'My grace is sufficient for you, for[1] power is made perfect in weakness.' Paul is no longer in danger of thinking too highly of himself; but no revelation in the third heaven could mean more for his authority than his frail person does. In his weakness the very power of Christ comes to full expression.[2] 'Χάρις is for Paul a δύναμις, a power'.[3]

Power as an Authenticating Sign

The power of signs and wonders and the power of the Holy Spirit are the means of Christ's working through Paul, Rom. 15: 19. This description of power is intended to elucidate the cryptic λόγῳ καὶ ἔργῳ of v. 18[4] and show how Paul can claim to have 'fully preached the gospel'. Preaching the gospel fully is inaugurating those powers whose origin is beyond Paul, but which are manifested in what he says and what he does.

Paul distinguishes between the mere word and something more important in I Thess. 1: 4, 5 and totally erases the line between his effort 'of the word' and the visible power which accompanies it in I Cor. 2: 4, 5. His speech (λόγος) and his proclamation (κήρυγμα) are not in persuasive words of wisdom, but are themselves 'in the demonstration of Spirit and power'. The counterpart of this demonstration is that Paul himself was there 'in weakness and in much fear and trembling' (v. 3).

Only from this background can we understand the reference in II Cor. 12: 11f. to the signs (σημεῖα) of the apostle. Paul claims that these signs were indeed present in his Corinthian ministry, being performed with 'signs and wonders (σημεῖα καὶ τέρατα) and mighty works (δυνάμεις)'. The reference seems to be a defense in the face of what Paul's opponents found missing in him,[5] but it is given so cryptically as to defy elucidation. Yet

---

[1] The reading δύναμίς μου of the Koine is secondary. The absence of μου, however, does not give the 'paradoxical sentence' a proverbial character (Windisch, *Korintherbrief*, p. 391).

[2] Τελεῖται (RSV, 'made perfect') means 'achieves its consummation' (BAG, p. 818).

[3] G. P. Wetter, *Charis* (Leipzig, 1913), p. 30.

[4] So Michel, *Römer*, p. 329.

[5] Schmithals, *Office*, pp. 36f. Cf. also Kümmel in the appendix to Lietzmann, *Korinther*, p. 213.

coming in the context of Paul's description of his weakness, the reference seems to be to the 'power and signs and wonders' of Rom. 15: 19. Whatever Paul's opponents had in mind, he means that these were not lacking in Corinth.

All these references to power visible in Paul's ministry serve to authenticate his work as truly effective and originating in the power of God. Together they serve to point beyond the limit of missionary preaching to the 'fullness of the gospel'. Together they are understood by Paul as inextricably bound up with his own weakness.

Power as Authority over the Community

Paul's word is something more than mere speaking in the initial proclamation of the gospel. It comes replete with power so that his word and his deeds together constitute his ministry. The gospel is fully preached by this power effective in word and deed. Moreover, Paul's concern for and authority over those whom he has begotten in Christ extends throughout his and their life in Christ, just as, and because, the gospel extends throughout their common life. Paul's continuing concern for the Christian community is but a facet of that power which has brought the fullness of the gospel. Just as the gospel cannot be confined to one point in the past but continues as the focus of God's weakness and power, so that weakness and power in Paul find continued application in his relationship to the community. If this is clear in II Cor. 13: 4, it is no less so in II Cor. 10: 1–6. By the 'weakness' of Christ Paul beseeches the Corinthians not to force him to show boldness, as he is confident they can, against those who accuse him of acting in a worldly fashion.

How is the objection to Paul, that he behaves in a worldly manner, related to his concern for Corinth's obedience? Paul cannot be accused of behaving immorally. While we can often distinguish between the anthropological designation ἐν σαρκί as a neutral expression, and the more derogatory ethical term κατὰ σάρκα (especially with περιπατεῖν, cf. Rom. 8: 4), κατὰ σάρκα does not necessarily mean anything different from the more neutral ἐν σαρκί (cf. II Cor. 5: 16). At least it is clear that if the charge against Paul concerns ethics or morality, he offers no defense. But what does Paul go on to say about his walking κατὰ σάρκα? He first of all admits to being ἐν σαρκί in v. 3 and says that his weapons are not σαρκικά but δυνατὰ τῷ θεῷ. This distinction between σαρκικός and δυνατός is arresting. Properly, for Paul the opposite of σάρξ is πνεῦμα. And clearly throughout his letters the antonym of δυνατός is ἀσθενής. Why, then, does Paul choose to contrast 'flesh' and 'power'? He interprets the charge as being an attack on his apostolic 'arsenal'. The designation of the apostle as behaving in a worldly fashion is, in reality, a denial of his being a πνευματικός. It is in distinction to πνεῦμα that the term σάρξ is used.[1] Therefore, Paul does not deny that he is in the world, i.e., ἐν σαρκί. But he rejects the implication that he carries on a worldly war. His weapons are 'divinely powerful'.[2] 'Fleshly' here must imply weakness.[3] And if the spirit is the opposite of flesh, and Paul's opponents style themselves πνευματικοί in distinction from him, they are claiming power or strength. At any rate, it is clear that nowhere in this passage is ethical behavior the subject under discussion. Even the disobedience against which his weapons will be effective is the disobedience of 'arguments' and 'obstacles to the knowledge of God'.

Paul rejects the charge by pointing to the power of his weapons. This power itself is qualified, for it is power τῷ θεῷ. Whatever the charge echoed in this passage, Paul rejects it not by calling himself either πνευματικός or δυνατός, but by admitting that he walks 'in the flesh' and stressing that nonetheless this is not the level on which he wages his battle. Hence, we have the distinction between σαρκικός and δυνατός rather than σαρκικός-πνευματικός or ἀσθενής-δυνατός. If Paul were to stress 'spirit' over against 'flesh', he would have to forfeit a distinction he wishes to make between himself and his opponents, who think of themselves as πνευματικοί. If, on the other hand, he were to stress ἀσθενής over against δυνατός, he would be avoiding a direct confrontation with their charge. Paul's defense does not rest in personal attributes, but in the fact that he

[1] Not to be understood ethically, Schmithals, *Gnosis*[2], p. 156.

[2] This colorless translation (RSV) of the dative τῷ θεῷ is perhaps the best. Most commentators take θεῷ as dative of advantage (Windisch; Lietzmann; BDF, par. 192), though it might be construed as an ethical dative.

[3] How closely the 'anthropological' or neutral designation of σάρξ can be identified with weakness is seen in Rom. 6: 19.

has weapons of divine power. Though 'flesh' and the claim that Paul walks κατὰ σάρκα are not again the subject of controversy in these four chapters, at the beginning of ch. 10 Paul sets the tone for his whole defense. He is not πνευματικός, it is true. But he is not the less confident for that. For he has at his disposal, even though he lives ἐν σαρκί, the very power of God itself.[1] The concrete utilization of this power which Paul has will be evident when he punishes every disobedience. In the meantime, he hopes for the completion of the Corinthians' obedience.

We have already seen in I Cor. 4 how Paul thinks of his continued responsibility for the Christian churches he has founded; he can even speak of reminding them of his ways in Christ (v. 17). It is but a small step from the responsibility he feels (grounded in the durative nature of the gospel) to the authority he manifests (grounded in the weakness and power of the word of the cross, and manifest in the apostle). Thus Paul will find out when he comes again soon 'not the talk' of some arrogant people in Corinth, but 'their power' (I Cor. 4: 19), 'for the Kingdom of God does not consist in talk, but in power' (4: 20). As in II Cor. 10: 1, here Paul leaves open the door for a change in the Corinthian situation before his arrival: 'What do you wish? Shall I come to you with a rod or with love in a spirit of gentleness?'

Paul's Identification of Weakness with Christ's Death

In order to understand his own apostolic life in these same terms of weakness and power, which characterize the event of Jesus and the gospel which continues to manifest that event, Paul must speak not only of his power, but of his weakness. Even the gospel is pre-eminently the 'word of the cross' and thereby characterized by its weakness *and* its power. Just as the cross simultaneously implies the concomitant idea of resurrection, we may expect Paul to imply something about his power even when dwelling on his 'weakness'.

The point of contact between Christ's death and Paul's weak-

[1] The distinction Paul makes here between what he *is* and what he *can do* is reminiscent of the distinction in I Cor. 1: 18ff. between 'wisdom' and 'power' as anthropological attributes (which they are not) and as divine entities affecting man (which they are).

ness is in Paul's suffering. In Phil. 3: 10 Paul speaks of the 'sufferings of Christ' when he actually refers to Christ's death. The reference to suffering is unusual, for Paul never describes Christ's death as a suffering, nor does he speak of any other sufferings of Christ. Since this connection is made elsewhere only in conjunction with Paul's own sufferings, it must be his device. In order to understand the death of Christ working in himself Paul connects this death with his sufferings and then speaks of Christ's sufferings, by which he actually means Christ's death.

This is clearly what has happened in II Cor. 1: 3ff. Paul begins his thanksgiving with a specific reference to God 'the father of all mercies and God of all comfort' (παράκλησις), 'who comforts us in all our affliction (θλῖψις), so that we are able to comfort those in every affliction on account of the comfort with which we ourselves are comforted by God' (vv. 3, 4). This theme of comfort and affliction turns, however, to 'sufferings' and comfort in v. 5. In the context, these παθήματα τοῦ Χριστοῦ can be nothing else than the equivalent of Paul's θλῖψις; and in the light of Phil. 3: 10, sharing Christ's sufferings means sharing Christ's death.

The theme of death and suffering has its opposite in resurrection and comfort. Παράκλησις is an eschatological-soteriological term denoting what Paul often calls 'life'.[1] Paul strengthens this identification by saying that his affliction is 'for your comfort and *salvation*', making certain that the eschatological-soteriological significance of the term is clear.

We shall return in a moment to this question of the relationship of Paul's suffering and comfort to that of the community. It is noteworthy here that Paul understands his tribulation/ suffering as Christ's suffering (Christ's death) and his comfort as the equivalent of the new life in Christ. The death and resurrection of Christ inform the life of the apostle with perfect analogies. The actual specification of tribulation/suffering is given in vv. 8–11. Paul means that his physical hardships and persecutions are to be understood as the equivalent of Christ's weakness (i.e., Christ's death) in this parallelism.

This identification is also made in II Cor. 4: 7–12. Here again we have the context of Paul's understanding of the on-going

---

[1] Cf. Str.-B., II, pp. 124–6.

nature of the gospel (vv. 1–6) in which the apostle finds the norm for his own activity. The apostle preaches not himself, but Jesus Christ as Lord with himself as servant (v. 5). The subordination of the apostle is necessary 'to show that ἡ ὑπερ-βολὴ τῆς δυνάμεως belongs to God' (v. 7). So it is that the apostle is afflicted (θλιβόμενος), perplexed, persecuted, struck down. But in all these, though it might seem he should despair of life itself, he need not. Each example of suffering carries with it a negative adversative phrase (ἀλλ' οὐκ κ.τ.λ.). These sufferings are not the apostle's undoing – they are the vehicle of the power of God itself. Thus Paul can comprehend them all in v. 10 within the amazing statement that he carries around in his body the death of Jesus that the life of Jesus may be manifested in his body. 'For always we who are living are being given up to death on account of Jesus, so that the life of Jesus may be manifested in our mortal flesh' (v. 11; cf. Gal. 6: 17). This is only an alternative way of saying that in his weakness God's power shines through.

A similar set of adversative phrases describes the apostle in II Cor. 6: 3–10. The commendation of the apostle, so much an issue in chs. 10–13, is found in being a διάκονος θεοῦ, described in vv. 3bff. in terms of human weakness (4b, 5), divine power (6, 7) and the adversative phrases of vv. 8–10. This ministry which Paul describes in these terms makes possible the acceptance of the 'acceptable time', the day of salvation. As in I Cor. 9: 12, the demands of salvation require the subordination of the apostle.

Finally, in I Cor. 4: 8–13 Paul presents the same picture of apostolic life in direct contrast to the supposed spiritual excellence of the Corinthians. They are filled; they have become kings! But God has exhibited the apostles as 'last of all, like men sentenced to death' (v. 9).

The Significance of the Weakness-Power Dialectic in Paul's Appropriation

In making the identification of his suffering with Christ's death, Paul has not taken over for himself the role of Christ as the suffering servant as has sometimes been assumed. To interpret Paul as 'continuing the work of Christ' in that literal sense

244

would be to miss the entire point of his emphasis on weakness and power in the apostolic life.

The mistake is tempting if we too sharply separate this weakness from this power. In three of the passages above in which Paul mentions his sufferings, he explicitly calls to mind the whole dialectic of weakness *and* power. This dialectic has its origins in the death and resurrection of Jesus, and its primary application in the gospel's being itself a manifestation of weakness and power. Paul's appropriation of the dialectic is derivative in the sense that it depends on the common Christian experience of sharing that death and resurrection. It is no less derivative in the narrower 'apostolic' application of identifying the apostle's entire mission with that gospel which manifests weakness and power.

In II Cor. 1: 3ff. Paul's suffering results in the comfort of the Corinthians. This would appear to be a case of vicarious suffering, were it not for the fact that Paul specifically says that the Corinthians themselves share in his sufferings (vv. 6b, 7). Yet if Paul is afflicted it is for their comfort and salvation, and if he is comforted it is for their comfort. Since they share the same sufferings that Paul experiences, the result of Paul's suffering is not the alleviation or removal of the Corinthians' sufferings. We can only understand the suffering and comfort of Paul to mean here his appropriation of death and resurrection. They are inseparable in the life of the Christian and in the life of the one who is in Christ. But Paul is not in Christ on behalf of others. He is in Christ with others.

There is only one way in which Paul can be distinguished from other Christians who also suffer and are comforted. As an apostle he has a commission to preach the gospel, the word of the cross. This gospel itself is weakness and power, grounded as it is in the event of Christ. In his ministry Paul reflects this same weakness and power. Not only does he experience it alongside all Christians, he makes it visible in himself.

Thus his suffering brings comfort and his comfort brings comfort, for his suffering and comfort are the reflection of that death and resurrection which itself brings the eschatological blessing of παράκλησις. This idea in II Cor. 1: 3ff. depends upon the indissolubility of weakness and power which reflects Christ's death and resurrection. The latter cannot be separated;

neither can the former. It is exactly when Paul is weak that he is strong (II Cor. 12: 10). So in II Cor. 6 all the woes of vv. 4b, 5 are yet also the blessings of vv. 6, 7, which include the power of God.

The same is true of II Cor. 4: 12. Death's being at work in Paul results in life's being at work in the Corinthians. But this is because in Paul's weakness (suffering) is already manifested the power (life) of Jesus which he carries around in his own body. Jesus' death brings life to the Christian, but not without Jesus' life. So Paul's death is also Paul's life, his weakness his power; and this weakness or suffering alone can stand for the union of the two, just as the cross stands for Christ's death and new life.

Paul's appropriation of the weakness-power dialectic is not his attempt to become one who continues the work of Christ. The work of Christ is the work of God and cannot be taken from God's hand. But the appropriation puts Paul into the life of the communities alongside of the gospel, itself power and weakness. This is how the authority of the gospel is to be understood. This is how the authority of the apostle is to be understood. In Paul's whole apostolic life one sees the manifestation of God's same act which one sees in the gospel itself.

Paul's role in making manifest what the gospel itself makes manifest is evident in several passages. In II Cor. 4: 2 he 'commends' himself by the open statement of the truth τῇ φανερώσει τῆς ἀληθείας. Paul can then move immediately from this commendation to the justification of 'his' gospel, v. 3: 'And if our gospel is veiled, it is veiled only to those who are perishing.' To those who are being saved, it shines in splendor; it is the power of God (I Cor. 1: 18). Just as the gospel shines in splendor, so his behavior makes manifest who and what the apostle is. But the apostle's gospel is simply the gospel in which he has a continuing role and commission. It is not his own private form of the gospel. Paul therefore goes on to elaborate on how he commends himself, giving the description of adversity in vv. 7–10. In summarizing this, vv. 10–11, he returns to the theme of 'making manifest': '...always carrying in the body the death of Jesus, so that the life of Jesus may also be *manifested* in our mortal bodies. For while we are living, we are always being given up to death on account of Jesus, so that the life of

Jesus may be manifested in our mortal flesh.' The Old Testament quotation from Psalm 115 and the references to 'speaking' are curious. What Paul 'speaks' must be (v. 5) 'Jesus Christ as Lord and ourselves as your servants'. Because he has faith in the final outcome of his life in Christ (v. 14), the apparent misery and despair of this life do not discourage the apostle. Indeed, he knows (v. 15) that ultimately it is all for the sake of those who receive the gospel, that grace may extend to more and more people. So 'speaking' from the context of this faith is nothing other than speaking the truth 'openly'. But that is itself a manifestion of the same power that is revealed in the gospel which speaks of Jesus as Lord and Paul as servant. The apostle's speech is ultimately nothing other than preaching the gospel, even when it is speech which describes what an apostle is like. This is so because in him as a person is being manifested the power also made manifest in the gospel. And just as the gospel is 'veiled' to those who are perishing, so his weakness may not appear in its true light. But both alike, because they are weak, are also strong. Paul speaks, in fact, the 'truth' in the sight of God. This is nothing other than speaking 'in Christ' (II Cor. 2: 17), which is Paul's way of equating his whole ministry with preaching the gospel.

This parallelism of Paul's 'making manifest' what the gospel also makes manifest is hinted at in II Cor. 2: 14 and made explicit by the unusual language in I Cor. 4: 8ff. In the latter, the context again speaks of the weakness and suffering of the apostle. Paul introduces his description by way of comparison with the Corinthians who have supposedly already become kings. The apostle would like to share their rule. Instead, he suspects that God has 'exhibited' the apostles as the least of all men. They have become a spectacle (θέατρον) to the world, to angels, and to men. The weakness of the apostles is not something which can go unnoticed. It is God's own display. If the connection we made earlier between vv. 8–13 and Paul's 'ways' in Christ is correct, this very display is intended to illustrate the gospel in which Paul has begotten the Corinthians.

In Rom. 16: 25–6 Paul suggests that 'his gospel' and the κήρυγμα Ἰησοῦ Χριστοῦ are the 'revelation of the mystery...now disclosed (φανερωθέντος) and made known to all nations'. This display of the gospel is what is also displayed in the apostle's

247

own life. God shows forth his power in man (cf. Rom. 9: 17, 22), and in Paul the weakness and power which is the gospel itself is shown forth. Paul sees in 'his' life what he sees in 'his' gospel.

There is no possibility that this view of apostolic life will usurp the proper role of the gospel, for the gospel is itself the norm and source of apostolic behavior. To its most stringent demands the apostle is completely subordinate. At the same time, if the gospel were not what it is, the continuing manifestation of God's weakness which is God's power, the apostle could not be what he is. That the whole of apostolic life and work is itself a reflection of the forces made manifest in the preaching of the gospel is only possible because that gospel itself continues to make manifest the power of God. The Christian stands 'in' the gospel throughout his life. He never ceases to need the 'word of life' to which he must hold fast. Nor does he, in Paul's churches, ever cease to need the apostle's own work which reflects the same power made manifest in weakness.

Conclusion

In summary, apostolic authority for Paul rests in the gospel but is evident in the apostle's own work at every turn just because, like that gospel, the apostle's life is weakness and power, God's weakness and power made visible in human history. Paul sees his life as making transparent what the gospel tells about, the power and weakness of God acting in those events which constitute the beginning of the new creation. There can be no question for Paul of the validity of his continuing concern for the churches, or of their obedience to his authority over them, for there can be no question of the continuing reality of God's acting to save man through the weakness and power of Christ's death and resurrection.

CHAPTER 9

CHARISMA AND CONTROL: THE SOCIOLOGY OF APOSTOLIC AUTHORITY

INTRODUCTION

The gospel is not an exclusive apostolic possession. On the contrary, the apostle is owned and authorized by the gospel. He does not stand as a unique and exclusive bridge between the gospel and the Christian, between the power he interprets and the goal of that interpretation, the Church. He mediates between the gospel and the Church, to be sure; he links cause and effect. But all Christians participate directly in the gospel itself. They do not stand in Paul or some other apostle, but in the gospel. They were not baptized in him, but in Christ. This has specific implications for understanding Paul's concept of apostolic authority. Just as the apostle must be understood in reference to his own autobiography and the relationship between his 'self' and that power which shapes it, so he must be understood in the context of a community in which every member has an autobiography which embodies his membership in Christ. The basic structure of that community and its relationship to Paul as one who 'authors' the ordering arrangement which the community itself manifests is the sociology of apostolic authority.

Analyzing Paul's description of apostolic authority in the opening chapters of Galatians, we found it necessary to introduce an unusual disjunction, suggesting that there might be a difference between his perception of the authority of the gospel and his perception of the Church's unity. More particularly, we found that the logic of Paul's position could have impelled him, had he allowed it, to conclude by denying Peter's apostolic authority. In fact there is no evidence that he does so. Paul seems instead to assume the role of an independent apostolic missionary, severing his ties with Antioch and striking out on his own.

If this is a plausible reading, it is important to understand some of its ramifications. First, Paul could avoid facing the problem of the unity of the Church in this concrete situation for his own reasons, but only for the moment. He could not evade the issue's larger implications. Nor would he wish to. He went to Jerusalem from Antioch as a proponent of the unity of the Church and in the name of that ideal. It is doubtful that he left Antioch any less convinced of this necessity. On the criteria he was using this unity depended on the primacy of the singular gospel. Other features were obviously pertinent for Peter and Barnabas, though they too seem to have been committed to the principle of unity. One can only say that in a manner of speaking their concept was more pragmatically informed than his.

This difference ultimately rests on Paul's decision to subordinate all things, even the Church, to the gospel. Here we encounter his primary vision of the 'unity' (as distinct from the singularity) of the gospel. If there is any carry-over between 'another gospel' in Galatian churches and Paul's rebuke of Peter, it suggests that Peter is guilty of living by a putative other gospel. Paul, of course, does not say this. He does not need to. He merely charges Peter with living out of accord with the gospel. For Paul, unity expresses itself in fitness, in accordance. It depends on the assumption that the gospel is normative not merely for preaching, but also for action and life within the community.

Like Galatians, I and II Corinthians make it clear that Paul will finally make no distinction between his authority to preach (his 'missionary' authority) and his authority to assess the adequacy with which the gospel is heard on the second day as well as the first. II Corinthians shows explicitly what is only implicit in the body of Gal. 3–6. For Paul this continuing responsibility of the missioner for the ordered and healthy life of the Christian community expresses its own sense of unity. In recognizing this we must keep in mind another distinctive feature of Paul's viewpoint. The relationship between gospel as missionary proclamation and gospel as the normative framework of Christian communal existence is reflected in the relationship between gospel and apostle. Both the Church and the apostle are to be subordinate to and manifestations of the one gospel. Hence, singularity and unity coalesce.

In this coalescence can be located the role of *imitatio Pauli* and admonitions such as that in Gal. 4: 12, 'become as I am'. This theme of imitation flows directly from Paul's perception of apostolic authority.[1] More dialectical is the way Paul's logical parallelism between apostle and community softens what we might otherwise expect to be hard lines separating the leader from the followers. There are occasions on which Paul seems scarcely to distinguish his role from the community's role. This feature is not unrelated to the admonition to become as Paul, for the seeming interchangeability is more than an admission that the apostle is, underneath and before all else, a Christian. It is directed at the community itself and not just at its individual members. It is the *Church* which is to become as Paul. And it is the Church which 'preaches' the gospel (I Thess. 1: 10) just as the apostle does. This attraction of the Church to the apostolic figure, and its relation to the apostolic paradigm, is brought full circle in I Thess. when Paul commends the Church for becoming his imitator (1: 8) and that even of the 'churches of God in Christ Jesus which are in Judea', 2: 14.

This raises the question of how Paul conceives of the apostolic role and its relation to other roles within the community. Specifically, is it χάρις or χάρισμα which lies behind the apostle? If the former, does this mean that the apostle is ultimately indistinguishable from any other Christian, that there is no role or status distinction? If the latter, in which case the role distinction is clear enough, does this mean that there are discernible apostolic attributes?

Perhaps the distinction between *charis* and charisma as a foundation for apostolic activity should not be drawn overly sharply.[2] Paul never explicitly ties the apostolic role to the notion of charisma,[3] but the apostle seems to be an important instance of what he regards as charismatic.

[1] Cf. ch. 8.

[2] E. Käsemann, 'Ministry and Community in the New Testament', *Essays on New Testament Themes* (London, 1964), p. 65.

[3] J. Wobbe, *Der Charis-Gedanke bei Paulus* (Münster i. W., 1932), pp. 74ff.; Campenhausen, *Authority*, p. 33, n. 12; A. Satake, 'Apostolat und Gnade bei Paulus', *NTS* 15 (1968-9), 96-105, cf. esp. p. 103.

THE APOSTLE AS A CHARISMATIC

If Paul did not coin the term χάρισμα,[1] he gave it the technical meaning we find in early Christian literature.[2] It is less well understood that at the same time he was projecting a sociological category of primary importance in his own understanding of authority. The key question is how this is related to his understanding of apostolic power. In order to answer that question we must briefly sketch the way Paul's idea of charisma interprets power and reinterprets it in the face of a dominant hellenistic tradition before him. The idea of *charismata* as a first century sociological category for the expression of authority depends on our seeing the spiritual gifts as a power phenomenon, and authority as the interpretation of power.[3]

Like most of the Greek religious world around him, Paul can regard *spirit* as something impelling and energizing, a view which fits comfortably with the animating power ascribed to spirit by the Old Testament.[4] This general view rests on the assumption that the spirit is a gift poured out in baptism, the common property of the man in Christ. As the spirit gives life (II Cor. 3: 6) so it pledges the certainty of life in the future

[1] Cf. BAG, p. 887; LSJ, p. 1979b. For the relevant problem of Philo's use of the term (*Leg. All.*, xxiii, 78), cf. Käsemann, 'Ministry', p. 64, n. 1.

[2] Its use outside Paul is limited. In the NT: I Tim. 4: 14; II Tim. 1: 6; I Peter 4: 10. In the Apostolic Fathers: Didache 1: 5; I Clem. 38: 1; Ignatius Smyr. inscript. (*bis*), Eph. 17: 2; Polycarp 2: 2.

[3] What follows is necessarily a brief sketch, both in terms of the exegesis of relevant Pauline texts and in the attention to modern sociological theory. Discussions of the charismatic outside Biblical interpretation have been dominated by the conceptual explorations of M. Weber. Weber built on the earlier work of R. Sohm, who isolated the phenomenon in similar ways but used a different vocabulary. The matter of vocabulary is important here also. When we speak of 'charismatic' in the Pauline context we mean something different from the ideal type of legitimate leader Weber has in mind, just as both uses diverge from the common parlance of today where 'charisma' is all but equated with magnetic personality and largely confined to political or para-political figures. In what follows we shall try to take seriously both Paul's use of the noun χάρισμα and Weber's sociological theory regarding the charismatic type, without simply collapsing one into another. It will help to remember our earlier distinction between leadership and authority (ch. 1). What we are after is not a profile of leadership but a description of authority.

[4] Bultmann, *Theol.*, I, p. 156. 'Its essence is power', Davies, *Paul*, p. 183.

(Rom. 8: 10; cf. Gal. 6: 8). It constitutes the 'indicative' character of the reality of reconciliation, or, to use Paul's favorite term, 'justification': '...God's love has been poured into our hearts through the Holy Spirit which has been given to us.' The energizing and impelling facet of this possession of spirit is found throughout the letters and in specific passages such as I Cor. 2: 4, 'in demonstration of the spirit and power'. The hendiadys refers to Paul's word of proclamation and its appearance originally among the Corinthians, and is reminiscent of the specific linking of power, spirit and gospel in I Thess. 1: 4. Hence, 'it can almost be said that "spirit" and "power" are synonymous'.[1] Nor is it difficult to see why specific capacities of the Christian are credited to this powerful spirit, such as working miracles (Gal. 3: 5).

In contrast to much of the Greek religious world, however, Paul also regards spirit in quite another framework. It is not merely impelling but also compelling. It approaches being an agency of government, as is evident in the dialectic of indicative and imperative.[2] The spirit is not merely gift, it is also norm. It is not merely enabling, it is also regulative. A description of this dialectic is found in Gal. 5: 25 ('if we live by the spirit, let us also walk by the spirit'). Its specific implications are found in catalogs of virtues deemed to be appropriate fruits of the spirit, such as that in Gal. 5: 22ff.

In some circles of hellenistic religion the bearer of concrete spiritual endowment, manifestations of the spirit (πνευματικά), is himself a religious type – the πνευματικός, the spiritual man.[3] In gnosticism this type reaches its culmination. The true gnostic defines himself by reference to his πνεῦμα, regarding all others as inferior, as σαρκικοί or ψυχικοί.[4] Most important, this mode of self-identification demands a static and essentialist view of the self in which individuation is subordinated to the

---

[1] Cf. the article 'πνεῦμα etc.' by H. Kleinknecht, F. Baumgärtel, W. Bieder, E. Sjöberg and E. Schweizer, *TDNT*, VI, pp. 332–455.

[2] R. Bultmann, 'Das Problem der Ethik bei Paulus', *ZNW* 23 (1924), 123–40; V. Furnish, *Theology and Ethics in Paul* (Nashville, 1968), pp. 224ff.

[3] Cf. R. Reitzenstein, *Die hellenistische Mysterienreligionen* (Stuttgart, 1927³/1956), pp. 69ff., 284ff., 333ff.

[4] On gnostic anthropology, in addition to the work of Reitzenstein cf. K. Niederwimmer, *Der Begriff der Freiheit im Neuen Testament* (Berlin, 1966), Schmithals, *Gnosis*², pp. 157ff.

generic form.[1] Such generic predominance is evident in the manifold gnostic mythical texts in which the career of the liberated gnostic constitutes a virtual repetition of the story of cosmogony, or anthropogony, as well as the story of soteriology. The narrative account of the dispatch of the revealing and redeeming figures, as in the Hymn of the Pearl, is the gnostic's own story. This storied form of gnostic myth is actually a surrogate for history. It is made necessary by the evacuation of history and contingency from the concept of the self. The resulting vacuum leaves the self to be understood exclusively in reference to transcendent substance. This also explains the curious way in which the gnostic approaches the matter of community. On the one hand he is genuinely and substantially (pneumatically) related to all others who have his knowledge. On the other, this relationship transcends mere temporal and geographical boundaries. It recapitulates the basic norms governing the place of man in his world. This one locus, being in the world, and its soteriological counterpart, being at one beyond the world, is the only *location* of humanity which counts. Human communities, therefore, are not the focus of strong gnostic attachments. Where there is no historical self there is no possibility of social intercourse which reflects one's sense of identity even while constituting it. Paul's indicative and imperative scheme would not only be senseless to the gnostic. It would be useless.

Not every pneumatic is a gnostic. But we may take the gnostic as one ideal type in order to illustrate a fundamental feature of this concept of pneumatic endowment. It expresses transcendent achievement by transcending historical contingency and social or communal responsibility.[2] This is true whether the pneumatic state is thought of as occasional and hence 'ecstatic' in the usual senses,[3] or permanent. From a phenomenological point of view, and only from that point of view, there is no distinction among ecstatics, pneumatics in the gnostic sense, and the non-gnostic θεῖος ἀνήρ.

[1] Cf. E. Schweizer, *TDNT*, VI, p. 432 and his essay 'Gegenwart des Geistes und eschatologische Hoffnung bei Zarathustra, spätjüdischen Gruppen, Gnostikern und den Zeugen des Neuen Testaments', *Neotestamentica* (Zürich, 1963), pp. 153–79 (pp. 167ff.).

[2] The best contrast within the hellenistic world would be with Stoicism and its understanding of society and πνεῦμα.

[3] Cf. Bultmann, *Theol.*, I, p. 157.

Paul's use of the hellenistic πνεῦμα idea reveals the difficulties he had with it. For him the spirit is given in baptism as a common Christian possession. This view must be correlated with his understanding of the ἐκκλησία as an entity which, if it is the eschatological people of God, is nevertheless in the world and subject to the vicissitudes of historical existence. The identity of the Christian cannot be thought of without practical reference to his social setting.

Yet Paul's understanding of the 'spiritual man' is not always uniform. We have, for example, an apparent distinction between *pneumatic* Christians and others in I Cor. 2: 13 – 3: 3. Whether Paul introduced it into the discussion is not clear. It is more likely that some Corinthians did. Paul is not yet able to address the Corinthians as πνευματικοί for they are still σαρκικοί (or σάρκινοι), immature, νήπιοι. To be sure, they are νήπιοι ἐν Χριστῷ, but it is just this which illustrates the very problem: How can Paul make such distinctions if the origin of Christians is the same and all have received alike the Spirit? This kind of internal discrimination runs counter to the basic thesis that spirit is an inaugural possession of all Christians. Yet Phil. 3: 15 shows that even if in I Corinthians Paul is using an alien vocabulary, he can discriminate this way.

Against this background we must look at Paul's references to charisma, an idea which dominates portions of that same Corinthian letter and provides a characteristically Pauline expression for spiritual gifts (χαρίσματα).[1] *Charismata* are *pneumatika*, but more than that, and more importantly, they are a fundamental expression of *individuation*. Not only can it be said that Christians possess spiritual gifts (I Cor. 1: 7; they are not deficient in any, such as knowledge), but the gifts of one are not another's, 7: 7. 'Each has his own charisma from God.' This same sense of individuation permeates Paul's reflections on the *charismata* in 12: 1ff. The one spirit, enabling gift for all Christians,[2] manifests itself in varieties of χαρισμάτων (12: 4). The

[1] Cf. χάρισμα πνευματικόν, Rom. 1: 11 and Michel's comment: 'Paul uses χαρίσματα in the sense of πνευματικά and thus takes up the argument with the hellenistic understanding of the penumatic role' (*Römer*, p. 39).

[2] This is the purpose of 12: 3. The idea that 'Jesus be cursed' is a gnostic touch (Schmithals, *Gnosis*², pp. 117ff.) has been refuted by B. Pearson, 'Did the Gnostics Curse Jesus?', *JBL* 86 (1967), 301–5.

specific list which follows is less important than Paul's conclusion: 'The one and same Spirit energizes all of these, apportioning to each one individually as he wills' (διαιροῦν ἰδίᾳ ἑκάστῳ καθὼς βούλεται, v. 11). Paul's articulation of the *charismata* is a response to the Corinthian urge to overvalue such gifts in general and some in particular. It is also a response to the larger problem behind the Corinthian attitude, the difficulty of bringing into harmony the individual and the social facets of the *pneumatikos*.

Paul's understanding of the Church makes necessary this bridge between the individual and his social setting. Thus it is no surprise to find the explication of *charismata* set in the context of Paul's metaphor of the σῶμα Χριστοῦ (12: 12–26). Just as the whole body does not function without the specific and distinctive contribution of its individual parts, so the whole Church does not function without respecting the individual *charismata* which are expressions of the one spirit. Paul makes it unmistakably clear that the Church as the common life of Christians is the proper goal toward which the energies of the *charismata* are to be directed. 'To each is given the manifestation of the spirit for the common good' (πρὸς τὸ συμφέρον, 12: 7). Establishing this goal is crucial and basic to the whole Pauline scheme at two particular points.

In the first instance, supplying the goal provides Paul with the criteria for discrimination among spiritual gifts. The particular circumstances of I Corinthians suggest that some who prized gifts most highly prized some more highly than others: gnosis and speaking in tongues in particular (1: 5; 14). Regarding the latter, Paul makes discriminatory judgments on the principle of church order, edification (14: 3, 4, 5, 12, 27). The Corinthians should 'let all things happen decently and in order'. With this emphasis on order (τάξις) and edification (οἰκοδομή) we make contact with Paul's apostolic image. In II Corinthians he repeatedly stresses his responsibility for building up the Church. Moreover, it is from this context that Paul comes to describe the *charismata* as διακονίαι, I Cor. 12: 4–6. 'Diakonia is thus a category which exceeds charisma in scope and content. A charisma can become diakonia if it is "bound" to the edification of the community.'[1] Commentators

[1] I. Hermann, *Kyrios und Pneuma* (München, 1961), p. 74.

have correctly stressed this unusual dimension in Paul's vision of pneumatic endowment,[1] the dimension of service. For Paul 'the test of a genuine charisma lies not in the fact that something supernatural occurs but in the use which is made of it. No spiritual endowment has value, rights or privilege on its own account. It is validated only by the service it renders.'[2]

Secondly, this understanding of charisma rearranges the concept of self. It trims and bounds the ἐγώ of the religious man. In the body of Christ every member's contribution is counted worthy and must be honored because all men possessing the spirit manifest that spirit in individual gifts. Nevertheless, this sense of individuation does not give license to individualism. Quite to the contrary, by stressing individuation Paul rescues the self from submersion in a principle like πνεῦμα where self and spirit become indistinguishable. The self is submerged only in the larger *body* where it does not lose, but finally gains, its true identity.

Hence, distinguishing among pneumatic gifts is only one function of Paul's understanding of charisma. Distinguishing among individuals while recognizing their common ties is a parallel function. This comes forcefully to expression in I Cor. 14: 4: 'He who speaks in a tongue edifies *himself*; he who prophesies edifies the church.' Where the spirit is valued for the spirit's sake and the spiritually endowed self is identified by reference to spirit alone, only the self is served. The ἐκκλησία as the σῶμα Χριστοῦ provides an alternative criterion to that of the spirit (self) of the hellenistic pneumatic.

Hence we are justified in speaking, as we did earlier, of charisma as an ordering principle. It orders the common life by establishing priorities and discriminating among competing manifestations of the spirit. And it orders the individual life by providing the coordinates of its locus within a common framework.

What Paul says in I Cor. 14: 4 is reminiscent of the problem he faced later in his experience with the Corinthians, when the superlative apostles appeared on the scene. 'Commending' oneself, like 'edifying oneself', is a disease to which those who have no point of reference beyond themselves are susceptible.

[1] Cf. J. Borsch, *Charismen und Ämter in der Urkirche* (Bonn, 1951), pp. 127ff.
[2] Käsemann, 'Ministry', p. 67.

In sharp antithesis to both manifestations of misplaced spiritualism Paul sets the priority of service, his own apostolic service and that of any bearer of charisma: service to build up the Church. In both instances this goal toward which the gift is directed dissociates the engifted from the gift, whereas his opponents would identify the two. In both instances Paul radically revises the concept of the charismatic self by insisting on its ultimate endowment and yet insisting that the endowment is beyond and other than the self. In both instances the self as a scale of reference is abolished, to be replaced by the concept of 'building up'.

To this larger context belongs the question of whether Paul regards the apostolic role as one kind of charisma. Only one text suggests this, I Cor. 12: 28, and it does so largely by association (vv. 30, 31) and context. But we must take care not to ask the wrong question. Even if the apostolic rank is a charisma, it cannot take precedence over any other charisma which builds up. There might be implied a distinction in capacity for that task,[1] but there is none in substance. Paul never considers the *charismata* as 'legitimate orders' in which the matter of authority may be already assumed, just as he has no core of 'leadership' in the churches, persons whose authority is so clearly circumscribed and subscribed to by others that he may call on these to carry out his recommendations.

Thus what is most remarkable about I Cor. 12: 28 is not that Paul identifies an 'office' with a charisma, if he does. What is remarkable is that the pattern of authority characteristic of the apostle is characteristic of every Christian, because the same response of obedient service is expected alike from each. Ultimately, all are responsible and obedient to the same thing: the gospel; for the same purpose: service to the Church.

When we speak of charisma as an ordering principle, we suggest two ways of viewing it. On the one hand it may be seen as a principle transcending a formless mass of spirit, as shown by its capacity to individuate the pneumatically endowed and grant his individual identity. On the other hand, it may be regarded as an attempt to 'rationalize' a concept of *homo religiosus* made chaotic when one tries to move immediately from an individual concept to a pluralistic one. How does any society become uni-

---

[1] Implied in the description of apostles as πρῶτον, I Cor. 12: 28?

fied and specific? What keeps it from being a mere multitude of individuals, in this case of spirit-endowed individuals? Paul himself suggests this process of rationalization when he includes 'helpers, administrators' (ἀντιλήμψεις, κυβερνήσεις) among the charismatics (I Cor. 12: 28).[1] The religious life has its most profound expression in the concrete, every-day reality of human social life visible in the cultically gathered Church,[2] a Church which therefore can number its administrators among its pneumatics.

This emphasis on the every-day reality of the holy destroys the common distinction between sacred and profane and regards the actual and at hand as somehow transformed. Parallel to Paul's concept of himself as a bearer of 'treasure in earthen vessels', it is intimately related to the dialectic of weakness and power which he invokes so frequently, especially in II Corinthians. It is the boast of the 'sufficient' man who knows his sufficiency to come from beyond himself and to be made real precisely in his insufficiency. As Käsemann emphasizes, there are no 'holy places and holy times' distinguished from other places and other times. Where and when the community gathers there is the holy. There are no spiritual persons set apart from others when all persons are 'spiritual'.

These two *effects* of the charisma idea, transcendent principle and rationalization, are but two ways of looking at the same phenomenon. Isolating that phenomenon on more general principles is our next task.

CHARISMA AND AUTHORITY

For Paul the transcendent norm for action is the 'gospel'. One knows what his responsibility is by reference to the need for 'building up'. For all charismatics, as for the apostle, this is tied to the idea that the gospel is a durative force in history. It is a contemporary mode of expression, a state of being; and it has a future. But can we speak of the 'normative' character of the charismatic as we can of the apostle? Does the charismatic somehow express or articulate the gospel itself, as the apostle does?

---

[1] As indeed he does by the general device of failing to separate, as would most modern interpreters, 'technical' service from substantive *charismata*.

[2] Cf. Käsemann, 'Ministry', *passim*.

Paul uses the category of 'love' to enunciate the gospel's demand. This love, demanded of one Christian for another, is based on a pattern of prior love to which the charismatic responds. Hence, 'building up' is the criterion for measuring the utility and adequacy, even the valence, of the spiritual gifts; love is the criterion for determining what builds up. Building up in love extends and reflects the 'gospel' message of love. Seen this way, there is no distinction between the external norms to which the apostolic self is adjusted, and by which it is measured, and the external norms by which the general picture of the Christian self is measured and adjusted. To be sure, the apostle is 'first' at least in the sense that without his original missionary efforts there would be no church to build up. But how closely the question of apostolic authority is linked to Paul's more general concept of authority is displayed quite forcefully, if innocently, when Paul includes the entire community in the task of missionary preaching, otherwise exclusively the prerogative and purpose of the gospel. A well-knit and functioning body, faithful to its original calling,[1] is itself a missionary unit.

This raises obvious problems, chief among which is the question of what happens when authority becomes stated in terms of legitimacy, as it eventually does in the life of early Christianity. It is obvious that legitimacy does not descend on the office holder and all other Christians alike, as does the spirit in its various charismatic manifestations. In time, expectations of obedience from the once charismatic Christians become more narrowly focused. Although they may still be urged to be obedient to the one who 'calls' them, they are expected to express that obedience by submitting to the authority of office holders as if that authority were one denied all others. Legitimate ecclesiastical authority replaces the more direct authority of the gospel. We no longer have an interpretation (authority) of the gospel (power), but an interpretation (legitimacy) of authority itself. Legitimacy is valued *per se* as a surrogate for authority.

The problem has been analyzed often enough with reference to the post-Pauline period, especially because it touches on a fundamental difference in perspective between Protestant and Catholic interpreters. Among Protestant exegetes few have been more concerned with it than E. Käsemann, and he perhaps

---

[1] *Ibid.*, p. 69.

nowhere more directly than in his germinal essay on 'Ministry and Community in the New Testament'.[1]

Käsemann begins with an analysis of the idea of charisma much like that provided above. The charismatic notion provides a point of definition for the pneumatic self and the Pauline pattern of the suffering and obedient apostle is related to this. From this last he draws the conclusion that the theological meaning of charisma is the Pauline doctrine of justification by faith (pp. 75ff.).[2] This in itself is an important clue to the way he will proceed, for Käsemann is interested in locating the theological center in a set of ideas which are embodied in concrete forms of life.[3]

The Church is the embodiment of the gospel understood as the doctrine of justification. For this reason Käsemann can turn to other evidence about the Church and read it equally well as a statement of theology, as he does with the deutero-Pauline tradition. Here, in the face of a growing gnostic provocation, 'the Pauline character of the communities in the province of Asia was being surrendered in favor of other ecclesiastical connections' (p. 86). This results in the need for firmly established Church government such as the presbyteries of Titus and the apostolic delegate in II Timothy. The latter is nothing less than a bridge from the apostle to the monarchial bishop. The apostles are there represented as companions of the historical Jesus in order 'to present the apostle as the guarantor of the Gospel tradition as later he is to appear as the guarantor and criterion of the canonical tradition' (p. 89). We do not need to multiply or rehearse the evidence at length. The point is that the Church appears 'before us in a new guise... as an institution purveying salvation' (p. 92). 'A *theologia gloriae* is now in the

[1] Cf. p. 251, n. 2 above. In what follows, references are given in parentheses.

[2] 'Paul's doctrine of the charismata is to be understood as the projection into ecclesiology of the doctrine of justification by faith and as such makes it unmistakably clear that a purely individualistic interpretation of justification cannot legitimately be construed from the Apostle's own teaching.'

[3] 'Paul's teaching on the subject of the charismata constitutes the proof, first, that he made no basic distinction between justification and sanctification and did not understand justification in a merely declaratory sense; further, that he binds justification by faith tightly to baptism, so that it is not permissible to drive a wedge into his gospel, separating the juridical from the sacramental approach; and finally, that he considers faith to be actually constituted by the new obedience' (*ibid.*, p. 75).

process of replacing the *theologia crucis*' (p. 92). The irony, of course, is that Paul tried to preserve the *theologia crucis* in the face of an earlier assertion of a *theologia gloriae*.

Central to Käsemann's understanding of the shift is the appearance of two principles, that of tradition and that of apostolic succession. He is clear about the close relationship between the concept and articulation of order in both Paul and his successors, and the 'theology' of each. Furthermore, 'we cannot overlook the fact that need and necessity were the godparents of this transformation' (p. 88), given the acute nature of the gnostic threat. Nor may a mere structural alteration of the relationship between community and office be the point of a theological critique. Paul himself teaches us to seek relevance 'not so much in the "that" as in the "how" of a thing' (p. 89). The change in structure may have been justified.

But it is a complete break. How are we to explain the fact that Pauline theology is 'forgotten and replaced' (p. 93)? Why has there, outside of the sects, never been a Church order which reflects the Pauline understanding of *charismata*? The development of the early Catholic Church makes plain the problem. Paul's vision opened wide the doors to enthusiasm and fanaticism. The 'order' was too disorderly. 'Are we driven to the conclusion that Paul, who spent his life fighting the Enthusiasts, was not capable of establishing Church tradition but only of causing its disintegration, because he asked too much of the Christian and of the fellowship of the Church and for this reason was himself one of the principal factors which led to the triumph of Enthusiasm?'

We cannot fully answer Käsemann's question here, for doing so would require plotting in detail the shift from the Pauline to the deutero-Pauline period. Whatever the reasons, however, it does seem a fact that Pauline perception of authority did not yield a lasting church order. Thus it is all the more remarkable that Paul is remembered and revered in early ecclesiastical tradition as a primary authority of the earliest Church. Such a reminiscence must certainly have been based on fact, the more so if Paul actually, albeit innocently, encouraged rather than disciplined the type of enthusiasm which Käsemann and others have suggested could thrive under him, an enthusiasm so closely related to the gnostic heresy of the second century.

We need to remember that tradition played a central role in Paul's perception of the gospel, and hence of apostolic authority. His attitude toward tradition was positive because it was a basic component of gospel. Tradition, therefore, exercises its control over the apostle Paul. But Paul, through adherence to the gospel, also exercises his control over tradition. This symbiotic relationship of tradition and gospel renders them inseparable. We cannot assume that Paul's 'gospel' (whether understood as centered in *justificatio impii* or elsewhere) is not itself 'controlled' by tradition. The 'control' is tight and operates in manifold directions. Nothing can be gospel without the base of tradition, and the apostle who reflects gospel therefore reflects this foundation. The tradition may not be tinkered with in order to restate the gospel, for the apostle has control over the tradition by virtue of his mandate to reflect the gospel based on it. Finally, the apostle is controlled indirectly by tradition through the agency of the gospel which he embodies. This well qualified attitude toward tradition is part of the legacy Paul bequeaths. If his successors requalified it or stripped it of this dialectical setting, they did so by subtracting the one essential ingredient: *the personal figure of the apostle himself as the focal plane on which is projected the true meaning of tradition,* and through whom pass these various lines of interrelationship.

Paul does not elaborate a complete church order, a polity. Nevertheless, there is an implicit theory of order embedded in the articulation of apostolic authority and its relationship to the functioning of charisma. For Paul, what holds true for the definition of the apostolic self also holds true for the definition of the Christian in general. Paul's argument against the pneumatics of I Corinthians betrays the same theological thrust and the same center of values as his argument against the superlative apostles in II Corinthians: They have no norm outside themselves, and therefore are doomed to commend themselves. Paul was quite sure there was a norm, and the personal figure of the apostle was its embodiment and manifestation.

If we are to probe more deeply into the implications of this for 'ordering' the common life of the Church, if we ask what could and could not emerge from Paul's conception of authority, the difficulties are great. The letters are in themselves not sufficient. To be sure they reveal that Paul can set right the

Corinthian celebration of the eucharist (I Cor. 11) and pre-
scribe for its notorious case of incest (I Cor. 5). He can recom-
mend a host of customs, such as those concerning the behavior
of women. With Paul's concept of charisma in hand, with its
principle of self-transcendence, we can understand how Paul
could counsel the slave or anyone else to remain where he was
called; and one problem, how to reconcile Paul's affirmation of
charismata with his specific 'legalistic' pronouncements, is at
least not insurmountable. Yet no amount of such detail would
reveal the outline of an 'order' in its full scope. Certainly we
cannot use the later tradition with any degree of confidence.
The Pastoral letters look at the Paul they wish to see, not the
Paul we wish to see. Much the same is true of Acts. We must try
a different approach.

CHARISMA AND SOCIAL ORGANIZATION

Argument about the proper understanding of charisma and its
relationship to later 'offices' of the Church received classical
expression in the work of R. Sohm and his debate with Harnack.[1] Sohm regarded the official leadership roles of the early
Church to be oriented exclusively to spiritual claims, thus ex-
cluding from the Church's very constitution the role of legal
authority. The Church was to be thought of as a spiritual body,
spiritually organized and directed, with no possibility of legal
appeal which could resolve conflict or provide direction. It was
in the very nature of the Church to regard all 'offices' as
charismatic. The principle of ecclesiastical law is antithetical
to the principle of the Church itself. Sohm did not deny the
existence of an early ecclesiastical structure. He merely denied
that legal forms were of its essence.

Understood this way, the discrepancy between the charismatic
and the legal mode has continued to be a basic premise in the
writing of early Church history. More than that, it has entered
general sociological theory through the influential work of Max
Weber. In *Economy and Society* Weber saw the charismatic as

[1] R. Sohm, *Kirchenrecht, I: Die geschichtliche Grundlage* (Leipzig, 1892);
A. Harnack, *Entstehung und Entwicklung der Kirchenverfassung und des Kirchen-
rechts in den zwei ersten Jahrhunderten* (Leipzig, 1910); R. Sohm, *Wesen und
Ursprung des Katholizismus* (Leipzig, 1912²; Darmstadt, 1967).

representative of a pure type of authority which stands in sharp contrast to the authority embodied in legal-rational or traditional systems.[1] It might seem that Paul is simply representative of authority perceived charismatically, as distinct from someone representing authority in a legal sense. Yet so are his opponents, and Paul's understanding of authority clearly diverges from theirs. Faced with the evidence of II Corinthians, we must search for a more precise understanding of charismatic authority which will allow a finer-grained distinction than that between spirit, or charisma, and law. We must be able to distinguish between one charismatic and another. To do so it will be helpful to call on Weber's work and its echoes in his successors, not to test its validity[2] but to sharpen our understanding of the anatomy of authority which Paul perceives, and its implications for the process of ordering social life.

Weber's use of the term 'charismatic' is not intended as an explication of the technical NT term. The charismatic is an ideal type whose features represent something of a combination of personality profile and action inventory.[3] He is a natural leader as distinct from an office-holder or a professional in the modern sense of the word. He is the bearer of gifts regarded as supernatural in origin; his authenticating sign is likely to be the miracle. The charismatic 'seizes the task for which he is destined and demands that others obey and follow him by virtue of his mission'. His claim to leadership is not derived from the assent of those who follow him, but stands outside them. They obey as their duty.

In every way the charismatic stands outside the bounds of rational or bureaucratic structures. He lives from the gift or bounty of others, by almost any but the usual manner of methodically acquiring money and property. The nature of his

[1] *ES*: i, 3, 1 : 2 (Vol. i, pp. 215ff.); i, 3, 4–5 (Vol. i, pp. 241–54); ii, 14, 1–3 (Vol. iii, pp. 1111–57). See above, ch. i.

[2] It is important to understand that Weber's work constitutes a conceptual sociological analysis and not an historical review, however well grounded (too well grounded? Cf. Shils, p. 274, n. 1 below) in historical observation his ideas may have been. The value of the work is not measured by its conformity to any one historical example of the charismatic leader, for instance, but by its utility in aiding our general conceptual understanding of social action and social relationships.

[3] Cf. esp. *ES*: ii, 14, 1–3 (Vol. iii, pp. 1111–57).

gifts being itself otherworldly, the charismatic inevitably turns away from the world. He is free from worldly attachments and duties of occupational and family life.

He is a natural leader in the sense that the mere fact of recognizing his personal mission establishes his power. The charisma with which he is endowed knows 'no formal or regulated appointment or dismissal, no career, advancement or salary, no supervisory or appeals body, no logical or purely technical jurisdiction and no permanent institutions in the manner of bureaucratic agencies which are independent of the incumbents and their personal charisma'.[1] This does not mean that charismatic authority implies no social structure. 'It indicates rather a definite social structure with a staff and an apparatus',[2] though Weber admits that the '"purer" charismatic authority in our sense is, the less can it be understood as an organization in the usual sense...'[3] The charismatic staff is chosen on the basis of its charismatic qualities. Within the staff conflicts are resolved by the personal and direct intervention of the charismatic leader. Should one of the staff prove deficient in the requisite qualities, that is a decision of the charismatic leader who has complete control over the staff's 'employment'. One phrase from Weber sums up the situation: '*Charisma is self-determined and sets its own limits.*'[4]

On those terms we could certainly fit the opponents of II Corinthians inside the charismatic camp. Within the limits of what we know about them, we can recognize their characteristics in the sketch culled from Weber's profile. But what of Paul? Does describing his opponents in this way automatically determine that Paul is to be placed among the bureaucrats and suggest that in the putative struggle between charisma and office Paul is a model of the second century office holder? If so, we are surely wrong in seeking to distinguish between legitimacy and authority. Moreover, we would have to revise our estimate of the difference between Paul and the deutero-Pauline tradition.

Both on Paul's word and on Weber's description, however, Paul himself has some claim to charismatic status. Weber lays

---

[1] *ES*: II, 14, 1: 1 (Vol. III, p. 1112).
[2] *ES*: II, 14, 1: 5 (Vol. III, p. 1119).   [3] *Ibid.*
[4] *ES*: II, 14, 1: 1 (Vol. III, p. 1112).